EXAM CRAM™

The Life and Health Insurance Exam Cram Sheet

This cram sheet contains the distilled key topics that are likely to appear on your licensing exam. Review this information as the last thing you do before entering the test room, paying special attention to areas in which you feel you need the most review. You should also review the glossary for a complete listing of definitions of terms included on the exam.

INTRODUCTION TO INSURANCE

- *Peril* is a cause of loss, such as an accident, fire, or flood.
- Insurers use the *law of large numbers* to predict how many losses will occur in a group of individuals. The larger the group, the more predictable the future losses will be for a given time period.
- Not all risks are equally insurable. Insurable risks possess certain characteristics that make the rate of loss fairly predictable.
- *Coinsurance* is an arrangement whereby the insurer and the insured share payment of covered losses in agreed proportions.
- A *foreign insurer* is an insurer conducting business in a state where it is not incorporated.
- *Independent insurance producers* sell products of several companies and work for themselves or other producers, and *exclusive* or *captive producers* represent only one company and have an agency relationship with that company.
- Producers may function as *agents,* representing the insurance company, or as *brokers,* representing the potential insured.

INSURANCE REGULATION

- *Misrepresentation* is falsely representing the terms, benefits, or privileges of a policy.
- It is illegal to permit discrimination between individuals of the same class or insurance risk in terms of rates, premiums, fees, and policy benefits because of their place of residence, race, creed, or national origin.
- *Churning* is the illegal practice of using misrepresentation to induce replacement of a policy issued by the insurer the producer is representing, rather than the policy of a competitor.

INSURANCE LAW

- An agent's authority will be one of three types:
  - Express, which is an explicit, definite agreement
  - Implied, which is not expressly granted under an agency contract, but actual authority possessed by the agent to transact the principal's business in accordance with general business practices
  - Apparent, which is the authority an agent seems to have because of certain actions undertaken on his or her part
- *Estoppel* is the legal principle that holds that anyone whose words or actions have caused a waiver of a right or privilege cannot later reclaim the waived right or privilege if a third party has relied upon it.
- Insurance contracts are conditional; when the loss occurs, certain conditions must be met to make the contract legally enforceable.
- *Representation* is a statement believed to be true to the best of one's knowledge.
- *Material fact* is a fact that is crucial to acceptance of the risk.

UNDERWRITING BASICS

- *Reserves* are funds set aside to pay future, existing, and ongoing claims.

GROUP INSURANCE

- Under a *noncontributory plan,* 100% of eligible employees must be covered; under a *contributory plan,* 75% of eligible employees must be covered.
- An *eligibility period* is the period of time, typically 30 or 31 days, in which an employee is eligible to enroll in a group plan; it immediately follows the *probationary period.*

W9-CML-421

SELLING LIFE INSURANCE

- With *capital conservation*, income is derived only from interest gained on the principal.
- With *capital liquidation*, both the interest and the principal are used to generate income, meaning that a smaller fund is needed because there is no concern for leaving the principal intact.
- *Accelerated benefits* are living benefits paid by the insurance company to cover medical and living expenses prior to death; the payments reduce the death benefit.

POLICY ISSUANCE AND DELIVERY

- When a producer completes an application, it is normal to collect the first full premium from the policyowner; the premium is a *conditional receipt* because the producer cannot guarantee that the policy will be issued.
- A *temporary insurance agreement* provides an applicant with immediate life insurance coverage while the underwriting process is taking place, regardless of the applicant's insurability.
- *Replacement regulations* require compliance with the following steps when the sale of a new policy will result in the termination or encumbrance of existing coverage:
  - List all existing life insurance policies to be replaced.
  - Give the applicant a completed *Comparison Statement,* signed by the producer, and a *Notice to Applicants Regarding Replacement of Life Insurance.*
  - Give the insurer a copy of any proposals made and a copy of the Comparison Statement with the name of insurer that is to be replaced.
  - Notify each insurer whose insurance is being replaced and, upon request, furnish a copy of any proposal and Comparison Statement.
  - Maintain copies of proposals, receipts, and Comparison Statements.

TYPES OF INSURANCE POLICIES

- *Whole life insurance* accumulates cash value and is designed to provide protection for the whole life of the insured.
- *Universal life insurance* is a flexible-premium and adjustable-benefit life insurance contract that accumulates cash value.
- *Variable universal life insurance* offers varying benefits, depending on the insured's investment choices.
- Applicable to juvenile policies, a *payor rider* waives all further premiums in the event of the death of the person who's paying the premiums.

- A *return of premium rider* provides that, in the event of the death of the insured within a specified period of time, the policy will pay, along with the face amount, an amount equal to all premiums paid to date.

POLICY PROVISIONS

- A lapsed policy can be reinstated, provided the following three conditions are met:
  - The policyowner pays all back premiums due plus interest.
  - The insured shows proof of insurability.
  - Less than 3 years have elapsed.
- An *assignment clause* stipulates that any transfer of policy rights must be filed in writing with the insurer.
- *Primary beneficiaries* are the first in line to receive life insurance policy proceeds; *contingent beneficiaries* receive the proceeds if the primary beneficiaries are deceased; *tertiary beneficiaries* receive the proceeds if the primary and contingent beneficiaries are deceased.
- *Free-look provisions* allow the proposed policyowner to return the policy for any reason within 10 days for a full refund.

POLICY OPTIONS

- The most common settlement options are
  - Interest only
  - Fixed period
  - Fixed amount
  - Life income
- The most common nonforfeiture options are
  - *Cash surrender value*
  - *Extended term insurance*
  - *Reduced paid-up insurance*
- The most common dividend options are
  - Cash dividend
- Accumulation at interest
- Paid-up additions
- *Reduced premium*, in which the policyowner directs the insurer to apply the dividend toward the next premium due.

ANNUITIES

- A *contract owner* is usually the one who pays for the contract.
  - An annuitant is the person on whose life the annuity policy has been issued.
  - The beneficiary is the one who receives any survivor benefits payable under the annuity upon the death of the annuitant.

EXAM CRAM™

Life and Health Insurance License

Your Vision • Our Solutions™

CERTIFICATION

800 East 96th Street, Indianapolis, Indiana 46240

Life and Health Insurance License Exam Cram

International Standard Book Number: 0-7897-3260-2

Library of Congress Catalog Card Number: 2004112114

Printed in the United States of America

20   17

Trademarks

All terms mentioned in this book that are known to be trademarks or service marks have been appropriately capitalized. Que Publishing cannot attest to the accuracy of this information. Use of a term in this book should not be regarded as affecting the validity of any trademark or service mark.

Warning and Disclaimer

Every effort has been made to make this book as complete and as accurate as possible, but no warranty or fitness is implied. The information provided is on an "as is" basis. The author(s) and the publisher shall have neither liability nor responsibility to any person or entity with respect to any loss or damages arising from the information contained in this book or from the use of the CD or programs accompanying it.

Bulk Sales

Que Publishing offers excellent discounts on this book when ordered in quantity for bulk purchases or special sales. For more information, please contact

> **U.S. Corporate and Government Sales**
> **1-800-382-3419**
> **corpsales@pearsontechgroup.com**

For sales outside the U.S., please contact

> **International Sales**
> **international@pearsoned.com**

Publisher
Paul Boger

Executive Editor
Jeff Riley

Acquisitions Editor
Carol Ackerman

Development Editor
Gus Miklos

Managing Editor
Charlotte Clapp

Project Editor
Elizabeth Finney

Copy Editor
Nancy Albright

Indexers
Ken Johnson
Mandie Frank

Proofreader
Tracy Donhardt

Technical Editor
Teresa Chapman

Publishing Coordinator
Pamalee Nelson

Multimedia Developer
Dan Scherf

Interior Designer
Gary Adair

Cover Designer
Anne Jones

The test is in 2 weeks – are you ready?

You need a quick and efficient way to make sure you have what it takes to pass.

Where do you go?

Exam Cram!

Why?

Que Certification Exam Cram titles have exactly what you need to pass your exam:

Property and Casualty Insurance Exam Cram
BISYS® Education Services
0-7897-3264-5
$34.99 US/$49.99 CAN/£24.99 Net UK

- Key terms and concepts highlighted at the start of each chapter
- Notes, Tips, and Exam Alerts advise what to watch out for
- End-of-chapter sample Exam Questions with detailed discussions of all answers
- Two text-based practice tests with answer keys at the end of each book
- The tear-out Cram Sheet condenses the most important items and information into a two-page reminder
- A CD that includes BISYS Practice Tests for complete evaluation of your knowledge
- Our authors are recognized experts in the field. In most cases, they are current or former instructors, trainers, or consultants—they know exactly what you need to know!

CERTIFICATION

About the Authors

About BISYS

The BISYS Group, Inc. (NYSE: BSG), headquartered in New York City, provides solutions that enable insurance companies, investment firms, and banks to expand their businesses and run their operations more profitably. BISYS currently supports more than 22,000 domestic and international financial institutions and corporate clients through several business units.

BISYS Education Services is the nation's premier provider of licensing preparation, continuing education, and professional development courses for life, health, long-term care, annuity, and property-casualty insurance products as well as investments. This unit complements its education services with a comprehensive compliance management solution that supports insurance and investment firms and professionals with a sophisticated suite of services that automate the entire licensing process.

BISYS Insurance Services is the nation's largest independent distributor of life insurance and provider of support services required to sell traditional and variable life and annuity products as well as long-term care and disability insurance. This unit is also the nation's second largest independent wholesale distributor of commercial property/casualty insurance.

BISYS Investment Services group provides administration and distribution services for approximately 380 clients, representing more than 2,200 mutual funds, hedge funds, private equity funds, and other alternative investment products, with approximately $750 billion in assets under administration. It also provides retirement services to more than 18,000 companies in partnership with 40 of the nation's leading banks and investment management companies and offers analytical research and competitive information through its Financial Research Corporation (FRC) subsidiary.

BISYS' *Information Services* group supports approximately 1,450 banks, insurance companies, and corporations with industry-leading information processing and imaging solutions, turnkey asset retention solutions, and specialized corporate banking solutions. Additional information is available at www.bisys.com.

Eric Alan Anderson is Director of Insurance Education for BISYS Education Services, based in Indianapolis, Indiana. He has almost 25 years of experience creating training and test preparation materials for the financial services industry. In addition to authoring 17 insurance training texts and editing 8 others, he has written newsletters and magazine articles and has developed materials for audio cassette/workbook, videotape, computer disk, and the Web. He has also taught basic English skills courses at the college level and has made presentations to national conferences of insurance associations.

Matt McClure is Editor of Life/Health Products for BISYS Education Services. He maintains 42 titles on BISYS Education Services' course list, including the *Life/Health Concepts* license preparation text and its supplementary review materials. Formerly a freelance writer and editor, his work has appeared in numerous nationally published books and magazines. He is a licensed life and health insurance producer.

Richard A. Morin, CIC, is a contract author based in Los Angeles, California. He has 35 years of experience writing and training on a broad range of subjects for the financial services industry. For several years he was an editor for a major insurance training publisher, and he has also worked as an insurance underwriter, a rating supervisor, and a licensed insurance and mutual fund sales representative.

About the Reviewer

Teresa Chapman has been in the insurance business since 1996, upon graduation from Ball State University in Muncie, IN. She started her career with State Farm Insurance Company as a Life and Health Underwriter. A series of moves with State Farm led to a variety of jobs; supervisor of Life and Health Policy Changes, and Life and Health compliance officer, and culminated in her decision to be a State Farm insurance agent located in Carmel, IN. Teresa now lives in Noblesville, IN, with her husband Trent, a State Farm auto claim representative, and their son, Christian.

We Want to Hear from You!

As the reader of this book, *you* are our most important critic and commentator. We value your opinion and want to know what we're doing right, what we could do better, what areas you'd like to see us publish in, and any other words of wisdom you're willing to pass our way.

As an executive editor for Que Publishing, I welcome your comments. You can email or write me directly to let me know what you did or didn't like about this book—as well as what we can do to make our books better.

Please note that I cannot help you with technical problems related to the topic of this book. We do have a User Services group, however, where I will forward specific technical questions related to the book.

When you write, please be sure to include this book's title and author as well as your name, email address, and phone number. I will carefully review your comments and share them with the author and editors who worked on the book.

Email: feedback@pearsonitcertification.com

Mail: Dave Dusthimer
            Editor in Chief
            Pearson IT Certification
            800 East 96th Street
            Indianapolis, IN 46240 USA

For more information about this book or another Que Certification title, visit our Web site at www.examcram.com. Type the ISBN (excluding hyphens) or the title of a book in the Search field to find the page you're looking for.

Contents at a Glance

Table of Contents

Introduction

Welcome to *Life and Health Insurance Licensing Exam Cram!* Whether this is your first or your fifteenth *Exam Cram* series book, you'll find information here that will help ensure your success as you pursue knowledge, experience, and certification. This introduction explains state insurance licensing programs in general and talks about how the *Exam Cram* series can help you prepare for your state insurance licensing exam. Chapters 1 through 19 are designed to remind you of everything you need to know in order to take—and pass—your state insurance licensing exam. The two sample tests at the end of the book should give you a reasonably accurate assessment of your knowledge—and, yes, we provide the answers and their explanations to the tests. Read the book and understand the material, and you stand a very good chance of passing the test.

Exam Cram books help you understand and appreciate the subjects and materials you need to pass state insurance licensing exams. *Exam Cram* books are aimed strictly at test preparation and review. They do not teach you everything you need to know to pass the exam. Instead, we present and dissect the questions and problems I've found that you're likely to encounter on a test. I've worked to bring together as much information as possible about state insurance licensing exams.

Nevertheless, to completely prepare yourself for any state insurance licensing test, we recommend that you begin by taking the Self-Assessment that is included in this book, immediately following this introduction. The Self-Assessment tool will help you evaluate your knowledge base against the requirements for a state insurance licensing exam under both ideal and real circumstances.

Based on what you learn from the Self-Assessment, you might decide to begin your studies with some more comprehensive self-study or classroom training, some practice with state insurance exam simulators, or an audio review program. On the other hand, you might decide to pick up and read one of the many study guides available from third-party vendors on certain topics. We also recommend that you supplement your study program with a visit to your state insurance department's website to get all the details about how to get your insurance license as well as how to schedule and take your insurance licensing exam.

Getting an Insurance License

Licensing is the way governments assure that only qualified individuals are allowed to practice certain important professions, such as being an insurance producer. Because insurance is regulated primarily at the state level, the rules for getting an insurance license vary somewhat from state to state.

Every state requires individuals to pass a qualification exam to get an insurance license. In addition, most states require individuals to meet a prelicensing education requirement before they can take the qualification exam. In some states, the prelicensing education requirement can be met through an approved self-study course—that is, you buy a book that has been approved in advance by the state insurance department and take an exam (not to be confused with the licensing qualification exam) that you send in to be graded. In other states, the prelicensing education requirement can be met only by attending an approved classroom course.

NOTE

This Exam Cram text is not approved to meet the prelicensing education requirement in any state. It is designed only as a supplementary aid to help you pass the state insurance licensing exam.

Besides fulfilling any prelicensing education requirement and passing the licensing exam, insurance license candidates must also submit a license application to their state insurance department and have it approved. In some states, the license application must be submitted before taking the license qualification exam; in some states, it must be submitted after passing the exam. Call your state insurance department's licensing division or visit its website to find out what you need to do in your state.

Taking a Licensing Exam

As with other aspects of insurance licensing, specific instructions on how to register for your qualification exam are available from the insurance department. Ask for a licensing information bulletin or a licensing candidate handbook, which will describe where and when exams are given, the fees you must pay, and the testing procedures.

One thing all state insurance qualification exams have in common is that they are closed-book exams. You will not be allowed to take any study materials or notes into the testing room. Even phones and calculators might not be allowed. In some states, the only items exam candidates are permitted to take into the testing room are their wallet and keys.

In most states, insurance qualification exams are given on computers. However, you will not need any computer or typing skills to take the exam. You will be instructed on how to answer questions and given a short practice test to get comfortable with the equipment before the actual qualification exam begins.

When you complete a computer-administered exam, the software tells you immediately whether you passed or failed. Your states will have its own rules for retesting in the event you don't pass. Those rules will be described in your licensing information bulletin/candidate handbook.

How to Prepare for an Exam

Whether or not your state has a prelicensing education requirement, you'll want to study in preparation for the license qualification exam. And even if your state has a prelicensing education requirement, you'll probably want to do some additional studying to make sure you are fully prepared for the exam. Your options for additional study include the following:

➤ *Self-study courses*—Publishers such as BISYS Education Services offer courses designed to allow you to study on your own for the licensing qualification exam. BISYS license training packages are available in either web-based or print-based formats and contain a number of components:

   ➤ A *Property-Casualty Concepts* text, which covers all the non–state-specific topics on the licensing exam

   ➤ Practice exams, which help you evaluate your comprehension of the material in the *Concepts* text

   ➤ Explanations to answers on the practice exams, so you know why each of your responses was right or wrong

   ➤ A state insurance law digest, which covers all the state-specific topics on the licensing exam

   ➤ An optional audio CD review program, which reviews the key information contained in the *Concepts* text

> ➤ An optional exam simulator, which gives you additional question-and-answer practice over the material covered in the *Concepts* text and the state insurance law digest

> ➤ *Classroom training*—Many colleges and commercial training companies offer classroom training for insurance license exams. Although classroom training generally costs considerably more than self-study, some individuals find that they learn best in a classroom situation. And of course, in many states, the prelicensing education requirement must be met with classroom study in any case.

> ➤ *Other sources*—There's no shortage of materials available on insurance topics. The "Need to Know More?" resource appendix at the end of this book will give you an idea of where we think you should look for further discussion.

In addition, you will surely find Que Publishing's *Exam Cram* insurance licensing preparation materials useful in your quest for insurance knowledge. *Exam Cram* books provide you with a review of the essential information you need to know to pass the tests. They focus on the detailed information in the *Concepts* texts available from BISYS Education Services. Together, the BISYS Education Services license training packages and the *Exam Cram* review materials create a powerful exam preparation program.

This set of required and recommended materials represents an unparalleled collection of sources and resources for insurance licensing qualification and related topics. Our hope is you'll find that this book belongs in that company.

What This Book Will Not Do

This book by itself will *not* teach you everything you need to know to pass your insurance licensing exam. It does not cover the state-specific topics that appear on the exam, usually dealing with laws that apply only in your particular state. That information, although it represents a small proportion of the entire exam, is critical to passing the exam. State-specific topics are covered in the state insurance law digests available from BISYS Education Services. This book reviews the rest of what you need to know before you take the test, with the fundamental purpose dedicated to reviewing the non–state-specific information on the insurance licensing exam.

What This Book Is Designed to Do

This book uses a variety of teaching and memorization techniques to analyze the exam-related topics and to provide you with ways to input, index, and retrieve what you need to know in order to pass the test.

This book is designed to be read as a pointer to the areas of knowledge on the test. In other words, you may want to read the book through once to get an insight into how comprehensive your knowledge of insurance is. The book is also designed to be read shortly before you go for the actual test and to give you a distillation of the topics covered by the exam in as few pages as possible. We think you can use this book to get a sense of the underlying context of any topic in the chapters—or to skim-read for Exam Alerts, bulleted points, summaries, and topic headings.

We draw on material from each state's exam outlines and from other preparation guides, in particular, BISYS Education Services' *Property-Casualty Concepts* text. Our aim is to walk you through the knowledge you will need and point out those things that are important for the exam (Exam Alerts, practice questions, and so on).

We demystify insurance jargon, acronyms, terms, and concepts. Also, wherever we think you're likely to blur past an important concept, we define the assumptions and premises behind that concept.

About This Book

We structured the topics in this book to build on one another. Therefore, the topics covered in later chapters might refer to previous discussions in earlier chapters. We suggest you read this book from front to back.

After you read the book, you can brush up on a certain area by using the Index or the Table of Contents to go straight to the topics and questions you want to reexamine. We use headings and subheadings to provide outline information about each given topic. After you pass the exam and obtain your insurance license, we think you'll find this book useful as a tightly focused reference and an essential foundation of insurance information.

Chapter Formats

Each *Exam Cram* chapter follows a regular structure, with graphical cues about especially important or useful material. The structure of a typical chapter is as follows:

➤ *Opening hotlists*—Each chapter begins with lists of the terms you need to understand and the concepts you need to master before you can be fully conversant with the chapter's subject matter.

➤ *Topical coverage*—After the opening hotlists, each chapter covers the topics related to the chapter's subject.

➤ *Alerts*—Throughout the topical coverage section, we highlight material most likely to appear on the exam by using a special Exam Alert layout that looks like this:

> This is what an Exam Alert looks like. An Exam Alert stresses concepts or terms that will most likely appear in one or more license exam questions. For that reason, we think any information found offset in Exam Alert format is worthy of special attention.

Even if material isn't flagged as an Exam Alert, *all* the content in this book is associated in some way with test-related material. What appears in the chapter content is critical knowledge.

➤ *Notes*—This book is an overall examination of entry-level insurance knowledge. As such, we touch on many aspects of insurance that open doors for further inquiry. Where a topic goes deeper than the scope of the book, we use notes to indicate areas of concern or further training.

> Cramming for an exam will get you through a test, but it won't make you a fully competent insurance professional. Although you can memorize just the facts you need in order to become licensed, your daily work in the field will rapidly put you in water over your head if you don't continue your insurance education.

➤ *Tips*—Besides *Alerts* and *Notes*, we also include tips to help you remember or distinguish certain information that may appear on your license exam.

> Pay special attention to Tips because they provide you with various techniques that may improve your exam score!

➤ *Exam Prep Questions*—This section presents a short list of multiple-choice test questions related to the specific chapter topic. Each question has a following explanation of both correct and incorrect answers. The practice questions highlight the areas we found to be most important on the exam.

➤ *Need to Know More?*—At the end of the book is a section titled "Need to Know More?" This section provides pointers to resources that we found to be helpful in offering further details on the book's subject matter. If you find a resource you like in this collection, use it, but don't feel compelled to use all these resources. We use this section to recommend resources that we have used on a regular basis, so none of the recommendations will be a waste of your time or money. These resources may go out of print or be taken down (in the case of websites), so we reference widely accepted resources.

The bulk of the book follows this chapter structure, but there are a few other elements that we would like to point out:

➤ *Practice Exams*—The sample tests, which appear in Chapters 25 and 27 (with answer keys in Chapters 26 and 28), are intended to test your comprehension of the material in this book. They are also intended to be in a similar format and degree of difficulty as the questions you are likely to see on the license exam. However, because the questions on the actual exam are kept highly confidential, you should expect that the questions on the actual license exam will be ones that you have never seen before.

➤ *Answer Key*—These provide the answers to the sample tests, complete with explanations of both the correct responses and the incorrect responses.

➤ *Glossary*—This is an extensive glossary of important terms used in this book.

➤ *Cram Sheet*—This appears as a tear-away sheet inside the front cover of this *Exam Cram* book. It is a valuable tool that represents a collection of the most difficult-to-remember facts, terms, and concepts we think you should memorize before taking the test.

You might want to look at the Cram Sheet in your car or in the lobby of the testing center just before you walk into the testing center. The Cram Sheet is divided under headings, so you can review the appropriate parts just before each test.

➤ *CD-ROM*—The CD contains the BISYS Education Services Exam Simulator, Preview Edition software. The preview edition exhibits most of the functionality of the commercially available version, but offers a reduced number of unit review questions and a 25-question practice exam. To get the complete set of practice questions and 100-question exam functionality, visit www.bisyseducation.com or call 800-241-9095.

Contacting the Source

Life and Health Insurance Licensing Exam Cram is a real-world tool that you can use to prepare for and pass your state insurance licensing exam. We're interested in any feedback you would care to share about the book, especially if you have ideas about how we can improve it for future test-takers. We'll consider everything you say carefully and will respond to all reasonable suggestions and comments. You can reach us via email at customerservice@bisys-education.com.

Let us know if you found this book to be helpful in your preparation efforts. We'd also like to know how you felt about your chances of passing the exam *before* you read the book and then *after* you read the book. Of course, we'd love to hear that you passed the exam—and even if you just want to share your triumph, we'd be happy to hear from you.

Thanks for choosing us as your license exam preparation coach, and enjoy the book. We wish you luck on the exam, but we know that if you read through all the chapters and work with the product, you won't need luck—you'll pass the test on the strength of real knowledge!

Self-Assessment

We include a Self-Assessment in this *Exam Cram* to help you evaluate your readiness to take and pass your state insurance license qualification exam. It should also help you understand what you need to master for an entry-level knowledge of the industry in which you are about to embark on a career.

Getting Prepared

Whether you attend a class to get ready for your exam or use self-study materials, some preparation for your insurance license qualification exam is essential. You want to do everything you can to pass on your first try.

You can get all the confidence you need from knowing that many others have gone before you. If you're willing to tackle the process seriously and do what it takes to gain the necessary knowledge, you can take—and pass—the insurance license qualification exams. In fact, the *Exam Crams* and the companion state license training packages from BISYS Education Services are designed to make it as easy as possible for you to prepare for these exams—but prepare you must!

 You can obtain an outline of exam topics, practice questions, and other information about insurance qualification exams from your state insurance department's website. If your state has contracted with an exam administration company to administer its insurance licensing exams (which is usually the case) you can get the exam information from the exam administrator's website. Contact your state insurance department for more information.

Put Yourself to the (Practice) Test

We have included in this book several review exam questions for each chapter and two practice exams at the end of the book. If you don't score well on the chapter questions, you can study more and then retake the review questions at the end of each part. When you have gone through all the chapters, take the first practice exam and then score yourself. Review by reading the explanations that accompany the answer key in the chapter following that exam. If you don't earn a score of at least 80% on the first practice exam, you'll want to do some additional study. Go back through this book, and also consult your notes and/or your text from any licensing exam preparation course you took. Then try the second practice exam in this book. Again, shoot for a score of 80% or better on your first try.

There is no better way to assess your exam readiness than to take a high-quality practice exam and pass with a score of 80% or better on your first try for that exam. When you take the same practice exam over and over, you begin to memorize the answers to the specific questions on that exam. It may help you improve your knowledge, but it spoils the value of the exam as an indication of how well you might respond to an exam containing questions over the full range of topics on your state's exam outline. Even though you must score only 70% to pass the actual exam, shoot for 80% on a practice exam to leave room for the fact that you might be nervous during the actual exam and that the questions on the actual exam might be more difficult than those on your practice exam.

If you did not score 80% or better on your first try, investigate the other study resources available (see the "Need to Know More?" addendum at the end of this book).

If you've given your utmost to self-study materials and then taken the exam and failed anyway, consider taking a class. For some people, self-study is not the optimal learning format. The opportunity to interact with an instructor and fellow students can make all the difference. For information about classes available in your area, ask your state insurance department or call BISYS Education Services (800-241-9095) to see whether there are schools using BISYS insurance licensing textbooks nearby.

One last note: Do not use practice exams as your only means of study for the exam. Next to not preparing at all, the best way to assure you'll fail your license qualification exam is to skip studying and go directly to taking question-and-answer practice tests to assess your readiness to take the exam. Practice exams are a gauge of how well you've comprehended your study material—they are not an accurate reflection of the questions you will see on your license qualification exam.

Other Preparation

Besides studying for the exam, there are some other things you should do to make sure you perform well on the exam:

➤ *Get a good night's sleep the night before the exam.* When you're tired, you're more likely to make careless—that is, needless—mistakes. Getting a good night's sleep will help assure that you feel refreshed and at your best.

➤ *Eat a nourishing breakfast the morning of the exam.* Your brain needs nutrients to function at its best—make sure you provide them! At the very least, you don't want your attention to be distracted by hunger while you're trying to concentrate on a question.

➤ *Give yourself plenty of time to get to the exam site.* Rushing to get somewhere can put you in a less-than-optimum frame of mind even if you end up arriving on time. Leave early to allow for unforeseen problems such as traffic delays. If you arrive well before the exam is scheduled to start, you can always use the extra time to go over your notes.

No Experience Required

Insurance license exams are designed so that they can be passed by individuals with no insurance industry experience or formal insurance schooling, other than any state-required prelicensing education requirement. So if you are completely new to this business, don't worry. Everything you need to know to pass your qualification exam can be obtained in the study materials referenced here.

In terms of having a successful insurance career after you pass your exam, the most important requirement is a sincere desire to help people solve their financial problems and reach their financial goals. However, there is certain background that can be an asset as you start out in the job. If you have run your own business, you already understand the type of self-discipline and motivation that will help you succeed in your insurance sales activities. If you have some prior sales experience—such as a customer service representative, real estate agent, or some other sales position—you'll probably have a comfort level with meeting people to discuss and solve their needs. But again, if you're new to insurance or to sales, have no fear on that account. You will have ample opportunity and resources for learning everything you need to know.

Onward to Exam and Career Success!

After you've undertaken the right studies and reviewed the many sources of information to help you prepare for the license qualification exam, you'll be ready to take a practice exam. When your scores are positive enough to indicate that you will get through the exam, you're ready to go after the real thing. Good luck!

Introduction to Insurance

Terms you need to understand:

- ✓ Insurance
- ✓ Risk
- ✓ Peril
- ✓ Hazard
- ✓ Exposure unit
- ✓ Stock insurer
- ✓ Mutual insurer
- ✓ Reciprocal insurer
- ✓ Fraternal insurer
- ✓ Lloyd's associations
- ✓ Assessment insurers
- ✓ Reinsurers

- ✓ Self-insurers
- ✓ Domestic insurer
- ✓ Foreign insurer
- ✓ Alien insurer
- ✓ Authorized or admitted insurer
- ✓ Unauthorized of nonadmitted insurer
- ✓ Insurance agents
- ✓ Insurance brokers
- ✓ Insurance solicitors
- ✓ Insurance consultants

Concepts you need to master:

- ✓ Methods of managing risk
- ✓ Law of large numbers
- ✓ Insurable interest
- ✓ Speculative risk
- ✓ Pure risk
- ✓ Insurable risk
- ✓ Indemnity

- ✓ Limit of liability
- ✓ Deductible
- ✓ Coinsurance
- ✓ Independent agency system
- ✓ Exclusive or captive producers
- ✓ Direct writing companies

The future is notoriously unpredictable. Every day, each of us faces the possibility that something might happen that would result in a personal financial loss. Sickness, disability, premature death, and damage or loss of property are examples of things that might cause a financial loss. We know that these things will happen to some people and not to others, but we do not know which things will happen to any particular person. In the face of this uncertainty, the idea and business of *insurance* was developed as a means for spreading the result of a financial loss among many persons, so the cost to any one person is small.

The basic mechanism behind insurance is relatively simple. The insurance company or *insurer* receives relatively small amounts of money, referred to as *premium*, from each of the large number of people buying insurance. A large uncertain loss is exchanged for a specific small amount of premium.

The agreement between the insurer and the *insured*, the person who is covered by the insurance, is established in a legal document referred to as a contract of insurance or a *policy*. The insurer promises to pay the insured according to the terms of the policy if a loss occurs. *Loss* is defined as reduction in the value of an asset. To be paid for a loss, the insured must notify the insurer by making a *claim*. The claim is a demand for payment of the insurance benefit to the person named in the policy.

Risk

To really understand insurance and how it works, you must first understand risk. *Risk* is the possibility that a loss might occur and is one of the reasons that people purchase insurance.

NOTE　Notice that risk is not the loss itself, but the uncertainty of loss. There are some losses that are certain to happen eventually, such as when a rug finally wears out after years of use, or the fact that a person will eventually die.

There are two types of risks, only one of which can be covered by insurance:

➤ *Speculative risk* is a risk that offers the opportunity for gain as well as the possibility of loss. Gambling is a common type of speculative risk. Insurance is not designed to protect against speculative risks. Examples are found in new business ventures, stock market investments, and race track bets.

➤ *Pure risk* is the possibility of loss only and is the type of risk that insurers accept—for example, the possibility of financial loss due to an accident, sickness, or premature death. The purpose of insurance is to make the person whole again, to restore the insured to his or her original financial position. Insurance is not designed to provide a person with the opportunity of making a gain or profit.

Perils and Hazards

A *peril* is the cause of a potential loss. Accident, fire, explosion, and flood are common perils that may be covered by insurance. A *hazard* is a condition that increases the seriousness of a potential loss or increases the likelihood that a loss will occur. Slippery floors, unsanitary conditions, and improperly stored gasoline are hazards Four types of hazards may contribute to losses:

➤ *Physical hazards* arise from material, structural, or operational features of a risk situation. Slippery floors or unsanitary conditions would be physical hazards.

➤ *Moral hazards* arise from people's habits and values. A moral hazard means that a person might create a loss situation on purpose just to collect from the insurance company. Filing a false claim is an example of moral hazard.

➤ *Morale hazards* arise out of human carelessness or irresponsibility. This means that an individual, through recklessness or thoughtless action, can increase the possibility for a loss. Failing to wear a seatbelt while driving is an example of morale hazard.

➤ *Legal hazards* arise from court actions that increase the likelihood or size of a loss. Legal hazards are illustrated by the growing tendency of people to file lawsuits and of courts to award enormous sums for alleged damages, or to require insurance payments that were not intended.

Managing Risk

Risks sometimes result in small losses, such as a stubbed toe or lost pocket comb. But risks may also result in serious financial losses, such as when a person is injured in a car accident or contracts a fatal disease. There are four ways of managing risk:.

1. The first method is to *avoid* risk. For example, a person might avoid the risk of being in an automobile accident by never getting into a car. However, not all risk is avoidable.

2. Risk may be *reduced*, or controlled, by examining the perils and seeing which ones can be eliminated. For example, a person reduces the risk of health problems by living a healthier lifestyle.

3. A risk is *retained* when a person decides to assume financial responsibility for certain events. The deductible amount on a health insurance policy is one way the insured retains some portion of the risk. In addition the premium may be reduced because he or she retains some of the risk.

4. The final method of managing risk is to *transfer* the risk to another party. This may be done through any of a number of legal mechanisms, such as hold harmless agreements or lawsuits. However, for many risks, the best way for individuals to transfer them is through insurance.

 Multiple methods may be employed simultaneously to manage the same risk. For example, purchasing an insurance policy to cover a significant exposure involves *risk transfer*, selecting a high deductible in order to reduce premiums involves an element of *risk retention*.

Law of Large Numbers

When an individual purchases insurance, the risk is transferred from the individual to the insurer. To make a successful business of accepting the transfer of individual risk, the insurer needs to have some idea of how many losses will actually occur.

Insurance companies cannot predict the losses expected for any given individual. However, using the *law of large numbers*, insurers are able to predict how many losses will occur in a group. The basic principle of this law is that the larger the group, the more predictable the future losses in the group will be for a given time period. The insurance company cannot reliably predict which people will die, but with a large enough population, statistics can accurately predict how many people in the group will suffer a loss. For example, experience might show that out of a group of 100,000 people aged 40, about 325 will die each year.

For the law of large numbers to operate, it is essential that a large number of similar risks, or exposure units be combined. An *exposure unit* is the item of property or the person insured. The exposure unit in life and health insurance is the economic value of the individual person's life. In property and casualty insurance it is the number of cars, homes, and so forth.

The degree of error in predicting future losses decreases as the number of individual exposure units in a group increases. Thus, the larger the group, the more closely the predicted experience will approach the actual loss experience. Insurance companies deal only with averages, in the sense of establishing actuarial predictions of loss experience. By providing for the average risk, the extremes in loss experience cancel each other out.

Actuaries are mathematicians who study and compile statistical data regarding exposure units and risks. This data is the basis for mortality and morbidity tables used to predict probable losses due to death (mortality) or sickness (morbidity) of large groups of people.

Insurance companies collect premiums to cover expenses, profits, and the cost of expected losses. The expected losses are based on the past experience of the average risk. The fact that some people never experience an automobile accident or that some live well beyond their life expectancy is immaterial, because other people are involved in accidents or die prematurely. Those insureds who suffer loss are compensated; many other insureds do not experience sizable losses.

Insurable Interest

A basic rule governing insurance states that before an individual can benefit from insurance, that individual must have must have a legitimate interest in the preservation of the life or property insured. This requirement is called *insurable interest.*

A person is presumed to have an insurable interest in his or her own life. An individual is also considered to have an insurable interest in the life of a close blood relative or a spouse. In these cases insurable interest is based on the love that individual would have for the family member and a real interest in protecting the life of that family member.

Insurable interest can also be based on a financial loss that will take place if an insured individual dies. Examples are two partners in a business, each of whom brings substantial expertise to that business. If one partner dies, the business could fail, resulting in a loss to the other partner.

 For life insurance, insurable interest must exist at the time of the application for insurance, but it need not exist at the time of the insured's death. In contrast, property and casualty insurance generally requires an insurable interest to exist only at the time of loss.

Insurable interest affects who may purchase a policy, but not who may benefit from a policy. For example, an individual could purchase life insurance on his or her own life and name a charitable organization as the beneficiary.

Because every person is presumed to have an insurable interest in his or her own life, the policy would be valid. As another example, a doctor who benefits from medical expense reimbursement payments may not have an insurable interest in the health of the insured, but the policyowner, usually the insured or the insured's employer, does have a personal or financial interest in keeping the insured healthy.

Insurable Risks

Not all risks are equally insurable. Insurable risks have certain characteristics that make the rate of loss fairly predictable, allowing insurers to adequately prepare for the losses that do occur. The more closely a risk aligns with the following characteristics, the more insurable it is.

Large Numbers of Homogeneous Units

The expected loss experience of a group of exposure units cannot be predicted with any certainty unless there are a large number of exposure units in that group. Risks are not considered insurable unless the insurance company has a large enough number of similar (homogeneous) risks and knows enough about their previous loss experience to be able to reliably predict possible future losses.

Loss Must Be Ascertainable

Because the purpose of insurance is to reduce or eliminate the uncertainty of economic loss, the insurer must be able to place a monetary value on the loss. In life insurance, monetary value is placed on the insured's human life value or ability to earn an income. In health insurance, economic loss is measured by lost wages or by actual medical expenses incurred. The potential loss must be measurable so that both parties can agree on the precise amount payable in the event the loss occurs.

Loss Must Be Uncertain

Because the purpose of insurance is to reduce or eliminate uncertainty, it is obviously not in the public interest to permit the writing of insurance for intentional acts, such as a man jumping off a skyscraper 2 days after purchasing an insurance policy. Uncertainty arises out of not knowing what is going to happen or being unable to predict what is going to happen to the individual exposure unit. If insurance is provided for certain losses, the element of chance is not a factor. Nor is there any element of uncertainty in losses occasioned by natural wear and tear or deterioration, depreciation, or defects in property covered under insurance.

With life insurance, the uncertainty rests not with *whether* a certain individual will die, but rather with *when* that individual will die and what financial obligations will be left behind when death occurs. With health insurance, the uncertainty rests less with *whether* a certain individual will have an accident or become ill sometime during his or her lifetime, but rather with *how much expense will be incurred* when an illness or accident occurs.

Economic Hardship

The nature of the loss must be such that an economic hardship would occur should the loss occur. For example, if a person loses 2 days of pay because of an injury, a loss occurs, but it is not significant enough to be covered by insurance.

The nature of the loss must be of such magnitude that it is worthwhile to incur the premium cost to cover potential loss. Thus, a comparison of the potential loss with the cost of premium is a major consideration to the insurance buyer.

Exclusion of Catastrophic Perils

Although the ability to predict future losses with a reasonable degree of accuracy is critical to the insuring function, certain types of perils do not lend themselves to prediction. Such perils, when they cause losses, do not establish a pattern of predictability that can be relied on for future predictions of anticipated loss. Examples of excluded catastrophic perils are war, nuclear risk, and floods.

Insurance Coverage Concepts

The following material reviews some of the concepts that are important for understanding how insurance works.

Indemnity

The concept of *indemnity* states that insurance should restore the insured, in whole or in part, to the condition he or she enjoyed prior to the loss. Restoration may take the form of payment for the loss or repair or replacement of the damaged or destroyed property.

In life and health insurance, the concept of indemnity has a slightly different meaning in that a person's economic value or human life value is the individual's present and future earning power. For example, a family is indemnified for the financial loss of the breadwinner by being provided with life insurance proceeds with which to replace present and future income and thus enable the family to maintain its lifestyle. An individual is indemnified for the financial loss of a broken arm by being provided with health insurance proceeds to pay the medical bills and perhaps to cover wages lost due to the injury.

Limit Of Liability

Although the term *limit of liability* is not used in the life and health insurance field as commonly as it is in the property and casualty field, it means the maximum amount the insurer will pay for a specified insured contingency.

 Life insurance policies usually use the term *face amount* to refer to the maximum liability of the insurer for a death claim. However, the face amount may not always be the maximum amount payable. In the case of a double indemnity provision, the limit of liability for an accidental death may be expressed as "twice the face amount" shown on the face of the policy.

Health and disability policies are more likely to specify a *maximum benefit* amount or period instead of a limit of liability. Basic medical insurance often has a maximum benefit amount (such as $10,000), and major medical insurance usually has a lifetime maximum benefit (such as $1 million). Disability income policies often limit benefits to a specified maximum benefit period (expressed in weeks or months). Within the maximum benefit limits found in health and disability policies there may be various *sublimits*—such as daily dollar limits on covered room and board charges, scheduled maximum amounts for various surgical procedures, and weekly dollar limits for disability income benefits.

Deductibles

Deductibles are a common feature of medical insurance coverages (the term has no application in life insurance). A *deductible* is simply the initial amount of a covered loss (or losses) that the insured must absorb before the insurer begins to pay for additional loss amounts. For example, if a basic medical expense policy pays losses only above a $250 deductible and an insured incurs $1,000 of covered medical expenses, the insured would have to pay the first $250 and the insurer would then pay the additional $750 of expenses.

Disability insurance usually has an *elimination period* or a *waiting period* that is similar to a deductible. The elimination period is simply a number of days that an insured must be disabled before disability income benefits become payable. For example, if a policy specifies an elimination period of 7 days and an insured is disabled for 30 days, the policy would pay benefits only for the 23 days following the elimination period.

> The purpose of a deductible is to minimize small nuisance claims and to keep premiums down. It might cost an insurer much more just to process the paperwork on $10 and $25 claims than the amount of the claims. Naturally, these costs would have to be reflected in insurance rates if such small claims were covered. Deductibles help eliminate this problem and keep rates down. Insurers usually offer a standard deductible, but give applicants the option of purchasing higher deductibles that result in even lower premiums.

Coinsurance

Coinsurance is another concept commonly found in medical insurance policies. It means that within a specified coverage range, the insured and insurer will share the allowable expenses. It is usually expressed in percentages (such as 20%–80%). For example, if a policy has a $500 deductible and a 20%/80% coinsurance provision for the next $10,000 of expenses, a $5,500 medical bill would be settled in the following manner: The insured would pay the first $500 (the deductible amount) and $1,000 of the additional expenses (the insured's 20% share); the insurer would pay the remaining $4,000 (the insurer's 80% share).

Types of Insurance

Insurers market a variety of insurance products. The most common products offered are property, casualty, life, health insurance, and annuities:

➤ *Property insurance* protects the insured against the financial consequences of the direct or consequential loss or damage to property of every kind.

➤ *Casualty insurance* protects the insured against the financial consequences of legal liability, including that for death, injury, or disability, or damage to real or personal property.

Almost every insured has a need for both property and casualty insurance coverage, whether personal or business (commercial). Some of the property and casualty coverages are sold together in special policies called *packages*.

➤ *Life insurance* is insurance coverage on human lives including benefits of endowment and annuities, and may include benefits in the event of death or dismemberment by accident and benefits for disability insurance. It is designed to protect against the risk of premature death—

dying too soon. Premature death exposes a family or a business to certain financial risks, such as burial expenses, paying off debts, loss of family income, and business profits.

➤ An *annuity* is a guaranteed income for the life of an annuitant. Annuities are designed to protect against the risk of living too long; that is, outliving one's financial resources and income during retirement.

➤ *Accident and Health or sickness insurance* protects the insured against financial loss caused by sickness, bodily injury, or accidental death and may include benefits for disability income. It may reimburse the insured for actual medical expenses incurred due to an accident or illness (hospitalization insurance) or it may provide protection for loss of income experienced by the insured during periods of disability due to accident or sickness (disability income insurance).

➤ *Variable life and variable annuity products* include insurance coverage provided under variable life insurance contracts and variable annuities. Variable products carry investment risk, that is, the insured may lose money due to a decrease in the price of the securities underlying the policy. For this reason, individuals selling such products are required to carry a Securities license as well as an insurance license.

➤ *Credit insurance* is a limited line of insurance, protecting the insured, who is usually a creditor, against the financial consequences should a debtor be unable to pay his or her debts due to illness or death. Other types of insurance, such as title insurance or crop insurance, may be authorized in individual states. These limited lines of insurance are more narrowly focused than the types of insurance listed above, generally falling within the broad scope of one of the types of insurance listed above.

Types of Insurers

Insurance is provided to the public by three major sources: private commercial insurers (profit-making), private noncommercial insurers (nonprofit service organizations), and the United States government (special nonprofit). Other types of private insurers include reciprocals, fraternals, Lloyd's, reinsurers, and selfinsurers.

Private life and health insurers are in the business to make a reasonable profit, and are, therefore, called *commercial insurers*. Stock and mutual insurers are private insurers. Private *noncommercial* service organizations, like Blue Cross and Blue Shield, operate on a nonprofit basis. A nonprofit status exists when profits are returned to subscribers in the form of reduced premium or expanded benefits (similar to mutual insurers).

Commercial Insurers

The most common types of insurers are commercial insurance companies.

Stock Insurers

A *stock insurance company*, like other stock companies, consists of stockholders who own shares in the company. The individual stockholders provide capital for the insurer. In return, they share in any profits and any losses. Management control rests with the board of directors, selected by the stockholders. The board of directors elects the officers who conduct the daily operations of the business. Capital stock companies control two-thirds of the premiums in the property and liability field and nearly one-half of the premiums in life insurance. If the board of directors declares a dividend, it is paid to the stockholders. Often a stock company is referred to as a *nonparticipating* company because policyholders do not participate in dividends.

Mutual Insurers

In a *mutual company*, there are no stockholders. Formation funds must be contributed by someone or some group. Because of the difficulties involved today in obtaining the funds to organize a mutual company, many mutual companies start as stock companies and then mutualize.

In a mutual company, ownership rests with the policyholders. They vote for a board of directors that in turn elects or appoints the officers to operate the company. Funds not paid out after paying claims and not used in paying for other costs of operation are returned to the policyowners in the form of policy dividends. As such, mutual companies are sometimes referred to as *participating* companies because the policyowners participate in dividends.

Nonprofit (Service) Organizations

Service insurers are unique to the health insurance field, and technically they are not insurers. They are organizations providing prepaid plans for hospital, medical, and surgical expenses. They do not provide cash benefits (except under certain limited conditions) to the plan subscriber, but instead pay the provider of medical services used by the plan subscriber to the extent covered in the contract. Best known of the service insurers are the various Blue Cross and Blue Shield plans. Blue Cross plans cover hospital expenses and Blue Shield plans cover medical and surgical expenses.

Other Types of Private Insurers

There are a few other types of private insurers.

Reciprocal Insurers

Reciprocal insurers are unincorporated groups of people providing insurance for one another through individual indemnity agreements. Each individual who is a member of the reciprocal is known as a *subscriber*. Each subscriber is allocated a separate account where his or her premiums are paid and interest earned is tracked. If any subscriber should suffer a loss provided for by the reciprocal insurance, each subscriber account would be assessed an equal amount to pay the claim. Administration, underwriting, sales promotion, and claims handling for the reciprocal insurance is handled by an *attorney-in-fact*.

Fraternal Insurers

Fraternal benefit societies are primarily life insurance carriers that exist as social organizations and usually engage in charitable and benevolent activities. Fraternals are distinguished by the fact that their membership is usually drawn from those who are also members of a lodge or fraternal organization. They operate under a special section of the state insurance code and receive some income tax advantages.

Lloyd's

Lloyd's of London is not an insurance company, but may be compared to a stock exchange. Just as an exchange provides facilities for its members but does not buy or sell securities itself, Lloyd's provides a meeting place and clerical services to its members who actually transact the business of insurance. Members may be individuals or corporations.

Members are grouped into syndicates, but they remain individually liable and responsible for the contracts of insurance they enter into. Their individual fortunes and resources are pledged as the capital behind their assumption of risk.

Assessment Insurers

An assessment company retains the right to charge policyholders additional premiums if those paid in are insufficient to meet claims.

Reinsurers

Reinsurance is a form of insurance between insurers. It occurs when an insurer (the reinsurer) agrees to accept all or a portion of a risk covered by another insurer (the ceding company). In the event of loss, the insured has no claim against the reinsurer. The ceding company is responsible for the coverage it has written, but it will have a legitimate claim against the reinsurer for any portion of its own loss that is reinsured.

Excess and Surplus Lines

Occasionally, it may be difficult to place a risk in the normal marketplace. If the risk is very large or unusual in nature, typical carriers may be unwilling to assume it. For some special risks, the only market may be with specialty carriers. *Excess and surplus lines* is the name given to insurance for which there is no market through the original producer, or insurance that is not available through authorized carriers in the state where the risk arises or is located. Such business must be placed through a licensed excess or surplus lines broker, who will attempt to place it with an unauthorized carrier.

Self-Insurers

Self-insurance is a means of *retaining risk*. For a risk to be truly self-insured, two important characteristics must be present: a large number of homogeneous exposure units, so that the law of large numbers can be used to predict expected losses; and sufficient liquid assets to pay claims and other costs of retaining risk.

The advantages of self-insurance are that money can be saved if losses are less than those predicted, expenses may be reduced by the elimination of such things as administrative costs and commissions, and the self-insurer has use of the money that would normally be held by the insurance company. The main disadvantages of self-insurance are that actual losses may be more than predicted, and expenses could be higher than expected if additional personnel have to be hired to administer the program.

The United States Government as an Insurer

The federal government provides life and health insurance through various sources. The federal government has offered a variety of military life insurance plans including United States Government Life Insurance (to veterans of World War I), National Service Life Insurance (in 1940) and Servicemen's Group Life Insurance. Additional occupations are eligible for federal government insurance provided through the Railroad Retirement Act, the Civil Service Retirement Act, and the Federal Employees' Compensation Act.

Because private insurance policies exclude catastrophic risks, the federal government has stepped in to provide War Risk Insurance, Nuclear Energy Liability Insurance, National Flood Insurance, Federal Crime Insurance,

Federal Crop Insurance, and insurance on mortgage loans. At the state level, governments are involved in providing unemployment insurance, workers compensation programs and second-injury funds, and state-run medical expense insurance plans.

Federal, state, and local governments provide *social insurance* to a segment of the population who would otherwise be without disability income, retirement income, or medical care.

Social Security provides survivor benefits in the event of death of a covered worker. These benefits include a lump-sum burial amount of $255 plus monthly income benefits to eligible survivors. Social Security also provides disability benefits in the event of the total disability of a covered worker. In addition, the program also provides retirement benefits to covered workers at age 65 or earlier if elected by the individual. The Medicare program is also part of Social Security and accordingly provides medical expense benefits for covered workers beginning at age 65. All these programs will be discussed in more detail in later chapters.

Medicaid is primarily a state governmental program that provides health care benefits for the financially needy. Medicaid is financed by the states with some federal subsidies.

Domicile and Authorization

Insurers may be categorized according to where they are domiciled and whether they are authorized to operate within a state.

Insurer's Domicile (Domestic, Foreign, and Alien Insurers)

An insurer is defined not only by its corporate status, but also by where it is located, or its *domicile of incorporation*. If an insurer is conducting business in the state where it is incorporated, that insurer is a *domestic insurer* in that state. If an insurer conducts business in a state where it is not incorporated, the insurer is a *foreign insurer* in that state. If an insurer is conducting business in a country where it is not incorporated, it is an *alien insurer* in that country. Therefore, an insurer incorporated in California is a domestic insurer when it is conducting business in California. The same company is a foreign insurer when it is conducting business in New York and an alien insurer when it is conducting business in Canada.

Authorized Versus Unauthorized (Admitted Versus Nonadmitted)

Before an insurance company can conduct business it must, by law, receive the authority to do so. Insurance statutes require a company to secure a license from the department of insurance to sell insurance in a particular state. After the insurer receives the license, it is considered *admitted* into the state as a legal insurer and is *authorized* to transact the business of insurance. Those insurers not licensed to transact insurance within the state are referred to as *unauthorized* or *nonadmitted*. This licensing power (sometimes companies are referred to as *licensed* and *nonlicensed*) is used to regulate company activities.

Types of Distribution Systems

Insurance companies market their products generally in one of two ways: by using producers to sell their products or by selling directly through mass marketing. The vast majority of policies are sold through producers.

Agency System

Companies that use producers to sell their products vary by whether the producers are employees or independent sales representatives.

Independent Insurance Producers

Independent Insurance Producers sell the insurance products of several companies and work for themselves or other producers. They sell their clients the policy that fits their needs best among the many insurers they represent and are paid a commission for each sale.

The independent producer owns the expirations of the policies he or she sells, meaning that the agent may place that business with another insurer upon renewal, if in the best interest of the client, and still retain control of the account and be entitled to the commission.

Exclusive Producers

Exclusive or *captive producers* represent only one company, and have an agency relationship with that company. These producers are sometimes referred to as *career agents* working from *career agencies*. Most often, these captive or career producers are compensated by commissions. A career producer's compensation will normally consist of first-year commissions and renewal commissions in subsequent years. If a producer hires, trains, and supervises other producers within a specific geographical area, he or she is referred to as a *general agent or managing general agent* (MGA). The MGA is compensated by commissions earned on business sold by him or herself as well as an overriding commission (overrides) on the business produced by the other producers managed by the general agent.

Direct Writing Companies

Direct writing companies usually pay salaries to employees whose job function is to sell the company's insurance products. Technically, these salaried employees do not function as producers. Commissions are usually not paid and the insurer owns all the business produced.

Mass Marketing

Mass marketing has grown in general use over the past several years. The most common types of mass marketing systems are direct-response, franchise, noninsurance sponsors, and vending machine sales.

Direct-Response

Direct-response marketing is conducted through the mail, by advertisement in newspapers and magazines, and on television and radio. Policies sold using this method have limited benefits and low premiums, such as disability only.

Franchise Marketing

The franchise marketing system provides coverage to employees of small firms or to members of associations. Unlike group policies where benefits are standard for classes of individuals, persons insured under the franchise method receive individual policies that vary according to the individuals' needs.

Noninsurance Sponsors

Noninsurance sponsors are being used more and more. The most common are banks and companies that issue credit cards. This marketing system reaches a select group of individuals who have a history of periodic payments.

Vending Machine Sales

Vending machine sales have traditionally been of travel accident policies sold from coin-operated machines at airports. A large amount of coverage is available at low premiums. The coverage is good only for the duration of a single trip.

Internet Insurance Sales

Advertising and selling insurance through the Internet are relatively recent developments in insurance distribution. Insurance company websites offer information about insurers, the various lines of insurance provided, and links to regulatory information, financial ratings, and quotation services, as well as "locator" services to put the consumer in touch with a local agent.

Insurance Producers

The term *producer* is becoming increasingly common for several reasons. Many states have replaced separate agent and broker licenses with a single producer license. In addition, a major law change in 1999 (discussed later in this course) removed prior legislative barriers between insurers, banks, and securities brokerages, allowing insurance to be sold by a wider range of professionals. Anyone who produces sales of insurance products is a *producer*.

Categories of Producers

Producers may function as agents, representing the insurance company, or as brokers, representing the potential insured. In some states, solicitors are still licensed and function as insurance producers.

Life and Health Agents

Generally, life and health insurance agents represent the insurer to the buyer with respect to the sale of life and health insurance products. The agents are appointed by the insurer and usually the agent's authority to represent the insurer is specified in the agency agreement between them, which is a working agreement between the agent and the insurer.

The life agent may receive the first premium due with the application but usually not subsequent premiums, except in industrial life insurance. The insurance company approves and issues the contract after receiving the application and premium from the applicant through the agent. The agent *cannot bind* coverage. This means that an agent cannot commit to providing insurance coverage on behalf of the insurance company.

Property and Casualty Agents

Agents appointed by property and liability insurance companies generally are granted more authority. These agents may *bind* or commit their companies by oral or written agreement. They sometimes inspect risks for the insurance company and collect premiums due. They may be authorized to issue many types of insurance contracts from their own offices.

Brokers

In contrast to the agent-client relationship in which the agent represents the insurer to the purchaser, a *broker* represents the buyer to the insurer. A broker may do business with several different insurers. Brokers are independent sales representatives who select insurance coverages from these various companies for their clients.

Brokers must be licensed just like agents, and generally their routine activities and functions are similar to that of agents. Brokers solicit applications for insurance and may collect the initial premium and deliver policies. Brokers do not have the authority to bind coverages.

Solicitors

A *solicitor* is a salesperson who works for an agent or a broker. Most often the solicitor will be licensed as a solicitor. The solicitor's primary functions are to solicit insurance, collect initial premiums, and deliver policies. Solicitors cannot bind coverage.

Insurance Consultants

A very small group of insurance professionals call themselves insurance consultants. *Consultants* are not paid by commission for the sales of insurance policies. Instead, they work strictly for the benefit of insureds and are paid a fee by the insureds they represent.

Exam Prep Questions

1. A social device for spreading the chance of financial loss among a large number of people is the definition of
   - ○ A. Hazard
   - ○ B. Risk
   - ○ C. Insurance
   - ○ D. Peril

2. Which of the following risks is most likely to be insurable?
   - ○ A. George is concerned about the financial impact his premature death would have on his family.
   - ○ B. Talyn is concerned about the financial impact large betting losses at the horse track will have on his retirement savings.
   - ○ C. John is concerned about the financial impact on his savings when his car eventually becomes worn enough to need to be replaced.
   - ○ D. Jewel is concerned about the financial impact losing her hat would have on her weekly spending money.

3. Roger refuses to travel by airplane. Roger is managing the risk of being in a plane crash by
   - ○ A. Reduction
   - ○ B. Avoidance
   - ○ C. Transference
   - ○ D. Retention

4. Chianna becomes injured in a car accident caused when she took her eyes off the road to answer her cell phone. This is an example of a
   - ○ A. Physical hazard
   - ○ B. Moral hazard
   - ○ C. Morale hazard
   - ○ D. Legal hazard

5. Mathematicians who study and compile statistical data regarding exposure and risks for insurance companies are called
   - ○ A. Solicitors
   - ○ B. Insuraries
   - ○ C. Underwriters
   - ○ D. Actuaries

6. Which of the following would not be an example of insurable interest?

   ○ A. Jose wishes to take out a life insurance policy on his own life to provide for his family in the event of his death.

   ○ B. Ana wishes to take out a life insurance policy on her mother to ensure that funeral costs will be covered when the time comes.

   ○ C. Juan wishes to take out a life insurance policy on his neighbor because his neighbor is a careless driver who Juan thinks is likely to die in a car accident.

   ○ D. Carla wishes to take out a life insurance policy on her best salesperson to protect the business from lost sales in the event of the salesperson's death.

7. Kim is injured in a house fire. When the bills come, the insurance company pays 80% of the cost and Kim pays the rest. This is an example of

   ○ A. Coinsurance

   ○ B. A deductible

   ○ C. Extraneous insurance

   ○ D. Policy limits

8. Hoosier Insurance Company is owned by the policyholders. Hoosier Insurance is a

   ○ A. Stock insurer

   ○ B. Mutual insurer

   ○ C. Nonprofit insurer

   ○ D. Fraternal insurer

9. Which of the following people represents several insurance companies but owns the policy expirations?

   ○ A. Independent agent

   ○ B. Exclusive agent

   ○ C. Direct writing agent

   ○ D. General agent

10. Which of the following can bind an insurance company by oral or written agreement?

   ○ A. Property/Casualty producer

   ○ B. Life producer

   ○ C. Broker

   ○ D. Solicitor

11. The ZYX Insurance Company is incorporated in Alabama. While doing business in Texas, it is

- O A. A domestic insurer
- O B. A foreign insurer
- O C. An alien insurer
- O D. An export insurer

12. Self-insurance is an example of which method of handling risk?

- O A. Acceptance
- O B. Transference
- O C. Avoidance
- O D. Reduction

Exam Prep Answers

1. **C is correct.** Insurance is a social device for spreading the chance of loss among a large number of people.

2. **A is correct.** Purchasing life insurance is a legitimate and practical use of insurance. The other answer choices do not reflect insurable risks.

3. **B is correct.** By not even getting on an airplane Roger has avoided the risk he is afraid to take.

4. **C is correct.** Carelessness is an example of a morale hazard.

5. **D is correct.** Actuaries study and analyze statistical data in order to project losses and develop premium rates.

6. **C is correct.** Juan has no personal or financial interest is his neighbor and is simply gambling. This is not an example of insurable interest, but all of the other answer choices are.

7. **A is correct.** When coinsurance applies, an insured may be required to pay a percentage of a health insurance cost known as a copayment.

8. **B is correct.** A mutual company is owned by its policyholders. A stock company is owned by its shareholders.

9. **A is correct.** An independent agent may represent many insurers but owns his or her accounts and is entitled to renewal commissions even if they shift to another company.

10. **A is correct.** Property/Casualty producers often have authority to bind coverage. Life insurance agents, brokers, and solicitors never have binding authority.

11. **B is correct.** Because ZYX is incorporated in Alabama, it is a foreign insurer within the jurisdiction of Texas.

12. **A is correct.** Self-insurance is an example of accepting risk because no other party will be involved if a loss occurs.

Insurance Regulation

Terms you need to understand:

✓ Pretext interview
✓ Rehabilitation
✓ Liquidation
✓ Temporary agent license
✓ Producer appointment
✓ Controlled business
✓ Misrepresentation
✓ Twisting
✓ Churning
✓ Defamation
✓ Discrimination
✓ Rebating

Concepts you need to master:

✓ Consumer report
✓ Investigative consumer report
✓ Disclosure authorization
✓ Company financial ratings
✓ Guaranty associations
✓ Unfair trade practices
✓ Unfair claims practices
✓ Self-regulation

Insurance is a public trust because it affects a large percentage of the general public and because it performs what can be construed as a public service by its very nature. The general public has an interest in making sure that insurance activity actually is provided as a service and not a disservice. Insurance is highly regulated to protect the public interest and to make sure coverage is available on an equitable basis.

Regulation of the insurance industry is divided among a number of authorities. The three major channels of regulation of the insurance industry are

➤ Federal regulation

➤ State regulation

➤ Self-regulation

 Most insurance regulation takes place at the state level, but there are some important regulations at the federal level. The National Association of Insurance Commissioners (NAIC) also plays an important role in insurance regulation.

Federal Regulation

Federal jurisdiction applies to individuals or companies whose activities affect interstate commerce, which includes most insurance activity. Federal regulation of insurance is primarily used as a means to oversee those areas not covered by state regulation of the industry. The most important sources of federal regulation are outlined in the following sections and include both legislative and judicial aspects.

Paul Versus Virginia

In the case of *Paul v. Virginia*, the Court's decision established, as law, that the transaction of insurance across state lines was not interstate commerce and therefore should be regulated by local law. This decision held for 75 years.

South-Eastern Underwriters Decision

In 1944 that decision was overturned by the Supreme Court, who said that insurance transacted across state lines was, in fact, interstate commerce. This decision had the capability of turning regulation of the insurance industry upside down.

McCarran-Ferguson Act

In order to waylay any impending confusion, Congress enacted the McCarran-Ferguson Act in 1945. This act stated that the federal government had the right to regulate the business of insurance, but only to the extent that such business is not regulated by state law. The main intent of the law was to exempt the insurance industry from most of the provisions of the federal antitrust laws.

Privacy Act Of 1974

In the 1970s the *Privacy Protection Study Commission* was established. The study found insurers to be one of the major collectors and users of personal information. The Commission's report resulted in the Privacy Act, which affected the way insurers obtained and handled personal information about applicants and insureds.

Disclosure Authorization

Applicants for insurance must be given *advance notice* of the insurer's practices regarding collection and use of personal information. Notice must be given promptly and in writing. Notice should be given in the following cases and in the following manner:

➤ If a third party is interviewed, the applicant must be given notice when the collection of information has begun.

➤ If only the applicant is interviewed, the applicant must be given notice when the policy is delivered.

➤ If a policy is being renewed, the insured must be given notice by the renewal date.

➤ If a policy is being reinstated, the applicant-insured must be given notice at the time the request is made.

➤ If an insured is requesting a change in benefits, the insured must receive notice at the time the request is made.

The notice must give the applicant or insured the following kinds of information:

➤ The people with access to personal information

➤ The kind of information to be collected

➤ The kind of information the insurer can receive without the applicant's prior approval

➤ The sources of information

➤ The persons to whom information may be disclosed without the applicant's prior authorization

Disclosure authorization forms are required by law to be prescribed and approved by the Commissioner. The disclosure form must be written in accordance with the plain language laws of the state and dated. Disclosure forms state the types of persons authorized to disclose private and personal information (for example, neighbors, employers, and previous or other insurers) and the kind of information that may be disclosed (for example, personal habits, work habits, and health habits such as smoking and drinking). The form must also state the reason information is collected and how it will be used. For instance, the *reason* personal information is gathered is because the applicant requested a life insurance policy; the information will be used by the underwriting department for the *purpose* of determining the applicant's risk category.

The applicant's signature on the disclosure form authorizes the insurer to collect and disseminate information in the manner described in the notice. The authorization is good only for a certain period of time. For example, if authorization is given to an insurer to collect information with regard to a claim settlement, the authorization is good for 30 months. At the end of this period another authorization must be obtained. The applicant or insured may request, and receive, a copy of the authorization form.

Personal information may be disclosed to persons other than the requesting parties under certain conditions. Among those to whom an insurer may disclose information are producers, other insurers, insurance organizations (such as the Medical Information Bureau), and insurance departments. This type of third-party disclosure may require authorization, but in some instances authorization is not required, as long as the applicant or insured has received proper notification of the insurer's information practices. In some cases information is passed on to those conducting scientific research, audits, or marketing approaches.

Penalties

The Commissioner of Insurance has the authority to investigate any insurer, or any agency used by the insurer to collect information, to determine whether the company is in compliance with the Insurance Act. If the Commissioner believes that a violation of the Privacy Act has taken place, he or she can conduct a hearing to determine the facts. If a violation is found, the Commissioner can issue a cease and desist order, but if the violator continues to violate the Privacy Act, the Commissioner can institute a fine of up to $10,000 for each violation. If the violation is one that happens with such frequency that it appears to be a general business practice, the fine for each violation can be up to $50,000.

The NAIC Model Privacy Act also provides for the enforcement of individual rights. The individual has the right to information concerning himself or herself, the right to correct inaccurate information, the right to know the reasons for being turned down for insurance, and the right to know any other adverse underwriting decision. These rights are those found under the Fair Credit Reporting Act.

A fine of $10,000, or up to one year in jail is the penalty for any person who obtains information that he or she has no legitimate reason to receive.

Fair Credit Reporting Act

When an application is submitted to a life or health insurance company, a consumer reporting agency may be hired to obtain personal information about the applicant to be used in the underwriting evaluation. To protect the consumer's right to privacy in this situation, the federal Fair Credit Reporting Act was passed in 1970. The Act sets up procedures for consumer reporting agencies to follow in their dealings with businesses to ensure that records are confidential, accurate, relevant, and properly used.

Consumer Reports

Consumer reports include written, oral, and other forms of communication that a consumer reporting agency has regarding a consumer's credit, character, reputation, or habits, which is used or collected to determine whether a consumer is eligible for credit, insurance, employment, or other purposes authorized under the Act. Consumer reports may be issued only to persons who have a legitimate business need for the information. Governmental agencies may also be provided with a consumer's name, present and former addresses, and present and past places of employment.

Investigative Consumer Reports

An investigative consumer report includes information on a consumer's character, general reputation, personal habits, and mode of living that is obtained through investigation—that is, interviews with associates and friends and neighbors of the consumer. Such reports may not be made unless the consumer is clearly and accurately told about the report in writing within three days of the date on which the report was first requested. The consumer must also be notified that he or she is allowed to request additional information. If that person requests such information in writing, the person who caused the investigative report to be made must make a complete and accurate disclosure of the report to the consumer about whom it is written. The disclosure must be made within five days of receipt of the report or when the report was first requested, whichever date is later. If there is an investigative consumer report prepared subsequent to the first one, any adverse information must be verified or must have been received during the three months preceding the subsequent report.

Pretext Interviews

A *pretext interview* is an interview whereby a person, in an attempt to obtain information about another person, pretends to be someone he or she is not, misrepresents the true purpose of the interview, or refuses to properly identify him- or herself.

Generally, pretext interviews are prohibited. However, such an interview may be conducted when there is evidence of criminal activity, fraud, or misrepresentation.

Consumer Reporting Agencies

Consumer reporting agencies collect information on individuals, prepare reports, and make the reports available to persons or organizations having a legitimate reason to receive such information. These agencies may operate for profit—for example, Experian or Equifax. Agencies also may be nonprofit, such as the Medical Information Bureau (MIB) or a credit union.

A consumer may choose to have his or her name and address excluded from any list provided by a consumer reporting agency in connection with a credit or insurance transaction that is not initiated by the consumer. The consumer simply needs to notify the agency that he or she does not consent to any use of a consumer report relating to the consumer in connection with any credit or insurance transaction that is not initiated by the consumer.

Credit agencies are required to provide a notification system, including a toll-free telephone number, to allow consumers to request exclusion of their information. This notification is valid for two years. If notification is made in writing on a signed notice of election form issued by the agency, it is valid until the consumer revokes the request. The consumer may revoke the request at any time.

Prohibited Information

Consumer reporting agencies are specifically prevented from putting information in their reports about

➤ Bankruptcies over 10 years old

➤ Suits and judgments over seven years old or in which the statute of limitations has expired, whichever period is longer

➤ Paid tax liens or accounts placed for collection or charged to profit that are over seven years old

➤ Arrests, indictments, or conviction of crime reports

➤ Any other adverse information that took place seven years prior to the report

These restrictions are not applicable when the consumer credit report is used in connection with a credit transaction of $150,000 or more, a life insurance policy of $150,000 or more, or when it concerns employment of an individual earning $75,000 or more.

Consumers' Rights

Consumers who feel that information in their files is inaccurate or incomplete may inform the consumer reporting agency of any information in dispute. The consumer reporting agency is then required to reinvestigate and record the current status of the disputed material (unless the agency has reasonable grounds to believe the dispute is frivolous or irrelevant) in a reasonable period of time.

If the agency's investigation finds that the information is no longer accurate or verifiable, it must be deleted promptly. If the dispute is not resolved after reinvestigation, the consumer may file a brief statement (not more than 100 words) concerning the problem. If this statement is filed, the consumer reporting agency must note it in future consumer reports that contain that information (unless it is determined to be frivolous or irrelevant). If credit or insurance is denied or charges are increased, based wholly or partially on information contained in a consumer report, the user of the information must notify the consumer of this fact and report the name and address of the consumer reporting agency that made the report. If credit or insurance is denied or charges are increased, wholly or partially due to information obtained from a person or organization *other* than a consumer reporting agency, the user of the information must disclose the nature of that information to the consumer if it has been requested within 60 days of the disclosure. It is the responsibility of the user of the information to inform the consumer of his or her right to request this information when the adverse action is communicated to him or her.

Penalties

Failure to comply with the provisions of the Act makes the guilty party liable to the consumer for the sum of actual damages sustained as a result of the noncompliance, punitive damages deemed proper by a court, and the costs of an action that enforces liability, plus reasonable attorney's fees. When the noncompliance is due to negligence, the guilty party must pay the consumer the sum of the consumer's actual damages, the costs of any successful action to enforce liability, plus reasonable attorney's fees.

False or Fraudulent Statements

Certain types of false or fraudulent statements have been specifically outlined in federal law as punishable by a fine, a prison sentence, or both. Federal law prohibits persons engaging in the business of insurance whose activities affect interstate commerce from knowingly, with the intent to deceive

➤ Making any false material statement or report that willfully and materially overvalues any land, property, or security in connection with any financial reports or documents presented to an insurance regulatory official or agency, or an agent or examiner acting for an insurance regulatory official for the purpose of influencing the actions of such individual.

➤ Making any false entry of material fact in any book, report, or statement of such person engaged in the business of insurance with the intent to deceive any person, including any officer, employee, or agent of such person engaged in the business of insurance regarding the financial condition or solvency of such business.

➤ Willfully embezzling, abstracting, purloining, or misappropriating any of the moneys, funds, premiums, credits, or other property of any person engaged in the business of insurance.

➤ Corruptly influencing, obstructing, or impeding the due and proper administration of the law under which any proceeding is pending before any insurance regulatory official or agency or any producer or examiner appointed by such official or agency to examine the affairs of a person engaged in the business of insurance.

The attorney general may bring a civil action in the appropriate United States district court against any person who engages in unfair and deceptive practices as defined in the law and, upon proof of such conduct by a preponderance of the evidence, the person will be subject to a fine of not more than $50,000 for each violation or the amount of compensation that the person received or offered for the prohibited conduct, whichever amount is greater.

Financial Services Modernization Act Of 1999

Also known as the Gramm-Leach-Bliley Act (GLBA), this legislation was passed in 1999 primarily to remove depression-era barriers between commercial banking, investment banking, and insurance. GLBA allows financial holding companies to engage in any activities that are financial in nature.

Regulation of these holding companies is managed on a functional basis. This means that regulatory authority is based on what activity is occurring, rather than on what type of company is engaging in the activity. For example, the sale of insurance is regulated by state insurance regulators even if the company making the sale is a bank or securities brokerage.

The law also requires that all the functional federal regulatory agencies establish appropriate information safeguards:

➤ To ensure the security and confidentiality of customer records and information;

➤ To protect against any anticipated threats or hazards to the security or integrity of such records;

➤ To protect against unauthorized access to or use of such records or information that could result in substantial harm or inconvenience to any customer.

Anyone about whom a company collects any information is a *consumer*. A *customer* is a consumer who has an ongoing relationship with the financial institution. Different states define *ongoing relationship* using different guidelines, so be certain you understand what it means in your state. GLBA protects the confidentiality of personal information. Business information is not covered under this statute. GLBA considers information to be *collected* when it is organized or can be retrieved by an individual's name or by an identifying number, such as a policy number. The source of the information is less important than how it is stored and organized.

Information that is publicly available, such as phone numbers listed in a telephone book, is not protected under GLBA. However, the fact that an individual has an insurance policy with a certain company is not public information, so publishing a list of policyholder names and listed phone numbers would not automatically be allowed.

In some cases, consumers and customers are given the opportunity to keep the company from sharing the information it has about them. This is known as the right to *opt out*. Health information, such as that acquired during a medical exam, is subject to a stricter *opt-in* standard, meaning that companies may not share some health information without getting specific permission to do so from the customer or consumer. However, companies are always permitted to share information with their affiliates.

GLBA requires that a company make two primary disclosures to customers: one at the time of the establishment of the customer relationship, and the second prior to the company disclosing protected information. The first disclosure is to be made at the time a consumer becomes a customer, usually by purchasing a policy. At this point, the company is required to give a clear and conspicuous disclosure to the new customer regarding its policies and procedures for customer privacy. The customer must, at least on an annual basis, receive an updated notice containing the same information.

The second disclosure required by GLBA explains the customer's right to opt out of information sharing. Each customer must be given the right to opt out and must be told explicitly how he or she may exercise that right. The notice must identify the products and services to which the opt-out right applies. The only other requirement is that the opt-out agreement must be in writing and may be electronic if the customer agrees. If the customer does not take advantage of this option within a reasonable time, the company may share the information with others.

Other Regulating Agencies

Some insurance products are regulated by both the federal and state government. For example, the Securities and Exchange Commission (SEC) and the state insurance departments regulate variable contracts.

State Insurance Regulation

Most insurance regulation takes place at the state level. The body of laws at the state level is called the *Insurance Code*. State regulation consists of statutes, rules, and regulations. *Statutes* are the body of law developed by the Legislative branch of government. They outline, in general terms, the duties of the Commissioner and the activities of the insurance department. *Rules* and *regulations* are developed by the insurance department to expand upon statutory requirements and carry out legislative intent.

Commissioner's Scope and Duties

The Insurance Code of each state authorizes the establishment of an insurance department to administer and carry out the insurance laws. In each state, a public official will head the department—the title of the official will be the *Commissioner*, *Superintendent*, or *Director* of insurance. The insurance laws of the state usually confer upon the Commissioner all the following powers and duties:

➤ To conduct investigations and examinations

➤ To make reasonable rules and regulations

➤ To hire employees and examiners, and delegate any power, duty, or function to such persons

➤ To examine the accounts, records, documents, and transactions of any insurer, agent, or broker

➤ To subpoena witnesses and administer oaths in order to further any examination, investigation, or hearing on insurance matters

➤ To issue orders and notices on decisions made or matters pending

➤ To issue insurance licenses and Certificates of Authority

➤ To impose penalties for violations of the Insurance Code, including but not limited to fines, suspensions, or revocations of licenses and Certificates of Authority, and requesting that the Attorney General prosecute a violator

➤ To approve insurance policy forms sold within the state

➤ To approve rates and rate increases for regulated lines of insurance

 Notice that the Commissioner does not make the insurance laws. He or she is simply in charge of making certain all insurance operations within the state are in compliance with the laws made by the State Legislature.

Regulating Insurance Companies

Before individuals can form an insurance company they must receive approval from the insurance department to organize. They must meet the requirements for incorporation, certificates of intention, and bylaws just as any other corporation. They are required to draw up a charter that states the proposed name of the insurer, location, lines of insurance to be sold, and method of operation. The insurance department will also conduct an investigation to ensure that the organizers are of good moral character.

The majority of individual life and health insurance is written by stock and mutual companies. A mutual company must have a minimum number of applications for insurance, the advanced premium payment for each application, and a surplus. A stock company must have a specified amount of capital, which is invested, and a surplus amount. In many states domestic insurers must deposit securities that insurance regulations specify as relatively stable and safe, such as government bonds.

Insurer Solvency

Insurance insolvency regulations govern such areas as the organization and ownership of a new company, capital and surplus requirements, reserves, accounting, investments, annual statements, and the rehabilitation and liquidation of impaired insurers. If an insurer gets into trouble, the insurance department will attempt to rehabilitate the company, or if this fails, handle the liquidation. In addition, insurance departments in many states have adopted regulations for the establishment of guaranty associations in the event that an insurer does, in spite of regulations and precautions, become insolvent.

Various state statutes impose capital and surplus requirements and the preparation of annual financial statements, and require periodic examinations of insurers by the insurance department. These laws establish initial financial requirements and help in the early detection of financial problems.

Investments

All states have regulations that are intended to assure that insurers invest only in high-quality assets to prevent insolvency. Life insurance companies may invest funds in concerns that are fairly stable in value. These safe investments include municipal bonds, corporate bonds, real estate mortgages, and even policy loans.

Taxation of Life Insurance Companies

Life insurance companies are taxed on both their investment income and underwriting profits. For stock insurance companies, investment income is taxed in the year it is earned; 50% of underwriting profit is taxed during the year earned, and the other 50% is taxed when paid out to stockholders.

The one-half of the underwriting income that is taxed becomes shareholders' surplus, and the half that has not been taxed becomes policyholders' surplus. Both types of surplus are collectively known as the *earned surplus* of an insurance company.

Mutual insurers pay out their underwriting income as dividends to policyholders, so this tax regulation does not generally apply.

Company Ratings

Producers have a responsibility to place coverage with financially sound carriers. There are several organizations that rate the financial strength of insurance carriers, based on an analysis of a company's claims experience, investment performance, management, and other factors. These organizations include A.M. Best Company, Standard & Poor's Insurance Rating Services, Moody's Investors Service, Duff & Phelps Credit Rating Company, and Weiss Ratings. The firms don't all rate every company, and each firm has a different criteria for which companies will be rated. Each firm also uses a different methodology for evaluating the financial strength of insurance companies. There are at least four different rating scales in use among the five firms (see Table 2.1).

Table 2.1 Scales in use by Financial Rating Services	
Firm	**Scale from Highest to Lowest**
A. M. Best Company	A++, A+, A, A-, B++, B+, B, B-, C++, C+, C, C-, D, E, F
Weiss Research	A+, A, A-, B+, B, B-, C+, C, C-, D+, D, D-, E+, E, E-, F+, F, F-
Standard & Poor's/Duff Phelps	AAA, AA+, AA, AA-, A+, A, A-, BBB+, BBB, BBB-, BB+, BB, & BB- , B+, B, B-, CCC, CC, D
Moody's Investors Service	Aaa, Aa1, Aa2, Aa3, A1, A2, A3, Baa1, Baa2, Baa3, Ba1, Ba2, Ba3, B1, B2, B3, Caa1, Caa2, Caa3, Ca1, Ca2, Ca3, C1, C2, C3

Consumers might find a rating meaningless, or even misleading, if it is not presented in the context of the scale. For example, an A+ rating sounds as if it belongs at the top of the scale, but only one rating service considers it the top possible rating. From other services, it may be the third or even the fifth highest rating.

Examination of Insurers

The state insurance department must examine the *financial affairs*, transactions, and general business records of domestic insurers in accordance with specific state insurance laws. Generally, these laws will state that the Commissioner of Insurance may examine the insurer's records as often as necessary but at least once every three to five years.

The nonfinancial regulatory activities of an insurance department fall under the broad heading of *market conduct*. Proper market conduct means conducting insurance business fairly and responsibly. A market conduct examination is when state insurance department investigators examine the business practices and operations of an insurer and its agents in order to determine their authority to conduct insurance business in the state. During a market conduct examination, state examiners investigate the records and practices of an insurance company and determine whether the company is in fact in compliance with state laws regulating the sales and marketing, underwriting, and issuance of insurance products. Some states conduct market conduct exams in conjunction with their regular financial examinations of insurers; others conduct independent market conduct exams.

Guaranty Associations

State guaranty associations are organized to protect claimants, policyholders, annuitants, and creditors of financially impaired or insolvent insurers by providing funds for the payment of claims and other related policy benefits. The association is composed of insurers authorized to transact insurance business within the state. Association membership exceptions include fraternal organizations and nonprofit companies. Member insurers are assessed certain sums of money to cover the association's operating expenses. If an insurer insolvency should occur, each member insurer will be assessed additional fees to cover the insolvency.

Guaranty associations are often compared to the Federal Deposit Insurance Corporation (FDIC), which protects bank depositors from bank failures. As with the FDIC, coverage by the guaranty association is subject to limitations, usually something like $300,000 for death benefits, $100,000 for life insurance cash surrender/withdrawal values, $100,000 for health benefits, and an overall cap for individuals.

Marketing and Advertising Life and Health Insurance

States often regulate the marketing and advertising of life and health insurance policies to assure truthful and full disclosure of pertinent information when selling these policies. As a rule, the insurer is held responsible for the content of advertisements of its policies. Advertisements cannot be misleading or obscure, or use deceptive illustrations, and must clearly outline all policy coverage as well as exclusions or limitations on coverage (such as preexisting condition limitations).

Most states require insurers to keep a permanent *advertising file* of all advertisements used in the state until the next regular examination of the insurer by the insurance department, or for a specified minimum number of years, such as 2 or 3.

Also, many states require the delivery of a Buyers Guide and Policy Summary or Outline of Coverage at the time of policy delivery. The Buyers Guide is a document providing basic information about the insurance policies, and the Policy Summary (life insurance) or Outline of Coverage (health insurance) is a written statement describing the elements of the policy being sold. Generally, it must include the agent's name and address, the name and office address of the insurer, and the generic name of the policy and each rider.

Producer Regulation

Producers may function as either an agent or a broker. Agents represent their *companies;* brokers represent their *clients.* Because both agents and brokers seek to serve both their clients and companies by matching coverage with need, it is important to know the difference between the two roles. Regardless of their role, producers are governed by the Insurance Code with respect to licensing and unfair trade practices.

Licensing Regulation

GLBA, passed in 1999, contained a small but important section on the regulation of insurance producers, stating that 29 states must have uniform or reciprocal licensing regulations in place by November 12, 2002, or the federal government would begin licensing agents and brokers. Ideas about uniformity and reciprocity of state licenses had already been in the works for years, and the National Association of Commissioners had even drafted a Producer Licensing Model Act (PLMA) that satisfied GLBA. In addition, the PLMA had the advantages of creating some standard statutory language, maintaining individual state authority over licensing, and maintaining important consumer protections.

License Required

Under the statutes of most states, no person is permitted to act as an insurance producer unless currently licensed as a producer for the class or classes of insurance involved.

Acting as a producer includes selling, soliciting, or negotiating insurance. In many states, adjusters, consultants, and service representatives must also be licensed, but they are not insurance producers.

PLMA streamlined the qualifications for insurance producers. Some states still require additional qualifications. The qualifications listed in the Model Act are as follows:

➤ Be at least *18* years of age

➤ Have not committed any act that is a ground for denial, suspension, or revocation of an insurance license

➤ Where required by the Commissioner, complete a prelicensing course of study for the lines of authority for which the person has applied

➤ Where required, pay the appropriate fees

➤ Where required, successfully pass the examinations for the lines of authority for which the person has applied

Exceptions To License Requirements

PLMA also defines a standard set of exemptions from the licensing requirements. Generally speaking, people who do not get paid commissions for selling insurance do not need a license. The list of exemptions according to PLMA includes the following:

➤ Insurers

➤ Officers, directors, or employees of an insurer or a producer who do not receive commission on policies written or sold in the state if the individual's activities are executive, administrative, managerial, clerical, or a combination of these, and are only indirectly related to selling, soliciting, or negotiating insurance

➤ Officers, directors, or employees of an insurer or a producer who do not receive commission on policies written or sold in the state if the individual's function relates to underwriting, loss control, inspection or the processing, adjusting, investigating, or settling of a claim on a contract of insurance

➤ Officers, directors, or employees of an insurer or a producer who do not receive commission on policies written or sold in the state if the individual is acting in the capacity of a special agent or agency supervisor assisting insurance producers where the person's activities are limited to providing technical advice and assistance to licensed insurance producers and do not include the sale, solicitation, or negotiation of insurance

➤ A person who secures and furnishes information for the purpose of group life insurance, group property and casualty insurance, group annuities, group or blanket accident and health insurance, or for the purpose of enrolling people under plans, issuing certificates under plans or otherwise assisting in administering plans, or performs administrative services related to mass marketed property and casualty insurance; where no commission is paid for the service

➤ An employer or association or its officers, directors, employees, or the trustees of an employee trust plan, to the extent that the individuals are involved in the administration or operation of a program of employee benefits for the employer's or association's own employees or the employees of its subsidiaries or affiliates, when the program involves the use of insurance issued by an insurer, as long as the individuals are not compensated in any manner by the insurer issuing the contracts

➤ Employees of insurers or organizations employed by insurers who are engaging in the inspection, rating or classification of risks, or in the supervision of the training of insurance producers and who are not individually engaged in the sale, solicitation, or negotiation of insurance

➤ A person whose activities are limited to advertising without the intent to solicit insurance through communications in printed publication or other forms of electronic mass media whose distribution is not limited to residents of the state, provided that the person does not sell, solicit, or negotiate insurance that would insure risks residing, located or to be performed in this state

➤ A person who is not a resident of a state who sells, solicits, or negotiates a contract of insurance for commercial property and casualty risks to an insured with risks located in more than one state insured under that contract, provided that the person is licensed as an insurance producer in the state where the insured maintains its principal place of business and the contract of insurance insurers risks located in that state

➤ A salaried full-time employee who counsels or advises his or her employer relative to the insurance interest of the employer or of the subsidiaries or business affiliates of the employer provided that the employee does not sell or solicit insurance or receive a commission

Nonresident Producer Licensing

The majority of states allow for reciprocity in nonresident licensing as required in GLBA. *Reciprocity* means a mutual exchange of privileges. In the case of producer licensing, it means the recognition of two states of the validity of licenses or privileges granted by the other.

Obtaining a License

Requirements for obtaining an insurance license are similar around the country. Generally, they require having reached a minimum age, satisfying education requirements, and passing a state examination.

Application for Examination

A resident individual applying for an insurance producer license has to pass a written examination unless exempt as discussed previously. The exam is developed by the Commissioner to test the knowledge of the individual concerning the lines of authority for which the application is made, the duties and responsibilities of an insurance producer, and the insurance laws and regulations of the state.

The Commissioner may, and generally does, make arrangements to contract with an outside testing service for administering examinations and collecting the nonrefundable fee as described by state law. Each individual applying for an examination must pay a nonrefundable fee. If the individual fails to appear for the exam as scheduled or fails to pass the exam, he or she must reapply for the exam and remit all the required fees and forms before being rescheduled for another examination. States may limit the frequency of application for examination.

Issuance of License

Licenses contain the licensee's name, address, and personal identification number; the date of issuance; the lines of authority; the expiration date; and any other information the Commissioner deems necessary.

Temporary Agent Licenses

In most states, temporary agent licenses may be issued for up to *180 days* without requiring an examination if the Commissioner considers the temporary license necessary for maintaining an insurance business in the following cases:

➤ To the surviving spouse or court-appointed personal representative of a licensed producer who dies or becomes disabled to allow adequate time for the sale of the insurance business, or for the recovery or return of the producer to the business, or to provide for the training and licensing of new personnel to operate the producer's business

➤ To a member of a business entity licensed as an insurance producer, upon the death or disability of an individual designated in the business entity application or the license

➤ To the designee of a licensed insurance producer entering active service in the armed forces of the United States of America

➤ In any other circumstance where the Commissioner considers the temporary license necessary to ensure the public interest will be served

The authority of any temporary license can be limited in any way the Commissioner considers necessary to protect insureds and the public.

Maintaining a License

After they are licensed, producers have to satisfy certain obligations in order to keep their licenses.

Change of Address

Every licensee must promptly give to the head of the insurance department written notice of any change of business address. Most states require this notice be made within *30 days*.

Assumed Names

An insurance producer doing business under any name other than the producer's legal name is required to notify the Commissioner before using the assumed name.

Office and Records

Every resident producer must have and maintain in the state issuing the license a place of business accessible to the public. The designated place of business must be where the licensee principally conducts transactions under the license. The licenses of the licensee and solicitors appointed by the licensee shall be conspicuously displayed in a part of the place of business that is customarily open to the public. The producer must keep at the place of business the usual and customary records pertaining to insurance transactions.

Continuation, Expiration, and Renewal of License

Producer licenses generally remain in effect unless revoked or suspended as long as the appropriate fee is paid and the continuing education requirements are met by the due date.

An individual insurance producer who allows his or her license to lapse may, within 12 months from the due date of the renewal fee, reinstate the same license without passing a written examination. However, a penalty of double the unpaid renewal fee will be required for any renewal fee received after the due date.

An insurance producer who is not able to comply with the license renewal procedures due to military service or some other extenuating circumstance (for example, medical disability) may request a waiver of those procedures. The producer may also request a waiver of any examination requirement or any other fine or sanction imposed for failure to comply with renewal procedures.

Notice of Appointment

If a producer is going to function as an agent of an insurer, the producer generally needs to be appointed by that insurer. To appoint a producer as its agent, the appointing insurer needs to file a notice of appointment within *15 days* from the date the agency contract is executed or the first insurance application is submitted. If an appointment fee is required, it will be paid by the appointing insurer. Any appointment renewal fees required in subsequent years are also paid by the appointing insurer.

In many states, the Commissioner verifies the eligibility of each producer appointed within the first *30 days* after being notified of the appointment. If the producer is found to be ineligible, the insurer is notified within *5 days*.

Like the insurance license, as long as the appropriate forms are filed and the appropriate fees are paid by the appointing insurer, appointments remain in effect until terminated or until the producer's license is revoked or terminated. If the filing of an appointment is late, additional fees may be charged.

Notice that producers are licensed by the state, and appointed by an insurer. Loss of an appointment does not necessarily mean that the producer has lost his or her license. It simply means that the producer may no longer represent that particular company although he or she is still licensed within the state.

Termination of Appointment

Subject to a producer's contract rights, if any, an insurer may terminate any of its appointed producers at any time. The insurer must give prompt written notice of the termination and the date to the insurance department (and to the producer when reasonably possible) and must file a statement of facts related to the termination and reasons for it.

If the appointment was terminated because the producer was found to have done something that would be grounds for revocation, denial, or suspension of his or her license, the insurer is obligated to notify the Commissioner, generally within *30 days*. If the insurer finds out after terminating the appointment that the producer did something while appointed that would have been grounds for revocation, denial, or suspension of an insurance license, the insurer has to notify the Commissioner when it makes the discovery. As long as this notification is made without malicious intent, whoever makes such notifications is immune from civil liability, and no civil cause of action may be brought against such person.

License Denial, Nonrenewal, or Revocation

The Commissioner may place on probation, suspend, revoke, or refuse to issue an insurance producer's license or may levy a civil penalty for any combination of the following causes, as listed in the PLMA:

➤ Providing incorrect, misleading, incomplete, or materially untrue information in the license application

➤ Violating any insurance laws, or violating any regulation, subpoena, or order of the Commissioner or of another state's Commissioner

➤ Obtaining or attempting to obtain a license through misrepresentation or fraud

➤ Improperly withholding, misappropriating, or converting any money or property received in the course of doing insurance business

➤ Intentionally misrepresenting the terms of an actual or proposed insurance contract or application for insurance

➤ Having been convicted of a felony

➤ Having admitted or been found to have committed any insurance unfair trade practices or fraud

➤ Using fraudulent, coercive, or dishonest practices, or demonstrating incompetence, untrustworthiness, or financial irresponsibility in the conduct of business in this state or elsewhere

➤ Having an insurance producer license, or its equivalent, denied, suspended, or revoked in any other state, province, district, or territory

➤ Forging another's name to an application for insurance or to any document related to an insurance transaction

➤ Improperly using notes or any other reference material to complete an examination for an insurance license

➤ Knowingly accepting insurance business from an individual who is not licensed

➤ Failing to comply with an administrative or court order imposing child support obligations

➤ Failing to pay state income tax or comply with any administrative or court order directing payment of state income tax

If the Commissioner does not renew or denies an application for a license, the applicant or licensee must be notified and advised, in writing, of the reason for the denial or nonrenewal of the license. The applicant or licensee may make a written demand for a hearing within a reasonable time as specified in state law.

A business entity's license may be suspended if the Commissioner finds that an individual licensee's violations were known or should have been known by one or more of the partners, officers, or managers acting on behalf of the business entity and the violation was not reported nor corrective action taken.

A civil fine may be imposed in addition to or instead of license denial, suspension, or revocation. Depending on the violation, fines can range from $100 to several thousand dollars. If a producer is in violation of civil law, the Commissioner can refer the matter to the state attorney general for criminal prosecution and possible imprisonment.

Regulated Practices

The following material reviews various practices that are prohibited or regulated by law.

License for Controlled Business Prohibited

Coverage written on a producer's own life or health and on the lives or health of such persons as the producer's relatives or business associates, is called *controlled business*. Because of the effect that controlled business could have on the insurance industry if people began becoming licensed solely to sell insurance to family and friends, the Commissioner limits such activities. Generally, a licensee is not permitted to earn commission or compensation from controlled business in excess of a stated amount (35%–50% of total compensation, depending upon the state) during a stated time period (usually a calendar year). If a greater proportion does come from controlled business, the practice is in violation of law and the license may be revoked or suspended.

Unfair Trade Practices

The Unfair Trade Practices Act is divided into two parts—Unfair Marketing Practices and Unfair Claims Practices. In each state, statutes define and prohibit certain trade and claims practices that are unfair, misleading, and deceptive.

Misrepresentations

A misrepresentation is simply a lie. It is a violation of Unfair Marketing Practices for any person to make, issue, or circulate any illustration or sales material, or to make any statement that is false, misleading, or deceptive.

Misrepresentations include (but are not limited to)

➤ Misrepresenting the benefits, advantages, or terms of any policy

➤ Misrepresenting policy dividends by implying or stating that they are guaranteed

➤ Misrepresenting the financial condition of an insurer by means of an inaccurate or incomplete financial comparison

➤ Misrepresenting an insurance policy by using any name or title that is untrue or misleading or by indicating that an insurance policy represents shares of stock

False or Deceptive Advertising

It is illegal for any person to formulate or use an advertisement or make a statement that is untrue, deceptive, or misleading regarding any insurer or person associated with an insurer.

Twisting

Twisting occurs when a producer convinces a policyowner to lapse or surrender a present policy in order to sell him or her another one, usually from a different company. This is not to say all policy replacements are wrong. If a producer proves to the policyowner that the protection he or she has is not the best available, and the policyowner decides to replace the old policy with a better one, that policyowner has been well served. However, the producer must be careful that the arguments used on the policyowner can stand the scrutiny of the Commissioner. Any attempt by the producer to misrepresent another insurer by falsely making statements about the financial condition of the company or by giving an incomplete comparison of policies can create legal liability.

Churning

Closely allied with twisting is *churning*, a term describing the practice of using misrepresentation to induce replacement of a policy issued by the insurer the producer is representing, rather than the policy of a competitor.

The impetus behind churning is to allow the producer to collect a large first-year commission on a new policy. Churning is the result of a producer putting his or her interests above those of the client.

False Financial Statements

It is a violation of Unfair Marketing Practices for any person to deliberately make a false financial statement regarding the solvency of an insurer with the intent to deceive others.

Defamation

It is illegal for any person or company to make any oral or written statements or to circulate any literature that is false, maliciously critical, or derogatory to the financial condition of any insurer, or which is calculated to injure anyone engaged in the insurance business.

Discrimination

It is illegal to permit discrimination between individuals of the same class or insurance risk in terms of rates, premiums, fees, and policy benefits, due to their place of residence, race, creed, or national origin.

Rebating

Splitting a commission with a prospect is prohibited in almost every state (California and Florida are exceptions). *Rebating* is any inducement in the sale of insurance that is not specified in the insurance contract. The offer of sharing commissions with the insurance applicant is an inducement in the sale of insurance that is not part of the insurance policy and, thus, rebating.

Rebates include not only cash but also personal services and items of value.

Illegal Premiums and Charges

It is unlawful for any person or insurer to collect premiums or make charges that are not specified in the insurance contract.

Boycott, Coercion, or Intimidation

It is a violation of the Act for any person or organization to commit or be involved in any act of boycott, coercion, or intimidation that is intended to create a monopoly or restrict fair trade in the transaction of insurance. For example, it is unlawful for a bank to force a person to purchase insurance from a particular company or agent as a condition for receiving a loan from the bank. The bank may require that adequate insurance be purchased or be in force to back such a loan but the bank cannot force or intimidate a person into purchasing coverage from a specific insurer as a condition for the granting of a loan.

Unfair Claims Practices

Claims settlement practices are regulated, in the public interest, for two main reasons:

➤ To settle claims regarding policyowners' money that insurance companies have collected

➤ To protect insureds when they are denied claims or claim payments are delayed or altered.

The Unfair Claims Practices provisions of the Unfair Trade Practices Act are designed to protect the insureds and claimants from any claims settlement practices that are unfair, deceptive, or misleading. The following are considered unfair claims practices:

➤ Misrepresenting pertinent facts or insurance policy provisions relating to coverage at issue

➤ Failing to acknowledge and act reasonably promptly on communications with respect to claims arising under insurance policies

➤ Failing to adopt and implement reasonable standards for the prompt investigation of claims arising under insurance policies

➤ Refusing to pay claims without conducting a reasonable investigation based on all available information

➤ Failing to affirm or deny coverage of claims within a reasonable time after proof of loss statements have been completed

➤ Not attempting in good faith to effectuate prompt, fair, and equitable settlements of claims in which liability has become reasonably clear

➤ Compelling insureds to institute litigation to recover amounts due under an insurance policy by offering substantially less than the amounts ultimately recovered in actions brought by such insureds

➤ Attempting to settle a claim for less than the amount to which a reasonable person would have believed he or she was entitled by reference to written or principal advertising material accompanying or made part of an application

➤ Attempting to settle claims on the basis of an application that was altered without notice, knowledge, or consent of the insured

➤ Making claims payments to insureds or beneficiaries not accompanied by statements setting forth the coverage under which the payments are being made

➤ Making known to insureds or claimants a policy of appealing arbitration awards in favor of insureds or claimants for the purpose of compelling them to accept settlements or compromises less than the amount awarded in arbitration

➤ Delaying the investigation or payment of claim by requiring an insured, claimant, or the physician of either, to submit a preliminary claim report and then requiring the subsequent submission of formal proof of loss forms, both of which submissions contain substantially the same information

➤ Failing to promptly settle claims where liability has become reasonably clear under one portion of the insurance policy coverage in order to influence settlement under other portions of the insurance policy coverage

➤ Failing to promptly provide a reasonable explanation of the basis relied on in the insurance policy in relation to the facts or applicable law for denial of a claim or for the offer of a compromise settlement

Some states have added another provision that makes it an unfair claim practice *to offer a settlement or payment in any manner prohibited by law.*

Penalties

Following an investigation and a hearing, if the insurance department finds that any person or insurer is engaged in any unfair trade or unfair claims practice, the Commissioner may issue a *cease and desist order* prohibiting the individual or company from continuing the practice. Failure to comply with the cease and desist order can result in a substantial fine (usually $10,000). In addition, fines and loss of license may also be imposed for any company or person guilty of violating the Unfair Trade Practices Act.

Self-Regulation

The last channel of regulation of the business is self-regulation, that is, those restraints from within the industry either by individual company conscience or by group pressure of insurance associations. There are several intercompany organizations or associations that impose "codes" on their members. In recent years, these industry associations have had a major impact on prelicensing and continuing education laws. For example, often the state Association of Life Underwriters will be the organization that is the major force in obtaining passage of these laws through the state legislature. Continuing education laws are designed to protect the consumer by mandating certain continuing educational requirements if a producer is to maintain his or her license.

The NAIC

The National Association of Insurance Commissioners (NAIC), an association of state Commissioners, although without legal authority as a group, also imposes a strong influence in the area of the industry's self-regulation.

The NAIC is the organization that has done the most to standardize law between the states. Although the wording—and sometimes the provisions themselves—differ from state to state, for the most part the differences are only slight as each state attempts to follow, in essence, the wording of the "model laws" established by the NAIC.

The model laws include the *Individual Accident and Sickness Policy Provisions Law, Standard Nonforfeiture and Valuation Laws, Fair Trade Practices Act, Unauthorized Insurers Service of Process Act, Insurance Holding Company System Regulatory Act, Variable Contract Law,* "group life definition and standard provisions bill," and "credit life and credit health insurance regulation bill."

Exam Prep Questions

1. Most insurance regulation takes place at the
   - ○ A. International level
   - ○ B. National level
   - ○ C. State level
   - ○ D. Local level

2. Applicants for insurance must be given advance notice, including all the following types of information *except*
   - ○ A. The persons who are collecting information
   - ○ B. The kind of information to be collected
   - ○ C. The sources of information
   - ○ D. The persons with access to personal information

3. Which of the following does *not* contain provisions protecting individual privacy?
   - ○ A. Gramm-Leach-Bliley Act
   - ○ B. Privacy Act of 1974
   - ○ C. McCarran-Ferguson Act
   - ○ D. Fair Credit Reporting Act

4. Consumer reporting agencies are prevented from putting information in their reports about all the following *except*
   - ○ A. Bankruptcies over 14 years old
   - ○ B. Suits and judgments over 10 years old if the statute of limitations has not expired
   - ○ C. Arrests, indictments, or conviction of crime reports
   - ○ D. Paid tax liens or accounts placed for collection more than 7 years previous

5. Under the Financial Modernization Act, an individual about whom a financial institution collects any information is a
   - ○ A. Customer
   - ○ B. Consumer
   - ○ C. Client
   - ○ D. Patron

6. Under the Financial Modernization Act, an individual with whom a financial institution has an ongoing relationship is a
   - ○ A. Customer
   - ○ B. Consumer
   - ○ C. Client
   - ○ D. Patron

7. The Commissioner of Insurance has all the following powers *except*
   - ○ A. Conducting investigations and examinations
   - ○ B. Making reasonable rules and regulations
   - ○ C. Promulgating insurance law
   - ○ D. Approving insurance policy forms sold within the state

8. Nonfinancial regulatory activities of an insurance department fall under the broad heading of
   - ○ A. Market regulation
   - ○ B. Conduct regulation
   - ○ C. Market conduct
   - ○ D. Insurance conduct

9. Associations organized to protect claimants, policyholders, annuitants, and creditors of financially impaired insurers are known as
   - ○ A. Insurance Associations
   - ○ B. Department Associations
   - ○ C. Liability Associations
   - ○ D. Guaranty Associations

10. Which of the following is *not* a requirement for obtaining a producer's license in most states?
    - ○ A. Have not committed any act that is grounds for denial or suspension of an insurance license
    - ○ B. Be at least 19 years of age
    - ○ C. Pay the required fees
    - ○ D. Complete any required prelicensing course

11. Which of the following people would be required in most states to obtain an insurance license?
    - ○ A. Rachel, a salaried employee of a large department store chain, who counsels her employer on insurance-related matters
    - ○ B. Ross, who works in an advertising agency, supervising the advertising business of a major insurer
    - ○ C. Phoebe, who works as an underwriter for a small insurer
    - ○ D. Chandler, who sells insurance to businesses only

12. A person licensed as an insurance producer in another state who moves to this state has how long after establishing legal residence to become a resident licensee without taking prelicensing education or an examination?
    - ○ A. 30 days
    - ○ B. 60 days
    - ○ C. 90 days
    - ○ D. 120 days

13. Which of the following individuals is least likely to be granted a temporary license?

   ○ A. Georgia, whose insurance producer-husband passed away unexpectedly, leaving her with a business to either learn or sell

   ○ B. Kim, who wants to try selling insurance on a temporary basis before investing the time and money into being licensed

   ○ C. Dave, an employee of a business entity, when the individual designated as the licensee in the business entity is disabled in an auto accident and unable to return to work for several months

   ○ D. Lee, whose insurance producer-fiancée was recalled to active duty by the Navy and appointed Lee her designee

14. Business written on the producer's own life or interests is known as

   ○ A. Controlled business

   ○ B. Personal business

   ○ C. Conflicted business

   ○ D. Producer business

15. Which of the following is considered an unfair claims practice?

   ○ A. Splitting a commission with a prospect

   ○ B. Failing to affirm or deny coverage within a reasonable time after receiving proof of loss

   ○ C. Convincing a policyowner to lapse or surrender an existing policy in order to sell another policy

   ○ D. Making any oral or written statement that is false, maliciously critical, or calculated to injure a competing producer

16. An organization that establishes model laws that are often adopted by states with only slight differences is the

   ○ A. National Association of Insurance Companies

   ○ B. National Association of Independent Commissioners

   ○ C. National Association of Insurance Consultants

   ○ D. National Association of Insurance Commissioners

Exam Prep Answers

1. **C is correct.** Most insurance regulation does take place at the state level, although some federal regulations apply.

2. **A is correct.** There is no requirement to provide information about the persons who are collecting the information.

3. **C is correct.** The McCarran-Ferguson Act exempted insurance companies from federal antitrust laws and established the right of states to regulate insurance. All the other answer choices involve laws that have provisions protecting individual privacy.

4. **C is correct.** There are no time limitations on reporting arrests or criminal convictions.

5. **B is correct.** The term "consumer" is used to describe a person who is the subject of information gathering.

6. **A is correct.** The term "customer" is used to describe an individual with whom a financial institution has an ongoing relationship.

7. **C is correct.** The Commissioner has no authority to make insurance laws, but does have authority to make rules and regulations, to conduct investigations and examinations, and to approve or disprove policy forms.

8. **C is correct.** "Market conduct" is a term that means nonfinancial activities and practices that may be investigated and regulated by the insurance department.

9. **D is correct.** Guaranty associations were established to protect policyholders and claimants in the event that an insurer becomes financially impaired or insolvent.

10. **B is correct.** In nearly all states the minimum age to qualify for a license is 18 years.

11. **D is correct.** Chandler is the only one actively selling insurance. In each of the other cases the individual is not acting as an insurance producer.

12. **C is correct.** If the person does not apply for a resident license within 90 days, the exemption is lost and the individual would be subject to prelicensing education and examination requirements.

13. **B is correct.** Temporary licensing is not intended to allow people to test the water before they are qualified to serve the public interest. Temporary licenses are commonly granted when a producer is no longer able to conduct business due to death, disability, or active military service.

14. **A is correct.** "Controlled business" means insurance on a producer's own life or interests, or those of family members or business associates.

15. **B is correct.** The other practices are all unfair trade practices, but they are not related to claims.

16. **D is correct.** The NAIC is the national organization that drafts and proposes model laws to the states.

Insurance Law

Terms you need to understand:

- ✓ Express authority
- ✓ Implied authority
- ✓ Apparent authority
- ✓ Waiver
- ✓ Estoppel
- ✓ Policy face
- ✓ Insuring clause
- ✓ Conditions
- ✓ Exclusions
- ✓ Aleatory contract
- ✓ Contract of adhesion
- ✓ Unilateral contract
- ✓ Executory contract
- ✓ Conditional contract
- ✓ Personal contract
- ✓ Warranty
- ✓ Representation
- ✓ Misrepresentation
- ✓ Concealment

Concepts you need to master:

- ✓ Presumption of agency
- ✓ Agent errors and omissions exposure
- ✓ Contract formation
- ✓ Offer and acceptance
- ✓ Consideration
- ✓ Competent parties
- ✓ Legal purpose
- ✓ Utmost good faith
- ✓ Parol evidence rule

Agency Law

An understanding of the law of agency is important because an insurance company, like other companies, must act through agents.

Agency Law Principles

Agency is a relationship in which one person is authorized to represent and act for another person or for a corporation. Although a corporation is a legal "person," it cannot act for itself, so it must act through agents. An agent is a person authorized to act on behalf of another person, who is called the *principal*.

In the field of insurance, the principal is the insurance company and the sales representative or producer is the agent. When one is empowered to act as an agent for a principal, he or she is legally assumed to be the principal in matters covered by the grant of agency. Contracts made by the agent are the contracts of the principal. Payment to the agent, within the scope of his or her authority, is payment to the principal. The knowledge of the agent is assumed to be the knowledge of the principal.

Presumption of Agency

If a company supplies an individual with forms and other materials (signs and evidences of authority) that make it appear that he or she is an agent of the company, a court will likely hold that a presumption of agency exists. The company is then bound by the acts of this individual regardless of whether he or she has been given this authority.

Authority

An agent has one of three types of authority:

➤ *Express authority* is an explicit, definite agreement. It is the authority the principal gives the agent as set forth in his or her contract.

➤ *Implied authority* is not expressly granted under an agency contract, but it is actual authority that the agent has to transact the principal's business in accordance with general business practices. For example, if an agent's contract does not give him or her the express authority of collecting and submitting the premium, but the agent does so on a regular basis, and the company accepts the premium, the agent is said to have implied authority.

Lingering implied authority means that the agent carries "signs or evidences of authority." By having these evidences of authority, an agent who is no longer under contract to an insurer could mislead applicants or insureds. When the agency relationship between agent and company has been terminated, the company will try, or should try, to get back all the materials it supplied to the former agent, including sales materials.

On the other hand, the public cannot assume that an individual is an agent merely because he or she says so. The agent must carry the credentials (for example, the agent's license and appointment) and company documents (such as applications and rate books) that represent him or her as being an agent for an insurance company.

➤ *Apparent authority* is the authority the agent seems to have because of certain actions undertaken on his or her part. This action may mislead applicants or insureds, causing them to believe the agent has authority that he or she does not, in fact, have. The principal adds to this impression by acting in a manner that reinforces the impression of authority. For instance, an agent's contract usually does not grant him the authority to reinstate a lapsed policy by accepting past due premiums. If, in the past, the company has allowed the agent to accept late premiums for that purpose, a court would probably hold that the policyowner had the right to assume that the agent's acceptance of premiums was within the scope of his or her authority.

Collection of Premium

All premiums received by an agent are funds received and held in trust. The agent must account for and pay the correct amount to the insured, insurer, or other agent entitled to the money. Any agent who takes funds held in trust for his or her own use is guilty of theft and will be punished as provided by law.

Agent's Responsibility to Insured/Applicant

An agent has a fiduciary responsibility to the insured, the insurer, the applicant for insurance, current clients, and so forth. The agent has a fiduciary duty to just about any person or organization that he or she comes into contact with as part of the day-to-day business of transacting insurance.

By definition, a *fiduciary* is a person in a position of financial trust. Thus, attorneys, accountants, trust officers, and insurance agents are all considered fiduciaries.

As a fiduciary, the agent has an obligation to act in the best interest of the insured. The agent must be knowledgeable about the features and provisions of various insurance policies and the use of these insurance contracts. The agent must be able to explain the important features of these policies to the insured. The agent must recognize the importance of dealing with the general public's financial needs and problems and offer solutions to these problems through the purchase of insurance products.

As a fiduciary, the agent must collect and account for any premiums collected as part of the insurance transaction. It is the agent's duty to make certain that these premiums are submitted to the insurer promptly. Failure to submit premiums to the insurer, or putting these funds to one's own personal use, is a violation of the agent's fiduciary duties and possibly an act of embezzlement.

The insured's premiums must be kept separate from the agent's personal funds. Failure to do this can result in *commingling*—mixing personal funds with the insured or insurer's funds.

Waiver and Estoppel

The legal doctrines of waiver and estoppel are directly related to the responsibilities of insurance agents. An insurer may, by waiver, lose the right of making certain defenses that it might otherwise have available.

Waiver is defined as the intentional and voluntary giving up of a known right. An insurance company may waive its right to cancel a policy for nonpayment by accepting late payments.

Waiver and estoppel often occur together, but they are separate and distinct doctrines.

Estoppel means that a party may be precluded by his or her acts of conduct from asserting a right that would act to the detriment of the other party, when the other party has relied upon the conduct of the first party and has acted upon it. An insurer may waive a right, and then after the policyowner has relied upon the waiver and acted upon it, the insurer will be estopped from asserting the right.

The agent must be alert in his or her words, actions, and advice to avoid mistakenly waiving the rights of the insurance company. As a representative of the company the agent's knowledge and actions may be deemed to be knowledge and actions of the company.

Agent's Responsibilities to Company

The agent's contract or agency agreement with the insurer will specify the agent's duties and responsibilities to the principal. In all insurance transactions, the agent's responsibility is to act in accordance with the agency contract and thus for the benefit of the insurer. In accordance with the agent's fiduciary obligation to the insurer and his or her agency agreement, the agent has a responsibility of accounting for all property, including money that comes into his or her possession. As part of the agent's working relationship with the insurer, it is important that pertinent information be disclosed to the insurer, particularly with regard to underwriting and risk selection. If the agent knows of anything adverse concerning the risk to be insured, it is his or her responsibility to provide this information to the insurer. To withhold important underwriting information could adversely affect the insurer's risk selection process. In accordance with agency law, information given to the agent is the same as providing the information to the insurer.

It is the agent's responsibility to obtain necessary information from the insurance applicant and to accurately complete the application for insurance. A signed and witnessed copy of the application becomes part of the legal contract of insurance between the insured and the insurer.

Finally, the agent has a responsibility to deliver the insurance policy to the insured and collect any premium that might be due at the time of delivery.

The agent must be prepared to provide the insured with an explanation of some of the policy's principal benefits and provisions. If the policy is issued with any changes or amendments, the agent will also be required to explain these changes and obtain the insured's signature acknowledging receipt of these amendments.

Company's Responsibility to Agent

The company is required to permit the agent to act in accordance with the terms of the agent's employment contract, and the company must recognize all the provisions of that contract.

In addition, the company must pay the agent the compensation agreed upon in the contract, must reimburse the agent for proper expenditures made on behalf of the principal, and must indemnify the agent for any losses or damages suffered without fault on the part of the agent but occurring on account of the agency relationship.

Potential Liabilities of Agent/Errors and Omissions (E&O) Exposure

Errors and omissions (E&O) insurance is needed by professionals who give advice to their clients. It covers negligence, error, or omission by the insurer or producer who is the insurer's representative. E&O policies protect producers from financial losses they may suffer if insureds sue to recover for their financial loss due to a producer giving them incorrect advice (error) or not informing them of an important issue (omission). Because a producer's office is very busy, he or she must take special care to follow strict procedures in regard to taking applications, explaining coverages, collecting premiums, submitting changes to policies upon an insured's request, and preparing claim forms.

Formation of a Life and Health Insurance Contract

The formation of a life or health insurance contract differs from the formation of other insurance contracts because the life or health producer usually does not have the authority to bind the insurer.

Contract Elements

Insurance policies are legal contracts and are subject to the general law of contracts. This is a distinct body of law that is separate from criminal law (crimes against society) and tort law (legal liability issues usually involving damages for negligence). A contract is a legal agreement between two or more parties promising a certain performance in exchange for a valuable consideration. Under the law, the following elements are necessary for the formation of a valid contract:

➤ Agreement (offer and acceptance)

➤ Consideration

➤ Competent parties

➤ Legal purpose

Agreement (Offer and Acceptance)

There can be no contract without the agreement or mutual assent of the parties. A common intention on all terms of the contract is essential to an agreement and no essential terms of the contract may be left unsettled. Further, the intention of the parties to a contract must be communicated to one another.

The parties to an insurance contract are the insurance company and the applicant, who may become the insured or may name another person to be insured. Unless otherwise indicated, it is assumed that the applicant is the prospective insured.

Offer

An offer is a proposal that creates a contract if accepted by another party according to its terms. If an applicant gives the insurer a completed application and pays the first premium, the application is an offer. If the policy is issued as applied for, the insurer accepts the offer.

There is no offer if the applicant sends the application to the insurance company without payment of the premium. Such an application is merely an invitation to the company to make an offer. The insurance company makes an offer by issuing the policy. The applicant accepts it by paying the first premium.

Acceptance

An acceptance must be unconditional and unqualified. If an insurance company, after receiving an application and premium payment, issues a policy with more restrictive coverage than that applied for, the company has made a counter offer.

For example, a *counter offer* occurs if an applicant applies for a standard health insurance policy, pays the premium, and receives a policy containing an exclusionary endorsement for specified physical conditions. The applicant must decide whether to accept the policy as modified. If he or she accepts the policy, there is a contract. If he or she rejects the modified policy, there is no contract, and the applicant is entitled to a return of his or her premium.

Consideration

Each party to the contract must give valuable consideration. In the insurance contract, the value given by the insurer consists of the promises contained in the policy contract. The consideration given by the insured consists of the statements made in the application and the payment of the initial premium.

The consideration may consist of any of the following:

➤ A monetary payment

➤ An act

➤ A forbearance from action

➤ The creation, modification, or destruction of a legal right

➤ A return promise

It is important to know that part of the applicant's consideration consists of the statements in the application. A great deal of importance is placed on the representations in the application because the insurance company's entire decision of whether to contract is based on its evaluation of the information in the application.

Competent Parties

For a contract to be binding, both parties must have the legal capacity to make a contract. To have the legal capacity to make insurance contracts, an insurance company must have authority under its charter to issue contracts and be authorized by the state to issue contracts. The company's representative must also be licensed by the state.

 The insured or applicant must be of legal age and be mentally competent to make an insurance contract. Applications of minors must usually be signed by an adult parent or guardian to comply with the legal age requirement for making contracts.

Legal Purpose

To be valid, a contract must be for a legal purpose and not contrary to public policy. An insurance contract is not against public policy where an insurable interest exists.

Parts of the Insurance Contract

Although it is not a legal requirement that all contracts be in writing, insurance contracts always are because of their complex nature. The number of pages that make up an insurance contract varies because of the types of insurance and the individual risks being insured, but all life/health insurance contracts contain four basic parts:

➤ Policy face (Title page)

➤ Conditions

➤ Insuring clause

➤ Exclusions

Policy Face (Title Page)

The *policy face* is usually the first page of the insurance policy. It includes the policy number, name of the insured, policy issue date, the amount of premium and dates the premium is due, and the limits of the policy. The policy face also includes the signatures of the secretary and president of the issuing insurance company. In addition, there are generally clauses required by law to give the insured information on his or her right to cancel, and a warning to the insured to read the policy carefully.

Insuring Clause

The *insuring clause* generally also appears on the policy face. It is a statement by the insurance company that sets out the essential element of insurance—the promise to pay for losses covered by the policy in exchange for the insured's premium and compliance with policy terms.

Conditions

This section spells out in detail the rights and duties of both parties. *Conditions* are provisions that apply to the insured and insurer. For example, the conditions include the reinstatement provision, suicide clause, payment of claim provision, and similar standard policy provisions.

Exclusions

In this section, the company states what it will not do. The *exclusions* are a basic part of the contract and a complete knowledge of them is essential to a thorough understanding of the agreement. Certain risks must be excluded from insurance contracts because they are not insurable.

Legal Requirements

When the courts have a case involving contracts, it looks at the "rules of construction" to interpret the contract. The rules of construction help identify and establish the intent of the parties to the contract.

Contract Construction

There are five major areas that the courts review in order to interpret the contract, establish the intent of the parties, and hand down a ruling.

Plain Language and Word Definitions

If the language of the contract is clear the courts do not have to interpret the meaning of the contract. The courts give the words in the contract their "ordinary meaning." In cases where ordinary words have been used in a technical capacity, the technical meaning of the word is accepted.

The Entire Contract

The courts look at the entire contract to determine the intent of the parties. It does not consider material added to the basic contract, nor does it take only parts of the contract to make a determination.

Interpretation in Favor of Valid Contract

Because the courts assume that when people make a contract they intend for it to be valid, the courts will, if possible, render an interpretation of the contract that makes it valid rather than invalid.

Unclear Contract of Adhesion Interpreted Against the Insurer

If a contract contains wording that is unclear the courts will interpret the language used against the writer of the contract, unless the wording used is required by law to be stated in a specific manner. Insurance contracts are *contracts of adhesion*, which means the insured had no part in determining the wording of the contract; therefore, the courts will interpret the contract in favor of the policyholder, insured, or beneficiary.

Written Contracts

If a contract contains unclear or inconsistent material between printed, typed, or handwritten text in the contract, the typed or handwritten material will determine intent.

Contract Characteristics

The insurance contract has certain characteristics not typically found in other types of contracts.

Utmost Good Faith

The insurance contract requires utmost good faith between the parties. This means that each party is entitled to rely on the representations of the other and each party should have a reasonable expectation that the other is acting in good faith without attempts to conceal or deceive. In a contact of utmost good faith, the parties have an affirmative duty to each other to disclose all material facts relating to the contract. That is not just a duty not to lie, but also a duty to speak up. Failure to do so usually gives the other party ground to void the contract.

Aleatory

An insurance contract is said to be *aleatory*, or dependent upon chance or uncertain outcome, because one party may receive much more in value than he or she gives in value under the contract. For example, an insured who has a loss may receive a greater payment from an insurer for the loss than he or she has paid in premiums. On the other hand, an insured might pay his or her premiums and have no loss, so the insurer pays nothing.

Adhesion

In insurance, the insurer writes the contract and the insured adheres to it. When a contract of adhesion is ambiguous in its terms, the courts will interpret the contract against the party who prepared it.

Unilateral

Insurance contracts are unilateral. This means that after the insured has completed the act of paying the premium, only the insurer promises to do anything further. The insurer has promised performance and is legally responsible. The insured has made no legally enforceable promises and cannot be held for breach of contract. For example, the insured may stop paying premium because he is not legally responsible to continue paying premium.

Executory

An insurance contract is an *executory contract* in that the promises described in the insurance contract are to be *executed in the future, and only after certain events (losses) occur.*

Conditional

Insurance contracts are also *conditional* contracts because when the loss occurs certain conditions must be met to make the contract legally enforceable. For example, a policyholder might have to satisfy the test of having an insurable interest and satisfy the condition of submitting proof of loss.

Personal Contract

Generally, insurance policies are personal contracts between the insured and insurer. Generally, insurance is not transferable to another person without the consent of the insurer. Fire insurance, for example, does not follow the property.

Warranties and Representations

A *warranty* is something that becomes part of the contract itself and is a statement that is considered to be *guaranteed* to be true. Any breach of warranty provides grounds for voiding the contract.

A *representation* is a statement *believed* to be true to the best of one's knowledge. An insurer seeking to void coverage on the basis of a misrepresentation usually has to prove that the misrepresentation is material to the risk.

 Under most state laws, an applicant's statements or responses to questions on an application for insurance (in the absence of fraud) are considered to be representations and not warranties.

An example would be a question on the application asking for your sex or date of birth. You represent yourself to the insurance company as being male or female and a certain age. The accuracy of these items is very important to the insurance company issuing the policy. If they are incorrect, they may be considered misrepresentations, and the policy may be voided as a result.

There is a difference between representation of a fact and an expression of opinion. A good example is a question on many applications: "Are you now to the best of your knowledge and belief in good health?" If the applicant answers "yes" while knowing in fact that he or she is not, there is a misrepresentation of actual fact. If, on the other hand, he or she has had no medical opinion and suffers from no symptoms recognizable to a layman, his or her answer is an opinion and thus not a misrepresentation.

Impersonation

Impersonation means assuming the name and identity of another person for the purpose of committing a fraud. The offense is also known as *false pretenses*. In the case of life insurance, an uninsurable individual applying for insurance may ask another person to substitute for him to take the physical examination.

Misrepresentation and Concealment

A *misrepresentation* is a written or oral statement that is false. Generally, in order for a misrepresentation to be grounds for voiding an insurance policy, it has to be material to the risk.

Concealment is the failure to disclose known facts. Generally, an insurer may be able to void the insurance if it can prove that the insured *intentionally* concealed a material fact.

Material information or a *material fact* is crucial to acceptance of the risk. For example, if the correct information about something would have caused the insurance company to deny a risk or issue a policy on a different basis, the information is material.

Fraud

Fraud is an intentional act designed to deceive and induce another party to part with something of value.

Fraud may involve misrepresentation and/or concealment, but not all acts of misrepresentation or concealment are acts of fraud. If someone intentionally lies in order to obtain coverage or to collect on a false claim, that would be a matter of fraud. If someone misrepresents something on an application (perhaps a medical treatment the person is embarrassed to talk about) without any intent to obtain something of value, no fraud has occurred.

Parol (Oral) Evidence Rule

The *parol evidence rule* limits the impact of waiver and estoppel on contract terms by disallowing oral evidence based on statements made *before* the contract was created. It is assumed that any oral agreements made before contract formation were incorporated into the written contract. After contract formation, earlier oral evidence will not be admitted in court to change or contradict the contract. An oral statement may waive contract provisions only when the statement occurs after the contract exists.

Exam Prep Questions

1. Ralph is a producer for Hoosier Insurance Company. His contract states that he is allowed to put the company's logo on his business cards and the door to his office. This is an example of

   ○ A. Express authority
   ○ B. Implied authority
   ○ C. Lingering implied authority
   ○ D. Apparent authority

2. Tom has always made a practice of having his policyholders mail their premium checks directly to him, and forwarding them on to the insurer, so that he is aware of anyone missing a payment and can contact policyowners directly if that should happen. His contract does not allow this, but the insurer is aware of the practice and has not asked him to stop. This practice is an example of

   ○ A. Express authority
   ○ B. Implied authority
   ○ C. Lingering implied authority
   ○ D. Apparent authority

3. Gina accepts the initial premium when she sells an insurance policy and sends it to the company with the application. Nothing in her contract mentions handling of initial premiums. This is an example of

   ○ A. Express authority
   ○ B. Implied authority
   ○ C. Lingering implied authority
   ○ D. Apparent authority

4. Albert's life insurance premium is due on the 10th of the month. Because he gets paid at the end of the month, he has always sent the premium late. The insurer has been accepting his premium this way for 3 years. A new CEO comes in and decides to crack down on late premiums, canceling Albert's policy for nonpayment of premium. Albert contests this decision legally and gets the policy reinstated. The decision to reinstate the policy is an example of

   ○ A. Estoppel
   ○ B. Waiver
   ○ C. Contract of adhesion
   ○ D. Express authority

5. When representing an insurer, a producer acting as an agent has a responsibility to act with the degree of care that

   ○ A. A licensed insurance producer would apply under similar circumstances

   ○ B. A reasonable person would apply under similar circumstances

   ○ C. A lawyer would apply under similar circumstances

   ○ D. Any person would apply under similar circumstances

6. Which element is not necessary for the formation of a valid contract?

   ○ A. Consideration

   ○ B. Competent parties

   ○ C. Written document

   ○ D. Legal purpose

7. The initial premium payment sent with an application constitutes which part of the formation of an insurance contract?

   ○ A. Consideration

   ○ B. Acceptance

   ○ C. Offer

   ○ D. Legal purpose

8. Life insurance contracts contain all the following except

   ○ A. Policy folder

   ○ B. Insuring clause

   ○ C. Conditions

   ○ D. Exclusions

9. Ken has paid only four premiums on his health insurance policy when he is hit by a car. The insurance company pays out nearly half a million dollars to cover his treatment and a lengthy stay in intensive care. This is an example of

   ○ A. Contract of adhesion

   ○ B. Aleatory contract

   ○ C. Unilateral contract

   ○ D. Utmost good faith

10. Carol applies for a life insurance policy and pays the initial premium. Carol has

   ○ A. Accepted an offer from the insurer

   ○ B. Made an offer to the insurer

   ○ C. Accepted a counter offer from the insurer

   ○ D. Made a counter offer to the insurer

11. The insurer looks at Carol's application and decides to offer Carol a modified policy, including an exclusion Carol did not request. The insurer has
   - ○ A. Accepted an offer from Carol
   - ○ B. Made an offer to Carol
   - ○ C. Accepted a counter offer from Carol
   - ○ D. Made a counter offer to Carol

12. The failure to disclose known facts is
   - ○ A. Misrepresentation
   - ○ B. Concealment
   - ○ C. Fraud
   - ○ D. Impersonation

Exam Prep Answers

1. **A is correct.** Express authority is spelled out in an agent's written contract.

2. **D is correct.** Apparent authority is the authority an agent appears to have because of past actions that have not been challenged by the insurance company.

3. **B is correct.** Implied authority is not expressly stated in an agent's contract but it is actual authority related to common business practices, such as accepting premiums for the insurer.

4. **A is correct.** Under the principal of estoppel, a pattern of past behavior may prevent the insurer from exercising a right it might have had if it had exercised it earlier.

5. **B is correct.** A producer has a duty to act with a reasonable degree of care when representing an insurer.

6. **C is correct.** Valid contracts do not need to be in writing. Oral contracts are legally binding.

7. **A is correct.** The premium is the consideration given by the insured in exchange for the insurer's promise to pay if a loss occurs.

8. **A is correct.** All life insurance policies include an insuring clause, conditions, and exclusions. There is no requirement for a policy folder.

9. **B is correct.** An aleatory contract is one that depends on chance or an uncertain outcome. Ken may have received far more in benefits than he paid as premiums, but others who pay premiums may never have a loss and never receive even a dollar in benefits.

10. **B is correct.** The act of submitting an application with a premium payment is an offer that is still subject to acceptance by the insurer.

11. **D is correct.** By not accepting the initial offer and offering alternative terms, the insurer has made a counter offer.

12. **B is correct.** The failure to disclose known facts is concealment. Intentionally giving false answers or misstating facts would be misrepresentation, and possibly fraud.

Underwriting Basics

Terms you need to understand:

✓ Applicant
✓ Policyowner
✓ Insured
✓ Beneficiary
✓ Standard risks
✓ Substandard risks
✓ Preferred risks
✓ Mortality
✓ Morbidity

Concepts you need to master:

✓ Adverse selection
✓ Insurance applications
✓ Attending physician's statement
✓ Agent's statement or report
✓ Inspection reports
✓ Investigative consumer reports
✓ Field underwriting
✓ Loss and expense ratios
✓ Insurance company reserves

When the prospect has agreed to purchase an insurance contract and submitted an application, three important functions must take place:

➤ The underwriting process begins.

➤ The application is approved and the policy issued (or declined).

➤ The producer delivers the policy to the policyowner.

Each of these activities is important—not only to provide the best possible service to the policyowners, but also to comply with state laws regulating the writing of life insurance policies.

It is important to clearly understand all the individuals who might be involved and the parts they play in the life insurance process. These might include the applicant, the insured, the policyowner, and the beneficiary. Although these are four separate roles, they may all be played by one person, or any combination of the four:

➤ *Applicant*—The individual who fills out the application and applies for the insurance

➤ *Policyowner*—The individual who pays the premium, accepts the policy when it is delivered by the agent, and has the special owner's rights, such as designating beneficiaries (usually, but not necessarily, also the applicant)

➤ *Insured*—The individual whose life is covered by the policy

➤ *Beneficiary*—The individual or individuals named by the policyowner receive the benefits of the policy

Most of the time, the applicant, policyowner, and insured are the same person. For example, a husband who applies for insurance on his own life will be the insured and most often will also be the policyowner.

The term *third-party ownership* refers to a situation where the policy is owned by someone other than the insured. For example, in a business situation, a corporation may apply for insurance on the life of a key employee. In this case, the corporation is the applicant and the policyowner, and the key employee is the insured. The corporation would also be the beneficiary.

The Underwriting Process

By definition, underwriting is the process of selection, classification, and rating of risks. Simply put, underwriting is a risk selection process. The selection process consists of evaluating information and resources to determine how an individual will be classified (standard or substandard). When this part of the underwriting procedure is complete, the policy will be rated in terms of the premium that the applicant will pay. The policy will then be issued and subsequently delivered by the producer.

Selection Criteria

An underwriter's job is to use all the information gathered from many sources to determine whether to accept a particular applicant. Individuals applying for individually owned life and health insurance receive more underwriting scrutiny than members of a group. The following concepts apply primarily to individual underwriting. The underwriter must exercise judgment based on his or her years of experience to read beyond the facts and get a true picture of the applicant's lifestyle. Are there any factors (occupation, hobbies, lifestyle) that make this individual likely to die before his or her natural life expectancy?

Is there any reason to anticipate that this individual will be ill or involved in an accident that will cause high medical expenses? An underwriter cannot, and is not expected to, foresee all circumstances.

An underwriter's purpose is to protect the insurance company insofar as he or she can against adverse selection—very poor risks and those parties with fraudulent intent. *Adverse selection* exists when the group of risks insured is more likely than the average group to experience loss.

For instance, in a randomly selected group of 1,000 25-year-old individuals, only two might be expected to die in a given year. Human nature is such that many healthy 25-year-olds do not see the need to buy life insurance and prefer to spend their money elsewhere.

It is only those 25-year-olds who are ill or perhaps employed in dangerous occupations who are likely to buy insurance. An underwriter must take care not to accept too many of these poorer-than-average risks or the insurance company will lose money.

Sources of Underwriting Information

The underwriter has various resources to provide the necessary information for the risk selection process:

➤ The application

➤ Medical exams and history

➤ Inspection reports

➤ The Medical Information Bureau (MIB)

➤ The agent

The *application* is a vital document because it is usually attached to and made a part of the contract. The producer must take special care with the accuracy of the application in the interest of both the company and the insured.

The application, which in actual form may vary from company to company, is divided into sections. Each section is designed to obtain specific types of information. The form of the application may differ from one company to another. However, most applications provide the following information:

➤ Part I: General Information

➤ Part II: Medical Information

➤ The agent's statement or report

➤ Proper signatures of all parties to the contract

Application Part I: General Information

Part I of the application asks for general or personal data regarding the insured. This would include such information as name and address, date of birth, business address and occupation, social security number, marital status, and other insurance owned. In addition, if the applicant and the insured are not the same person, the applicant's name and address would be included in Part I.

Application Part II: Medical Information

Part II of the application is generally designed to provide information regarding the insured's past medical history, current physical condition, and personal morals. If the insurance applied for qualifies as "nonmedical", the producer and the insured will complete Part II of the information. In some cases, the proposed insured is required to take a medical examination, and Part II of the application is completed as part of the physical exam.

Part II of the application provides information regarding the past medical history of the insured by asking questions related to the types of illnesses and accidents experienced by the insured—periods of hospitalization and any surgery and reasons for visits to any physician.

In addition, Part II requires information regarding the current health of the insured by asking for current medical treatment for any sickness or condition and types of medication taken. The name and address of the insured's physician is also required.

Usually Part II of the application will also include questions regarding alcohol and any drug use by the insured. Avocations and high-risk hobbies are also usually reported on Part II. Generally, any plans for a prolonged trip or stay in a foreign country are also reported in Part II.

Attending Physician's Statement

Another source of medical information available to the underwriter is an *Attending Physician's Statement (APS)*. After a review of the medical information contained on the application or the medical exam, the underwriter may request an APS from the proposed insured's doctor.

Medical Examinations and Testing

Medical examinations, when required by the insurance company, are conducted by physicians or paramedics at the company's expense. Usually such exams are not required with regard to health insurance (thus the importance of the agent in recording medical information on the application). The medical exam requirement is much more common with life insurance underwriting than with health insurance underwriting.

Simplified issue life insurance requires no medical exam and asks only very basic health-related questions on the application. Usually this type of insurance is available in only low face amounts to reduce the risk of adverse selection against the company.

AIDS Considerations

Beginning in the decade of the 1980s, state legislatures and the insurance industry began developing responses to AIDS and two related conditions:

➤ AIDS-related complex (ARC), which is caused by the same virus as AIDS—HIV-III—but may have less severe symptoms

➤ Positive test results for antibodies of human T-cell lymphotropic virus type III (HTLV-III)

That these are diseases, like any other disease, is a key point of insurance legislation. Many states instruct insurers to treat AIDS, ARC, and HTLV-III infection exactly as they treat other disease or illness in these ways:

➤ Underwriting decisions must be applied in the same manner as for other diseases.

➤ Provisions regarding coverage limitations, deductibles, exclusions, coinsurance, and similar clauses must be applied in the same way as for other diseases.

➤ Claim settlement considerations (such as when an illness begins or when a new claim should be submitted, rather than being considered a continuation of an old claim) must be on the same basis as other diseases.

State legislatures that have adopted specific AIDS insurance regulations often pointedly prevent insurers from attempting to identify in the applicant population those who appear likely to develop an AIDS-related condition. For example, insurers may be specifically prohibited from looking at certain characteristics of individuals in order to attempt to predict these health conditions, especially characteristics such as sexual orientation, marital status, and geographical area of residence. Instead, insurers are expected to develop sound statistical bases (just as they do for conditions such as heart disease or cancer) to draw on in making decisions to do the following:

➤ Accept or reject an applicant

➤ Rate an applicant as a standard or substandard risk

➤ Renew, not renew, or cancel a policy

Currently, state laws vary widely in regard to using certain tests to detect AIDS antibodies and using the results to make underwriting decisions. Blood tests for the AIDS virus prior to policy issuance are a common underwriting requirement. Typically, the proposed insured must sign a *consent form* before the blood test is performed. AIDS testing is almost always required whenever a large amount of insurance is applied for. Each insurance company sets thresholds for the ages and amounts of insurance for when medical underwriting (including blood tests for the AIDS virus) will be required.

Test results are confidential and certain procedures must be followed to inform the applicant of any positive results. A signed *release form* is required whenever test results will be disclosed to any party who is not otherwise entitled to the information.

Agent's Statement

The *agent's statement* is part of the application and requires that the agent provide certain information regarding the proposed insured. Generally, this includes information regarding the producer's relationship to the insured;

data about the proposed insured's financial status, habits, and general character; and any other information that may be pertinent to the risk being assumed by the insurer.

The application will also record information regarding the policyowner/insured's choices with regard to the mode of premium (monthly, annually, and so forth), the use of dividends, and the designation of a beneficiary.

Finally, the signatures of the insured (and the policyowner if different from the insured) are required in the appropriate places on the application. Usually, the producer also signs the application as a witness to the applicant's signatures.

Inspection Reports

To supplement the information on the application, the underwriter orders an inspection report, which covers financial and moral information about the applicant, from an independent investigating firm or credit agency. This information is used to determine the insurability of the applicant. If the amount of insurance applied for is average, the inspector will write a general report in regard to the applicant's finances, health, character, work, hobbies, and other habits.

The inspector will make a more detailed report when larger amounts of insurance are requested. This information is based on interviews with the applicant's associates at home (neighbors, friends), at work, and elsewhere.

Investigative Consumer Reports

An "*investigative consumer report*" includes information on a consumer's character, general reputation, personal habits, and mode of living that is obtained through investigation—that is, interviews with associates and friends and neighbors of the consumer.

NOTE Such reports may not be made unless the consumer is clearly and accurately told about the report in writing. This consumer report notification is usually part of the application. At the time the application is completed, the producer will separate the notification and give it to the applicant.

Medical Information Bureau

Another source of information that may aid the underwriter in determining whether or not to underwrite a risk is the Medical Information Bureau (MIB). This is a nonprofit trade association that maintains medical information on applicants for life and health insurance.

The MIB maintains a database of medical information and avocation risks on applicants for life and health insurance. For every 10 applicants, the MIB will have a file on one or two. MIB information is reported in code form to member companies in order to preserve the confidentiality of the contents. The database does not contain any details about the risk. The codes simply alert companies to the fact that there was information obtained and reported by a member company on this particular impairment or avocation risk. The report does not indicate any action taken by other insurers, nor the amount of life insurance requested.

Underwriters compare the MIB file against the information contained in the application. If the MIB file contains a code for a condition that should be listed on the application but isn't, the underwriter inquires more specifically about that area. For example, an MIB file might contain a code indicating high cholesterol levels, but the application indicates that the applicant had no ongoing medical conditions. This would prompt the underwriter to investigate whether the applicant had misrepresented his or her health status or perhaps had been able to reverse the condition.

In addition to tracking medical and avocation information, the MIB also reports the number of times information has been requested on an individual in the previous 2 years. There are two reasons for this report, which is called the Insurance Activity Index (IAI). The first reason is to allow insurance companies to identify people who frequently replace their insurance policies.

Because most of the costs associated with issuing a policy occur in the first 1 or 2 years, insurance companies are interested in identifying individuals who are likely to cancel their policy after only a year.

The IAI may also identify situations where an individual is loading up on insurance policies by applying for a series of smaller policies that might fall below the radar screen for other underwriting requirements. By purchasing several small to midsize policies, an individual may be trying to avoid drawing attention to the accumulation of an extremely generous death benefit. An insurer may not refuse to accept a risk based solely on the information contained in an MIB report. There must be other substantiating factors that lead an insurer to decide to deny coverage. The MIB must provide explanations to applicants who are denied coverage, allowing consumers to challenge possibly inaccurate information about their medical history.

Field Underwriting

A key element in the underwriting process is the role of the insurance producer. The producer is in a position to see and talk to the proposed insured, to ask the questions contained on the application, and to accurately and completely record the answers to those questions.

Thus, one of the most important functions of the producer is the completion of the application. Much of the information reported on the application becomes the basis upon which to accept or reject the proposed insured. In addition, a signed and witnessed copy of the application becomes part of the policy, the legal contract between the insured and the insurer.

 As a field underwriter, the producer can help expedite the underwriting process by the prompt submission of the application, by scheduling the applicant for a physical exam (if necessary), and by assisting the home office underwriter with other requirements such as obtaining an APS.

The most important element of this process for the producer is the accuracy, thoroughness, and honesty displayed when completing the application. Answers to questions must be recorded accurately and completely by the producer.

If the proposed insured is rated or declined for the insurance, it is the producer's role as a field underwriter to explain the reasons for the underwriting action. Seldom is an individual declined for life insurance but it does happen that he or she might be classified as substandard and thus a rated or substandard policy may be issued in lieu of the one applied for. When this occurs, the producer must be prepared to not only explain the reasons for the substandard rating but also to explain the rated policy that the company has issued.

Classification of Risks

As was previously stated, underwriting is the process of selection, classification, and rating of risks. Risk classification refers to the determination of whether a risk is standard or substandard based on the underwriting or risk evaluation process. Basically, a standard risk is simply an average risk.

Standard Risks

Standard risks are those who bear the same health, habit, and occupational characteristics as the persons on whose lives the mortality table used was compiled. Most insurers offer special but higher rates to persons who are not acceptable at standard rates because of health, habits, or occupation. This is sometimes called "extra risk" insurance. Some companies have coined euphemistic names for it in order to avoid the rather insulting implication that persons offered this type of coverage are *substandard*. There are several methods of determining the extra rate for the substandard class of risk:

➤ *Rated-Up Age*—This plan assumes that the insured is older than his or her actual age, which is a way of saying that he or she will not live as long or remain as healthy as a "standard" risk. Thus an impaired risk of age 35 may be issued a policy as applied for but with the rate of age 40. This method is no longer widely used.

➤ *Flat Additional Premium*—A constant (that is, not varying with age) additional premium is added to the "standard" rate.

➤ *Tabular Rating*—Applicants are classified on the basis of the extent to which mortality of risks with their impairment or degree of impairment exceeds that of the "standard" risk. Percentage tables are developed and used to calculate the amount of extra premium to be charged for any class of impaired risks. Extra percentage tables are usually designated as "Table A," "Table B," and so forth. Each usually reflects about a 25% increase above 100%, or "standard."

➤ *Graded Death Benefits*—The insured pays the standard premium for, say, $20,000 of insurance but receives a policy with a face amount of perhaps $15,000. After some time has elapsed the company may increase the amount of insurance periodically and when the company considers the substandard condition to no longer exist, the full $20,000 of coverage would be granted.

Preferred Risks

If a substandard risk presents an above average risk of loss, a *preferred risk* presents a below average risk of loss. In an effort to encourage the public to practice better health, the insurance industry has developed preferred risk policies with lower (or preferred) premium rates.

Those applicants who may be eligible for preferred risk classification are those who

➤ Work in low-risk occupations and do not participate in high-risk hobbies (scuba diving, skydiving, and so forth)

➤ Have a very favorable medical history

➤ Presently are in good physical condition without any serious medical problems

➤ Do not smoke

➤ Meet certain weight limitations

Determination of Premiums (Rating Considerations)

The final step in the underwriting process is the rating of the risk or the determination of the premium. There are three factors used in determining insurance rates:

➤ Mortality (life insurance rates) or morbidity (health insurance rates)

➤ Interest

➤ Expenses

Mortality or Morbidity

If underwriters could predict exactly how long each insured would live, they could charge a premium for each risk that was precisely correct for covering the policy face amount, and expenses, while taking into account the interest to be earned on the premium paid. Of course underwriters cannot do this on individual policies, but they can predict the probability of numbers of deaths for a large group of people. This is an example of the *law of large numbers* in action.

Insurance companies have kept the kind of records required to produce precise predictions, and the result is called a *mortality table*. The table is based on statistics kept by insurance companies over the years on mortality by age, sex, and other characteristics.

The deaths per 1,000 (*mortality rate*) is taken from the mortality table and converted into a dollar-and-cents rate. For instance, if the mortality rate for a particular age group is 3.00, it means, on the average, three out of every 1,000 can be expected to die at that age. An insurance company needs to collect $3 from each of 1,000 policyowners in order to have sufficient premium to pay out $1,000 in benefits for the three who are expected to die in that age group.

Health insurance policies use related but much more complex statistics to determine *morbidity rates*. *Morbidity* is the likelihood that a person will suffer an accident, contract a disease, or otherwise require medical care. For many years, insurance companies have kept records that document the outcome of insuring various types of risks. For instance, they know that older people are more likely to become ill than younger people, so health insurance premiums tend to be higher for older people. Similarly, insurers know that people employed in certain occupations are more likely to be injured than those in other occupations. These determinations are based on what has happened in the past, the company's and the industry's experience.

In order to set rates for health insurance, however, insurers need to consider not only how often people will become ill or injured, but how much it will cost when they do. Insurers look at how frequently claims happen among a particular population, or the *claim frequency rate*, as well as the average dollar amount per claim. These two figures are multiplied to create the *aggregate claim* amount, which is a primary element in calculating health insurance rates.

Interest

Because premiums are paid in advance of claims, insurance companies have money to invest to earn interest. This interest helps to lower the premium rate. It is assumed that all premiums are paid at the beginning of the year and all claims paid at the end. Therefore, it becomes necessary to determine how much should be charged at the beginning of the year, assuming a given rate of interest, to have enough money at the end of the year to pay all claims.

Expenses

Using the cost of mortality and discounting for interest, there is enough money to pay claims, but we have no money to pay operation expenses. The premium without expense loading is a "net" premium. (Do not confuse "net" as it is used here with the same term sometimes used to indicate a participating premium minus dividends paid.)

An *expense loading* is added to the net premium in order to

➤ Cover all expenses and contingencies

➤ Have funds for expenses when needed

➤ Spread cost equitably among insureds

Loading consists of four main items:

➤ *Acquisition Costs*—All costs in connection with putting the policy on the books are charged as incurred in the insurance accounting. In most cases, these costs will be so proportionately high in comparison to ensuing years that they must be amortized over a period of years. One of the highest acquisition costs is the producer's first-year commission.

➤ *General Overhead Loading*—Clerical salaries, furniture, fixtures, rent, management salaries, and so forth, must be considered when determining expenses. The allocation of these costs is unaffected by the size of the premium and probably little affected by the face amount, but is most likely affected by the number of policies.

➤ *Loading for Contingency Funds*—After a level premium policy has been issued, the premium can never be increased. However, unforeseen contingencies could make the rate inadequate. Assessment companies reserve the right to charge additional premiums in such a case. Legal reserve companies establish contingency reserves to draw on in such cases.

➤ *Immediate Payment of Claims*—In rate-making, it is assumed that all claims are paid at the end of the year. This is not literally true, of course. Relying on the law of large numbers, it is safe to assume that claims will be spread throughout the year.

The *gross annual premium*, the amount the policyowner actually pays for the policy, equals the mortality risk discounted for interest, plus expenses. By definition, the *net premium* is the mortality risk discounted for interest, without any expense adjustment.

The risk factor increases with age. This is the reason that some life insurance policy premiums increase periodically. For example, the premium for a 1-year renewable and convertible term insurance policy increases each year because each year the insured is one year older and thus the mortality risk is greater. This can result in very expensive premiums as the insured becomes older.

The *level premium* concept was devised to solve this problem of increasing premiums. Mathematically, the level premiums paid by the policyowner are equal to the increasing sum of the premiums caused by the increased risk of mortality. Accordingly, in the early years of the policy, the level premiums paid are actually more than the amount necessary to cover the cost of mortality.

Conversely, in the later years of the policy, the premiums paid are less that the amount necessary to cover the increased cost of mortality. This "shortage" in the later years of the policy is accounted for by the overcharges (plus interest earned) in the early policy years.

Premium Mode

After the single premium amount has been determined, the company will break this amount into smaller amounts (annual, semiannual, quarterly, or monthly) that will be more convenient for the insured to pay.

This frequency of payment is called the *premium mode*. This is important because the insurance company invests the premium amounts it receives and uses the income as part of the eventual settlement. The more payments the insured wants to break his premium into, the higher the total premium, to include the interest lost by not receiving money for coverage in advance and increased administrative expenses.

Loss Ratios

Loss and expense ratios are basic guidelines to the quality of company underwriting. A *loss ratio* is determined by dividing losses by total premiums received. Loss ratios are often calculated by account, by line of insurance, by "book of business" (all accounts placed by each producer or agency), and for all business written by an insurer. Loss ratio information may be used to make decisions about whether to renew accounts, whether to continue agency contracts, and whether to tighten underwriting standards on a given line of insurance. An *expense ratio* is determined by dividing an insurer's operating expenses (including commissions paid) by total premiums.

 When the combined loss and expense ratio is 100%, the insurer breaks even. If the combined ratio exceeds 100%, an underwriting loss has occurred. If the combined ratio is less than 100%, an underwriting profit, or gain, has been realized.

For example, let's assume that the ABC Insurance Company realizes $3 million in underwriting losses for all term insurance policies. This same block of business also generates $10 million in premium. The loss ratio in this case would be 30% ($3 million divided by $10 million).

Further, let's assume that the ABC Insurance Company has operating expenses totaling $2 million for this same block of term insurance. The expense ratio would therefore be 20% ($2 million divided by $10 Million).

Because the combined loss and expense ratio equals 50%, the ABC Insurance Company has an underwriting gain or profit on this block of term insurance.

Insurance Fund Reserves

Insurers are required to follow certain regulations and laws to be certain they will have the money needed to pay claims as they arise. Funds set aside to pay future, existing, and ongoing claims are known as *reserves*. Reserves are accounting measurements of an insurer's liabilities to its policyholders. Theoretically, the reserve is the amount together with interest to be earned and premiums to be paid that will exactly equal all the company's contractual obligations. Companies must also keep enough on hand to pay claims that might arise should some major catastrophe occur on a local, regional, or national basis. Because insurance premiums are paid in advance, an insurance company always has a certain amount of money that it has not yet earned by providing protection. This amount, too, is considered a reserve, called an *unpaid premium reserve*. When a policy is canceled before its term ends, unpaid premium is ordinarily returned to the former policyowner.

A life insurance reserve is a fixed liability of the insurer. By law, a portion of every premium must be set aside as a reserve against the future claim from the policy as well as other contractual obligations, such as cash surrender and nonforfeiture values. Accordingly, the policy reserve is equal to the premiums paid plus the interest earned on those premiums and other policy obligations.

Insurance companies demonstrate their solvency to the state insurance departments by showing their assets as well as adequate funds to cover their reserve obligations. In addition to its assets, the insurer must show that it will continue to receive future premiums plus interest in order to cover its reserve obligation.

Exam Prep Questions

1. John fills out an application for a life insurance policy to insure his own life, and for which he plans to pay the premiums. John is playing all the following roles *except*
   - ○ A. Applicant
   - ○ B. Policyowner
   - ○ C. Insured
   - ○ D. Beneficiary

2. Life insurance that requires no medical exam and asks only basic medical questions is known as
   - ○ A. Simplified policy
   - ○ B. Simplified issue
   - ○ C. Simplified risk
   - ○ D. Preferred risk

3. In many jurisdictions, testing for the presence of HIV infection requires all the following *except*
   - ○ A. A signed consent form before the blood test is performed
   - ○ B. A signed release form whenever test results will be disclosed to any party who is not otherwise entitled to the information
   - ○ C. Medical oversight of any testing by a specialist in HIV research
   - ○ D. Confidentiality of results in the absence of a signed release form

4. Which of the following is *not* likely to be contained in an MIB report?
   - ○ A. Mr. Jones reported a heart condition on an insurance application two years ago.
   - ○ B. Mr. Smith was turned down for insurance by two companies in the past year.
   - ○ C. Mr. Green's information has been requested 14 times in the previous two years.
   - ○ D. Mr. Brown reported a hobby as a flight instructor a year ago.

5. If an applicant is rated or declined an insurance policy, the reasons for this decision will be explained to the applicant by
   - ○ A. The producer
   - ○ B. The underwriter
   - ○ C. The insurer
   - ○ D. The Insurance Commissioner

6. A is a 25-year-old who drinks very occasionally, does not smoke, and does not have any known health problems. A would probably be classified by an insurer as

◯ A. A standard risk

◯ B. A substandard risk

◯ C. A superstandard risk

◯ D. A preferred risk

7. Which of the following does *not* have an impact on insurance premium rates?

◯ A. Mortality or morbidity

◯ B. Interest rates

◯ C. Producer certification

◯ D. Expenses

8. To be certain the insurer has the money available to pay claims as they arise, it is required to maintain

◯ A. A risk-based capital ratio

◯ B. Reserves

◯ C. Expense ratios

◯ D. Reinsurance

Exam Prep Answers

1. **D is correct.** Obviously John is the applicant and the insured. Because he will pay the premiums, he is also the policyowner.

2. **B is correct.** Simplified issue life insurance is a form of coverage that does not require a medical exam and asks only basic medical questions on the application.

3. **C is correct.** Consent forms, release forms, and confidentiality of results are required. There is no requirement for medical oversight by a research specialist.

4. **B is correct.** MIB reports do not include any information about the action taken by insurers.

5. **A is correct.** The producer is the person who has direct contact with an applicant, and it is the producer's duty to explain any adverse underwriting decision.

6. **A is correct.** This person probably falls into the standard risk category.

7. **C is correct.** Mortality or morbidity, interest rates, and expenses all influence insurance premiums. A producer's status has no effect on insurance rates.

8. **B is correct.** Reserves are the funds insurers put aside to cover claims and other contingencies.

Group Insurance

Terms you need to understand:

✓ Employee group
✓ Multiple employer group
✓ Trust group
✓ Association group
✓ Labor union group
✓ Creditor group
✓ Contributory group
✓ Noncontributory group

Concepts you need to master:

✓ Adverse selection
✓ Probationary period
✓ Eligibility period
✓ Nondiscriminatory classifications
✓ Enrollment percentage

Group insurance provides coverage to many people under one policy. It gets its name from the requirement that several people must first be members of a group before they become eligible to purchase the insurance.

A person who is covered by group insurance does not receive a policy as proof of insurance. As the master policyowner, the group receives and holds the insurance policy. The insured group members receive a *certificate of insurance* that certifies the coverage, the benefits under the policy, the name of the covered individual or individuals, and the name of the beneficiary if applicable.

Types of Groups

The first type of group would be the employees of an eligible employer. This is called an *employee group* or an *individual employer group*. The employer is the policyowner and establishes the eligible class of employees to be covered under the group policy.

Usually, this classification will include all full-time employees (including the employer). Further, the classification can also specify full-time, salaried, nonunion employees. By classifying the employee group in this manner, the employer is legally able to exclude certain groups of employees (part-time, union, and so forth) from the eligible class of covered employees. The eligible class of employees may also include retired employees.

A second type of group could be composed of several employers forming a trust fund to combine their workers for life insurance eligibility. This is known as a *multiple employer group*. The trusts are called *multiple employer trusts* (*METs*).

A policy may be issued to the trustees of a *trust group* if the fund has been

➤ Established by two or more employers in the same or related field

➤ Established by one or more labor unions or associations (this is known as a "Taft-Hartley Trust")

The trustees are the policyholders of the plan that covers eligible employees. This type of plan must not be for the benefit of the employer, union, or association. The individuals who may be considered "employees" as defined by this section are the same as those previously listed under employee group.

A third type of organization eligible for group insurance includes members of labor organizations, such as the United Auto Workers. An *association* or *labor group* must have the following characteristics to be considered an authorized group:

➤ Have a constitution and bylaws

➤ Be organized and maintained in good faith for purposes other than obtaining insurance

➤ Have insurance for the purpose of covering members, employees, or the employees of members for the benefit of persons other than the association or its officers or trustees

Credit group insurance is written to provide payment of the insured's debt when he or she dies prematurely or is disabled due to accident or sickness. The creditor is the policyowner and the debtor the insured. Benefits under credit insurance are not permitted to exceed the amount of indebtedness.

Group Premiums

Group insurance policies are often able to provide coverage at a lower premium than individual policies. One reason for this is that the administrative costs to cover a group of 50 people are much lower than the administrative costs involved in writing 50 separate policies.

Group insurance premiums are based on the experience of the group as a whole. Premium may be paid entirely by the policyowner, or it may be paid jointly by the policyowner and the insured.

If the insured contributes money toward the premium, the plan is considered contributory. In most states, at least 75% of the eligible employees must participate under a contributory plan. If the premium is paid entirely by the policyowner, the plan is considered noncontributory. All the eligible members must participate in noncontributory plans.

Group Underwriting Considerations

Group life insurance is usually written on a group basis as opposed to an individual basis. In other words, the underwriter focuses on the group as a whole, rather than individual members. Each group participant completes a very short application form, which usually consists of the individual's name, address, social security number, dependent information, and beneficiary designation.

For group insurance enrollments, there are no medical questions. Thus, no medical underwriting takes place. However, evidence of insurability must be furnished by an employee who wants to join a contributory group after the period of eligibility has ended.

It is therefore possible for individuals in poor health to receive group insurance benefits because there is no medical underwriting. All eligible participants obtain coverage. However, some underwriting—that is, risk selection—is done to help protect insurers from adverse selection. This underwriting is done on the characteristics of the group rather than the individual medical status of each person insured.

Adverse Selection

Adverse selection is the tendency for poor risks to seek and be covered for insurance more often than average risks. Thus in a group situation, the underwriter must consider such things as the type of work done, the ages of the participants, and the probability of this particular group being an adverse risk to the company. For example, a group of coal miners presents a much different risk than a group of bank employees.

When a group is written, the underwriter wants the business to stay on the books and thus is concerned about the financial stability of the company. If the company has a history of financial problems—bankruptcy, layoffs due to no work, seasonal employment—possibly the group may be declined for these financial reasons.

The insurer does not necessarily want a group in which there is no turnover. If the loss experience is to be favorable, employees must leave the group due to retirement or terminations and new (younger) employees must take their place. This turnover of employees helps bring some stability in terms of loss experience and possible adverse selection.

Adverse Underwriting Decisions

A risk will be rejected when the insurer believes the applicant cannot be profitable at a reasonable premium or with reasonable coverage modifications. If a risk is rejected based on information in an investigative report, the applicant must be notified and given the name and address of the reporting company. In health insurance, when renewal is denied, the insured must be given a written explanation for nonrenewal or be notified that the explanation is available upon written request.

Probationary Period

Often, individuals coming into a covered group will be required to serve a *probationary period* before becoming eligible for group coverage. It costs the insurer money to enroll an individual in a group plan. Some groups experience high turnover among membership. It would be prohibitively expensive, for example, to cover all workers in a business as of the first day of employment in businesses with high turnover.

To avoid this expense, the insurer usually requires that employees be on the job a specified period of time before the insurance is put into force. This period of time is often 90 days, though it can be longer or shorter.

Eligibility Period

If the group plan is noncontributory, all individuals become immediately covered after the probationary period. If the plan is contributory, the employees must first fulfill the probationary period, and then must enroll within the eligibility period to avoid medical underwriting. This is one way insurers protect against adverse selection.

The eligibility period typically runs for 30 or 31 days after the probationary period expires. If the group member does not apply during the eligibility period, he or she is generally required to take a medical exam before being eligible for coverage.

 If an individual does not enroll during the eligibility period, but wants to enroll later, he or she will generally be required to take a physical examination and will be selected on an individual basis, as if the policy were an individual policy.

Requirements in Group Underwriting

The following factors and requirements represent the underwriting criteria for group health insurance.

Statutory Requirements

There are only a few statutory requirements affecting the underwriting of group policies. Perhaps the most significant are laws prohibiting discrimination.

Nondiscriminatory Classifications

An eligible group must not discriminate in favor of particular individuals. For instance, if an employer has five typists in the same job classification (job title and salary range), the employer cannot single out one typist to receive benefits greater than the other four typists. Therefore, employees will be grouped under classifications, such as, "all eligible full-time employees," "all clerical workers," "all hourly employees," "all salaried employees," "all executives," "employees working one year or more," or "employees earning not less than $10,000 but not more than $15,000."

Optional Requirements

Optional requirements are usually imposed by the insurance companies, rather than by state law.

Employer Control

The employer should be in charge of enrollment, premium payment, benefit selection, and all other areas of administration that are not an insurance company function.

Group Size

Most insurers require a minimum number of employees or plan participants before a group health insurance plan may be written. This requirement may vary depending on state laws. Typically, the minimum group size for health insurance is 10 but it could be as low as five or some other number.

Predetermined Coverage Amount

The underwriter should determine that individual coverage is based on some plan other than individual selection.

Enrollment Percentage

The insurance company requires that a majority of eligible individuals be members of the group of insureds. For example, under a plan of insurance where an employer pays the entire premium, and the employee does not contribute to the premium payment (noncontributory plan), 100% of all eligible employees must be covered. Under a plan where both the employer and the employee contribute toward the premium payment (contributory plan), 75% of all eligible employees must be covered.

Insurance Incidental to Group

The underwriter should determine that the group has not been formed only for the purpose of purchasing insurance. If individuals could form a group for the purpose of obtaining insurance, the chance of adverse selection would increase dramatically.

Eligibility

The underwriter should first determine that the business is one that the insurer will cover. Because death and illness rates differ in different parts of the country, underwriters may take geographic *location* into account. Certain parts of the country also are more prone to catastrophic loss from natural disasters.

Composition of Group

The underwriter should determine that the group is of such nature that there is a reasonably steady flow of new members into the group. A new insurer also may establish a preexisting condition provision in the group contract that excludes coverage for any condition that exists before the effective date of coverage. This provision will normally exclude these conditions for a period of 6 or 12 months after the effective date of coverage.

Generally, there will also be a requirement that only employees currently working at least 25 hours per week are eligible for coverage.

Funding of Group Insurance

Several mechanisms for funding group insurance have been developed. Alternative funding allows employers to absorb some of the risk and save premium dollars (and increase cash flow).

For example, a *shared funding arrangement* allows the employer to self-fund health care expenses up to a certain limit. The employer can select a deductible and pay covered expenses for any individual incurring claims up to that maximum, at which point the insurer assumes the risk.

Under a *retrospective premium* arrangement, the insurer agrees to collect a provisional premium but may collect additional premium or make a premium refund at the end of the year based on the actual incurred losses.

A *minimum premium* plan is where the employer agrees to fund expected claims and the insurer funds excess claims. The employer and insurer agree to a trigger beyond which the insurer is liable. The employer is responsible for a minimum premium consisting of administrative expenses, reserves, and a premium for stop-loss to fund claims over the trigger.

A large employer may elect to fully self-fund, or may self-fund a plan but contract for *administrative services only* (ASO).

Exam Prep Questions

1. The baker's union and the butcher's union worked together to form a trust to provide insurance to their employees. This type of group is called

   - ○ A. An employee group
   - ○ B. A multiple employer trust
   - ○ C. A Taft-Hartley trust
   - ○ D. A labor group

2. Jimmy's Print Shop and Bryan's Boutique join to form a trust to provide insurance to their employees. This type of group is called a

   - ○ A. An employee group
   - ○ B. A multiple employer trust
   - ○ C. A Taft-Hartley trust
   - ○ D. A labor group

3. The candlestick maker offers insurance to its employees. This type of group is called a

   - ○ A. An employee group
   - ○ B. A multiple employer trust
   - ○ C. A Taft-Hartley trust
   - ○ D. A labor group

4. The United Auto Workers union provides insurance to its employees. This type of group is called

   - ○ A. An employee group
   - ○ B. A multiple employer trust
   - ○ C. A Taft-Hartley trust
   - ○ D. A labor group

5. General Electricians offers insurance to its employees. About 80% of the eligible employees are currently covered under the plan. The plan is most likely

   - ○ A. Contributory
   - ○ B. Noncontributory
   - ○ C. Inclusive
   - ○ D. Noninclusive

6. Group insurance generally does not require

   - ○ A. Stringent medical underwriting
   - ○ B. A short application form
   - ○ C. A minimum level of participation among the eligible insureds
   - ○ D. A master policyowner to hold the policy

7. Sara is hired to work at a restaurant. She is not eligible to join the group insurance plan for 30 days. This is an example of
   - ○ A. The introductory period
   - ○ B. The weeding out period
   - ○ C. The probationary period
   - ○ D. The eligibility period

8. Marie has worked at the restaurant for more than a year, but she never participated in the insurance program. She decides that it is now time to join. She is required to undergo a medical exam because she is signing up after
   - ○ A. The probationary period has expired.
   - ○ B. The weeding out period has expired.
   - ○ C. The introductory period has expired.
   - ○ D. The eligibility period has expired.

9. Which of the following group underwriting characteristics is generally required by law?
   - ○ A. Employer control
   - ○ B. Predetermined coverage amount
   - ○ C. Nondiscriminatory classifications
   - ○ D. Insurance incidental to group

10. Kelsy's Printing funds all the claims in a year, regardless of the amount of the claim. Kelsy's insurer manages the paperwork for the claims. What option is Kelsy's Printing using?
    - ○ A. Retrospective premium
    - ○ B. Minimum premium
    - ○ C. Variable premium
    - ○ D. Administrative services only

11. Al's Print Shop pays a provisional premium at the beginning of the year. At the end of the year, Al's insurer has the right to change that premium by charging more or issuing a refund. Al's policy is funded using which premium option?
    - ○ A. Retrospective premium
    - ○ B. Minimum premium
    - ○ C. Variable premium
    - ○ D. Administrative services only

12. PDQ Printing pays for all the routine claims. PDQ's insurer pays for excess or unexpected claims beyond a specified trigger point. PDQ's policy is funded using which premium option?
    - ○ A. Retrospective premium
    - ○ B. Minimum premium
    - ○ C. Variable premium
    - ○ D. Administrative services only

Exam Prep Answers

1. **C is correct.** When one or more labor unions or associations form a trust it is known as a Taft-Hartley trust.

2. **B is correct.** A multiple employer trust (MET) exists when individual employers join together to provide group insurance to their employees.

3. **A is correct.** An individual employer offering group insurance to its workers is an example of an employee group.

4. **D is correct.** This is an example of a labor union group.

5. **A is correct.** Usually, at least 75% participation is required for contributory groups. Because 100% participation is required for noncontributory groups, this is not a noncontributory group.

6. **A is correct.** Underwriters consider the overall group, but there is no individual underwriting of the covered individuals and no medical exams required.

7. **C is correct.** A probationary period is an initial period of time a person must work before being eligible for group insurance.

8. **D is correct.** Under contributory plans, if an employee does not enroll during the initial eligibility period the insurer may require a medical exam.

9. **C is correct.** State law requires nondiscriminatory classifications. The other answer choices are examples of insurance company requirements.

10. **D is correct.** Kelsy's is self-funding losses and using an insurer only for administrative services.

11. **A is correct.** Under retrospective premium rating the insurer will adjust the premium at the end of the year based on the amount of actual losses.

12. **B is correct.** Under a minimum premium plan the employer self-insures the normal and expected claims up to a given amount and the insurer funds only the excess amounts.

Selling Life Insurance

Terms you need to understand:

✓ Inter vivos transfers
✓ Testamentary transfers
✓ Accelerated benefits
✓ Viatical settlement
✓ Buy-sell agreement
✓ Key person life insurance
✓ Deferred compensation

Concepts you need to master:

✓ Costs associated with death
✓ Human life value approach
✓ Needs approach
✓ Capital conservation
✓ Capital liquidation
✓ Estate planning
✓ Split-dollar plan

Meeting Consumer Needs

The loss of human life is tragic in many ways. The financial results alone of such a loss can be devastating. If the principal breadwinner dies, the spouse might not be able to maintain the family on social security benefits. If there were two breadwinners in the family, the surviving spouse might not be able to maintain the family's lifestyle on his or her income alone. The death of a single parent might leave dependent children without an adequate source of support.

The Importance of Insurance

Life insurance products are designed to provide a number of unique and powerful features. But the one benefit all life insurance products have in common is that they provide financial security—a measure of certainty in an area marked by risk and change. And although different clients may find different life insurance products appealing in their particular circumstances, the one reason they all buy life insurance is to obtain that measure of financial security.

Studies show that less than half of American adults own individual life insurance, and the average American adult has just $45,000 of life insurance. Relying on the group life insurance provided at work can build a false sense of security, because coverage is usually insufficient for family needs and generally ceases when employment terminates. Experts agree that few people protect their own "full value" with life insurance, leaving their families at risk.

Costs Associated with Death

When an individual dies, he or she typically leaves behind certain costs associated with death, which include

➤ Doctor and hospital bills from a final illness or accident

➤ Funeral expenses

➤ Estate taxes

➤ Debts (credit cards, loans)

In addition, to those individuals leaving behind a family or others who are financially dependent on them for support, the following financial needs will immediately become apparent:

➤ Mortgage payments

➤ Immediate income needs—to pay for groceries, utilities, car payments, and other day-to-day living expenses

➤ Longer-term needs—money to pay for children's education, retirement income for a spouse

The insurance producer is the person most qualified to help potential insureds select the contract of insurance that will best meet their needs.

This needs analysis can be accomplished by identifying the specific financial objectives of the individual by means of a fact-finding interview. This interview covers the following financial needs:

➤ Cash needs to cover the expenses of dying (funeral, taxes, last illness, and so forth)

➤ Cash needs for payment of debts (charge cards, loans, bank notes, and so forth)

➤ Home mortgage payments

➤ Family income needs during the dependency period and in later years

➤ Educational funds for children's college education

➤ Retirement income needs

➤ Health insurance needs, such as hospitalization insurance and disability income coverage

After the needs analysis is complete, the producer should make recommendations about the amount and type of insurance needed by the individual. These recommendations should consider the following:

➤ Should the coverage be permanent or term insurance, or a combination of the two?

➤ How much premium can the individual afford to pay?

➤ Should the premium be level, increasing, or decreasing?

➤ Is the individual insurable?

Human Life Value Approach

The human life value concept puts a dollar value on an individual based on the earning potential of the insured, calculated and projected over a period of years (capitalized), taking into account four factors:

➤ The individual's net annual salary

➤ The individual's annual expenses

➤ The number of years the individual has left to work (the present to retirement age)

➤ The value of the individual's dollar as it depreciates over time (capitalized rate)

The human life value concept is a way of determining what a family would lose in income by the death of the principal wage earner. By this method, if the insured died, the family could be reimbursed for that loss.

Needs Approach

Looking at the needs of an individual and his or her dependents is considered the best method for determining the amount and kind of insurance a prospect should buy. Basically, the needs method looks at such things as

➤ Needs for last illness and burial expenses

➤ Maintenance income for the family for a period of time after the death of the principal wage earner

➤ Education for dependent children

➤ Continuing income for the surviving spouse, and so forth

After determining needs, the agent must find out how much the prospect can afford to pay in premium and make further adjustments to the proposed plan based on the prospect's financial position, keeping in mind the various term policies and riders.

Income Periods

A typical married couple with children will have fluctuating income needs based on the changes in their family. To properly determine how much life insurance protection they will need if an income-earner dies, their needs should be divided into three different income periods. The first period is called the *family dependency period* because the surviving spouse will have children to support during this time, which means the family's income needs will be greatest during this period. When the children are no longer dependent on the surviving spouse, he or she enters the *preretirement period*. Because the surviving spouse qualifies for social security survivor benefits only when he or she has dependent children in his or her care or after reaching the age of

60, this period is also referred to as the *blackout period*. Usually, the surviving spouse's income needs lessen during this period. The final period is called the *retirement period*. During this period, the surviving spouse's working income ceases and his or her social security and outside retirement benefits begin.

Because the surviving spouse's standard of living does not lessen, he or she will require an income comparable to the preretirement period during this time.

Capital Conservation and Capital Liquidation

There are two methods used to calculate the amount of life insurance needed to supply an individual or family with the desired amount of capital to generate income if an income-earner should die prematurely. *Capital conservation* (sometimes called *capital retention*) and *capital liquidation* (sometimes called *capital utilization*) differ in how capital is used to generate income for the surviving family.

Under the capital conservation method, income is derived only from interest gained on the principal. But under the capital liquidation method, both the interest and the principal are used to generate income. Generally, this means that a smaller fund is needed when using the capital liquidation method because there is no concern for leaving the principal intact.

Some individuals find the smaller fund required an attractive feature of the capital liquidation method, but the capital conservation method has two significant advantages:

➤ *It generates income indefinitely.* No matter how long the survivor lives, the capital conservation fund remains intact and generates interest. Under capital liquidation, however, the fund generally gets smaller and eventually disappears. Survivors who live longer than expected will outlive their source of income.

➤ *It creates a legacy.* Under capital conservation, when funds are no longer needed, they can be given away to loved ones or charity. Legacies are uncertain under capital liquidation because they depend on the survivor dying prematurely.

Estate Planning

Life insurance can also create an immediate estate for the insured and provide funds that will help preserve the greatest amount of value in the estate.

The field of estate planning is very complicated. It requires expertise in the areas of wills, taxes, law, and life insurance. Some of the items to be considered when planning an estate are

➤ The needs of the beneficiaries

➤ The type and amount of property that is in the estate

➤ How to best administer the estate to fulfill the wishes of the insured

➤ The amount of insurance needed to cover expenses and costs

➤ How to dispose of any business interest

➤ Who will settle and administer the estate

There are two methods of distributing the estate; *inter vivos transfers,* or *testamentary transfers.*

Inter vivos transfers are made while the estate owner is still alive. Transfers can be made as

➤ Gifts

➤ Trusts

➤ Policy ownership under rights of survivorship

Testamentary transfers are made by will after the death of the estate owner. If the estate owner dies without leaving a will, which is called *dying intestate*, the property will be transferred as an intestate distribution under the laws of the state.

Other Sources of Funds

In determining the amount and kind of insurance an applicant needs, the agent must consider other sources of income or benefits the applicant currently has, or for which he or she may be eligible under other insurance plans, government programs (such as social security), and retirement plans (pensions, IRAs, Keoghs, and so forth). Some other sources of funds to be considered are

➤ Medicare

➤ Medicaid

➤ Group retirement plans

➤ Savings

➤ Investments

➤ Other income (for example, income from property rental)

➤ Annuities

➤ Other insurance

Living Benefits

The primary reason to own life insurance is the death benefit—the money the beneficiaries will receive when the insured dies. But life insurance can also provide benefits for the policyowner while he or she is living.

The living benefit of the most prevalent type of life insurance is the cash value it accumulates. Throughout the years of premium payments, part of these payments accumulates for the insured as a cash value. This cash accumulation may be used as collateral for policy loans or later as retirement income. Many policies allow withdrawals from the policy's cash value, which can be used to meet emergencies or to pay off debts. Participating policies also pay dividends, which are another form of living benefit.

Although not all types of life insurance policies accumulate cash values or make payments to policyowners, you should recognize these *"living benefits"* of life insurance:

➤ Loan values

➤ Retirement income

➤ Cash withdrawals

➤ Dividends

Advantages as Property

A life insurance policy's cash value can be used as a collateral for borrowing money. Suppose an insured goes to a bank to borrow money. The bank will want to determine the type and amount of property the individual can call on to pay off the loan should his or her income be suspended. Life insurance can act as collateral or "back-up" property for the loan.

Another advantage of life insurance as property is one you have already learned—it creates an immediate estate.

Suppose a man invests in a piece of land. He may have to wait years and years for that land to appreciate. Its value may never quite reach what he had anticipated. If that man were to die the day after buying the land, whether he paid cash for it or not, his family might have difficulty getting the money back that was invested.

Not so with life insurance. The instant a life insurance policy goes into effect, the insured policyowner has established a fund that will be paid to her or her beneficiary—even if only one premium payment has been made. There is no waiting for the property to appreciate in value; no worrying whether the value will actually rise as expected.

There are other advantages to life insurance as property:

➤ The entire premium to purchase the policy does not have to be paid up front, and paying in installments is convenient.

➤ *Safety of principal* is of considerable concern to anyone purchasing property. How safe is your money? Is it subject to market fluctuations, depreciation, or other loss? A $100,000 life insurance policy will pay that amount to the beneficiary at the death of the insured as long as premiums are met and there are no outstanding loans against the policy.

➤ As for *return on investment*, as you'll see later in the course, life insurance offers plans that can be very advantageous, especially with regard to taxation of cash values.

➤ Many kinds of property require *physical maintenance or upkeep*. Houses must be painted, car engines tuned, livestock fed, and so on. Apart from paying premiums, a policyowner has no other obligations with regard to life insurance.

➤ Finally, *managerial care* is a frequent concern of property owners. Stocks and bonds, real estate, and similar investments require constant attention with regard to market conditions, taxation, and so on. No managerial care is required of a policyholder toward a life insurance policy.

Comparing Insurance Policies

Life insurance cost comparison methods are used to compare the cost of one life insurance policy against another in order to guide prospective purchasers to policies that are competitively priced.

Comparative Interest Rate Method

This analysis examines the rate of return that must be earned on a hypothetical side fund in a "buy-term-invest-the-difference" plan so that the value of the side fund will be exactly equal to the surrender value of the higher premium policy at a designated point in time. The higher the comparative interest rate (CIR), the less expensive the higher-premium policy relative to the alternative plan. Outlays and death benefits are held equal. The CIR method requires a computer because the final interest rate is found through trial and error.

Interest-Adjusted Net Cost Method

To compare two different policies, it is not enough just to compare premiums. A lower premium does not automatically mean a low-cost policy. Cost indexes have been developed to help measure the cost of a policy.

This analysis is conducted over a set time period considering a policy's premiums, death benefits, cash values, and dividends, recognizing the accumulated interest over the set time period. The NAIC Model Life Insurance Solicitation Regulation requires two interest-adjusted cost indexes for a policy—a *surrender cost index* and a *net payment cost index*.

These indexes show average annual costs and payments per $1,000 of insurance on a basis that recognizes that $1 payable today is worth more than $1 payable in the future. Both assume that the insured will live and pay premiums for a period of years. Most companies provide these index numbers on both a guaranteed and an illustrated basis.

Traditional Net Cost Method

The *surrender cost index* method uses a complicated formula, but the basic process works like this. The policy's premiums and dividends are accumulated over a period of years (say 10 or 20) at some assumed annual rate of interest, often 4% or 5%. Then the total accumulated dividends are added to the cash value at the end of the period (plus any terminal dividends), and this total is subtracted from the accumulated premium payments. In other words, the projected total cash value of the policy at some point in the future is subtracted from the total premium payments to that same point in the future to find out how much the policy cost. This net cost is averaged over the number of years in the period to arrive at the average cost-per-thousand for a policy that is surrendered for its cash value at the end of the period.

Interest Adjusted Cost Method

The *net payment cost index* is developed in the same way, but it does not assume the policy is surrendered at the end of the period. The same formula is used, but the cash value element is omitted. Instead, this index provides an estimate of the policyowner's average annual out-of-pocket net premium outlay, adjusted for time value of money.

Cost indexes can be a significant help to life insurance consumers. It's important, however, to understand that in using cost indexes, the consumer should compare index numbers only for similar kinds of plans and only for the kind of policy for the consumer's age and the amount he or she intends to buy. Policy features and company service could offset small differences in cost index comparisons.

In addition to providing death benefits—the most obvious purpose of a life insurance policy—life insurance serves a number of other purposes that may fulfill the needs of individuals and businesses. The next two sections discuss personal and business uses of life insurance.

Personal Uses of Life Insurance

Life insurance is the only financial services product that guarantees a specific sum of money will be available at exactly the time that it is needed. From a personal perspective, life insurance may be used to provide

➤ Peace of mind and financial security for a family

➤ Cash for funeral costs and related expenses

➤ Cash to pay off a home mortgage

➤ A college education for surviving children

➤ Income for a family and surviving spouse

➤ Cash for emergencies or to supplement retirement

➤ A means of maintaining a family's lifestyle

➤ Funds to preserve an estate and avoid a forced liquidation of capital to pay estate taxes and debts

➤ Bequests to non–family members or to charitable or civic organizations

➤ Advance payment of proceeds prior to death through accelerated benefits or viatical settlements

If an insured has a terminal illness, a life insurance policy may be his or her last substantial source of money. The life insurance benefits may be made available for medical expenses and living expenses prior to death through accelerated benefit provisions or viatical settlement agreements.

Accelerated benefits are living benefits paid by the insurance company that reduce the remaining death benefit. The government does not consider accelerated death payments to be taxable income, and the policyowner gets between 50–95% of the policy's full benefit.

Under a *viatical settlement*, the policyholder sells all rights to the life insurance policy to a viatical settlement company, which advances a percentage (usually 60%–80%) of the eventual death benefit. The viatical settlement company then receives the death benefit when the insured ultimately dies.

Beginning in 1997, proceeds from viatical settlements and accelerated benefits are not taxable as income. Although accelerated death benefits may require a life expectancy of one year or less, viatical settlements may be available for a person who has up to five years to live.

Charitable Uses of Life Insurance

Another use of life insurance is for charitable purposes. In accordance with tax laws, a policyowner may purchase a life insurance contract on his or her life, pay the premiums, and designate a charitable organization as the beneficiary—such as a church, school, hospital, or similar organization. Generally, the premium paid by the insured-donor is tax deductible.

Business Uses of Life Insurance

There are generally three types of business organizations: the sole proprietorship, the partnership, and the corporation. Regardless of business type, a business has the same need as an individual—protection against premature death and the delivery of cash exactly when it is needed.

This cash need relates to the disposition of a business interest upon the death of the sole proprietor, a partner or a corporate stockholder. Disposition of the deceased's business asset usually means the sale of the business, retention of the business within the family or liquidating the business. The difference between a sale and liquidation is that a sale will usually result in the family receiving a fair market value for the business interest. Liquidation is a forced sale that may only bring one-tenth of the true business value.

In some situations, liquidation of the business is necessary or mandated by law. However, liquidation is the least desirable method of disposing of the deceased's business interest. The sale or retention of the business requires

➤ Proper planning and implementation of business agreements

➤ A willing and competent successor/buyer

➤ Cash with which to implement the plan

Sole Proprietorship

A sole proprietorship is an unincorporated form of business whereby an individual owns and manages a business. Even though a sole proprietorship may have several employees, it is the sole proprietor who is generally directly responsible for the success of the business.

The sole proprietor has *unlimited liability* with regard to the business operation. Creditors can claim both the sole proprietor's business assets as well as personal assets. When the sole proprietor dies, the business also dies. This business asset becomes part of the deceased's estate and is commingled with other personal assets subject to taxation, the payment of debts, and claims of creditors.

Generally, the business is the principal asset in the sole proprietor's estate. It is also normally the only source of income for the family. Upon the death of the sole proprietor, family income ceases and, unless adequate planning has occurred, the business may have to be liquidated for a fraction of its value in order to pay estate settlement costs.

Life insurance can be used to solve the problems created by the death of the sole proprietor. Life insurance may fund a *business continuation agreement* (also known as a *buy-sell agreement*) by providing necessary cash with which to keep the business doors open until possibly the business can be sold at its fair market value for the benefit of the family. Life insurance can also be used to provide funds for a competent employee or other qualified person to purchase the business from the surviving family members.

Partnership

A partnership is a legal, non-incorporated business relationship involving two or more individuals who each contribute their unique skills, talents, and capital for the purpose of owning and operating a business enterprise. As a partnership, each partner has unlimited liability with regard to partnership functions. As such, business creditors may claim personal assets for payment of debts.

Generally, by law, when a partner dies, the surviving partner(s) must dissolve the business. The survivor becomes a liquidating trustee and in essence liquidates the business and his or her own job, eliminating the family's principal source of income. Disposition of the deceased's business asset is required in order to settle the deceased's estate.

To a large degree, the problems created by the death of a partner can be resolved by means of a properly drawn buy-sell agreement. If there are only two or three partners, a *cross-purchase* plan may be advisable in which each partner is bound by the terms of the plan and agrees to purchase a share of the deceased partner's interest. If there are more than two or three partners, the *entity type* plan is usually recommended, whereby the partnership agrees to purchase the interest of a deceased partner.

The key element for partnership planning is the funding of the agreements.

Life insurance is the ideal choice to guarantee that the required amount of money will be delivered exactly when it is needed. A cross-purchase plan covering two partners would require that each partner own, pay the premium, and be the beneficiary of a life insurance policy on the life of the other partner.

If the partnership consisted of six partners, each partner would be the owner of five policies for a total of 30 life insurance policies. This is the reason why an entity agreement is usually recommended if there are more than two or three partners. Under an entity agreement involving six partners, the partnership would own six policies.

The principal advantages of the funded buy-sell agreement include

➤ A fair market value is established, funded with life insurance, for the benefit of the surviving family.

➤ Buyers of the partnership interest are predetermined and legally bound by the agreement.

➤ The partnership and employee's jobs are secure.

➤ The necessary funding to implement the plan is readily available.

Corporations

A corporation is an "artificial person." It is a legal entity that is owned by its stockholders. One of the characteristics that distinguishes a corporation from the other business forms is that its life is *unlimited*. When a working stock-holder dies, the corporation continues. Another distinguishing characteristic is that stockholders have limited liability. A stockholder's risk is limited to his or her investment in the corporation. Personal assets are generally safe from the claim's of creditors.

Corporations may be classified as closely held or publicly held. A close corporation is typically one that is owned by a few stockholders, often members of the same family. A publicly owned corporation may be owned by several thousand stockholders, such as General Motors. This discussion of corporate insurance needs will be limited to the close corporation.

The death of a stockholder in a closely held corporation means the loss of services of this key person and quite possibly loss of business income. However, the most immediate effect will be the loss of income to the deceased's family. The choices available to the family are to sell the deceased's stock, attempt to live off of any dividends that the corporation may pay, or assume a working position within the corporation.

Probably, the most desirable alternative is to sell the deceased's stock.

Attempting to live on dividend income only will probably not enable the surviving family members to maintain their standard of living for very long.

Assuming the surviving spouse has inherited the deceased stockholder's shares, he or she may not be knowledgeable or competent enough to assume the position of the deceased within the corporation. In addition, the surviving stockholders may not want a new, inexperienced stockholder working in the corporation. Thus, the purchase of the deceased's stock becomes a viable alternative, provided there has been adequate planning and there is cash available for the stock purchase.

Business planning to resolve the problems created by the death of a stock-holder involves the implementation of a stock purchase or stock redemption plan. A *stock purchase plan* is similar to a cross-purchase partnership plan, whereby a price is determined and each stockholder agrees to purchase a proportionate share of the deceased shareholder's stock. The purchase price is naturally funded with life insurance and each shareholder owner, premium payor, and beneficiary of a life policy on the lives of the other stockholders.

This arrangement is feasible when there are only a few shareholders.

In situations with several shareholders, the stock redemption plan is better.

Stock Redemption Plan

Under a *stock redemption plan*, the corporation is the owner, beneficiary, and premium payor of the life insurance policies, and the corporation agrees to purchase the deceased's stock.

The advantages of the life insurance–funded corporate buy-sell plan include

➤ The establishment of a fair price for the stock

➤ A binding agreement that identifies the buyers

➤ Corporate assets and jobs are secure

➤ Guaranteed delivery of the purchase price

Section 303 Stock Redemption

Section 303 stock redemption is a special type of stock redemption that permits a corporation to *partially* redeem a shareholder's stock for purposes of providing cash to cover estate settlement costs. Tax laws generally require that stock redemption be total to avoid taxing the proceeds payable to the family as a dividend. The Internal Revenue Service will permit a partial redemption by the corporation to pay funeral expenses, taxes, and related estate settlement costs.

Key Person Life Insurance

Key person life insurance protects the corporation from the financial loss sustained when a key employee (the owner, for example) dies. In addition to the corporate owner, a key person could be a sales manager, a vice president, and so forth. When a key person dies, the corporation could experience a loss of income, impaired credit standing, loss of jobs, and customers. To offset this financial impact, the corporation may purchase a life insurance policy on the life of the key person. The corporation would be the owner, premium payor, and beneficiary of the policy. The face amount of the policy would generally relate to the amount of lost corporate income plus the costs of hiring and training a replacement for the deceased key person.

Deferred Compensation

Deferred compensation is an executive benefit that enables a highly paid corporate employee to defer current receipt of income such as an *executive bonus* and have it paid as compensation at a later date (retirement, death, or disability) when presumably the employee will be in a lower tax bracket. Generally, the employee will enter into an agreement with the employer that specifies the amount of money to be paid, when it will be paid, and the conditions under which the deferred compensation may not be paid.

The agreement will specify that the amount deferred will be paid as a retirement benefit or in the event of the premature death or disability of the employee. It will further indicate that the individual will forfeit the right to this sum of money if he or she leaves the employer except for retirement, death, or disability.

The advantage of this agreement for the employee is avoidance of current taxation because receipt of the money is deferred and therefore not subject to income tax until it is actually received.

The principal advantage for the employer is that the services of the employee are usually secured for life because the employee will forfeit the right to the deferred compensation except for retirement, death, or disability. In addition, deferred compensation can be viewed as a desirable executive benefit and thus enable the employer to attract and retain key personnel. Funding for the deferred compensation may be life insurance contracts, disability income policies, annuities, mutual funds, and so forth.

Split-Dollar Plan

Split-dollar plans are not actually types of life insurance policies but rather methods of purchasing life insurance. Under a split-dollar arrangement, a plan of permanent life insurance is jointly purchased by the employee and the employer. Permanent life insurance is used because it provides guaranteed cash values.

The employer's share of the premium is an amount equal to the annual increase in the policy's cash value. Accordingly, in the early years of the plan, the employee's cost will be higher than in the later years when the policy will contain higher amounts of cash value and the employer's share of the premium will be greater.

The death benefit is also shared between the employee and the employer in proportion to the amount of the premium each is paying. Usually, the employer is the policyowner and thus has control of the policy including its cash value.

Split-dollar plans are an attractive benefit, whereby a key employee is able to purchase life insurance at an attractive cost because of the joint premium payments.

Exam Prep Questions

1. Which of the following should not be taken into account when a producer makes recommendations as to the amount and type of insurance needed by an individual?

   ○ A. How much premium can the individual afford to pay?

   ○ B. Should the premium be level, increasing, or decreasing?

   ○ C. How much commission does the product offer?

   ○ D. Is the individual insurable?

2. Ana wishes to purchase enough insurance to support her husband for the rest of his life if she should die prematurely, and then leave a sizeable inheritance for her children upon his death. Which method should be used to calculate the amount of insurance necessary?

   ○ A. Capital conservation

   ○ B. Capital liquidation

   ○ C. Human life value

   ○ D. Needs analysis

3. The type of estate transfer made while the estate owner is still alive is called a(n)

   ○ A. Inter venous transfer

   ○ B. Inter vivos transfer

   ○ C. Testamentary transfer

   ○ D. Trustee transfer

4. The type of estate transfer made after the estate owner dies is called a(n)

   ○ A. Inter venous transfer

   ○ B. Inter vivos transfer

   ○ C. Testamentary transfer

   ○ D. Trustee transfer

5. Suki dies without leaving a will. The distribution of her estate will be handled by a(n)

   ○ A. Intestate distribution

   ○ B. Inter vivos distribution

   ○ C. Testamentary distribution

   ○ D. Vivos testate distribution

6. Ken has terminal cancer and wants to access the death benefit of his life insurance policy to pay medical expenses. How might he be able to do this?

○ A. He won't be able to access the policy funds until after his death.

○ B. He may access the funds through accelerated benefits.

○ C. He may access the funds through a viatical settlement.

○ D. He may access the funds either through a viatical settlement or by using the accelerated benefits provision.

7. Shane is a master carpenter in business for himself. His business is probably operated as

○ A. A corporation

○ B. A sole proprietorship

○ C. A partnership

○ D. A limited liability company

8. Which of the following would not be financed by using life insurance?

○ A. A buy-sell agreement

○ B. A Section 303 stock redemption

○ C. A cross-purchase agreement

○ D. A split-dollar plan

9. Which of the following are costs associated with death?

○ A. Doctor or hospital bills from a final illness or accident

○ B. Paying off debts such as credit cards or other loans

○ C. Taxes

○ D. All of the above

10. An insurance producer analyzed Bonita's life insurance needs, taking into account Bonita's net annual salary, her expenses, her current age, and depreciation of the dollar over time. This producer was using

○ A. The analytical approach to needs analysis

○ B. The human life value approach to needs analysis

○ C. The needs approach to needs analysis

○ D. The planning approach to needs analysis

11. An insurance producer analyzed Dwight's life insurance needs, taking into account the amount of money Dwight anticipated needing for his funeral and the amount of income that would be required to maintain his family's standard of living in the event of his death, including projected college costs and the costs of supporting his spouse. This producer was using

○ A. The analytical approach to needs analysis

○ B. The human life value approach to needs analysis

○ C. The needs approach to needs analysis

○ D. The planning approach to needs analysis

12. Wilma's husband died 3 years ago, leaving her with two children in grade school. Wilma is most likely in which income period?

   ○ A. The family dependency period
   ○ B. The preretirement period
   ○ C. The retirement period
   ○ D. The grieving period

Exam Prep Answers

1. **C is correct.** The producer is supposed to serve the client's needs. The amount of commission should not be a factor in any recommendations.

2. **A is correct.** The primary concern here is capital conservation.

3. **B is correct.** A transfer made while the estate owner is still alive in an inter vivos transfer.

4. **C is correct.** This is an example of a testamentary transfer.

5. **A is correct.** This is an example of an intestate distribution.

6. **D is correct.** Both options make funds available prior to death.

7. **B is correct.** Shane has no partners and probably has no need to incorporate.

8. **D is correct.** A split-dollar plan is a method of purchasing life insurance, rather than a plan financed using life insurance.

9. **D is correct.** All of the choices are costs that might be associated with death.

10. **B is correct.** This is an example of using the human life value approach.

11. **C is correct.** This is an example of using the needs approach to needs analysis.

12. **A is correct.** This is an example of the family dependency period.

Policy Issuance and Delivery

Terms you need to understand:

✓ Conditional receipt
✓ Binding receipt
✓ Temporary insurance agreement
✓ Replacement
✓ Fiduciary

Concepts you need to master:

✓ Personal delivery
✓ Delivery by mail
✓ Constructive delivery
✓ Policy retention

Collection of Premium

The producer is encouraged to collect the initial premium with the application.

Evidence shows that this procedure is most effective in having the insured accept the policy when it is issued. If the insured does not pay the initial premium at the time of application, chances increase that he or she will not accept the issued policy. Another point the producer can make to the applicant is that if the applicant waits to pay the premium, he or she may become uninsurable, or may die before the policy takes effect. Remember, the policy is effective only after the initial premium has been paid.

When the initial premium is not paid with the application, no contract is in force. The applicant is not making an offer to the insurer. He or she is merely inviting the insurer to make an offer by issuing the policy. Because there is no insurance in force under these circumstances, when the producer delivers the policy and collects the initial premium, there may be additional underwriting requirements to be satisfied. Most commonly, the insurance company may require that the insured sign a health statement verifying that no change in health has occurred since the date of the application.

Receipts for Premium

When the underwriting process is complete and the applicant has been approved, the life insurance policy will be issued by the insurance company. The coverage is not effective until the policy is delivered and the initial premium has been paid. Usually the applicant will pay the initial premium with the application. When this occurs, the producer will provide the applicant with a receipt for the initial premium, and the effective date of coverage will depend on the type of receipt issued.

Conditional Receipt

After the producer has completed the application, it is normal to collect the first full premium from the policyowner. The receipt for this premium is generally a *conditional receipt*.

This type of receipt is conditional because the producer cannot guarantee that the policy will be issued. The conditional receipt explains to the proposed insured that the policy will be issued subject to the approval of the insurance company.

According to the conditional receipt, if the proposed insured should die before the policy is issued, one of the following will occur:

➤ The proceeds will be paid to the beneficiary named in the policy if the company *would have* issued the policy to the proposed insured if he or she had been living.

➤ The proceeds will not be paid to the policy's beneficiary if the company *would not have* issued the policy. Instead, the premium will be returned.

For example, an applicant has paid the initial premium and completed and signed the application. The producer provides the applicant with a conditional receipt that basically states that the applicant is covered as of the date of the application (or receipt), provided he or she is insurable as a standard risk. Thus, if the applicant were to die before the policy was issued, the beneficiary would receive the face amount of the policy.

On the other hand, if the applicant was found to be a substandard risk, the conditional receipt is null and void and no coverage would be effective until the substandard policy was delivered and additional premium paid. If the policy is not issued as applied for (a substandard rating, for example), no coverage would be in force until the applicant accepts the substandard policy and pays the additional premium required by the rating.

This receipt makes the coverage effective on the date of the application, if the applicant is found to be insurable under the company's general underwriting rules in effect at the time of application. However, some conditional receipts make coverage effective on the date of application or the date of the medical examination, whichever is later.

Binding Receipt

A few companies use an *"unconditional"* or *binding receipt* that makes the company liable for the risk from the date of application. This coverage lasts for a specified time or until the insurer issues the policy or notifies the applicant the policy is being refused. The specified time limit is usually 30–60 days.

NOTE

With a binding receipt, regardless of the applicant's insurability, he or she is covered following completion of the application and the payment of the initial premium and remains covered for the length of the specified term or until notified of refusal. Use of this type of receipt is rare for life insurance policies, though it is commonly used for auto or homeowners insurance.

Inspection Receipt

Occasionally, a situation will arise where the proposed insured wants to examine the policy carefully before actually purchasing it. In this situation, the policyowner does not pay the first full premium at the time the application is completed. The policyowner signs an inspection receipt for the policy, examines the policy, and then pays the first full premium.

Temporary Insurance Agreement

This type of receipt or agreement provides the applicant with immediate life insurance coverage while the underwriting process is taking place whether or not the individual is insurable. In this instance, the insurance protection applied for becomes effective immediately, within the limitations stated in the temporary insurance agreement or receipt.

The insurer has the right to cancel this coverage if the applicant fails to meet the company's normal underwriting requirements. However, claims incurred during the underwriting period will be paid in line with the terms of the receipt, whether or not the application would ultimately have been approved.

For example, an applicant submits the initial premium and application and is provided with a temporary insurance agreement that states that coverage is effective immediately and will continue during the underwriting process. If the applicant should die during this period, the coverage is in force regardless of the individual's insurability or risk classification as a result of the underwriting process.

Submitting the Application and Initial Premium

It is important for the producer to submit the application, initial premium, and any questionnaires or other forms to the home office underwriter promptly. The producer should review all forms for completeness and be sure that they are properly signed. Not only does this ensure good relationships with the home office underwriter, but also it is extremely important to the applicant.

Unnecessary delays in issuing the policy can cause the applicant undue anxiety and result in a loss of confidence in the producer.

Because producers are handling money belonging to their clients, it is extremely important that an accurate record of such transactions be kept. It is also wise for the producer to keep copies of applications and other information. This avoids unnecessary delay or other problems if the originals are lost.

Issuing the Policy

A life insurance policy may be *issued as applied for*, *modified*, or even *amended* if the applicant does meet the underwriting standards of the insurance company. Although uncommon, an insurer may issue a waiver with the policy that states that death by a particular event will not be covered. This might be done if the insured had a particularly hazardous occupation or hobby. More commonly, an insurer might issue a more limited form of policy or one at lower limits.

Delivering and Servicing the Policy

Generally, policies are delivered in person by the producer or are delivered by mail.

Personal Delivery

Because delivery is necessary to complete the sale of a life insurance policy, the best way to assure delivery is to do it in person. If a conditional receipt has not been previously issued, the insurer may require the producer to obtain a statement of good health at the time of policy delivery. In addition to knowing the policy has been delivered, this method also gives the producer an opportunity to

➤ Thoroughly explain all coverage provisions, exclusions, and riders to the applicant/policyowner. Although most policies contain a provision barring a producer from changing the policy contract in any way, the company may be liable for errors made by the producer if the producer incorrectly represents the policy being sold. It is important for the producer to sit down with the insured at the time of policy delivery and explain all policy provisions, particularly the exclusions, and any riders that may restrict the coverage given in the policy.

➤ Review the purpose of the policy and how it fits into the policyowner's total life insurance plan.

➤ Reinforce the relationship and good will established with the client.

➤ Allow the producer to explain the possible need for additional coverage.

➤ Ask the insured for referrals under favorable circumstances.

Mailing the Policy

Legally, the policy is considered "delivered" when it is mailed or turned over to the policyowner or someone acting on his or her behalf. Some companies do mail policies directly to policyowners. However, many prefer to have the producer make a personal delivery.

In some cases, a *constructive delivery* is deemed to occur when the insurer mails a policy to its producer for actual delivery to the policyowner, because the insurer has issued the policy and released it for delivery. However, a legal delivery has not yet occurred if the insurer requires personal delivery for verification of good health at the time of delivery, or if the policy is being provided to the applicant merely to review and inspect at that time and not necessarily to buy.

Handling a Claim

A claim and its payment are the end result of the insurance process. With respect to life insurance, it means the insured has died and the beneficiary stands ready to collect from the insurer what is due. Unlike property or casualty insurance, claims made on a life insurance policy are rarely negotiated. They are either paid or denied. When proof of the death of the insured arrives at the insurer's claims department, the records are checked to make sure the policy was in force at the time of death and that the person to whom the policy proceeds are to be paid is indeed the rightful beneficiary.

Payment of Claims

When an insured dies, the life insurance company should be notified as soon as possible. In many cases, the family of the deceased is too grief-stricken and shocked even to think about such matters as notifying the insurer. It is the agent's responsibility, in such a case, to make sure that the company is notified of the claim at the earliest possible moment.

After a company has been given the proper forms, there is usually little or no delay in payment of the claim, especially when it is obvious that the claim is valid—the policy is in force, the beneficiary is available, there is no evidence of suicide within the limitations of the suicide clause, and so on. When an insurer is notified of a valid claim, the claim will be paid in very short order, usually within a few days.

Good will is one of the life insurance industry's most valuable selling tools.

This is one of the many reasons why most life insurance companies pay a valid death claim as soon as possible after they receive the proper notification and proof of death.

 In most jurisdictions, life insurance companies are required to pay death claims within a specified period of time after proper notification of the claim and receipt of a death certificate. This period is usually two months (60 days).

Should there be a delay in a death claim payment, the usual reason is that the company has not been properly notified of the insured's death. A formal proof of death form of some type is usually required by the company, in addition to a death certificate completed by the attending physician or the coroner. When an insured dies, the agent should complete any proof of death form the company requires, have it signed by the necessary parties, and forward it to the company as soon as possible along with a death certificate.

Payment Less than Face Amount

In property or casualty insurance, the amount of claims paid is often less than the face amount of the policy. In contrast, life insurance is generally paid for the full face amount of the policy. There are three exceptions to this.

The first exception is when there is an outstanding loan against the cash value of a policy. The amount of the loan, plus any interest outstanding, is deducted from the face amount of the policy before payment is made to the beneficiary.

The second exception is when there is a premium payment due. With insurance premiums, as with many other types of bills, there is a grace period of somewhere between a week and a month after the due date but before the policy expires. If the insured dies within this grace period, the amount of the premium due is deducted from the face amount of the policy before payment is made to the beneficiary.

The third exception happens when an error is made in determining the age or gender of the insured when the policy was issued. If such an error is discovered at the time of death, the insurance company will compute the face amount that the premium would have purchased if the accurate information was used and pay that amount to the beneficiary.

Such errors are not an unusual occurrence in the life insurance business. Some are intentional, but most are simply mistakes. In either event, the discrepancy is not material enough to void the policy. Just remember that unless one of these three exceptions applies, the full face amount of the policy is paid.

Producer Responsibilities upon Insured's Death

When the producer is informed of an insured's death, he or she has a number of things to do:

➤ First, notify the company immediately. On occasion, a beneficiary, the beneficiary's legal representative, or an heir of the deceased will notify the company directly of the insured's death. In these instances, the company will then contact the producer or will advise the beneficiary to do so.

➤ Next, the producer should contact the person designated to receive proceeds of the policy or that person's legal representative.

➤ The company will require a completed form of some type that serves as an official proof of the insured's death. The agent should help the beneficiary complete a proof of death form and send it to the company with a death certificate.

➤ Most of the information on the proof of death form can be obtained without actually questioning the distraught family members of a deceased insured. Because this is true, the producer should personally complete the form, and then take it to the beneficiary for signing.

➤ An insured may have policies from more than one company. Therefore, the producer may be meeting one or more producers from other companies when attempting to settle a death claim. The important thing at this point is to render the best possible service to the beneficiary.

➤ If the insured chose a particular settlement option at the time the policy was bought, this option should be explained to the beneficiary. The logical person to explain this settlement option is the producer, who is on hand to answer questions and give a detailed explanation of the option. In some cases, the beneficiary may have the right to choose or change the settlement option.

The insured may have chosen a particular settlement option at the time the policy was purchased but may have given the beneficiary the right to change it. Alternatively, the insured may not have selected a settlement option at all.

In this case, it is entirely up to the beneficiary. In either situation, the producer explains all the available options to the beneficiary.

Policy Replacement

Technically, *replacement* means any transaction in which new life insurance or a new annuity is to be purchased, and it is known, or should reasonably be known, that as part of the transaction, existing life insurance or annuity will be

➤ Lapsed, forfeited, surrendered, or terminated

➤ Converted to reduced paid-up insurance, continued as extended term insurance, or reduced in value by the use of nonforfeiture benefits or other policy values

➤ Amended to produce a reduction in the benefits in the term for which coverage would otherwise remain in force or for which benefits would be paid

➤ Reissued with reduction in cash value

Replacement, simply, is the purchase of one life insurance policy to replace another. Because of the cash values that can build up in a policy and the favorable loan interest rates in older policies, replacement can be disadvantageous to consumers. However, there are good reasons to replace a policy, particularly if it does not meet the current needs of the consumer.

Commissions paid to producers for selling a new policy are particularly lucrative. For this reason, unscrupulous producers have persuaded consumers to give up old policies for new ones, even if it was not in the best interests of the policyholder.

When replacement of life insurance is involved, the producer must comply with all pertinent federal and state regulations. Each state has rules and regulations regarding replacement of life insurance products, which are designed to protect the interests of the insuring public. Frequently, it is not in the best interests of the insured to replace existing life insurance with a new policy:

➤ New insurance requires the applicant to prove insurability.

➤ Premiums may be higher for a new policy.

➤ New policy provisions will have to be complied with, such as a new incontestable period.

➤ The existing policy's provisions might be more liberal than a new policy's provisions.

➤ Generally, a new policy will not have any current cash values.

The National Association of Insurance Commissioners (NAIC) has adopted a Model Life Insurance Replacement Regulation. The majority of states have replacement regulations based on this model.

Duties of Producers

Generally, the duties of the producer include obtaining, along with the application, a signed statement from the applicant as to whether insurance is to be replaced and submitting the statement to the insurer.

If replacement is involved, the producer is required to

➤ List all existing life insurance policies to be replaced.

➤ Give the applicant a completed *Comparison Statement*, signed by the producer, and a *Notice to Applicants Regarding Replacement of Life Insurance* (a copy of the forms should be left with the applicant).

➤ Give the insurer a copy of any proposals made and a copy of the Comparison Statement with the name of insurer that is to be replaced.

The producer must take special care when replacing an existing policy with a new policy to make sure that the insured is not misled into purchasing a policy that is to the insured's disadvantage. The producer also needs to be aware of his or her own errors and omissions liability, particularly in the area of replacement.

Duties of the Insurer

The duties of the replacing insurer include

➤ Making sure that all replacement actions are in compliance with state regulations

➤ Notifying each insurer whose insurance is being replaced, and upon request, furnishing a copy of any proposal and Comparison Statement

➤ Maintaining copies of proposals, receipts, and Comparison Statements

Each state has established time limits for the performance of duties. You should check your state's regulations to learn specific time limits, such as

➤ The time within which a producer must supply the applicant with a Comparison Statement

➤ The time and manner within which the producer must notify the insurer of replacement activities

➤ The time within which the insurer must notify the insurer being replaced that such action is in operation

➤ The time within which the insurer being replaced must respond to the replacing insurer and the applicant

Also, individual state law specifically outlines the method in which records are to be maintained and the length of time the records are to be made available.

Policy Retention

The producer becomes involved with the client after original application and delivery at times of change. The client's needs change at such times as marriage, the birth of a child, and death. The producer acts as the representative of the company in changing beneficiaries, adding amounts of insurance, and facilitating payment of claims. The effectiveness of the producer at these times will lead to retention of the account for the lifetime of the client—often over generations.

Professionalism and Ethics

All business transactions are based to a certain extent on trust. When it comes to life insurance, the trust factor is especially significant.

Fiduciary Responsibility

Insurance producers have a fiduciary duty to just about any person or organization that he or she comes into contact with as a part of the day-to-day business of transacting insurance. By definition, a *fiduciary* is a person in a position of financial trust. Attorneys, accountants, trust officers, and insurance producers are all considered fiduciaries.

As a fiduciary, producers have an obligation to act in the best interest of the insured. The producer must be knowledgeable about the features and provisions of various insurance policies as well as know the use of these insurance contracts. The producer must be able to explain the important features of these policies of the insured. The producer must recognize the importance of dealing with the general public's financial needs and problems and offer solutions to these problems through the purchase of insurance products.

As a fiduciary, the producer must know and comply with the state's insurance laws. Many of these laws are for consumer protection. It is the producer's duty to comply with these laws and protect the interest of the insured at all times.

Summary of the Producer's Responsibilities

The insurance producer is a key person in the process of marketing, underwriting, and delivery of insurance policies. As a marketing representative of the insurer, it is the producer's responsibility to represent and market the insurer's products in an ethical and professional manner. This requires knowledge of various insurance products, being aware of a prospect's insurance needs and problems, and the ability to solve these needs with the proper insurance products.

The producer also has a responsibility to be aware of insurance laws that pertain to marketing of insurance products, such as state-required standards for advertising and sales literature. Generally all advertising, sales presentations, and illustrations must be truthful and must not misrepresent or omit material information.

Exam Prep Questions

1. Lee applies for a policy, pays the initial premium and receives a conditional receipt on March 14. On March 15, he passes the medical exam with flying colors. On March 16, an undiagnosed brain aneurysm bursts, killing Lee instantly. On March 17, the insurer receives the results of the medical exam, which includes no information about the aneurysm. On March 19, the insurer receives the notice of claim. The insurer will

- ○ A. Pay the claim.
- ○ B. Return the premium.
- ○ C. Pay the claim plus the amount of the first premium.
- ○ D. Pay the claim minus a processing fee.

2. Rich applies for a policy, pays the initial premium, and receives a binding receipt on Friday, September 1. On Monday, September 4, the underwriting department decides not to issue the policy and places the file in a pile for notification letters to be sent out at the end of the week. On Wednesday, September 6, Rich is killed in a auto accident. On Thursday, September 7, the insurer receives the notice of claim. The insurer will

- ○ A. Return the premium and not pay the claim, because the underwriting decision had been made.
- ○ B. Return the premium and not pay the claim, because death occurred before the policy was issued.
- ○ C. Pay the claim, because a binding receipt assures coverage until the potential insured is notified of a rejection.
- ○ D. Pay the claim, because any receipt assures coverage until the potential insured is notified of a rejection.

3. Brit purchases a policy and tells the producer he wants immediate coverage, regardless of the underwriting outcome. To meet Brit's demand, the producer is most likely to

- ○ A. Accept the premium and set up a temporary insurance agreement.
- ○ B. Accept the premium and issue an inspection receipt.
- ○ C. Accept the premium and issue a binding receipt.
- ○ D. Accept the premium and issue a conditional receipt.

4. A policy may be issued all of the following ways *except*

- ○ A. As applied for
- ○ B. As a modified or amended policy
- ○ C. As an exchange policy, covering someone other than the original applicant
- ○ D. With a waiver excluding death by a certain cause

5. Which of the following statements is true about submitting the application, premium, and other forms to the insurance company?

- ○ A. The application and any questionnaires must be signed by the beneficiary.
- ○ B. The producer must keep accurate records of all transactions involving the applicant's money.
- ○ C. Because coverage is effective immediately, it is not necessary to send the forms to the home office underwriter more often than weekly.
- ○ D. A life insurance policy may be issued only as applied for or rejected.

6. Which of the following statements describe the best use of a producer's time when personally delivering the policy?

- ○ A. Mr. Jones delivers a policy and makes a special point of finding out how the insured's son performed in the gymnastics competition.
- ○ B. Ms. King delivers a policy and reiterates the same sales pitch she used to make the initial sale.
- ○ C. Mrs. Ritley delivers a policy and restates the advantages of the policy and how it can be amended to meet future insurance needs.
- ○ D. Mr. Bourne delivers a policy early in the morning, before the client is home, so that he can simply leave the policy in the mailbox.

7. Which of the following statements is false?

- ○ A. Replacement is illegal.
- ○ B. Replacement is the purchase of one life insurance policy to replace another.
- ○ C. Replacement laws are designed to protect the interests of life insurance purchasers.
- ○ D. Replacement laws concern themselves with the use of false and misleading statements used in the sale of insurance.

8. Alice decides to buy a policy. She pays the first premium and the producer issues a receipt and tells her that she is covered immediately, until she is notified that the policy is either issued or declined. What kind of receipt has Alice received?

- ○ A. Conditional receipt
- ○ B. Binding receipt
- ○ C. Inspection receipt
- ○ D. Premium receipt

Exam Prep Answers

1. **A is correct.** The conditional receipt was based on underwriting acceptance. There would have been no reason for the underwriter to decline this application.

2. **C is correct.** The binding receipt guarantees coverage until the applicant is notified otherwise.

3. **A is correct.** The temporary insurance agreement provides immediate coverage while the underwriting process is taking place.

4. **C is correct.** Life insurance policies cannot be exchanged to cover a different insured.

5. **C is correct.** This is a common business practice.

6. **C is correct.** The other answer choices do not reflect good use of the producer's time.

7. **A is correct.** Replacement transactions are not illegal when they are in the best interests of the insured.

8. **B is correct.** A binding receipt provides immediate coverage.

Types of Insurance Policies

Terms you need to understand:

- ✓ Term insurance
- ✓ Whole life insurance
- ✓ Adjustable life insurance
- ✓ Universal life insurance
- ✓ Variable life insurance
- ✓ Variable universal life insurance
- ✓ Industrial life insurance
- ✓ Credit life insurance
- ✓ Endowment policy
- ✓ Riders

Concepts you need to master:

- ✓ Renewable term insurance
- ✓ Convertible term insurance
- ✓ Level term insurance
- ✓ Increasing term insurance
- ✓ Level premiums
- ✓ Face amount
- ✓ Cash values
- ✓ Nonforfeiture value
- ✓ Policy loan
- ✓ Family income policy
- ✓ Family maintenance policy
- ✓ Family protection policy
- ✓ Retirement income policy
- ✓ Joint life policy
- ✓ Juvenile policy
- ✓ Double indemnity
- ✓ Waiver of premium
- ✓ Accelerated benefits
- ✓ Viatical settlements

All life insurance provides a death benefit. This benefit is easy to understand. The living benefits—such as loan values, retirement income, and cash withdrawals—set certain life insurance policies apart from others. These additional benefits add to the enormous versatility that life insurance has to meet a wide variety of needs.

Life insurance can be structured to provide

➤ A guaranteed death benefit only, using term insurance

➤ A guaranteed death benefit plus cash accumulation, using one of many types of permanent insurance

➤ A guaranteed death benefit plus premium flexibility, using universal life

➤ A guaranteed death benefit plus premium and investment flexibility, using variable or variable universal life

➤ Liquidity for estates, using survivorship life

Term Insurance

Term insurance is designed to provide life insurance protection for a limited period of time. It might be for 1 year or 10 years, but the face amount of the policy is payable only if the insured dies during the time specified in the policy.

If the insured survives the limited term of the policy, the insurance company has fulfilled its part of the contract and no payment or refund is due.

Term insurance can be compared to a fire policy on a home. The fire policy is purchased to protect the homeowner from financial loss. However, if the home does not suffer a fire loss, the homeowner's premium is not returned. The homeowner had the peace of mind that comes with insurance protection, but no cash value accumulation or refund.

Characteristics of Term Policies

The *premiums* for a term policy are usually level over the length, or term, of the policy. At the end of the policy, the policyowner may purchase another policy. The new policy almost always requires a higher premium than the expired policy. This new, higher premium, will then be in effect for the length of the new term.

Types of Term Policies

Term policies are defined by the nature of the coverage, the options available under the contract, and the way the face amount of the policy changes throughout the life of the policy. The *face amount*, or *face value*, of the policy is the amount of money listed on the face page (first page) of the policy. This is the amount that will be paid in the event of the insured's death.

Renewable Term

A *renewable term* policy is one that may be renewed at the end of the specified period of time for another term period *without evidence of insurability*.

Thus, a 1-year renewable term policy expires after 1 year but is renewable for additional 1-year periods. A 5-year renewable term policy can be renewed for subsequent 5-year periods. Renewability may be limited to a certain number of renewals or to a specified age, such as 85. The renewable feature must be written into the original policy at the time of purchase.

When a renewable term policy is being renewed, however, the rates will be based on the age the insured has reached at the time of renewal. This is why premiums for renewable term coverage are often called *step-rate* premiums.

Convertible Term

A term policy that is *convertible* allows the policyowner to convert or exchange the temporary protection for permanent protection without evidence of insurability. Usually, this conversion feature is used to convert term insurance to some form of whole life insurance. If the conversion privilege is exercised it will be at the attained age, meaning the premium paid for the new policy will be based on the insured's age at the time of conversion. Like the renewability provision, the conversion privilege must generally be written into the contract and spells out the terms of the policyowner's right to convert.

At the time conversion to permanent insurance is made, the insured generally has a choice of two ages: the present age (called attained age) or the age at the time the original term policy was purchased (called original age).

Premium amounts depend to some extent upon the age of the insured. If the insured converts to permanent insurance using original age, the premiums will be lower than if attained age is used.

When using original age, the policyowner must pay an additional sum, usually consisting of the difference between the lower term premiums over the years, and the higher premiums he or she would have been paying if the permanent protection had been bought originally. The policyowner is also required to pay the interest that the insurance company could have earned on those higher premiums, if it had invested them for those extra years.

By paying the difference in back premiums and interest, the policyowner is building an accumulated value in the policy much more quickly than if he or she simply begins paying the higher premiums as for the attained age. The cash value will be well on its way to a meaningful amount.

Some life insurance companies place a time limit on the conversion privilege. This limit is usually based on the expiration date of the original term policy.

The number of years excluded from the conversion privilege on a convertible term policy varies from company to company. For instance, some companies state that the policy must be converted as much as 5 years before expiration of the original policy, after which point, the right to convert is lost.

Reentry Term

A *reentry option* (also known as *reissue*) is also a common feature of term policies. This option gives the insured the opportunity to provide evidence of insurability at the end of the term in order to qualify to renew the policy at a lower premium rate than the guaranteed rate that is available without evidence of insurability. Essentially, the renewing insured is reviewed as a new applicant for term insurance.

Level Term

Level term provides a level death benefit and level premium during the policy term. For example, if an individual purchases a 10-year term policy with a face amount of $100,000, both the premium and the face amount will remain constant for the entire 10-year period.

Assuming the level term policy is issued as renewable and convertible, every time the policy renews for a subsequent term period, the policy's premium will increase due to the increased age of the insured. For example, an insured has purchased $50,000 of 1-year renewable and convertible term insurance.

Each year the policy is simply renewed at the same face amount by the payment of the new, higher premium. A new application is not required nor is a new policy issued. The only thing that changes is the age of the insured and subsequently the policy's premium.

Decreasing Term

Decreasing term is also temporary protection for a specified period of time. The face amount decreases throughout the life of the policy down to zero at the date of policy expiration. The annual premium for a decreasing term policy remains level during the term of the policy. A common use for decreasing term insurance is to cover a home mortgage. The policy amount decreases each year at the same rate as the balance on the mortgage.

Decreasing term is usually written as convertible but generally is not renewable at the end of the term period. The convertible feature allows the policyowner to convert to permanent insurance usually at any point during the decreasing term of the policy for the available amount of insurance at that point in time. Mortgage life insurance is an example of decreasing term.

Increasing Term

Increasing term is another type of term insurance, which is not used as often as level or decreasing term. Increasing term is basically the opposite of decreasing term. The death benefit increases over the life of the policy, and the premium remains level.

Indeterminate Premium Term

Indeterminate premium term is a type of term insurance where the premium may fluctuate between the current premium charge and a maximum premium charge that is stipulated in the insurer's premium tables, based on the insurer's mortality experience, expenses, and investment returns.

Interim Term

When a person wants immediate protection and is thinking of starting a permanent insurance policy in the near future, *interim term* may be used to cover the period of time before permanent protection is to begin. Many companies write interim term on an automatically convertible basis. That is, they provide the insured with temporary term protection that will covert automatically at some future date, usually no later than 11 months. The premium for the interim term is based on the age at application. The premium for the permanent coverage is also based on attained age when permanent protection begins.

Advantages and Uses of Term Insurance

Some of the advantages and uses of term insurance are

➤ Initially, the cost of term insurance is low, making it useful for individuals or businesses who may have a large need for insurance but limited financial resources to pay for it.

➤ As temporary protection, it is often used to help cover temporary needs. For example, decreasing term is frequently used to cover the decreasing financial obligation associated with debts.

➤ Term insurance can be flexible. Frequently it is used to provide additional protection for an insured. For example, a husband has a relatively small whole life policy and becomes a father of twins. His responsibilities have suddenly changed and there is a need for possibly large amounts of additional life insurance. Term insurance could provide the solution to this problem. Often, the additional insurance is added to the existing policy by means of a rider.

Disadvantages of Term Insurance

Some of the disadvantages associated with term insurance are

➤ Over a long period of time, renewable term insurance becomes very expensive. Although initially the level term premium is low, it increases with each renewal, based on the increased age of the insured and the increased risk of mortality for the insurance company. Thus, a relatively low premium at age 35 becomes an expensive and sometimes prohibitive premium at age 55 or 60.

➤ Even though the premium for decreasing term remains level for the life of the contract, this level premium pays for less and less insurance. In the later years of a decreasing term policy, the actual cost of the remaining insurance tends to be expensive.

➤ One of the disadvantages of term insurance is its very nature—it is temporary protection for a limited period of time. If the policy is not renewable or the increasing cost of the policy is prohibitive, the insured can be left without insurance at a time (older age) when he or she needs the protection the most.

➤ Term insurance is pure death protection only. It offers no living benefits, such as guaranteed cash values.

➤ Even if the term policy is renewable, it generally is not renewable beyond a certain age such as age 65 or 70. Again, there is the danger of losing or not being able to afford the protection at these ages.

Whole Life Insurance

Whole life insurance, sometimes known as permanent insurance or ordinary insurance, is designed to provide protection for the whole life of the insured.

Characteristics of Whole Life Policies

Whole life policies have a number of common characteristics.

Level Premiums

Through mathematical science, the premiums for most permanent insurance policies are designed to remain level during the entire period the policy is in force. In the early years of the contract, the insured actually pays in more premium than is needed to provide the current year's insurance protection, and in later years pays in less than is needed. The net result is that the premium remains the same for the entire period of the contract. In addition, the company has the opportunity to use the money and to invest it at a favorable return. This helps reduce the cost of insurance.

Level Face Amount

Not only does the premium remain level for the life of the policy, but so does the face amount of the policy. Generally, the policy's basic face amount will not change for the life of the policy.

Guaranteed Cash Value

As the policyowner continues to pay the premiums, the cash value in the policy accumulates year by year. The amount of pure insurance protection the insurance company must provide decreases as the amount of cash value increases.

Usually, in the first couple of years of the policy, the cash value is equal to zero. Over the life of the policy, there is a steady increase in the amount of the cash value until age 100 when the cash value is exactly equal to the policy's face amount. An increasing number of people do live past the age of 100, but they are so rare that they may be ignored statistically. Insurance company statistics generally assume that everyone has died by age 100.

 The cash value built by whole life policies may be used by the policyowner in several ways, including withdrawing part or all of the cash value or taking a loan using the policy as collateral.

Nonforfeiture Value

The cash value in the policy belongs to the policyowner. If he or she wishes to, some or all of the cash value may be withdrawn from the policy. Any withdrawal of cash value will reduce both the face value of the policy and the amount of cash value available.

The policyowner is entitled to this living benefit at any time. If the policyowner decides to cease paying premiums, he or she may cash the policy in for the available cash value.

Policy Loans

The cash value can also be loaned to the policyowner. The term, *loan* is used, but this loan does not have to be repaid unless the policyowner elects to repay it. Just as with a partial withdrawal of the cash value, a cash value loan (for the available amount of cash at that point in time) that is not repaid will reduce both the face amount of the policy and the cash value available. For example, an insured dies with a $10,000 whole life policy that has an outstanding loan of $1,000, the beneficiary would receive $9,000.

As a policy loan, it is also subject to interest. In order to meet the obligations of all of its policyholders, a life insurance company invests the dollars it receives. These investments earn interest at a rate close to estimates made in advance. When the policyowner takes a policy loan, the amount the company has available to invest is reduced by the amount of the loan. This means that the company will earn less interest than estimated, unless it makes up that amount from some other source. In this instance, the other source available to the company is annual interest charged.

When a policyowner takes out a policy loan, he or she usually continues to pay premiums on the policy. As long as the premiums are paid regularly, the cash value in the policy will generally rise faster than the loan plus the loan's interest. If the policyowner does not pay the premiums, the policy may lapse. If the policy loan and the interest on it become greater than the total cash value of the policy, the policyowner no longer has sufficient collateral for the loan, and the policy will lapse. The company must warn the policyowner before cancellation to give the policyowner the opportunity to take action to keep the policy in force. To avoid cancellation of the policy, the policyowner can pay enough of the loan and interest to reduce the total outstanding amount to a figure lower than the total cash value of the policy or pay off the entire loan plus interest.

Types of Whole Life Policies

Whole life policies may be categorized according to how the premium is paid.

Continuous Premium Whole Life

Continuous premium whole life is the most common type of whole life insurance sold. These policies stretch the premium payments over the whole life of the insured (to age 100).

 This type of policy is often referred to as *straight life* insurance.

Limited Payment Whole Life

Many policyowners want the lifetime insurance protection afforded by the whole life policy, but do not like the thought of paying premiums for their entire lives. *Limited payment whole life* policies allow the policyowner to pay for the entire policy in a shorter period of time. The premium for any whole life policy can be broken down into any desired number of installments.

Because the limited pay policy is paid up sooner than the whole life policy, all other factors being equal, the limited pay policy would have a larger annual premium than the whole life policy. Because the premiums are accelerated, the cash values of limited pay policies build at a faster rate than for whole life policies. This means that, for example, the loan value for a limited pay policy after 5 years would be more than for a whole life policy owned for the same length of time.

Common forms of limited payment whole life are 20-payment life (meaning payments spread over 20 years), 30-payment life, and life paid up at age 65.

For example, 20-pay life means premium payments for 20 years but lifetime (to age 100) protection. Life paid up at 65 means premium payments to age 65 but the policy provides lifetime protection.

Single Premium Whole Life

The most extreme version of a limited pay policy is one that can be paid for with only one premium. For this reason it is called a *single premium whole life* policy.

The premium for such a policy might be many thousands of dollars. The advantage offered by a single premium policy is that the policyowner will pay less for the policy than if the premiums stretched out over several years.

By the same token, the person insured by a single premium policy could die shortly after the single premium was paid, thus making the cost of insurance coverage much higher than it might have been had premiums been scheduled over a period of many years.

Indeterminate Premium Whole Life

Indeterminate premium whole life policies are nonparticipating contracts that were developed to compete with participating policies. These policies employ a *dual premium* concept—a maximum premium and discounts that may reduce the premium. The discounts vary with insurance company investment performance, but the actual premium charged will never be more than the maximum premium specified in the contract.

Current Assumption Whole Life

Current assumption whole life (also known as *interest-sensitive whole life*) offers flexible premium payments that are tied into current interest rate fluctuations. The insurance company reserves the right to increase or decrease the premium within a certain range depending on interest rate fluctuations. During a period of relatively high interest rates, premiums could be reduced. During periods of low interest rates, premiums could be increased within certain limits. Usually, any premium adjustment is made on an annual basis.

Economatic Whole Life

Economatic whole life is a whole life-type policy with a term rider that uses dividends to purchase additional paid-up insurance. Let's assume that an individual wants $100,000 of whole life but can't quite afford it. Instead, he purchases $70,000 of whole life with $30,000 of term insurance. Thus, he has $100,000 of death protection at a lower cost.

As policy dividends are declared, they are used to purchase additional paid-up insurance. As the paid-up insurance is added, an equal amount of term insurance is removed from the policy, thus maintaining the full face amount of $100,000 at no additional cost. In reality, the cost of the insurance may decrease as the term amounts are eliminated if a level term rider was used. If a decreasing term rider were used, the reduction of the term insurance would become automatic, but a level premium would be paid for the decreasing term.

When the paid-up additions equal $30,000, the insured now owns $100,000 of whole life but only pays an economical premium for $70,000.

Advantages and Uses of Whole Life Insurance

Some of the advantages and uses of whole life insurance are

➤ The principal advantage of whole life is that it is permanent insurance and can be used to satisfy permanent needs, such as the cost of death, dying, and final burial expenses.

➤ The level premium enables the policyowner to know exactly what the cost of insurance will be and offers a form of forced savings.

➤ Whole life builds a living benefit through its guaranteed cash value, which enables the policyowner to use some of this cash for emergencies, as a supplemental source of retirement income and for other living needs.

Disadvantages of Whole Life Insurance

Some of the disadvantages of whole life insurance are

➤ The premium paying period may last longer than the insured's income-producing years.

➤ It does not provide as much protection per premium dollar as term insurance.

Flexible Policies

Ordinary whole life policies offer premiums, cash values, and face amounts that are determined at the time the policy is purchased, and unless the policyowner takes out a loan or partial withdrawal, generally do not change over the life of the policy.

Flexible policies, in contrast, offer the policyowner the opportunity to change one or more of these components in response to changing needs and circumstances. Each type of policy offers different types of flexibility.

Adjustable Life Insurance

Adjustable life is a policy that offers the policyowner the options to adjust the policy's face amount, premium, and length of protection without ever having to complete a new application or have another policy issued. Adjustable life introduces the flexibility to convert to any form of insurance (such as from term to whole life) without adding, dropping, or exchanging policies. Adjustable life is based on a money purchase concept.

The basic premise becomes not so much which type of policy does a person buy but rather how much premium is to be spent. For example, if an applicant, age 25, states that he or she can afford to pay a $500 annual premium, it then becomes a matter of using this premium commitment to meet the individual's needs and to identify the type of insurance to be purchased.

To further illustrate, let's assume the 25-year-old applicant is married with three children and a large home mortgage and has no other life insurance. This person naturally needs a large amount of insurance. Based on the $500 premium, it might be recommended that all or most of that premium be used to purchase several hundred thousands of term insurance.

In later years, this same individual may adjust the premium, the face amount, or the period of the death protection to meet current needs. For example, the insured is now 50 years old and possibly is planning for retirement. The same $500 premium could now be used for some form of permanent insurance protection with guaranteed cash values. The temporary protection is changed to permanent coverage and the death benefit (face amount) would be reduced due to the insured's age and premium commitment.

If the insured makes an adjustment in the policy that results in a higher death benefit, proof of insurability may be required for the additional coverage.

Universal Life

Universal life was the insurance industry's answer to the extremely high interest rates we experienced in the decade of the 1970s. Traditional whole life contracts have earned 3 1/2%–5% interest. In an effort to be more competitive, many insurers developed universal life products with relatively high interest rates (8%, 10%, 12%). Universal life is a flexible premium, adjustable benefit life insurance contract that accumulates cash value.

A prime feature of universal life is premium flexibility. Premiums paid into a universal life policy accumulate and, together with interest, make up the policy's cash value. After sufficient cash value is accumulated, the policyowner has considerable flexibility with regard to subsequent premium payments.

A policyowner under a universal life insurance contract may increase the death benefit without buying another policy, although he or she may have to prove insurability. Also, the policyowner has the freedom to reduce the death benefit. Neither an increase nor a decrease in death benefit requires the issue of a new policy.

Universal Life Sales Charges

In earlier model universal life policies, a charge or *load* is deducted from each premium after the first-year premium to cover sales and administrative expenses. The remainder of the premium goes into a cash value account. From this cash value account the monthly amount needed to pay for the desired death benefit is deducted, usually on a monthly basis. When the policyowner pays more premium than is required to provide the desired death benefit plus other costs, the universal life policy accumulates cash values.

As mentioned, a part of the premium goes to pay sales and administrative charges. A typical sales load is 7.5%. Thus, for a $1,000 premium payment, 7.5%, or $75, would be deducted, and the $925 balance would go into the cash value account. Load charges range generally from about 7.5% to as high as 10%.

More recent universal life policies have adopted a *back-end* (deducted whenever the policyowner withdraws cash from the policy) sales load. These back-end loads usually take the form of service charges for withdrawals from the policy, or policy surrenders, and for coverage changes. By postponing these sales loads until later, universal life policies could be illustrated showing more attractive returns than the earlier policies that subtracted the sales load at the front end.

These back-end loads often decrease to zero over a period of years. For example, if a universal life policy has a 10-year decreasing back-end load, the charge would be 10% in the policy's first year, 9% in the second year, and so on until withdrawals could be taken without any charge after the 10th policy year.

Universal Life Cash Value Adjustments

Two adjustments are made to the cash value account of a universal life policy, usually on a monthly basis. The first adjustment is a charge against the account to pay the cost of the desired insurance coverage.

The second adjustment is a credit to the cash value account of interest at the current rate. The current rate consists of two parts:

➤ Guaranteed interest, which is guaranteed for the life of the policy, and usually about 4%

➤ Excess interest earned by the insurer. This will vary greatly with the current level of interest rates.

Current interest, then, is equal to guaranteed interest plus excess interest.

The cash value account isn't always fully credited with interest at the current rate. For some policies, there is an additional load that is generated by simply not paying excess interest on the first $1,000 in the cash value account. Thus, this load is the difference between the guaranteed interest rate and the current rate. For example, in a universal life policy with a guaranteed interest rate of 3.5% and a current interest rate of 8%, the annual load would be 4.5%, and would amount to $45, 4.5% of the first $1,000 of cash value.

The current interest rate is commonly set once a year and guaranteed for the entire policy year. However, not all companies will guarantee their current rate for a full year, instead choosing periods as short as 3 months.

Universal Life Death Benefits

There are two options regarding the death benefit payable under a universal life policy:

➤ *Option A* (or option 1) provides a level death benefit equal to the policy's face amount. As the policy's cash value increases, the mortality risk decreases. Thus, the cost of the death protection actually decreases over the life of the policy and accordingly more of the premium can be placed in the cash account. This is exactly the same concept that applies to whole life.

➤ *Option B* (or option 2) provides for an increasing death benefit equal to the policy's face amount plus the cash account. Unlike option 1, the mortality risk remains at a level amount equal to the policy's face value. Thus, the policyowner will incur a higher expense for the cost of the death protection over the life of the policy and less of the premium will be deposited in the cash account.

Universal Life Policy Loans and Withdrawals

Universal life provides cash value loans in the same manner that whole life or any permanent plan of insurance does. If a loan is taken, it is subject to interest, and if unpaid, both the interest and the loan amount will reduce the face amount of the policy.

Many universal life policies will also permit a partial withdrawal or surrender from the cash account. In such a case the policyowner withdraws the desired cash directly from the cash value account and pays a small service charge for doing so. No interest of any kind is credited by the insurer or paid by the policyowner on the amount withdrawn.

Partial withdrawals may be repaid, although any money paid back will be treated as a premium payment and thus subject again to expenses charges if it is a *front-end* (deducted from each premium payment) load policy. With a current interest rate of 10% and a typical expense charge of 7.5%, the cost of a partial withdrawal that is repaid after 1 year is 17.5%, plus the amount of the service charge.

A universal life contract may be surrendered for its cash values whenever the policyowner wants, although a surrender charge (or service charge) is usually applied.

Universal Life Premium Requirements

A featured benefit of the universal life contract is the flexibility of premium payments. As long as there is sufficient cash value to pay the monthly cost-of-insurance deductions, the policy will continue in force and policyowners may pay premiums in whatever amounts and at whatever times they want.

If the monthly cost-of-insurance deductions cause the cash value account to reach zero, coverage under the contract expires. However, there is a grace period, usually 30–60 days, during which the policyowner is given the opportunity to pay enough premium to keep coverage in force.

Variable Life Insurance

Primarily, *variable life insurance (VLI)* is a whole life policy designed to protect the policyowner and the beneficiaries from the erosion of their life insurance dollars due to inflation. Thus, it could be said that variable life is designed to be a hedge against inflation.

Historically, during periods of inflation, the stock market usually has kept pace with inflationary trends by increasing in value. In recognition of this fact, the insurers have established *separate accounts*, which consist primarily of a portfolio of common stock and other securities-based investments. It is these separate accounts that support variable life policy benefits. Policyowners are allowed to choose among various sub-accounts within the separate account that offer different investment objectives, and they can transfer their policy funds among them.

In contrast, the insurer's general account consists primarily of safe, conservative investments such as high-grade bonds, real estate, certificates of deposit, and so forth. The premium from traditional life insurance contracts is placed in the company's general account and the entire contract is fully guaranteed by the insurer.

Variable Life Death Benefits

Because the value of the securities in the separate account are subject to change, the death benefit of the variable life policy can also change. If the value of the separate account increases, the death benefit may increase. A drop in the investment results of the separate account may cause a decrease in the death benefit from the value in the previous year. However, the death benefit will never fall below the guaranteed minimum, which is the same as the original face value of the policy.

Variable Life Cash Values

Cash values in a VLI policy are determined on a *daily* basis according to the investment experience of the separate account, with no minimum amount guaranteed. So, although there is a guaranteed death benefit, there is no guaranteed cash value.

The cash value may be withdrawn at any time on surrender of the policy. The exact amount payable will be the cash value calculated at the time the policy is surrendered.

Typically, up to 90% of the cash value of a VLI policy may be borrowed, subject to interest at a rate of 6%–8% compounded annually. The minimum that will be loaned is generally $100. Loans may be partly or fully repaid at any time as long as the insured is alive and the policy is in force.

Variable Life Premiums

Variable life premiums are fixed and payable on a regular schedule, as are whole life premiums. If the policyowner defaults on a VLI premium payment, he or she has a 31-day grace period in which to pay the overdue premium. If the premium is not paid by the end of this period, the policy lapses.

Variable Life Regulation as a Security

Because VLI places considerable investment risk on the policyowner and offers few guarantees, the federal government has declared that variable contracts are securities. They are thus regulated by the Securities and Exchange Commission (SEC), the National Association of Securities Dealers (NASD), and other federal bodies.

Variable life producers must be registered with the National Association of Securities Dealers (NASD). This registration may be obtained by passing the NASD Series 6 or Series 7 exam.

The variable life product is regulated by the Securities Act of 1933, the Securities and Exchange Act of 1934, and the Investment Company Act of 1940. The following is a brief review of these acts as they apply to variable life insurance:

➤ The Act of 1933 requires a prospectus be delivered at or before the point of sale of a variable life product.

➤ The Act of 1934 requires registration of the company and the company's sales representatives with the federal authorities.

➤ The Act of 1940 provides for the registration of separate accounts as an investment company.

At the time of solicitation, variable life illustrations may not be based on projected interest rates greater than 12%. This is known as the *12% rule* and it prevents both the producer and the policyholder from assuming excessive and unrealistic rates of return. A variety of policy performance illustrations at different rates would be the preferred method for clearly explaining variable life products. Producers should also stress that rates are not guaranteed and historical performance may not be duplicated in the future.

Other requirements of the federal laws include a mandatory 45-day free-look provision from the date of policy application. Also, variable life policyowners have voting rights. Under the Act of 1940, the policyowner is allowed one vote for each $100 of cash value. The policyowner must be permitted to convert to traditional whole life insurance within 24 months of policy issuance.

Variable Life Regulation as Insurance

Variable life insurance is also regulated by the state insurance departments as an insurance product. In effect, VLI is a dually regulated product. In addition to compliance with securities laws, variable life is subject to the state insurance laws:

➤ Producers must be licensed on a state level to sell life insurance.

➤ In some states, producers are required to have a separate state variable contracts license.

➤ All variable contracts must be filed and approved by the state insurance department

Variable Universal Life

Although variable life is essentially whole life with a separate account, *variable universal life* is essentially universal life with a separate account. It combines the investment features of variable life with the flexibility of universal life. For example, variable universal life premiums are not payable on a fixed schedule, as is the case with variable life. For this reason, variable life is sometimes referred to as *scheduled premium variable life*, and variable universal life is sometimes called *flexible premium variable life*.

Like universal life, variable universal life offers policyowners a choice of two death benefit options and access to the policy's cash value through withdrawals as well as loans. It also uses monthly deductions from the cash value to pay for the cost of insurance. Rather than crediting cash values with current interest rates, however, the cash value varies with the value of the investments in the separate account, as with variable life. As with variable life, policyowners also can choose among a number of sub-accounts that offer different investment objectives and transfer their policy funds among them.

Also like variable life, variable universal life is dually regulated as a security and insurance. All the regulatory requirements we described previously for variable life insurance apply to variable universal life.

 Policyowners naturally hope that the cash value of their policies will grow, but with investments of any kind there's always the possibility of a loss. If there should ever be a lack of funds in a policy's account to pay for insurance coverage, the policyowner is given a grace period to deposit enough money in the account to cover the minimum needed to keep the policy in force.

Advantages and Uses of Flexible Policies

Some of the advantages of flexible policies are

➤ Flexible policies provide the opportunity to customize the policy to the needs and wants of the insured.

➤ Flexible policies may include a securities component, which is considered an effective hedge against inflation.

➤ Premium flexibility enables policyowners to pay what they can, when they can. This provides the opportunity to increase cash value when the policyowner has the resources to do so. It also provides the opportunity for policyowners to skip payments without losing insurance protection.

Disadvantages Of Flexible Policies

Some of the disadvantages associated with flexible polices are

➤ Flexible policies that include a securities component may not have guaranteed returns. Returns may be low, or even negative, in policies based on separate securities accounts.

➤ Some policyowners need the forced discipline of a mandated premium schedule to ensure that they regularly contribute enough to ensure adequate cash value growth.

Industrial Life Insurance

The industrial policy is written for a small face amount, usually $2,000 or less, and the premiums are payable as frequently as weekly, and occasionally, monthly. It derived its name from the fact that it was originally sold in England to the industrial class of factory workers. This form of insurance was originally sold in America to workers in industry.

The insured would determine how much he could pay each week and the face amount would be determined by the amount of premium the insured could pay. A company representative would call on the insured each week, usually at home, to collect the premium, which usually ranged from 5 cents to 1 dollar. The policy benefit was used primarily to pay for *last illness* and *burial expenses*.

This method of distribution is very expensive for two reasons. First, the mortality rates are higher for industrial policyowners because these insureds tend to have higher than average health risks and poorer than average living standards. Second, having the agent collect the premium each week at the customer's home increases the cost of this type of policy.

With the rising incomes of workers, increasing consumer awareness, the introduction of social security, and the growth of group life insurance, the need for industrial life has decreased considerably over the last several decades. Today, industrial life represents about 1% of life insurance in force.

Industrial Life Policy Provisions

Most of the provisions found in individual life insurance policies are also found in industrial life insurance. However, consideration should be given to these provisions and their unique application to industrial policies. Because the face amount of the policy is so small and the cost of this type of insurance is expensive, certain provisions do not have the same impact on industrial insureds as on individual insureds:

➤ A 31-day grace period (28 days for weekly premium policies) is provided.

➤ The application is not required to be part of the policy.

➤ Medical examinations are not required.

➤ Cash values do not accumulate sufficiently to provide loans.

➤ Settlement options do not apply because of limited cash value.

➤ Suicide provisions are not included in the policy because of the small benefit amount.

➤ Nonforfeiture provisions do not allow the cash option until premiums have been paid for 5 years (compared to 3 years for ordinary policies).

➤ Dividends are used to reduce the premium payment or to purchase paid-up additions.

Home Service Life Insurance

Today we find a variation in the industrial life concept known as *home service life* insurance. The home service policy is written for a small face amount, usually $10,000 to $15,000 in face value, and is typically sold on a monthly payment plan, either by automatic bank payment or a payment by mail. These insurance policies are subject to the same requirements for standard policy provisions as regular life insurance policies.

Credit Life Insurance

The unexpected death of an individual who has time payment obligations can create serious problems for his or her family. *Credit life insurance* provides that, in the event of the death of an insured debtor, the outstanding balance is usually paid off in full.

Credit life insurance can be written on a group basis or in individual credit life policies. It is usually written as a decreasing term type of coverage so the amount of insurance reduces as the amount of the obligation reduces. Level term insurance may also be written, which would remain level for the term of the loan. The benefits are payable to the policyowner (the creditor) and are used to reduce or extinguish the unpaid indebtedness. Most commonly, credit life insurance provides protection for 10 years or less.

Usually, the individual debtor pays the total premium. The premium is added to the finance contract amount so that, in effect, the insurance premium is being financed along with the item being purchased. The insurance company receives full premium up front. Life insurance companies write credit insurance through lenders such as banks, retailers, auto dealers, credit unions, and finance companies.

If a debtor prepays or refinances the loan, he or she is entitled to cancellation of the credit insurance and a refund of the unearned premium.

Credit Life Policy Provisions

Some of the major provisions found in credit life insurance policies are those that provide the following:

➤ Insureds must be given a certificate of coverage under the creditor's group policy, including their rights and obligations under the policy.

➤ The number of insureds under the policy must be maintained at a specified level (usually 100); if participation drops below that number, the insurer may not insure new debtors.

➤ The debtor's coverage will terminate when the debt is paid off, transferred to another creditor, refinanced, or becomes significantly overdue.

➤ Unlike standard group insurance policies, the policy does not have a conversion privilege.

Specialized Policy Forms

There are a number of life insurance policies that have been designed to fit specialized situations. Some of the more frequently used forms will be discussed here. These forms are merely combinations or modifications of whole life or term life policies. Many of these special policy names vary by company, and many companies have produced variations of these basic combinations.

Endowments

The *endowment policy* is another category of permanent insurance. As with other types of policies, the endowment pays a death benefit upon the death of the insured. And like the limited pay policy, the premiums are paid only for a specified period of time. So if the insured is alive at the end of the premium paying period, the policyowner would receive the face amount maturity benefit and the insurance coverage would terminate. Thus, the policy endows at the end of the premium-paying period.

An endowment policy has all the same elements as a whole life policy. The primary difference is that it matures earlier (at a specified age or date), so the cash value must build up more rapidly and the premium is higher per $1,000 of coverage.

The accelerated growth of the cash values of endowment policies resulted in legislation against them. According to the Tax Reform Act of 1984, any policy issued after January 1, 1985, that endows before age 95 will not qualify as life insurance. That means that the policy's cash value accumulation and its death benefit would be taxed. The endowment policy is included in this book because some state insurance exams still cover it, and because some clients may own existing endowment policies acquired before January 1, 1985.

Endowments were purchased for various periods of time—that is, 10 or 20 years, or to age 65.

Another version of the endowment concept was the *pure endowment*. This policy offered no life insurance protection. The pure endowment provided for the payment of the policy's face amount only if the insured lived to the maturity date. If the insured died prior to the endowment date, all benefits were forfeited. Because this was essentially a high-risk savings plan (all savings were lost upon early death), it was rarely sold.

Family Income Policies

Family plans are uncommon, but still included in most state exams. Combining whole life insurance with *decreasing term coverage*, the *family income policy* provides temporary protection and permanent coverage. The family income policy provides an income to be paid upon the death of the family breadwinner.

The payout period, which is determined when the policy is purchased, is scheduled to last until the family's income needs diminish. Family policies are usually sold for periods of 10, 15, or 20 years. Coverage is provided by combining decreasing term insurance with a permanent policy. This may be accomplished by means of a special policy or by actually adding term insurance to a permanent policy.

The family income portion of this type of coverage is supplied by a decreasing term policy. Income payments to the beneficiary begin when the insured dies and continue for the period specified in the policy, which is usually 10, 15, or 20 years *from the date of policy issue*, and *not* from the date of the insured's death. So the longer the insured lives, the less insurance will be needed to meet the income obligations of the policy. That's why decreasing term insurance is used for a family income policy. So, for example, if Kim has a 15-year family income policy and Kim dies 2 years after purchasing this policy, Kim's family can expect to receive income benefits for 13 years.

To prevent what might be a burden if the insured dies close to the end of the family income protection period, some companies permit an arrangement whereby the beneficiary would receive an income guaranteed for some specified period of time—say 5 years—should the insured die within the family income protection period.

The amount of monthly income provided by the family income policy depends on the amount of insurance bought. A typical arrangement might be

$10 of monthly income for each $1,000 of insurance. Some companies may offer more. For example, if Kim purchases a $75,000 family income policy, Kim's family might expect to receive $750 per month during the family income protection period following Kim's death.

The death benefit from the permanent insurance protection of the family income is usually paid in a lump sum when the insured dies, even if that occurs after the family income protection period. However, some family policies stipulate that if the insured dies before the end of the family income protection period, the proceeds will be paid at the end of that period. The amount paid is the face value of the policy.

Family Maintenance Policies

Family maintenance policies are similar to family income policies because they both provide an income to be paid to the insured's beneficiary. The difference is that with a family maintenance policy, coverage is provided by combining level term insurance with a permanent policy. A family maintenance policy provides income for a stated number of years *from the date of death of the insured*, provided the insured dies before a predetermined time. The family maintenance portion of the coverage comes from a level term policy.

Here's how it works. Let's say Sandy, age 30, wants to provide funds for family maintenance for at least 15 years following Sandy's death, as long as death occurs *before* age 45. If Sandy were to die 10 years later, at age 40, this family maintenance policy would pay monthly income to Sandy's beneficiary for 15 years *from the date of Sandy's death*. The permanent insurance portion of the family maintenance policy pays a lump sum for the face value of the policy to the insured's beneficiary either when the insured dies or at the end of the family maintenance payout period, whichever is stipulated in the policy.

The Family Policy (Family Protection Policy)

Some companies offer contracts that provide coverage on each of the family members at the time the policy is issued. These combination policies or family plans customarily provide coverage on the principal breadwinner equal to four times the spouse's and five times the children's coverage amounts. For example, Bob's policy might provide $100,000 on himself, $25,000 on his wife, and $20,000 on each child. In this example, the wife and children's coverage would ordinarily be term insurance and Bob's would be a permanent policy.

These additions to Bob's permanent coverage are sometimes referred to as *riders*, a concept we'll look at later in this unit. *Spouse term rider* and *family rider* are common names for that coverage.

Under a family policy, term insurance coverage is provided without additional premium for children born or adopted after the policy is issued. The term insurance expires on each child as he or she reaches a specified age— 18, perhaps 21, sometimes as late as 25. Coverage on the children is usually convertible to any permanent insurance without evidence of insurability.

Retirement Income Policy

The *retirement income policy* accumulates a sum of money for retirement while providing a death benefit. Upon retirement, the policy pays an income such as $10 per $1,000 of life insurance for the insured's lifetime or a specified period. These policies are expensive and cash value accumulation is high to pay for the monthly income. As the cash value in the policy approaches the face amount, the face amount must be increased to maintain the policy's status as life insurance.

Joint Life Policies

Although most life insurance is written on the life of one person, policies are available to insure the lives of two or more people. A *joint life policy* may pay the face amount upon the first death among the persons covered by the policy or upon the last death among the persons covered by the policy. Under a *first-to-die joint life policy*, the contract comes to an end at the first death and there is no further insurance protection for the other person or persons covered by the policy.

Suppose Esther, Sarah, and Rebecca are three sisters who have a $50,000 joint life policy covering all three of their lives. The proceeds are to be shared equally by the survivors upon the first sister's death. So, when Esther dies, Sarah and Rebecca would each receive $25,000. Suppose Sarah dies soon after Esther. The last surviving sister will receive nothing more from the joint-life policy, because it terminated at the first sister's death.

Survivor life insurance, or *second-to-die insurance*, covers two lives and guarantees payment only when the second insured dies. Premiums are usually payable until the second death.

Second-to-die policies are very useful in estate planning. When a surviving spouse dies, the policy can provide money to pay taxes on assets that may have been sheltered at the first death by the marital deduction. The money also can be used in certain business applications. Premiums on a survivorship policy can be significantly less than if the two lives were insured separately.

Juvenile Policies

Juvenile insurance can be any type of coverage—whole life, limited payment life, or term insurance—depending on the purpose of having the policy. The criterion for juvenile insurance is that it be written on the life of a person who is not yet considered an adult for life insurance purposes. In most places, this includes anyone who is under the age of 15 (16 in Canada).

A popular juvenile policy is called the *jumping juvenile* policy. It is normally purchased by a parent for a child. The face amount of this policy might be for as little as $1,000 initially. At the time the child turns age 21, however, the face amount automatically jumps by an amount usually five times greater than the original face amount with no increase in premium and no evidence of insurability required.

Minimum Deposit Policies

Minimum deposit or *financed insurance* is technically a method of paying for insurance and not a type of policy. It is a high cash and loan value whole life policy. Such policies were devised in the late 1950s to take advantage of the fact that at the time, the Internal Revenue Service allowed the interest paid on a policy loan to be deducted in full for income tax purposes. Thus a prospect could buy such a policy and immediately borrow back the loan value so that, in effect, his or her initial premium outlay was very small. Since that time, however, the IRS has placed restrictions on the interest deduction when the loan is to finance insurance, so its popularity has diminished.

As it is currently used, the cash value of a permanent policy is used to pay the premiums on that policy through the use of policy loans. To achieve sufficient cash value, the first two of these premium payments must be paid by the policyowner; then loans may be used, but only if during the first 7 years of the policy at least four of the seven annual premiums are paid from funds other than policy loans. This is a rule imposed by the IRS.

Modified Premium Policies

A *modified premium policy* is an ordinary life policy in which the premium obligation is redistributed. Premiums are lower during the first 3–5 years of the policy, usually only a little more than would be paid for a level term policy for the same period of time. After this initial period, the premiums go up so that they're somewhat higher than would be paid for an ordinary whole life policy.

Graded Premium Plan

A *graded premium plan* is similar to modified whole life in that initially the premium is very low. Unlike modified life, which has one increase to a higher, level premium for the life of the contract, graded premium policies provide an increase in premium each year for the first 5–10 years of the policy. At the end of this step-rate premium period, the premium remains level for the life of the policy.

It should be noted that graded premium (and modified life) policies build cash value but the amount of the cash value is usually less because of the smaller outlay of premium. Typically, a graded premium policy will have very little, if any, cash value during the graded premium period.

Mortgage Redemption

The *mortgage redemption policy* or rider is simply decreasing term insurance. The benefit amount of the term element is intended to be sufficient to pay off the unpaid remainder of the mortgage loan if the insured dies before paying it off.

Multiple Protection

Multiple protection policies are combinations of whole life and term whereby the amount of protection is higher in the early years of the policy and less in the later years. For example, the current death benefit may be described as equal to two times the benefit at age 65 (double protection). If the age 65 (and thereafter) benefit is $5,000, the insured has $10,000 of protection up to age 65. In essence, the additional death benefit prior to age 65 is term insurance.

Index-Linked Policies

As a hedge against high inflationary periods, many companies offer policies with face amounts increasing by the amount of inflation. The policy amounts are generally linked to the Consumer Price Index (CPI). There are two ways of providing this additional coverage. Either the premium is increased every year to cover the increased insurance amount, or the life insurance company makes assumptions about what it expects the increases to be at policy inception and the insured pays the same (but higher than average) premium over the life of the policy.

Deposit Term Insurance

Deposit term insurance is a level term insurance policy that has a much higher premium for the first year than for subsequent years. The initial premium is significantly higher than the average premium needed to cover the cost of mortality during the term period. The excess front-end premium (the deposit) is then set aside to earn interest, and these dollars (deposit plus interest) will be applied to reduce the premium payments required in the following years. The premium levels are set so that the entire deposit will be exhausted when the final annual premium is paid. In effect, this arrangement provides a method of paying a portion of the premium in advance.

For example, the annual premium for a 10-year level term policy for a particular insured may be $500 (total outlay of $5,000). The same type of policy may be purchased as a deposit term contract for an initial premium of $2,500 followed by annual premiums of $200 (total outlay of $4,300). The initial deposit and interest are used to make up the difference in premium. Mathematically, the insurance company actually receives an equal amount of premium for these two policies when the time factor and interest earnings are taken into account.

Pre-need Funeral Insurance

Funeral insurance or pre-need burial insurance is a type of life insurance used to pay for an insured's funeral at a particular funeral home. Funeral insurance pays the face amount on an insured's death. Really, it is just a contract to provide a preplanned funeral and cemetery services funded by a life insurance contract or annuity. Typically, the funeral home has the insured buy a life insurance policy on him- or herself, naming the funeral home as the beneficiary. The funeral home usually is paid a commission on the policy sale as well. The policy purchased will have an increasing face amount so that the funeral will be fully funded, even if burial costs increase.

Advantages and Uses of Specialized Policies

Some of the advantages and uses of specialized policies are

➤ Specific combinations of term and permanent insurance can be used to match the need exactly.

➤ The cost of the policy may be lower than ordinary whole life insurance.

Disadvantages of Specialized Policies

Some of the disadvantages of specialized polices are

➤ Policies set up to meet a specific need might become obsolete if the need changes over time.

➤ Certain policies, if not set up carefully, might incur negative tax consequences.

Insurance Policy Riders

Riders take their name from the concept that they have no independent existence. They have force and effect only when they are attached to a policy.

Riders are special policy provisions that provide benefits that are not found in the original contract, or that make adjustments to it. These special provisions are, in effect, attached to the policy or "ride" it. A rider can also refer to a term policy that is attached to a permanent policy to provide additional or specially needed coverage. Riders can be used to enhance or add benefits to the policy or they can be used to take benefits away from the policy.

A *waiver* is a type of rider that is usually used to exclude benefits and for which no premium is charged. For example, for underwriting reasons, a waiver may be attached to a policy that excludes benefits for death by a specified cause, such as a particularly hazardous hobby or occupation. The other riders discussed in this section usually require the payment of a relatively small additional premium for the benefits provided. The payment of the rider premium does not increase the cash value of the policy, but only pays for the benefits provided by the rider.

Accidental Death (Double Indemnity)

An accidental death benefit (ADB) rider may be added to an insurance policy to provide an additional amount to be paid to the beneficiary should the insured die as the result of an accident. This amount, usually referred to as the *principal sum*, is usually the same as the face value of the policy and is therefore often referred to as *double indemnity*. It could, however, be three or more times the face value.

Whatever the amount, the accidental death benefit may be paid only when the insured dies as the result of an accident.

Accidental death benefits apply if the insured dies in an accident or within a specified period of time after and as the result of an accident. The period of time permitted between the accident and the insured's death also varies, but it's most often 3 months, or 90 days.

Certain causes of death are usually excluded:

➤ Death as a result of self-inflicted injury

➤ Death while committing a crime

➤ Death as a result of war

➤ Death as passenger in an aircraft other than a regularly scheduled commercial flight

➤ Death as a result of riot or insurrection

The accidental death benefit usually ceases either 5 years before or after an individual's normal retirement age—that is, ages 60, 65, or 70 unless the accident occurs prior to that age. Note, however, that the rider itself can stipulate that the accidental death benefit is to apply for the entire lifetime of the insured, or for the length of the contract. If a policyowner is paying an extra premium for the accidental death benefit and reaches the age at which this benefit no longer applies, the premium drops.

An accidental death benefit rider to a policy may also include additional benefits for dismemberment. If so, it is called an accidental death and dismemberment (AD&D) rider. The dismemberment portion of this rider provides for the payment of the *capital sum* (the face amount) in the event that, due to an accident, the insured loses two arms, two legs, two hands or the irrecoverable loss of vision in both eyes. Loss is generally defined as the actual severance or removal of the arm or leg as a result of the accident. Again, the loss usually must occur within 90 days of the accident.

Waiver of Premium

The *waiver of premium rider* exempts a disabled policyowner from needing to pay premiums during the term of disability, while keeping the policy in force. For the waiver of premium to apply, the disability must be permanent and total. *Total,* as it is used here, can have two connotations:

➤ The insured is prevented (by disability) from engaging in his or her usual occupation.

➤ The insured is prevented from engaging in any work for gain or profit.

Technically, the first definition of *total* sometimes applies for a stated period of time, and then the second definition might take over as the criteria for deciding whether the disability is total. That is, the company may state that for the first year, all that's necessary to qualify a disability as total is that the insured be prevented from engaging in his or her usual profession. After the year has elapsed, the company will then apply the broader definition of *total*—whether the insured can engage in any (not just his or her own) work for gain or profit. Understanding what constitutes *permanent disability* is somewhat more standardized. In most instances, whether the disability is considered permanent involves a waiting period after the onset of disability. If this waiting period elapses and the insured is still disabled, in the judgment of a company authorized physician, the disability is considered permanent. The length of the waiting period involved varies by company, usually ranging from 3–6 months.

During this waiting period, the permanency and totality of the insured's disability have not yet been established, so the policyowner must continue making normal payments. When the disability proves to be permanent and total, the company refunds the premiums paid during the waiting period, because they were paid while the insured was, in fact, disabled.

Although premiums are being paid by a company under the waiver of premium rider, the policy remains in full force in every respect, as if the policyowner personally were making the payments. This means that the cash value of a policy in this situation, and any dividends if it is a participating plan, continue to increase at the usual pace.

What happens when a disabled policyowner recovers from a disability? Suppose John, who is both the policyowner and the insured, was disabled for 2 years, during which time the company paid more than $1,000 in premiums for him under the waiver of premium rider. John has now recovered, so he simply begins paying his premiums again, starting with the next premium when it falls due.

The waiver of premium rider is usually not available when the policyowner reaches a specified age, commonly 60 and sometimes 65. When the waiver of premium rider expires due to the insured reaching a certain age, the company lowers the premium to compensate for the loss of the benefits the rider provided—unless, of course, the company provides waiver of premium benefits free of charge.

If the insured should become disabled shortly before the age at which the rider expires, he or she would still be eligible for the benefit under the waiver of premium rider of the policy. This is true even if the waiting period extends past the normal cut-off age of 60.

When a waiver of premium rider is attached to a policy, the company cannot arbitrarily drop the rider. It must remain a part of the policy as long as the policyowner continues to pay premiums as agreed. However, if the policy should ever lapse and then be reinstated, the company can refuse to reinstate the waiver of premium rider.

Waiver of premium riders usually contain exclusions for suicide, military service, or injury received while committing a crime.

Because premiums on a universal life policy may fluctuate considerably, most companies provide a *waiver of monthly deduction* rider on a universal life policy that guarantees only the monthly cost of insurance, not the total premium the insured was paying. Under waiver of monthly deduction, the policy's cash value will remain intact and continue to earn interest.

Some companies, however, will waive the guaranteed minimum annual premium on a universal life policy, rather than just the monthly cost of insurance. In this case, the rider is usually called *waiver of premium* and the policy's cash value will grow not only with the interest credited, but also by the amount of the additional premium payments less the cost of insurance.

Disability Income Rider

Under the disability income rider, the company guarantees the policyowner a regular monthly income for as long as he or she remains totally and permanently disabled. The amount of the income is usually based on the face amount of the policy—$X per month per $1,000 of coverage, for instance. In addition, most disability income riders include waiver of premium. For example, if a policyowner has the disability income rider on a $100,000 policy and the company guarantees $10 per month on each $1,000 of coverage, the policyowner will receive $1,000 per month.

An income under the disability income rider continues for the length of the disability. However, a waiting period is required by most companies to ensure that the disability is, in fact, permanent (by the company's definition) and total (as determined by a company-approved physician). As in the case of the waiver of premium rider, this waiting period is usually 3–6 months.

Although the disability income rider usually includes the waiver of premium rider, it is possible to have one without the other. It's essential that you understand the difference between these two important riders:

➤ The waiver of premium rider states that the company will pay the premiums on the policy during the insured's total and permanent disability.

> ➤ The disability income rider stipulates that the company will pay the policyowner a monthly income during any period of total and permanent disability.

 Remember, the amount paid under the waiver of premium rider depends on the amount of the policy's premium. The amount paid under the disability income rider is based on the face amount of the policy.

Payor Rider

With most juvenile insurance policies, a parent is the policyowner and pays for the coverage; the child, of course, is the insured. If the parent dies, premium payments will probably cease, so the policy would lapse. Policyowners can protect their (and their child's) interest in the policy through a *payor rider*.

This rider states that if the person who's paying the premiums should die or become disabled before the child has reached a specified age—usually 21 or 25—the company will waive all further premiums until the child reaches that age. This waiver can apply for death only, or for death and disability.

Because the payor is, in effect, insured for the amount the premiums will cost the company in the event of the payor's disability or death, the payor must prove insurability.

Guaranteed Insurability

There are times when an insured discovers that due to some circumstance, usually health reasons, he or she has become uninsurable. There may be some existing life insurance, but the insured wants more coverage and discovers he or she is no longer able to purchase it. There is a rider that will guarantee that the insured can purchase more permanent insurance at specified ages, without proof of insurability. This is the *guaranteed insurability rider (GIR)*, sometimes referred to as the *insurance protection rider (PIR)* or *future increase option*.

This rider guarantees that on specified dates in the future (or at specified ages or upon the event of specified occurrences such as marriage or birth of a child), the insured may purchase additional insurance without evidence of insurability.

As the option age is reached, the insured normally has 90 days in which to exercise the option or it is lost. The rate for this additional coverage will be that for his or her attained age, not the age at which the policy was issued. The rider generally expires at the insured's age 40.

The amount of insurance that can be purchased on the option dates is usually limited to the amount and type of the base policy. Thus, if the insured had a $10,000 whole life policy with the guaranteed insurability rider, he or she could purchase up to an additional $10,000 of whole life coverage on the option dates.

Return of Premium

The *return of premium rider* was developed primarily as a sales tool to enable the agent to say, for example, "In addition to the face amount payable at your death, we will return all premiums paid if you die within the first 20 years." The rider is simply an increasing amount of term insurance that always equals the total of premiums paid at any point during the effective years. In reality, the rider does not return premium but pays an additional amount at death that equals the premiums paid up to that time—as long as death falls within the time specified in the rider. By purchasing this rider, the policyowner is buying term insurance and is, of course, charged for it accordingly.

Return of Cash Value

The *return of cash value rider*, not often used, was designed to offset the invalid complaint, "When I die, the company confiscates the cash value." Such a complaint is based on lack of understanding of the mathematics involved in a level face value life insurance policy. However, if the agent can say, "We can attach a rider returning the cash value in addition to the face amount," the objection is more easily answered than if it is necessary to explain the mathematics involved. The return of cash value rider is similar to the return of premium rider because it is merely an additional amount of term insurance that is equal to the cash value at any point while effective. By buying it, the policyowner is simply getting additional term insurance. In reality, this rider does not return the cash value; it pays an additional amount of insurance equal to the cash value.

Cost of Living

With the *cost of living rider*, the policyowner has the option of increasing the death benefit of his or her policy to match any increase in the cost of living index (usually the CPI-U, the Consumer Price Index-All-Urban). This is accomplished either by changing the face amount of an adjustable life policy (and increasing the premium accordingly) or by attaching an increasing term rider to the base term or whole life policy and billing the policyholder for the additional coverage. (There is usually a cap on the increase—for example, 5%.)

Any increase in the death benefit, of course, will mean an increase in premium. Any subsequent decreases in the index will not result in lowering the policy's death benefit.

Suppose Louise has a whole life policy with a face value of $100,000 and a cost of living index rider. If the CPI-U has gone up by 2%, Louise may increase the face value of her policy by $2,000 up to $102,000.

Note that this increase will result in Louise's premium being raised. Note also that when the CPI-U goes up, Louise is not required to increase the face value of her policy accordingly.

Additional Insureds

Riders are also commonly attached to life insurance policies to provide coverage on the lives of one or more additional insureds. Usually these are term insurance riders covering a spouse, one or more children, or all family members in addition to the insured policyholder. Many companies will issue additional insured riders on request. As discussed earlier in this unit, some companies actively market combination coverage policies for family members under the label *family protection policy*.

Substitute Insured Rider

Although it seems unusual to allow the substitution of insureds in life insurance, the *substitute insured rider* permits a change of insureds. This rider is also known as an *exchange privilege rider*.

The ability to substitute or exchange insureds is desirable, for instance, in business-owned life insurance, when a key employee or business executive is insured for the benefit of the corporation. Should this employee terminate employment or retire, the insurance can be switched over to apply to the employee's replacement, subject to evidence of insurability. This way, the policy can continue (rather than be terminated and a new policy issued) with the same face amount, and with premiums calculated based on the new insured's age, sex, and so forth.

Accelerated Benefits

Beginning in the 1980s, many companies offer an accelerated benefits rider, sometimes known as a *living benefits* rider. This rider allows policyowners who are terminally ill, or who require long-term care or permanent confinement to a nursing home, to collect all or part of their death benefit while they are still alive. This can help relieve some of the financial distress caused by an insured's inability to continue working and the rising costs of health care.

The purpose of this benefit is to provide the terminally ill person with necessary cash with which to take care of expenses related to the terminal illness—that is, medical expenses or nursing home expenses. Death benefits payable under the policy are reduced by any amounts paid under this rider. Most companies charge an additional premium to add this benefit, but some plans charge for the option only if it is used.

Living Benefit Provisions

Long-term care (LTC) insurance, which reimburses health and social service expenses incurred in a convalescent or nursing home facility, can be marketed as a rider to life insurance policies.

LTC rider benefits are similar to those found in a LTC policy. The benefit structure includes the following:

➤ Elimination periods of 10–100 days are imposed.

➤ Benefit periods of 3–5 years or longer are available.

➤ Prior hospitalization of at least 3 days may be required.

➤ Benefits may be triggered by impaired activities of daily living.

➤ Levels of care include skilled, intermediate, custodial, and home health care.

In addition, certain optional benefits may also be provided, such as adult day care, cost of living protection, hospice care, and so forth.

There are two approaches to the LTC rider concept. The generalized or independent approach recognizes the LTC rider as independent from the life policy, because the benefits paid to the insured will not affect the life policy's face amount or cash value. The integrated approach links the LTC benefits paid to the life policy's face amount and/or cash value.

The living benefit or *living needs* rider combines life insurance and LTC benefits, drawing on the life insurance benefits to generate LTC benefits. In a sense, it's like borrowing from the life insurance to pay LTC benefits. Under the LTC option, up to 70–80% of the policy's death benefit may be used to offset nursing home expenses. Under the Terminal Illness option, 90–95% of the death benefit may be used to offset medical expenses. Of course, payment of LTC benefits reduces the face amount of the life policy.

Viatical Settlements

If a chronically or terminally ill insured does not have an accelerated death benefits rider under his or her life insurance policy or wants another option, he or she may want to consider a *viatical settlement*. Under a viatical settlement contract, the insured, or *viator*, sells his or her life insurance policy to a viatical settlement provider for a reduced percentage of the policy's face value.

After the exchange, the viatical settlement provider becomes the owner of the policy and the beneficiary. While the viator lives, the provider must continue to pay premiums to keep the policy in force. When the insured dies, the viatical settlement provider receives the entire death benefit.

Due to the delicate nature of viatical settlements, some states require viatical settlement providers and brokers to be licensed before entering into viatical settlement contracts.

Although a few providers may enter into a viatical settlement contract with a policyowner based on old age, most will only solicit contracts from terminally or chronically ill insureds. A *chronically ill* person is either unable to perform at least two activities of daily living (eating, toileting, transferring, bathing, dressing, or continence) or needs substantial supervision due to cognitive impairment. A person is considered *terminally ill* if he or she is not expected to live more than 24 months due to a medical condition. Tax laws require viators to be chronically or terminally ill to receive payments from viatical settlements tax-free.

During the underwriting process, the viatical settlement provider will contact the insured's physician and/or clinic to verify records and determine his or her life expectancy. The issuing insurer of the life insurance policy will also be contacted to confirm policy terms and ascertain whether any outstanding policy loans exist. Throughout this process, the insured's information may be shared only with the appropriate people involved in the settlement to protect his or her privacy. If the issuing insurance company has a favorable rating and the settlement is in compliance with state laws, the provider will issue the viator an offer.

Exam Prep Questions

1. What type of insurance is designed to provide life insurance protection for only a limited period of time?
   - O A. Whole life insurance
   - O B. Variable life insurance
   - O C. Term life insurance
   - O D. Universal life insurance

2. A flexible premium, adjustable benefit life insurance contract that accumulates cash values is called
   - O A. Whole life insurance
   - O B. Variable life insurance
   - O C. Term life insurance
   - O D. Universal life insurance

3. Christy has a term policy that will enable her to switch over to a whole life policy at any time during the first half of the term without providing evidence of insurability. What type of policy is this?
   - O A. Level term insurance
   - O B. Renewable term insurance
   - O C. Convertible term insurance
   - O D. Reentry term insurance

4. Which of the following is not an advantage of whole life policies?
   - O A. Low initial cost
   - O B. Permanent coverage
   - O C. Guaranteed cash value
   - O D. Nonforfeiture values

5. Janice and Julie are identical twins who both work as teachers and live next door to each other. They each purchase a $75,000 whole life policy at the same time. Janice chooses continuous premium whole life, and Julie chooses a 20-pay whole life policy. Which sister is probably paying a higher premium?
   - O A. Janice is probably paying more.
   - O B. Julie is probably paying more.
   - O C. They are probably paying the same amount.
   - O D. It is not possible to determine from the information provided.

6. Gerald has a state insurance license but no other training or licenses. Gerald can sell any of the following except a(n)
   - O A. Adjustable life insurance policy
   - O B. Economatic life insurance policy
   - O C. Indeterminate premium life insurance policy
   - O D. Variable universal life insurance policy

7. LaKita buys a policy that enables her to adjust the face amount, premium, and length of protection without having to complete a new application or have a new policy issued. LaKita has a(n)

   ○ A. Adjustable life insurance policy

   ○ B. Economatic life insurance policy

   ○ C. Indeterminate premium life insurance policy

   ○ D. Variable universal life insurance policy

8. What type of policy combines whole life insurance with decreasing term coverage?

   ○ A. Family stability policy

   ○ B. Family maintenance policy

   ○ C. Family income policy

   ○ D. Family protection policy

9. What type of policy combines whole life insurance with level term coverage?

   ○ A. Family stability policy

   ○ B. Family maintenance policy

   ○ C. Family income policy

   ○ D. Family protection policy

10. What type of policy combines whole life insurance on one family member with term coverage on other family members?

   ○ A. Family stability policy

   ○ B. Family maintenance policy

   ○ C. Family income policy

   ○ D. Family protection policy

11. Tim has a life insurance policy that will pay $100,000 if he dies before age 65 and $50,000 if he dies after age 65. Tim probably has a

   ○ A. Juvenile policy

   ○ B. Minimum deposit policy

   ○ C. Joint life policy

   ○ D. Multiple protection policy

12. Minimum deposit policies have become less popular due to tax regulations, but they can still be used as long as a certain number of the initial payments are made from sources other than cash value. How many payments must be made from other sources?

   ○ A. 2 of 7

   ○ B. 3 of 7

   ○ C. 4 of 7

   ○ D. 5 of 7

13. What provision might eliminate all future premiums in the event of total and permanent disability?

   O A. Guaranteed insurability

   O B. Return of premium

   O C. Accidental death

   O D. Waiver of premium

14. Which of the following provisions reflects a guarantee that at specified ages, dates, or events, the insured may buy additional insurance without a medical exam?

   O A. Guaranteed insurability

   O B. Return of premium

   O C. Accidental death

   O D. Waiver of premium

Exam Prep Answers

1. **C is correct.** This is an example of term insurance.

2. **D is correct.** This is the definition of universal life insurance.

3. **C is correct.** This is an example of convertible term insurance.

4. **A is correct.** Whole life policies provide level premiums, but term insurance could provide the same coverage at a lower cost.

5. **B is correct.** Because Julie decided to pay her entire policy premium in a shorter period of time, her premiums will be higher.

6. **D is correct.** To sell this type of contract a producer must pass an NASD exam and be registered to sell securities.

7. **A is correct.** This is an example of adjustable life insurance.

8. **C is correct.** This is an example of a family income policy.

9. **B is correct.** This is an example of a family maintenance policy.

10. **D is correct.** A family protection policy combines whole life insurance for the policyowner with term coverage for other family members.

11. **D is correct.** This is an example of a multiple protection policy.

12. **C is correct.** At least four payments must be made from sources other than policy loans. This is an IRS rule.

13. **D is correct.** If a waiver of premium provision applies, no future premium payments will be required if the insured becomes totally and permanently disabled.

14. **A is correct.** A guaranteed insurability provision locks in the right to purchase additional insurance regardless of changing circumstances.

Policy Provisions

Terms you need to understand:

- ✓ Insuring clause
- ✓ Consideration clause
- ✓ Ownership clause
- ✓ Grace period
- ✓ Reinstatement
- ✓ Incontestability
- ✓ Assignment
- ✓ Beneficiary
- ✓ Primary beneficiary
- ✓ Contingent beneficiary
- ✓ Per capita
- ✓ Per stirpes

Concepts you need to master:

- ✓ Ownership rights
- ✓ Policy loans
- ✓ Automatic premium loan
- ✓ Misstatement of age or sex
- ✓ Free look
- ✓ Revocable beneficiary designation
- ✓ Irrevocable beneficiary designation
- ✓ Succession of beneficiaries
- ✓ Class designations
- ✓ Simultaneous death act
- ✓ Common disaster provision
- ✓ Facility of payment provision

An insurance policy is a legal contract. Life insurance policies contain provisions setting forth the rights and duties of parties to the contract. Although it is necessary to look beyond the actual wording of the policy contract and into the statutes and court decisions for a full interpretation of these provisions, they are, nevertheless, the basis of the agreement between the company and the policyholder (and the beneficiaries, heirs, and assignees of the policyholder).

This chapter summarizes standard provisions, restrictions, and limitations in life insurance policies. It also reviews beneficiary provisions and permitted exclusions and limitations on coverage.

Standard Provisions

There are no "standard" policies in life insurance in the sense that there are in the property and casualty insurance field. However, many states have provisions that are required in all life policies so that the following provisions have become more or less standard in such policies.

Insuring Clause

The *insuring clause* contains the basic promise of the life insurance company to pay a specified sum of money, in a lump sum or an equivalent income stream, to the beneficiary upon the death of the insured. It sets forth the basic agreement between the company and the insured.

Consideration Clause

The *consideration clause* is the second important clause found in every life insurance policy. As its name implies, the consideration clause deals largely with the consideration paid by the policyowner for life insurance protection- -the premium.

Part of the insuring clause states that the company promises to pay the policy benefits in consideration of the premium payments. The consideration clause identifies the fact that the policyowner must pay something of value for the insurer's promise to pay benefits. This valuable consideration is the premium.

Execution Clause

The *execution clause* simply says that the insurance contract is executed when both parties (the company and the policyowner) have met the conditions of the contract.

Payment of Premium

The *payment of premium provision* specifies when, where, and how premiums are to be paid. Usually premiums are to be paid in advance either at the company's home office or to the agent. The various modes of paying the premium will also be identified, such as monthly, quarterly, semiannually, and annually.

In addition, most insurers permit the premium to be paid by means of a monthly bank draft. This method is referred to by such names as monthly bank or automatic check plan (the actual name of the option may vary by company). The insurer simply sends a monthly premium notice to the policyowner's bank and the bank sends the insurer a check for the monthly premium.

The least expensive way to pay the premium is annually or by a monthly bank plan. The other premium modes require the payment of a service charge added to the basic premium. For example, an annual policy premium might be $300. The monthly premium might be $25.50, which would total $306 of premium in a year.

Ownership Rights

The policyowner has certain rights regarding the policy owned. The first of these is the right to name the person or persons to receive the policy's proceeds in the event of the death of the insured. That is, the policyowner can name the beneficiary.

The policyowner also has the right to decide how the proceeds of the policy are to be paid. A number of options are available regarding the way in which insurance benefits may be distributed, including leaving the decision to the beneficiary. But the initial right to select how the policy proceeds are to be paid out belongs to the policyowner.

The policyowner also has the right to assign the policy. For example, the policyowner could borrow funds from a bank and assign the policy to the bank as collateral security for the loan. When the loan is fully repaid, the policy would be reassigned back to the policyowner. A policy may also be assigned permanently and irrevocably. This is called an *absolute assignment*. For example, the policyowner might want to make a gift of a policy to his daughter. He would accomplish this by making an absolute assignment.

The policyowner might state that a creditor (such as the bank mentioned previously) has the right to take whatever amount is necessary from the policy's proceeds to pay a debt if the insured should die before the debt is repaid. Or the policyowner might sign a contract that says a creditor can obtain a portion of the policy's cash value if the policyowner fails to pay the debt as agreed. In either event, the policyowner is using the right to assign the policy.

Another right the policyowner has is to use the policy's cash value. As pointed out previously, permanent policies accumulate a cash value that may be borrowed. Any cash value accumulated by a policy must be turned over to the policyowner in the event the policy lapses, or in the event the policyowner surrenders the policy. The policyowner also has the right to decide on what schedule he or she will pay for the coverage--annually, semiannually, quarterly, or monthly. Later the policyowner might decide that the chosen premium payment schedule is inconvenient. He or she can then exercise the right to change the schedule.

The policyowner has the right to decide how to use any dividends paid by the company. There are a number of choices regarding dividends available to the policyowner. For right now, you just need to be aware of the policyowner's right to designate how dividends may be used.

Finally, with convertible term life insurance, the policyowner can change coverage to permanent protection. That is, he or she can convert the policy.

Third-Party Ownership
In typical instances, the owner of an insurance policy is also the applicant and the insured. However, for any of several reasons, it might be advantageous for the policy to be owned by a third party. The three parties would then be the insured, the insurer, and the policyowner.

Ownership of a policy by a third party usually means that the value of that policy will not be included in the estate of the insured. This can be of great benefit when the insured has a very large estate, but is short on liquidity.

Applicant Control or Ownership Clause

When the proposed insured is a minor, the applicant can be the minor's parent or other relative or legal guardian. In such a situation, the applicant--let's say a parent who's applying for insurance on his or her son's life--will probably want to maintain control of the policy until the insured is "of age." This can be accomplished by including a clause that designates the parent--the applicant--as the controller or owner of the policy. Because this clause designates the applicant as the person in control of the policy, it is called the *applicant control clause* or the *ownership clause*.

Besides the parent/child relationship, other common situations of this type are the guardian/child and grandparent/grandchild relationships.

Grace Period

If the policyowner fails to make the premium payment, the company won't immediately cancel the policy; it will allow a specified period of time in which to pay the overdue premium. We call this period of time the *grace period*.

This grace period is of tremendous advantage to the policyowner. For instance, suppose the premium payment has simply been forgotten; or suppose the policyowner intends to make the payment, but is short of funds for a few days. Because of the grace period, life insurance protection is still available and the beneficiary would still receive the proceeds if the insured died within that period even without the premium having been paid. The amount of the premium owed, however, is deducted from the proceeds.

The grace period can vary, but for most ordinary life policies it's 1 month (30 or 31 days).

Reinstatement

When a policy lapses due to nonpayment of a premium, it can generally be reinstated, provided three conditions are met. These conditions are spelled out in the *reinstatement clause* of the policy:

➤ The policyowner must pay all back premiums due plus interest on this amount and must repay any policy loans or other indebtedness against the policy.

➤ The insured must show proof of insurability.

➤ Less than 3 years must have elapsed (this period may be more or less in some states).

Any statements made on the reinstatement application are subject to a new incontestable period (usually 2 years).

If the policy has not been in force for some time, the policyowner might think it is better to simply purchase a new policy rather than pay back premiums plus interest to reinstate the lapsed policy. However, there are several reasons for considering reinstatement:

➤ The lapsed policy may have more liberal policy provisions.

➤ The older policy may offer lower interest rates on policy loans.

➤ Suicide and incontestable clauses may no longer apply if the policy is 2 years old or older.

➤ The lapsed policy probably has a lower premium than a new policy.

This last point is especially true if the policyowner had purchased the lapsed policy 10 or 15 years earlier. Instead of paying attained age rates for a new policy, the policyowner could reinstate the lapsed policy at original issue age rates.

Policy Loan Provisions

Policy loan provisions are found in policies that include cash values. After a policy has been in force for a specified period of time (usually *3 years*), it must contain some cash value, which may be borrowed by the policyowner.

NOTE

A policyowner always has the right to surrender or cash in a policy in exchange for the full cash value. But in many cases, a policyowner might want to make only a partial withdrawal of the available funds and not fully surrender the contract, so a policy loan is often a more appropriate solution.

Generally, a policyowner may borrow up to the amount of the current cash value *less any indebtedness against the policy* (previous loans and interest charges). The insurance company will charge interest on cash value loans. The amount of interest is usually relatively nominal and regulated by state laws. Often, if the policyowner agrees to pay the interest in advance, the amount charged will be reduced. A slightly higher interest rate is charged if it is paid at the end of a loan year. Most states allow the insurer to use an adjustable rate of interest in lieu of a fixed loan rate.

If the loan amount and interest due are not paid, these amounts will be considered an indebtedness against the policy and will result in a reduced death benefit should the insured die while the indebtedness is outstanding. In most policies, after the policy has been in effect a certain number of years, failure to repay the loan or to pay interest on it will not void the policy unless or until the total amount of the loan and accrued interest equals or exceeds the cash value of the policy, and then only after 30 days' notice has been mailed to the last known address of the policyholder and his assignee, if any.

The insurer may defer a loan request for up to 6 months from the date of the loan application unless the reason for the loan is to pay premiums due.

Automatic Premium Loan Provision

The *automatic premium loan provision*, when included, enables the company to use, automatically, whatever portion of the cash value is needed to pay premiums as they fall due. This keeps the policy in force when it would otherwise lapse due to nonpayment of premiums. Because only permanent insurance policies have cash value, the automatic premium loan provision applies only to permanent policies.

Even with the automatic premium loan provision, of course, the policy must have sufficient cash value to pay the premium due. This means that the automatic premium loan provision is meaningless if the policy has no cash value.

Money lent to the policyowner under the automatic premium loan provision is treated just like any other loan of the policy's cash value. This means that interest is charged on the loan, and the cash value payable on surrender or death is reduced by the loan amount outstanding.

One final point: Just because this provision has the word *automatic* in its title, don't get the idea that it's automatically included in every policy. In many instances, this provision must be requested and written into the policy.

Incontestability Clause

The *incontestability clause* states that after the policy (term as well as permanent) has been in force a certain length of time, the company can no longer contest it or void it, except for nonpayment of premiums. The length of time varies, but it's usually 1 or 2 years.

If the company discovers some reason to void the policy during the contestable period--the first year or two the policy is in force--it can take such action. After the policy has been in force for the specified period, even if fraud is discovered, the company cannot void the policy. This provision makes the life insurance contract a little different from other types of contracts. Usually, contract law specifies that if a fraudulent contract has been enacted, it may be voided or canceled at any time. The incontestable provision limits the period of time in which the insurer may contest the insurance contract as to any misrepresentations or fraud on the part of the applicant.

Suicide Clause

The *suicide clause* is designed to prevent people who are contemplating suicide from obtaining life insurance. To accomplish this, the clause states that if the insured commits suicide within a specified period of time, the policy will be voided.

 The length of time varies, but it's usually the same as the incontestable clause time limit: 1 or 2 years.

After the period of time specified in the policy has elapsed, the company will pay the claim even if the insured commits suicide. If suicide occurs within the time limit, however, the company usually refunds any amount the policy-owner has paid for the coverage. In other words, the company refunds the premiums paid. When refunding premiums in the case of suicide occurring within the specified time limit of the suicide clause, the company usually doesn't pay any interest that the premium has earned because the interest earned is used to offset part of the costs the company incurred in setting up the policy.

One final point: When included in a policy, the suicide clause applies whether the insured is sane or insane at the time he commits suicide.

Entire Contract

A life insurance policy is a contract between the insurer and the insured. Each party has obligations and rights that are spelled out in the contract. In order to make sure that there will be no misunderstanding of what each insurance contract provides, one of the provisions contained in every policy states that the insurance policy itself and the application, when attached to the policy, make up the entire contract between the parties. No company rules, no oral understandings or the like have any bearing on the contract unless they are included in the policy or the attached application.

In addition to the rights and obligations of the insurer and the insured, the policy conditions also designate any restrictions, limitations, or exclusions of the policy. You'll learn about formal exclusions in detail later. For now, let's assume that John qualifies for life insurance coverage. However, his hobby is road racing. The insurer might issue a policy on his life with an exclusion-- a provision that states, in this case, that no claim will be paid if John is killed while participating in a sports car race.

Standard policy conditions--the rights and obligations of the insurer and the insured--are included when the company's standard contract is printed. If it's necessary to adjust the standard contract to satisfy the particular situation of a given policyowner, the alterations can simply be inserted (often typed) into the contract at the time the policy is issued. If a policy provision is typed into the contract, of course, the company must make certain that the policyowner knows the provision has been inserted and that he or she accepts it.

On occasion, it's necessary to amend a life insurance policy after it has been issued. This occurs when a policyowner requests that the company add some coverage after the policy has been issued. In such instances, the company simply types or prints up the necessary addition to the policy--or stamps the data on the policy itself--to amend the policy contract. Such changes or additions are called *riders, endorsements,* or simply *amendments*. For common additions to policies, most companies have printed forms that can be attached to the policy. In addition, some very short common amendments can simply be rubber-stamped onto a policy. A producer is never permitted to make a change in a policy, whether at the request of a policyowner or for some other reason. Only authorized company officers can make changes or amendments in life insurance policies.

Assignment Clause

When a policyowner assigns a policy, he or she transfers rights in the policy--either all of them or a stipulated portion--to another party. The *assignment clause* in a policy states that any assignment the policyowner decides to make must be filed in writing with the company or it will not be valid when the claim is paid.

Suppose Henry decides to borrow some money from the bank. He assigns enough of his policy proceeds to the bank to repay the loan should he die before repaying it himself. Through an oversight, both Henry and the bank forget to notify the insurer of the assignment. If Henry dies before paying off the loan, the insurance company will pay the entire face amount (proceeds) to the beneficiary because the assignment wasn't filed with the company.

Keep in mind in this section that the type of beneficiary designation has a great deal to do with the policyowner's capability to assign policy rights. For example, if the beneficiary has been named irrevocably, he or she must agree in writing to the assignment.

Collateral, Partial, Conditional Assignment

A policyowner, as you know, names the beneficiary of the policy. Under normal circumstances, the proceeds of the policy go directly to this named beneficiary upon the insured's death. However, the policyowner can, if so desired, direct that a certain amount of the money is to go to another party.

Suppose a man borrows $5,000. He uses the proceeds of his life insurance policy as part of the collateral for the loan. To do this, he signs an agreement that states that if he should die before repaying the entire $5,000, a portion of the proceeds of his policy is to be paid to the assignee--the person or party he's borrowing from--to pay off any outstanding loan balance. Because the policyowner is using his policy as collateral for a loan, this is known as a *collateral assignment*.

Because just part of the proceeds are assigned, we sometimes call a collateral assignment a *partial assignment*.

In addition, the assignee is to receive a portion of the proceeds only under certain conditions, the main one being that a balance remains on the loan when the insured dies. Because this condition must exist, this collateral or partial assignment is also referred to as a *conditional assignment*.

Obviously, a lending institution or bank won't lend more than the face amount of the policy under a collateral assignment alone. In fact, most institutions probably won't lend an amount equal to the face amount, but will limit the loan to something less than the face amount of the policy. Because this is the case, under a collateral, partial, or conditional assignment, the policyowner is usually assigning only part of the policyowner rights in the policy.

Absolute, Voluntary, Complete Assignment

It sometimes happens that the policyowner decides to sell or make a gift of a life insurance policy by assigning all rights in the policy to the assignee. For instance, a man might want to give a policy on his life to his son. This type of assignment is made voluntarily, so it's sometimes called a *voluntary assignment*.

A voluntary assignment usually involves turning all rights--including the right to use the cash value--over to the assignee. For this reason, it can be called an *absolute* or *complete* assignment.

When an *absolute assignment* is made, the original policyowner usually has no means of recovering surrendered rights. In effect, he or she has designated another policyowner to take over--a change in the ownership of the policy is taking place. This type of assignment is usually permanent.

Beneficiaries' Assignment Rights

In some cases, the policy's beneficiary can assign a portion of the proceeds (or all of them, technically, although this is unlikely) in about the same manner as the policyowner. However, unless the beneficiary has been named irrevocably, there is actually little to assign.

A *revocable beneficiary* has only an expectancy as far as the policy is concerned. He or she expects to receive the proceeds--unless the policyowner changes the designation to another person. This makes it unlikely that a lending institution will advance money on the strength of this expectancy.

An *irrevocable beneficiary*, on the other hand, has more than a mere expectancy in the policy; receiving the proceeds upon the insured's death is more likely because the policyowner cannot designate another person in his or her stead. An irrevocable beneficiary, then, is more likely to find a lending institution willing to lend money on the strength of the policy than is a revocable beneficiary.

One final point about assignments made by beneficiaries: If the beneficiary dies before the insured does, any assignment made by the beneficiary is no longer valid in most jurisdictions, unless the policyowner agrees in writing that the assignment remains valid if the beneficiary should die first. The proceeds of the policy are paid just as if the assignment had never existed, then, unless a written agreement to the contrary exists.

Misstatement of Age or Sex

If the insured's age or sex is misstated on the application, the insurer has the right to adjust the policy's benefits to reflect the amount that the premiums paid would have purchased based on the correct age or sex of the insured. The insured's age is a factor in computing the amount of premium to be paid. If a man said he was 30 at the time his policy was issued, and it came to light upon his death 20 years later that he was actually 32 when the policy was issued, this means that the insured has been paying a lower premium than he should have been for the entire 20 years.

The *misstatement of age clause* in an insurance policy provides that when a discrepancy in age exists, if the insured is alive the company must adjust the amount of future premiums and request payment of the additional premium the policyowner should have paid. If the insured has died, the company must compute the amount of insurance that the actual premium paid would have purchased at the insured's correct age and pay the beneficiary that amount.

For example, suppose an insured purchases a policy with a face amount of $50,000. He states his age at the time of purchase as 30 when, in fact, he was

34. Let's assume that the premium he was paying would purchase only $47,000 of insurance at age 34. After he dies, the error in age is discovered. His beneficiary will receive $47,000 in proceeds rather than $50,000.

Misstatement of age is not an unusual occurrence in the life insurance business. Some misstatements of age are intentional, but most of them are simply mistakes. In either event, the difference in actual and stated ages is not material enough to void the policy. Most policies contain this misstatement of age clause to rectify this situation should it occur. You should be aware that if an overstatement of age occurs, the company will reduce premium payments or adjust the face amount of the policy upward if the insured dies before the error is discovered.

The same concept applies for misstatement of sex. Due to life expectancy (females have longer life expectancy), males pay more for life insurance than females. Therefore if the insured's sex has been misstated on the application, an adjustment in the death benefit will be made. If the mistake was found while the insured was alive, an adjustment in the premium would be made.

This provision allows the insurer to make a change in the policy even though the error is discovered beyond the incontestability period.

Medical Examinations and Autopsy

Some states require life insurance policies to include a provision that gives the insurer the right and opportunity at its own expense to conduct a medical examination of the insured as often as reasonably required when a claim is pending, and to make an autopsy in case of death where it is not forbidden by law.

Modifications Clauses

Modifications or changes in the policy, or any agreement in connection with the policy (such as changes in the beneficiaries, face amount, or additional coverage), must be endorsed on or attached to the policy in writing over the signature of a specified officer or officers of the company. No one else has any authority to make changes or agreements, to waive provisions, or to extend the time for premium payment.

Some modification clauses also specifically state that no agent has the right to waive policy provisions, make alterations or agreements, or extend the time for payments of premiums.

Policy Change Provision (Conversion Option)

The policy may contain a provision that permits the insured to exchange a policy for another type of policy form permitted by the company. This exchange is usually made from one policy type to another policy form with the *same face amount*.

If the exchange is to a policy with a higher premium, the insured merely has to pay the higher premium and no proof of insurability would be required. If the exchange is to a policy form with a lower premium, proof of insurability may be required because this could result in adverse selection against the insurer.

For example, if Charlie discovers that he has only 6 months to live, he might decide to exchange his higher premium 20-pay life for 1-year term insurance with the same face amount. The insurer's risk has increased while its premium income has decreased. Thus, Charlie has to prove insurability.

Free Look

No policy of individual life insurance can legally be delivered or issued for delivery in most states unless it has printed on or attached to it a notice stating in substance that during a period of 10 days (some companies allow 20 days) from the date the policy is delivered to the policyholder, it may be surrendered to the insurer together with a written request for cancellation of the policy and in such event, the policy shall be void from the beginning and the insurer shall refund any premium paid. This provision allows the policyholder an opportunity to review the entire contract and reevaluate the purchase decision.

Beneficiary Provisions

The *beneficiary* is the person or interest to whom payment of the life insurance proceeds will be made upon the death of the insured. The beneficiary provision enables the insured or the policyowner to direct the payment to any person he or she chooses.

A variety of different parties or interests may be designated as beneficiaries under the life insurance policy. The beneficiary can be a person or an institution, such as a foundation or charity. A specifically designated person, more than one person, or a class or classes of persons also may be named as beneficiaries. The insured may name his or her estate, an institution, a corporation, a trust, or any other legal entity as a beneficiary.

As you should recall, to form an insurance contract, the policyowner must have an insurable interest in the insured at the time of application but not necessarily at the time of death. After a policy is in effect, the policy remains valid even if the insurable interest of the policyowner ceases to exist.

A beneficiary is not required to have an insurable interest, but often does. In many cases, a spouse, parent, or child of the insured person is named as the beneficiary, so the beneficiary does happen to have a coincidental insurable interest in the life of the insured. Nonetheless, there is no need to change a beneficiary designation if the original family relationship changes.

For example, a couple is married and each spouse is the owner and beneficiary of a life insurance policy covering the other spouse's life. Insurable interest exists at the inception of the insurance contract. Later, this married couple divorces. Legally, the policies remain valid, even though insurable interest has ceased, and there is no obligation to change the beneficiary designations.

However, more than likely, there will be a change in ownership rights, or the beneficiary designations, or both, or the policies will be surrendered when a marriage terminates. If there are children from the marriage, ownership rights may be transferred to the children or the children may be designated as new beneficiaries. If there are no children, the policies will probably be surrendered, because people generally don't continue to pay life insurance premiums when financial and emotional interest in an insured has ceased.

Revocable Versus Irrevocable

One of the rights of the life insurance policyowner is the right to designate a beneficiary and to change that beneficiary designation at will. Almost all life insurance beneficiary designations are *revocable* (changeable). Usually the insured retains the right to change the beneficiary, unless he or she has specifically given up that right. Most policies have a revocable beneficiary.

It is possible, however, for the owner of the policy to give up the right to change the beneficiary designation at will. In such cases there is an *irrevocable* beneficiary and the designation cannot be changed without the consent of the beneficiary. An irrevocable designation might be used when a court orders a husband in a divorce settlement to continue payment on an insurance policy on his own life, with an irrevocable beneficiary designation on behalf of his wife (the primary beneficiary) and his children (the contingent beneficiaries).

In the event that the irrevocable beneficiary dies before the insured, the right to select the beneficiary may revert to the policyowner on a *reversionary* basis.

When an irrevocable beneficiary is named, the policyowner gives up the usual ownership rights to the policy and cannot exercise them without the consent of the beneficiary. For example, the policyowner could not take out a policy loan without the consent of the irrevocable beneficiary.

Even when an irrevocable beneficiary designation has been made, the designation can be changed if the irrevocable beneficiary agrees to it.

Succession of Beneficiaries

Every policy has a *primary beneficiary*. The word *primary* means first or most important. Therefore, if Jane is named the primary beneficiary, she is the first person in line to receive the proceeds of the life insurance policy.

 It's possible to name more than one primary beneficiary for the proceeds of an insurance policy. So if Jane and her brother Bob are both named primary beneficiaries, they will both receive their shares of the proceeds before any others.

Because there's no guarantee that a beneficiary will outlive the insured, it might be wise to name a *contingent beneficiary* as well. Whether the contingent beneficiary receives anything depends upon--or is contingent upon--something happening to the primary beneficiary that keeps him or her from receiving the proceeds. Thus, a contingent beneficiary will receive the proceeds of the policy only if the primary beneficiary dies before the insured.

It is also possible to designate a *tertiary beneficiary*. A tertiary beneficiary occupies the third level in the succession of beneficiaries and is entitled to receive the life insurance proceeds following the death of the insured, provided that both the primary and contingent (secondary) beneficiaries have died before the insured.

After the death of the insured, the proceeds belong to the beneficiary. What is left after the beneficiary dies, of course, depends on the settlement option selected to go into effect at the death of the insured. If a lump-sum benefit is paid, the insurance company has no further obligation to the beneficiary. If an option other than a lump-sum payment is selected, or an arrangement is made where benefits continue over a period of time, the beneficiary should name his or her own beneficiary.

If the primary beneficiary dies before the insured and there is no contingent or tertiary beneficiary, the insured's estate automatically becomes the beneficiary.

Naming of Beneficiaries

Careless wording of beneficiary designations can result in undesirable consequences. A tremendous amount of time is spent each year in courtroom litigation attempting to determine the beneficiaries and heirs. For this reason the life insurance producer should insist that the applicant word his or her beneficiary designation carefully. For example, if the insured designates his wife (not specifically named) as the beneficiary, a problem may arise. If the insured has married several times, it may be difficult to identify the true beneficiary.

In such a case, does *wife* mean the insured's present wife or does it mean his wife at the time the beneficiary was designated? Or does it apply to a wife who is now caring for the insured's minor children? Who was the intended beneficiary in such a case? It is important that the beneficiary be designated by full name to avoid misunderstanding.

If children are designated as a class to receive the proceeds, and if it is apparently the intention of the insured that an adopted child be included, a disposition of the proceeds will be made to follow that intention.

The insurer will make every effort to make a disposition of the proceeds of the policy in compliance with the wishes of the insured, as long as the insured makes his intention clear. Otherwise, the insurer must distribute the funds according to the *apparent* intent of the insured or pay the funds into court and seek a judicial determination of the proper distribution.

Designation Options

Beneficiary designations may stipulate that the proceeds be paid to a minor, a trust, or the insured's estate.

A Minor as Beneficiary

Naming a minor as the beneficiary of a life insurance policy presents problems. The most immediate of these problems is that a minor would not be competent legally to receive payment of and provide receipt for the policy proceeds should the insured die before the minor came of age. If an insurance company paid the policy proceeds without a proper receipt from the beneficiary, it might be liable to pay the proceeds again when the beneficiary reached his or her majority.

To avoid this, insurance companies may hold onto the proceeds, paying interest on them until the beneficiary reaches legal age. Or the company may insist that a trustee or guardian be appointed for the minor, someone who is legally entitled to receive and manage the policy proceeds.

If a minor becomes eligible to receive life insurance proceeds due to the death of both parents, any part of their estate left to the minor would have to be administered by a general guardian, regardless of whether it includes life insurance proceeds. Thus the life insurance proceeds would be paid to that guardian. Some parents anticipate this problem by establishing a trust to administer the life insurance proceeds and all other property in the estate of the parents in the event that both parents die leaving minor children.

A Trust as Beneficiary

Up to this point, we've talked about beneficiaries of policies as if they were always one or more individuals--living human beings. However, this is not always the case. For example, if Jack wants to, he can name his estate as the beneficiary of his policy. The same is true of a company or a trust. All of these may be named as a beneficiary, as can the surviving stockholders of a closely held corporation.

A trust is formed when the owner of property (the grantor) gives legal title of that property to another (the trustee) to be used for the benefit of a third individual (the trust beneficiary). This fiduciary relationship enables the trustee to manage the property in the trust for the benefit of the trust beneficiary only. The trustee legally must not benefit from the trust.

When a trust is designated as the beneficiary of a life insurance policy, the policy proceeds provide funds for the trust. Upon the death of the insured, the trustee administers the funds in accordance with the instructions set forth in the trust provisions.

Although there are many benefits in naming a trust as beneficiary of an estate or a life insurance policy, particularly for minor children, there are drawbacks as well. A trustee will charge a fee for managing a trust. The way the trust property is managed is often left up to the trustee, leaving the trust beneficiary powerless to intervene if the trust is poorly managed. Also, the trustee may not provide resources for the trust beneficiary as he or she or even the grantor would have wanted; the trust beneficiary must request resources from the trustee, and he or she cannot make free use of the property in the trust.

Life insurance trusts are often used to provide management of insurance proceeds on behalf of a beneficiary. Rather than allow the insurance company to administer the proceeds, a policyowner might want the proceeds to be invested, managed, and paid out on a discretionary basis through the use of a trust.

An *inter vivos trust* is one that takes effect during the lifetime of the grantor. A *testamentary trust* is a trust created after the grantor's death, according to the provisions of the grantor's will.

The Insured's Estate as Beneficiary

The insured's estate can be named as beneficiary. The insured may direct that the policy proceeds be payable to his or her executors, administrators, or assignees. Such a designation might be made by an insured in order to provide funds to pay estate taxes, expenses of past illness, funeral expenses, and any other debts outstanding prior to the settlement of the estate. Designating the insured's estate as beneficiary aids in the settlement of the estate by avoiding the need to sell other assets of the estate to pay these last expenses.

Frequently, it is not desirable to name the estate as beneficiary. When money enters an estate and there is no will, the court handling the disposition of that estate is required to distribute the assets according to state law, which may or may not be the way the deceased would have wanted.

In addition, estate costs are usually determined by the size of the probate estate. This means that adding life insurance policy proceeds to the probate estate increases the costs of settling the estate. When policy proceeds go into an estate, they could also be tied up for a considerable period of time, especially if the estate is involved in a dispute.

Finally, when a policyowner leaves policy proceeds to a named beneficiary, there are ways to protect these funds from the beneficiary's creditors. When the proceeds go into the estate, however, the heirs receive the proceeds in the form of cash, which makes the money more vulnerable to creditors.

Class Designations

Another way of designating beneficiaries of life insurance policies is by group or by class, rather than by individual name. An example of such a designation would be "all my children" or "my brothers and sisters still living." This designation saves the policyowner the trouble of making changes should the membership of the group be altered due to births or deaths.

Let's use an example to see how beneficiaries may be designated by class. In 1995, Julio purchased a life insurance policy and listed as the beneficiaries "all my children." At the time he purchased the policy, Julio had three children--Maria, Jose, and Elizabeth. All three were, therefore, the beneficiaries of Julio's policy.

In 1997, Elizabeth dies, so the beneficiaries are Maria and Jose, Julio's surviving children. In 1998, Julio's wife has twins, Raoul and Margaret, at which point the beneficiaries to Julio's policy are Maria, Jose, Raoul, and Margaret.

By designating his beneficiaries by class rather than individually by name, Julio saved himself the trouble of having to change the beneficiaries after Elizabeth's death and then again after Raoul and Margaret were born. More importantly, Julio made sure that the policy proceeds would be distributed according to his wishes--that is, that all his children would share those proceeds.

If Julio had designated his beneficiaries individually by name rather than by class, it could have led to confusion and, worse, the distribution of the policy proceeds in a manner not in accordance with Julio's wishes. For example, suppose Julio had named Maria, Jose, and Elizabeth as beneficiaries and then neglected to eliminate Elizabeth as a beneficiary after her death. If Julio had died, part of the policy proceeds might have been paid into Elizabeth's estate and distributed according to state law rather than to Julio's remaining children as he intended.

Per Capita and Per Stirpes

Suppose when Zeke dies he has a $150,000 life insurance policy that names his three sons--Abe, Ben, and Carlos--per capita primary beneficiaries. Each of the three sons would receive $50,000.

Under a per capita beneficiary designation, if one of the named beneficiaries is already dead when the policy matures, the remaining beneficiary or beneficiaries divide his or her share, in addition to receiving his or her own. In the situation we've just described--three sons, named per capita primary beneficiaries of a $150,000 policy--if Carlos dies before the father, when the father dies Carlos' share is divided equally between the other two sons, who would each receive $75,000.

Under a *per stirpes* (meaning *through the root*) designation, the proceeds belonging to the deceased brother would not go to the other beneficiaries. In this case, the deceased brother is the *root* if he has heirs of his own. To those heirs--usually his children--the proceeds of the father's policy pass through the root (him) to his children.

So, if we have three brothers named primary beneficiaries per stirpes of a $150,000 policy, but Carlos has died, followed by the death of the father, each surviving brother would receive $50,000, with Carlos' $50,000 share passing on to his heirs.

The Uniform Simultaneous Death Act

Beneficiary designations may seem perfectly clear when read in a life insurance policy. Nevertheless, if an insured and the primary beneficiary are both killed at the same time, problems arise. How can it be determined who died first?

Many states have adopted the Uniform Simultaneous Death Law. Under it, if there is no evidence as to who died first, the policy will be settled as though the insured survived the beneficiary.

Accordingly, the life insurance proceeds would be paid to the estate of the insured, not the estate of the beneficiary. Of course, if contingent beneficiaries are designated, the proceeds would be payable to them. If there is clear evidence that the beneficiary survived the insured, the proceeds are payable to the beneficiary's estate.

Let's say Melvin is the insured and his wife Melody is the primary beneficiary of the policy. Their children, Mike and Melissa, are the contingent beneficiaries.

Melvin and Melody are killed in a plane crash. If Melody, the primary beneficiary, lived longer than Melvin, she should get the proceeds and they should be paid into her estate. The proceeds would then go to people designated in her will or in accordance with state intestacy laws if she has no will.

If Melvin lived longer than Melody, the contingent beneficiaries, Mike and Melissa, should receive the proceeds. If there were no contingent beneficiary, the proceeds would go to the insured's estate. The insured's will would then designate who should receive the money, or, if he or she had no will, the intestacy laws would control the disposition.

As a practical matter, it is often impossible to determine whether one person outlived another in this type of situation. To deal with this type of problem, the Uniform Simultaneous Death Act has been adopted by most states.

The Uniform Simultaneous Death Act states that if the primary beneficiary and the insured die in the same accident and there's no proof that the beneficiary actually outlived the insured, the proceeds are paid as if the primary beneficiary had died first. This means that the proceeds of the policy are paid to any named contingent beneficiary(ies) or into the estate of the insured if contingent beneficiaries were not named. But if there's any kind of proof--such as a witness who says he saw the primary beneficiary move, thus showing signs of life, after an accident that kills both the beneficiary and the insured--the primary beneficiary outlived the insured and the money must be paid to the primary beneficiary's estate.

Common Disaster Provision

There are times when it is most desirable to avoid this problem of the primary beneficiary living a short time longer than the insured and receiving the proceeds of the policy. It can be accomplished by using a *common disaster provision*.

A policyowner can make certain that the rights of the contingent beneficiary are protected by including a common disaster provision in the policy. This provision simply writes into a policy that the primary beneficiary must outlive the insured a specified length of time in cases of simultaneous (or nearly simultaneous) death; otherwise, the proceeds are paid to the contingent beneficiary.

The common disaster provision paves the way, legally, for the policyowner to make certain that the contingent beneficiary receives the proceeds if both the insured and the primary beneficiary die within a short time of each other. The policyowner requests this provision in the policy. It states that the primary beneficiary must outlive the insured a specified period of time--usually 10, 15, or 30 days--in order to receive the proceeds. This provision comes into play most frequently when the insured and the primary beneficiary are killed in (or die as a result of) a common disaster, an accident of some kind.

 As an example, suppose you buy a life insurance policy, naming your wife the primary beneficiary and your son the contingent beneficiary. You want to protect the rights of your son, in respect to the policy, in the event you and your wife die in a common disaster. You should protect these rights especially if you die first, because in that case, the proceeds might pass on to your wife and then into her taxable estate upon her death a short time later. You can prevent this by adding a common disaster provision to your policy.

Spendthrift Clause

One of the unique features of life insurance is that the life insurance proceeds are exempt from the claims of the insured's (deceased's) creditors as long as there is a named beneficiary other than the insured's estate. A similar provision with reference to the beneficiary is the *spendthrift clause*.

A person who spends money extravagantly is known as a spendthrift. The insured can protect the proceeds of an insurance policy from the actions of a spendthrift beneficiary through the use of a spendthrift clause. This clause in a life insurance policy provides the following:

➤ The proceeds will be paid in some way other than a lump sum.

➤ The proceeds or payments to be made to the beneficiary are protected from the beneficiary's creditors while they are still held by the insurance company.

The spendthrift clause is designed to protect the proceeds of a life insurance policy from the beneficiary's spending habits and creditors. The spendthrift clause also prevents the beneficiary from

➤ *Transferring the proceeds*--assigning payments to a creditor

➤ *Commuting the proceeds*--taking the present value of future payments in a lump sum

➤ *Encumbering the proceeds*--borrowing money on the strength of the proceeds of the policy

If the beneficiary fails to pay his or her creditors as agreed, one or more of them may be forced to take legal action to recover the money. If the beneficiary is receiving payments from a life policy that has a spendthrift clause, the creditors cannot attach those payments before they are made to the beneficiary. After the beneficiary has received the payments, however, the creditors can take steps to attach those payments.

Facility of Payment Provision

The *facility of payment provision* enables the insurer to select a beneficiary if the named beneficiaries cannot be found after a reasonable time. This provision is most commonly found in group life insurance contracts and industrial life policies. Typically, this provision is found in policies with relatively small death benefits, such as industrial life. Normally, the insurer would select someone who is in the family's immediate bloodline (a brother, sister, aunt, uncle, and so on).

Exclusions and Limitations

Life insurance policies used to be written with a number of exclusions. Most life insurance policies today no longer contain these exclusions. However, because many policies containing exclusions of one kind or another are still in force, you should know about the most common ones.

Aviation Exclusion

The *aviation exclusion* restricts payment of benefits in case of death from aviation activities, except when the insured was a fare-paying passenger or commercial crew member. Among the types of aviation restrictions still found are these:

➤ Exclusion of all aviation-caused or aviation-related deaths except those of fare-paying passengers on regularly scheduled airlines. Some policies do not include the phrase, "regularly scheduled airlines," thus covering nonscheduled flights also, but only for a fare-paying passenger.

➤ Exclusion of deaths in military aircraft only or death while on military maneuvers.

➤ Exclusion of pilots, crew members, student pilots, and (sometimes) any-one with duties in flight or while descending from an aircraft--for example, parachuting.

Companies using any or all of these restrictions will cover civil aviation deaths for an extra premium.

War or Military Service Exclusion

In wartime, it has been common for companies to include restrictions that limit the death benefit paid to usually a refund of premium plus interest or possibly an amount equal to the policy's cash value. Often in the past, the policy's benefits were suspended during a war or an act of war. The term, "act of war" has been used to describe the Korean and Vietnam conflicts.

Today, most insurers will provide some form of life insurance coverage for those on military duty. Traditionally, there are usually two types of restrictions or clauses that may be used. The *status clause* excludes the payment of the death benefit while the insured is serving in the military. The *results clause* excludes the payment of the death benefit if the insured is killed as a result of war.

Hazardous Occupation or Hobby Exclusion

By today's underwriting standards, few applicants are declined life insurance because of their occupations. For example, firefighters and police personnel can purchase life insurance at standard rates. Even commercial airline pilots can usually purchase life insurance (although possibly at higher than standard rates).

Much of the underwriting attention is focused on the applicant's avocations or hobbies. If an applicant participates in a hazardous hobby such as auto racing, sky diving, scuba diving, and so forth, the amount of insurance that may be purchased may be limited, or an extra premium may be charged due to the additional risk. Depending on the hobby, the death benefit may be excluded if death was caused as a result of the hazardous avocation.

Prohibited Provisions

By law in most states, life insurance policies are *not* permitted to contain the following provisions:

➤ A provision that limits the time for bringing any lawsuit against the insurance company to less than 1 year after the reason for the lawsuit occurs.

➤ A provision that allows a settlement at maturity of *less* than the face amount plus any dividend additions, less any indebtedness to the company and any premium deductible under the policy.

➤ A provision that allows forfeiture of the policy because of the failure to repay any policy loan or interest on the loan if the total owed is less than the loan value of the policy.

➤ A provision making the soliciting agent the agent of the person insured under the policy or making the acts or representations of the agent binding on the insured. (The agent must only be an agent of the company, not the insured.)

The law of the state in which the policy is sold governs the contract. The policy may not contain a provision by which the laws of the home state of the insurer govern the policy provisions.

Exam Prep Questions

1. How long is the typical grace period?

   ○ A. 10 days

   ○ B. 30 days

   ○ C. 60 days

   ○ D. 90 days

2. Which of the following is true about an automatic premium loan provision?

   ○ A. It applies only to term policies.

   ○ B. It is automatically included in all policies.

   ○ C. It keeps the policy in force when it would otherwise lapse due to nonpayment of premiums.

   ○ D. Money used to pay premiums is treated as a partial withdrawal and not subject to interest charges.

3. The incontestable clause is usually in effect after

   ○ A. 2 years

   ○ B. 4 years

   ○ C. 5 years

   ○ D. 6 years

4. Harry decides to borrow some money from a bank and use life insurance cash values as collateral. What type of assignment will Harry probably use to secure the loan?

   ○ A. Voluntary assignment

   ○ B. Partial assignment

   ○ C. Complete assignment

   ○ D. Absolute assignment

5. Carol has a policy on her ex-husband that she wants to give to their daughter. Carol no longer wants any control over this policy. What type of assignment will Carol probably use to accomplish this?

   ○ A. Collateral assignment

   ○ B. Voluntary assignment

   ○ C. Partial assignment

   ○ D. Conditional assignment

6. Carl purchased a life insurance policy when he was 44. The insurer accidentally recorded his age as 42. When the mistake is discovered in a review of the files 5 years later:

   ○ A. The policy will be canceled due to misrepresentation.

   ○ B. The policy will not change, because the incontestable period will have passed.

   ○ C. Carl will be charged the difference in premium between his actual age and his stated age, along with the interest on the back payments.

   ○ D. Carl will be credited the difference in premium between his actual age and his stated age, along with the interest on the back payments.

7. How long is the free look period in most states?

   ○ A. 5 days

   ○ B. 7 days

   ○ C. 10 days

   ○ D. 30 days

8. When Tom dies, Rosemary receives the death benefit. If Rosemary had died before Tom, George would have received the benefit. Which statement is true?

   ○ A. Rosemary is the primary beneficiary and George is the contingent beneficiary.

   ○ B. Tom is the primary beneficiary and Rosemary is the contingent beneficiary.

   ○ C. Rosemary is the contingent beneficiary and George is the primary beneficiary.

   ○ D. George is the contingent beneficiary and Rosemary is the tertiary beneficiary.

9. John leaves his $300,000 estate to his three children to split equally according to a per stirpes distribution. One of his children dies before John does. Upon John's death, which of the following is true?

   ○ A. The proceeds are split three ways, between the remaining children and John's estate.

   ○ B. The proceeds are split two ways, between the remaining children only.

   ○ C. The proceeds are split three ways, between the remaining children and the beneficiary of the deceased child's estate.

   ○ D. The proceeds are split four ways, between the remaining children, John's estate, and the deceased child's estate.

10. Alice and Ken are in a fatal car crash that kills them both. Alice is the primary beneficiary of a policy on Ken's life. What happens to the policy proceeds?

○ A. The proceeds are retained by the insurance company.

○ B. The proceeds are paid to Alice's estate.

○ C. The proceeds are paid to any contingent beneficiaries, or to Ken's estate.

○ D. The proceeds are paid directly to Ken's estate.

Exam Prep Answers

1. **B is correct.** It is 30 or 31 days in most cases.

2. **C is correct.** The provision is designed to keep a policy in effect when cash value is available to pay the premium.

3. **A is correct.** This is the period of time that applies in most states.

4. **B is correct.** This is an example of a partial assignment.

5. **B is correct.** This is an example of a voluntary assignment.

6. **C is correct.** The adjustment will be made based on Carl's true age.

7. **C is correct.** It is 10 days in most states.

8. **A is correct.** Rosemary is the primary beneficiary. George would only have been eligible to receive the benefit if Rosemary died before he did.

9. **C is correct.** Under a per stirpes distribution the proceeds due a deceased beneficiary are protected and will be paid to that person's heirs or estate.

10. **C is correct.** Under the Simultaneous Death Act, it will be assumed that Ken survived Alice and the benefits will be paid to Ken's estate if there are no contingent beneficiaries.

Policy Options

Terms you need to understand:

- ✓ Interest only payments
- ✓ Fixed period installments
- ✓ Fixed amount installments
- ✓ Life income
- ✓ Straight life income
- ✓ Refund annuity
- ✓ Life income certain
- ✓ Joint and survivor income
- ✓ Cash surrender value

- ✓ Extended term insurance
- ✓ Reduced paid-up insurance
- ✓ Cash dividend
- ✓ Accumulation at interest
- ✓ Paid-up additions
- ✓ Reduce premium option
- ✓ Accelerated endowment
- ✓ Paid-up option
- ✓ One-year term option

Concepts you need to master:

- ✓ Settlement options
- ✓ Withdrawal provisions
- ✓ Third-party rights

- ✓ Nonforfeiture options
- ✓ Dividend options

The life insurance policy provides important policy options. These options give the life insurance contract flexibility to meet the needs of the insuring public. Of particular value are the settlement, nonforfeiture, and dividend options available under a life insurance contract.

Settlement Options

At one time, life insurance policy proceeds were paid only in the form of a lump-sum cash payment. This often created as many problems for the beneficiary as it solved. For instance, the beneficiary, who is the sudden recipient of a large amount of cash, might have little or no idea of how to use or invest the money. An immature beneficiary might launch into a great spending spree and be broke in a short period of time.

To avoid situations such as these, the life insurance industry developed methods by which the proceeds of a policy could be paid in forms other than a lump sum. These methods of receiving policy proceeds in other than a lump sum are known as *settlement options* or *payment options*.

Most policy proceeds are still distributed in a lump sum. It is important that policyowners and beneficiaries understand that settlement options are available and that such options may be tailored to meet individual needs. When a settlement option is chosen, the proceeds of the policy are left with the company. The insurance company invests the proceeds and guarantees that the funds will earn interest.

 Unless the policyowner specifies an irrevocable settlement option, the beneficiary may select any of the same options available to the policyowner when the proceeds become payable, even if that option differs from that originally selected by the policyowner.

If there are any outstanding policy loans, they are always deducted from the settlement option chosen. All dividend accumulations, paid-up dividend additions, and any term insurance riders will serve to increase the benefits of the settlement option chosen.

There are four frequently used optional modes of settlement:

➤ Interest only

➤ Fixed period installments

➤ Fixed amount installments

➤ Life income

In addition, most companies will agree to distribute the proceeds under any reasonable and actuarially sound mode.

Interest Only Option

The first settlement option to be described is the *interest option*, sometimes also called the *interest only option*. Under the interest option, the life insurance company keeps the proceeds of the policy for a limited time and invests them for the beneficiary, paying the interest earned as income to the beneficiary.

Under the interest-only option, the policyowner may provide a means by which the beneficiary can withdraw all or part of the principal amount of the policy proceeds. The right of withdrawal can take several forms. Consider this example.

The insurance company holds $100,000 of proceeds at interest. Interest is paid to the beneficiary at the rate of so many dollars per month. In addition, the beneficiary may withdraw, at any time, any amount up to the full $100,000 principal. In this situation, the beneficiary can withdraw all or part of the principal, if so desired. The policy can also be arranged so that the beneficiary cannot withdraw any of the principal amount or cannot make any withdrawals for a specified number of years or until a specified age is reached.

If the beneficiary dies while money is still on deposit with the company, the money is paid to the deceased beneficiary's estate or to a secondary beneficiary (or beneficiaries) named in the policy. If the insured indicated that the contingent beneficiary should continue to receive income, the company pays the contingent beneficiary in the designated manner.

When the insured has not elected a settlement option for the contingent beneficiary, that beneficiary can select the manner in which the proceeds are to be paid.

Fixed Period Option

The *fixed period option*, along with the remaining two options that we'll look at, is actually a form of annuity. Under the fixed period option, the beneficiary receives a regular income, comprised of both principal and interest, for a specified period of time. So under this option the principal amount gradually decreases to zero.

Three factors that determine the amount the beneficiary or payee will receive each time a payment is made under the fixed period option are

➤ The principal amount

➤ The interest earned on the principal

➤ The length of time the payments are to be made

For example, if the policy proceeds total $100,000, earn 6% annual interest, and are to be paid out over a 10-year period, the beneficiary can expect to receive approximately $1,100 each month for a total of $132,000. However, if the proceeds are paid out over a 15-year period, the beneficiary would receive approximately $845 per month for a total of $152,100. Note that in both examples the total amount paid exceeds the policy proceeds because of the interest earned.

As with other settlement options, if the primary beneficiary dies before receiving the full amount of the policy's proceeds, the money remaining is paid to the contingent beneficiary, if one is named in the policy, or into the estate of the primary beneficiary.

Fixed Amount Option

The third type of settlement option is the *fixed amount option*, under which the payee receives payments but the length of time for the payments is not specified. The amount of each periodic installment is established ahead of time and payments continue until the combination of principal and interest has been exhausted.

The three factors that determine how long the payee will receive payments under the fixed amount option are

➤ The specified amount of each payment

➤ The principal amount, or the amount of the policy proceeds

➤ Earnings on the principal, or the interest

Suppose the beneficiary is to receive $10,000 per year from $100,000 in policy proceeds that are earning 6% interest annually from the insurer. Payments would extend over a 14-year period and total approximately $140,000. But if the annual payment were increased to $15,000, the income would last for only 8 years and total $120,000. Just as with the fixed period option, the company guarantees that the total amount paid until the proceeds are exhausted will exceed the policy proceeds because of the interest earned.

In guaranteeing that the payee will receive more money in the long run by taking the proceeds in the form of an income stream, the company is encouraging the payee to leave the proceeds with the company. It also increases its total assets, thus increasing overall earnings for the company—and the payee.

Life Income Option

The fourth settlement option is the *life income option*. As its name implies, the life income option provides for payment of installments for the entire lifetime of the payee. Just as with an annuity, there are at least four distinct methods in which these installments can be paid. Many companies offer additional options. The most common methods of payment are

➤ Straight life income (or life only), in which the payee receives a specified income for as long as he or she lives

➤ Refund annuity, in which an income is paid for the lifetime of the payee, and to a second payee if the first payee dies prior to having received an amount equal to the full proceeds of the policy

➤ Life income certain, in which the payee receives installments for life, with a second payee receiving the payments if the first payee dies before the end of the years specified in the "certain" period—for example, a period certain of 5, 10, or 20 years

➤ Joint and survivor life income, in which two payees are recipients of the income for the lifetime of the first payee, and the surviving payee the recipient of income of a lesser amount (usually two-thirds or one-half) for the rest of his or her life

Using these four settlement options, some custom tailoring may be done between the policyowner and the company. For instance, an insured policyowner might specify in her policy that if she should die, her husband is to receive only the interest on the proceeds until he reaches age 62; from that point on, he is to receive a life income certain for 20 years.

Additionally, because a beneficiary's needs change from time to time, most companies will allow the policyowner to change the settlement option as necessary during his or her lifetime.

Withdrawal Provisions

The *withdrawal provision* is used in connection with settlement options. Under this provision the proceeds of a policy are held by the insurance company and earn interest. The insured has the right to withdraw the funds but may withdraw only a limited amount each year. Quite often this withdrawal provision is used to pay for college.

Other Settlement Arrangements

Many policies are written with no provision for any special arrangements in the settlement of proceeds. However, a large number of companies will permit other settlement arrangements. Special settlement arrangements are sometimes desirable in order to accomplish the estate planning objectives of some insureds, and insurance companies will cooperate with almost any arrangement that is reasonable.

An insurance company does not provide trustee services. If an insured, for example, requested a settlement arrangement whereby the insurance company would make payment of the proceeds to two beneficiaries "according to their needs," the insurance company would probably reject the settlement arrangement because it would require the insurance company to make a judgment determination.

Companies have rules to avoid arrangements that are uneconomical to administer. For example, a company may specify that a minimum of $1,000, or in some cases $2,000, may be placed under a settlement option. It may prescribe that minimum installments payable shall be not less than a certain amount per installment. A company may set a time limit for holding proceeds at interest, such as for the lifetime of the primary beneficiary or the lifetime of a contingent beneficiary.

Third-Party Rights and Creditor's Rights

Although the life insurance contract is between the policyowner and the insurer, after the insured dies, a contractual arrangement exists between the insurer and the beneficiary. The beneficiary may sue the insurer if payment is not received upon proper proof of death.

Likewise, after the insured dies, the proceeds of a life insurance policy belong to the beneficiary, and the insured's creditors have no right to them. The beneficiary's creditors, however, may have a right to the life insurance proceeds. Even the cash value of life insurance is generally protected from creditors.

The only exception to these statements is if the premiums that paid for the insurance were from embezzled funds.

Advantages of Settlement Options

One of the principal advantages for the insured or beneficiary in selecting one of the various settlement options is freedom from investment concerns. If a beneficiary elects a lump-sum settlement of the death benefit, he or she must decide how to use or invest the money. In essence, by electing a settlement option other than a lump sum, the beneficiary is trusting in the expertise and knowledge of the insurance company to administer these proceeds and provide some form of income.

Another advantage of settlement options is the fact that any of the options will guarantee a greater return than simply taking the face amount of the policy. A $100,000 policy will generate a greater death benefit than $100,000 if these proceeds, consisting of principal and interest, are paid to a beneficiary over a period of time.

Nonforfeiture Options (Guaranteed Values)

Nonforfeiture options assure that any cash value accumulation in a life insurance policy is made available to the policyowner should he or she stop paying the premiums for any reason.

 The amount of cash value and the rate at which it accumulates depends upon the type of policy purchased by the policyowner. The amount and rate vary from company to company and often from one type of policy to another. In many states, however, permanent policies are required to have at least a small cash value by the end of the policy's third year.

The following are common nonforfeiture options in cash value policies:

➤ Cash surrender value

➤ Extended term insurance

➤ Reduced paid-up insurance

Cash Surrender Value

With the *cash surrender option*, the policyowner can receive the cash accumulation as cash. The minimum cash value is determined by a formula established by law. A portion of each premium paid is allocated to the policy reserve that is a fixed liability of the insurance company. The balance of the premium is used to cover certain expenses (acquisition costs, administrative expenses, agents' commission, and so forth). In the early years of the policy (the first two or three), all the premium is used for the reserve requirement and other liabilities and expenses, so there is no cash value in the early years of the policy.

Usually about the third year of the policy, these initial expenses are covered and the policy's guaranteed cash value begins to grow. As the cash value grows so do the values associated with the nonforfeiture options. With the cash surrender option, life insurance protection ceases. If the policyowner has borrowed money on a policy loan, the amount yet to be repaid plus interest will be deducted from the cash surrender value.

If Sherry has a policy with a stated cash value of $1,500 and she still owes $350 (including interest) on a previous loan from this cash value, for example, the company would give her on the cash surrender value option a total of $1,150 ($1,500 less $350).

Reduced Paid-Up Insurance Option

Another nonforfeiture option is called the *reduced paid-up insurance option*. Under this option, the policyowner essentially uses the cash value of a present policy to purchase a single premium insurance policy, at attained age rates, for a reduced face amount.

Remember the following about the reduced paid-up insurance option:

➤ After the face amount of protection has been determined, it remains the same for the duration of the contract, and the new policy will build cash values for the policyowner.

➤ No further premiums need be paid on the reduced policy—it's paid up because it's a single premium policy.

➤ The new protection is computed at the attained age of the insured (who may also be the policyowner).

➤ A full share of expense loading is usually not included in the premium on the reduced coverage, because the costs of setting up the coverage are greatly reduced.

 All reduced paid-up policies are of the same type of insurance as the original policy, except all riders, including those for disability and accidental death, are eliminated.

Extended Term Option

The third nonforfeiture option is called the *extended term option*, in which the policyowner can use the policy's cash value accumulation as a single premium to purchase paid-up term insurance in an amount equal to the original policy face amount. The length of the term depends on the net cash value that is applied as a net single premium at the insured's attained age.

Typically, the extended term nonforfeiture option goes into effect automatically if the policyowner isn't available to make a choice or simply fails to exercise an option.

If a policy loan is outstanding at the time the extended term option is exercised, the company will first deduct the loan outstanding from the cash surrender value of the policy to cancel out the outstanding loan. The reduced cash value will provide term coverage for a shortened period of time and for a face amount that is likewise reduced by the amount of the loan outstanding.

Insurance Dividends

Many life insurance policies have a provision allowing the policyowner to participate in the favorable experience of the insurance company through dividends. Most, although not all, of these *participating policies* (sometimes referred to as *par policies*) are sold by mutual life insurance companies rather than by stock companies.

Policies that do not pay dividends are called *nonparticipating* (*nonpar*) policies.

Usually the premium for a participating policy is calculated using very conservative assumptions, including an allowance for future dividend payments. The amount, or even the existence, of policy dividends is never guaranteed. But by charging a slightly higher initial premium for participating policies, a company can be fairly sure that it will be able to return at least a small dividend.

As a matter of practice, many companies declare and pay dividends annually. The policyowner is usually offered several options for the settlement of these dividends. The following represents a list of possible dividend payment options. Although these are the most frequently used options, the list is not all inclusive:

➤ Cash dividend

➤ Accumulation at interest

➤ Paid-up additions

➤ Reduced premium

➤ Accelerated endowment

➤ Paid-up option

➤ One-year term option

Policy Dividend Sources

The source of funds from which life insurance policy dividends are paid is the same (basically) as the three factors used in premium computations:

➤ *Mortality*—The mortality tables tell us that a certain number of persons (insureds) in each age group will probably die during the next year. If fewer people die than predicted, the life insurance company experiences a savings in mortality.

➤ *(Assumed) interest*—A life insurance company estimates that invested money will earn a given rate over the long run, usually around 4%. If a company assumes its investments will earn 4% but the invested premiums actually earn 8%, the company has earned greater interest than it thought it would.

➤ *Operating expenses or loading*—Past experience tells a company that it will cost so many dollars per $1,000 coverage to keep the company going. Such costs as accounting, rent, office equipment, and the like are relatively predictable. Let's say, however, that a given company installs a new accounting system that saves several thousand dollars. These savings help reduce operating expenses or loading.

In each of the cases outlined above, the company ends up with excess funds or surplus over those needed to pay claims, pay operating expenses, and make a respectable profit. Life insurance policy dividends are paid out of such funds.

Dividend Options

The policyowner has several options available with respect to the receipt of dividends when they are paid and notifies the insurer regarding which option he or she selects.

Cash Dividend Option

One dividend option is simply to have the company issue the policyowner a check for the dividend amount. This is known as the *cash dividend option*.

Accumulation at Interest Option

The policyowner can let dividends accumulate at interest with the company. The company will invest the policyowner's money and add interest earnings to the initial amount of the dividends as such earnings accrue. Of course, any interest is currently taxable. The interest on invested dividends builds up, or accumulates. For this reason, this dividend option is called the *accumulation at interest option*.

If an insured policyowner should die with a credit to the policy for accumulated dividends and interest, the dividends, plus any accrued interest, are paid to the beneficiary of the policy because this money belonged to the policyowner.

Keep in mind, with respect to leaving dividends to accumulate at interest, that this money has nothing to do with the cash value accumulation of a permanent policy. This means that dividends left at interest can be used in a cash emergency—the policyowner can withdraw them—without in any way affecting the cash value of the policy.

Paid-Up Additions Option

If a policyowner decides to use dividends as a single premium to buy additional life insurance protection, the additional coverage is fully paid for, or paid up, with that premium. For this reason, we call this option the *paid-up additions option*.

The amount of paid-up addition per $1 of dividend is based on the insured's age at the time the paid-up addition is purchased. The amount of the paid-up addition to a life insurance policy is therefore dependent on the amount of the dividend and the insured's attained age.

No new policies are issued. The base policy is simply amended to reflect the additional paid-up values. Each of these additions will also develop cash value. The face amount and the additions make up the total death benefit if the policy matures as a death claim. Should the policyowner elect to surrender the policy for its cash value prior to that time, both the cash value of the policy and the addition would be paid. When this arrangement is chosen, the insured need not prove insurability for the purchase of the additional coverage.

If another dividend option is chosen originally and the policyowner later decides to change to the paid-up additions option, any previous dividend amounts generally cannot be used to purchase these additions. However, the policyowner can use current and future dividends to purchase paid-up additions.

The type of insurance purchased as a paid-up addition is usually restricted to the same type as provided in the original policy. If a policyowner is insured by a whole life policy and decides to use policy dividends to purchase paid-up additions, the paid-up additional insurance will be whole life insurance.

There is one more point concerning paid-up additions: the *loading charges*—the share of the company's operating expenses—borne by each policy. When current dividends are used to buy paid-up additions, no agent's commission is involved, nor is there any investigation of insurability. This means that the operating expenses of putting this coverage in force are lower than original policy expenses.

Reduce Premium Dividend Option

The policyowner can direct the insurer to apply the dividend toward the next premium due on the policy, which is called the *reduce premium dividend option*. Usually if this option has been elected, the premium notice will show the gross premium minus the dividend and the policyowner simply pays the net amount. If the dividend equals or exceeds the premium amount, the premium payment may be suspended entirely.

Accelerated Endowment

As discussed in the text, endowment policies lost their tax advantages in 1985 and have been rare since that time. However, you may still encounter a policyowner with an endowment policy using dividends to accelerate the endowment.

Paid-Up Option

This option actually enables the policyowner to pay up the policy early. For example, the insured has a 20-pay life. By using the dividends over the life of the policy, it may be paid up after 16 or 17 years instead of the full 20 years.

One-Year Term Dividend Option

If the policyowner chooses to do so, he or she can direct the company to use the dividends on the policy to purchase term insurance—term coverage that will be in force for a full year. We call this option the *1-year term dividend option*.

Under the 1-year term dividend option, the dividend money is used to buy term coverage of 1 year's duration, based upon the attained age of the insured, with the amount usually limited to the current cash value of the policy. If there is more than enough dividend money to buy that amount of 1-year term coverage, any excess dividend money still belongs to the policyowner. These extra funds can be applied under other available dividend options.

In addition, the company usually will require a medical examination for the term coverage only if the original policy has been in force and another dividend option has been in effect for several years. If this option has been in effect since the original policy went in force, the company usually requires no additional proof of insurability under the 1-year term dividend option.

A company's board of directors can declare a policy dividend annually if a surplus exists. This doesn't mean that the policyowner has to decide which dividend option to select every time the dividend is declared. The policyowner can set up any one of the options we've been discussing as a permanent option to be handled automatically by the company every time dividends on the policy are made available.

Exam Prep Questions

1. Ken is receiving interest only payments on the settlement of his father's life insurance policy. If Ken dies before the lump sum is paid to him, what happens to the balance of the money?

   ○ A. It is retained by the insurer.

   ○ B. It is paid to any contingent beneficiary named in the original policy, or if there is no contingent beneficiary, it is paid to Ken's estate.

   ○ C. It is paid to any primary beneficiary named in the original policy, or into Ken's father's estate.

   ○ D. It is paid directly into Ken's estate.

2. Which of the following is not a factor in determining the amount the beneficiary will receive each time a payment is made under the fixed period option?

   ○ A. The age of the beneficiary

   ○ B. The principal amount

   ○ C. The interest earned on the principal

   ○ D. The length of time payments are to be made

3. Which of the following is not a factor in determining the amount the beneficiary will receive each time a payment is made under the fixed amount option?

   ○ A. The specified amount of each payment

   ○ B. The principal amount

   ○ C. The interest earned on the principal

   ○ D. The capital amount

4. Walter is the beneficiary of his mother's life insurance policy. He wants to make sure the proceeds will last not only as long as he lives, but also as long as his wife is alive. Walter should select the

   ○ A. Straight life income option

   ○ B. Refund annuity option

   ○ C. Life income certain option

   ○ D. Joint and survivor life income option

5. Which of the following does not affect the payment of life insurance dividends?

   ○ A. Mortality

   ○ B. Assumed interest

   ○ C. Morbidity

   ○ D. Operating expenses or loading

6. Which of the following is true about paid-up additions?
   - ○ A. The dividends are used to purchase additional insurance protection.
   - ○ B. The additional protection is almost always restricted to term insurance.
   - ○ C. The single premium for the added coverage will be based on the insured's original age.
   - ○ D. The operating expenses of putting this coverage in force are higher than original policy expenses.

7. Emily has chosen to receive the payout from her husband's life insurance policy so that she will receive an income for the next 15 years. At the end of that time, the entire proceeds from the policy will have been paid out. Emily has selected the
   - ○ A. Interest only option
   - ○ B. Fixed period option
   - ○ C. Fixed amount option
   - ○ D. Life income option

8. Heath has chosen to receive the payout from his wife's life insurance policy in such a way that he will have an income for the remainder of his life, regardless of how long he lives. Heath has selected the
   - ○ A. Interest only option
   - ○ B. Fixed period option
   - ○ C. Fixed amount option
   - ○ D. Life income option

9. Jim has selected to receive only the interest from his mother's life insurance policy. When Jim dies, his children will receive the lump-sum benefit in addition to the benefit from his life insurance policy. Jim has selected the
   - ○ A. Interest only option
   - ○ B. Fixed period option
   - ○ C. Fixed amount option
   - ○ D. Life income option

10. Carmen has selected to receive $10,000 per month until the principle and interest on her husband's life insurance policy has all been paid. Carmen has selected the
   - ○ A. Interest only option
   - ○ B. Fixed period option
   - ○ C. Fixed amount option
   - ○ D. Life income option

Exam Prep Answers

1. **B is correct.** The money would be paid to a contingent beneficiary or to Ken's estate.

2. **A is correct.** Under the fixed period option the age of the beneficiary is irrelevant.

3. **D is correct.** The specified amount of payment, principal amount, and rate of interest are all factors. The term capital amount is not used.

4. **D is correct.** The joint and survivor option will pay benefits as long as Walter or his wife is alive, regardless of who dies first.

5. **C is correct.** Morbidity is a concept that relates to the development of health insurance premiums.

6. **A is correct.** With this option additional amounts of insurance are purchased.

7. **B is correct.** This is an example of the fixed period option.

8. **D is correct.** This is an example of the life income option.

9. **A is correct.** This is an example of the interest only option.

10. **C is correct.** This is an example of the fixed amount option.

Annuities

Terms you need to understand:
✓ Annuity
✓ Contract owner
✓ Annuitant
✓ Beneficiary
✓ Immediate annuity
✓ Deferred annuity
✓ Single premium annuity
✓ Level premium annuity
✓ Flexible premium annuity

Concepts you need to master:
✓ Accumulation period
✓ Annuity period
✓ Accumulation units
✓ Annuity unit
✓ Life annuity
✓ Refund life annuity
✓ Life annuity certain
✓ Joint and survivorship annuity
✓ Joint life annuity
✓ Tax-sheltered annuity
✓ Retirement income annuity
✓ Equity-indexed annuity
✓ Market-value adjusted annuity

Purposes of Annuities

Life insurance is designed to protect the insured against premature death. An *annuity* is designed to protect the annuitant against the risk of living too long and possibly outliving his or her financial resources during retirement. Annuities offer a benefit unknown to other types of financial vehicles: a payout you cannot outlive. Other investments and savings can be depleted and leave an individual with no other resources in dire financial straits. Annuity payments, however, can be arranged to last for life.

Like all insurance, annuities are designed to transfer a risk from consumers to an insurance company. In the case of annuities, the risk being transferred is the risk of outliving your savings. Annuities are not technically "life" insurance, but because annuities are sold by life insurance companies, a basic understanding of the types of annuity policies available is necessary to qualify for a producer license.

Distribution of a Lifetime Income

Suppose you had a sum of money with which to support yourself for the rest of your life. If you spent too much each month, you would run out of money before you died. If you spent too little, you would not maximize the use of that money—you would die before it was all used up. An annuity eliminates this uncertainty by converting a sum of money into a series of period payments that can be guaranteed to last a lifetime, and sometimes longer.

From the standpoint of the consumer, it could be said that life insurance offers protection against dying too soon, and an annuity offers protection against living too long.

Accumulation of a Retirement Fund

Suppose you don't have a sum of money that will serve as a fund for your retirement. Well, an annuity can be structured to allow for the accumulation of such a fund over time so that when retirement finally arrives, income payments begin. These payments will continue as long as you live and even afterward to your spouse if he or she survives you.

Annuities exist to distribute a lifetime income or to accumulate a sum of money, if necessary. Generally, this accumulation is designed to be used for retirement.

How Annuities Work

Like an insurance policy, an annuity is a contract between a purchaser and an insurance company. The purchaser pays the premium and generally is the *contract owner*. The contract owner has certain rights under the contract.

For example, the contract owner names the *annuitant*. The annuitant is the insured, the person on whose life the annuity policy has been issued. In most cases, the annuitant is the intended recipient of the annuity payments. Many times the contract owner and annuitant are the same person, but not always.

The contract owner also names a *beneficiary*, who receives any survivor benefits payable under the annuity upon the death of the annuitant.

The Accumulation Period

Most annuities have an *accumulation period*, which may be initiated by the payment of a single lump sum or the first of a series of premium payments. During this accumulation period, the principal earns interest and grows year by year. A so-called *fixed annuity* specifies a fixed, guaranteed minimum rate of interest that will be paid on the principle amount invested in the annuity.

Under this arrangement, the contract owner knows exactly the minimum return that will be earned during the accumulation period. The insurer simply invests each premium in its general investment account and credits the current interest to the annuity's cash value, but never less than the minimum guaranteed.

A *variable annuity* offers a variable, non-guaranteed rate of interest that offers the potential—but not a promise—to act as a hedge against inflation.

In all types of annuities, the principal earns interest. The first year's interest is added to the original principal, and the combined sum then earns more interest in the second year. In other words, we earn interest on interest, or *compound interest*, in the second and every subsequent year.

The interest earned by the annuity contract is generally not currently taxed as it is with other savings investment vehicles. This untaxed interest goes right on earning even more interest, which is also untaxed currently and added to principal. This tax advantage is an important reason why people buy annuities.

The Annuity Period

The *annuity period* starts when the annuitant begins receiving a series of installment payments from the annuity. Each periodic annuity payment is made up partly of the premium deposits and partly of the interest those deposits have earned. The interest portion of the payment is taxable as income because it was not taxed as it was earned. The premium portion of the payment is not taxed because annuity premiums are paid with dollars that were taxed before they were paid into the annuity.

Of course, nobody knows exactly how long the annuitant is going to live. However, insurance companies have studied average life expectancies over many years, so that using the law of large numbers, the insurance company has a pretty good idea how long the average person will live. Some people will die before their life expectancy is up, leaving uncollected benefits for the people who live longer than their life expectancy.

An annuity is really a combination of three things: the premium deposits, the interest earned, and a mortality factor. Even after the annuitant has exhausted all deposits and interest, he or she can still collect annuity payments for life due to the insurer's acceptance of longevity risk.

Fixed Payout

For a fixed annuity, the cash value accumulation at the beginning of the annuity period is simply "annuitized." That is, the accumulation is converted into a stream of periodic payments using actuarial principles that take into account the expected longevity of the annuitant, interest earned by the principal balance during the annuity (payout) period, and related factors. The result is a fixed dollar amount payout that remains the same for the rest of the contract.

Variable Payout

A different payout measure is used for variable annuities. The payout can change, reflecting the investment experience of the principal.

Nonforfeiture Options

An annuity contract owner that stops making premium payments during the accumulation period does not lose the value accumulated in the annuity to that point. The contract holder may have several *nonforfeiture options*, rights to the cash value accumulation up to the point the premiums stopped.

A common option is to permit the contract to become a paid-up contract with the annuitant receiving annuity payments based on that amount.

Another option is to surrender the contract for its cash value and take a lump-sum payment. Surrender, however, is not available after annuity payments begin. Most companies will level some kind of surrender charge, which often scales downward as time goes on.

Immediate and Deferred Annuities

There are two categories of annuities, based on when annuity payments are to begin. These are immediate and deferred annuities.

A contract is an *immediate annuity* if income payments to the annuitant are to begin one payout interval (for example, one month or one year) after purchase of the annuity.

A contract is a *deferred annuity* if income payments are to begin at some further point in the future—perhaps as much as several years from the date of purchase.

Even with an immediate annuity, payments don't begin on the very next day after the contract is purchased. Instead, payments begin after one full payment period from the date of purchase has elapsed. If the contract calls for monthly installments for example, payments will begin 1 month after the date of purchase. If the contract calls for annual payments, the annuitant will receive the first payment one year after the date of purchase.

Annuity benefit payments are made on either an annual, semiannual, quarterly, or monthly basis. Because the longest period between benefit payments is a year, it follows that payments on an immediate annuity will begin no later than 1 year from the date of purchase. However, if the contract provides for monthly benefit payments, with an immediate annuity, payments could begin as soon as 1 month from the date of purchase.

Because an immediate annuity has no accumulation period during which additional premium payments may be made, an immediate annuity must be paid for with a single premium and is known as a *single premium immediate annuity (SPIA)*.

A deferred annuity can also be a single premium contract or *single premium deferred annuity (SPDA)*. In fact, such persons as professional athletes frequently buy single premium deferred annuities while their incomes are quite high. This deferral period allows a deferred annuity to be used as an accumulation vehicle during the annuitant's working years as well as a source of lifetime income after retirement.

Deferred Annuity Death Benefits

In the case of a deferred annuity contract, the annuitant could die before annuity payments were scheduled to begin. In such cases, the contract beneficiary is paid the cash value of the contract.

For fixed annuities, that amounts to the premiums credited to the contract (that is, net of any front-end loads), plus interest, minus any surrender charges. Some companies waive the surrender charges in such cases.

For variable annuities, the cash value depends on the investment experience of the funds supporting the annuity, which could be more or less than the total premium paid into the policy. However, some companies agree to pay a death benefit at least equal to the amount of premium the policyowner paid into the annuity (sometimes plus interest), even if the funds have fallen to a lower amount by the time of death. Other companies pay a *stepped-up* death benefit on variable annuities: If the fund previously grew to a high level but had fallen to a lower level at the time of death, the death benefit would equal the previous higher level of the fund. Although these proceeds do not represent death protection like the benefits from a life insurance policy, we may still call the amount refunded from a deferred annuity a death benefit.

Annuity Premiums

Let's look at the various ways to pay for an annuity.

Single Premium

One of the most common ways to pay for an annuity is with a single premium. An annuity purchased by a single lump-sum payment is called a *single premium annuity*. For example, a life insurance policy could be cashed in at retirement and the cash value used to buy a single premium annuity that will provide income for the rest of the individual's life.

Level Premium

A second method of buying an annuity is the *level premium annuity*. Under this arrangement the premiums are paid in periodic installments over the years prior to the date on which annuity income begins. Level premiums have a "forced savings" aspect to them, much like making regular deposits into a passbook savings account. A common level premium arrangement is the annual premium annuity in which the premiums are paid in yearly installments up to the time the annuity benefits begin. Premiums can also be paid semiannually, quarterly, or monthly.

Flexible Premium

A *flexible premium annuity* is like the level premium annuity because annuity premiums are made over a period of time, usually years, until annuity benefits are scheduled to begin. The difference is that with a flexible premium annuity, the purchaser has the option to vary the amount of each premium payment, as long as it falls between a minimum and maximum amount—say, between $200 and $10,000. The timing of the payments is also flexible—that is, they needn't be paid on a fixed schedule.

The flexible premium annuity can be advantageous to persons whose incomes may be subject to considerable fluctuation or who, for whatever reason, cannot pay for an annuity all at once or with periodic premiums that are the same amount each time. If an annuity is used to fund an IRA, it must provide flexible premium payments.

Determining Annuity Payouts

There are five factors used to determine annuity payouts:

➤ Annuitant's age

➤ Annuitant's sex

➤ Assumed interest rate

➤ Income amount and payment guarantee

➤ Loading for company expenses

The annuitant's age is important, because the company must determine how long it's likely to have to make income payments to the annuitant. If Mr. A, age 60, and Mr. B, age 65, both had $100,000 to fund the payment of a life-time annuity benefit, the amount of Mr. A's payment would have to be lower than Mr. B's because the insurance company would expect to pay Mr. A's benefit 5 years longer than Mr. B's.

The annuitant's sex is also a factor used in most states to determine premiums because women tend to live longer than men. However, some states have adopted unisex titles that disregard gender in determining annuity payouts.

As you know, life insurance companies invest premium dollars and earn a certain rate of interest on these investments. When determining payouts for annuities, the companies estimate, or assume, that invested dollars will earn a specified interest rate and that these earnings can increase the amount of the benefits paid out. This assumption is known as an *assumed rate of interest*, and it is the third factor in determining annuity payouts.

The fourth factor in annuity premium computation is the cost of any guarantees the company has made concerning the total amount (or total number of payments) to be paid. As we'll cover in more detail later, some annuity payout options provide that payments will continue for at least a certain period of time even if the annuitant dies earlier. In such cases, the annuity payout is reduced to cover the cost of the guarantee. The longer the guaranteed payment period, the more the annuity payout is reduced. Finally, to administer annuity contracts, companies incur operating expenses. Payout amounts, therefore, must have an expense factor added to them.

Variable Annuities

Except as otherwise indicated, the annuities we've been discussing up to this point have been fixed annuities—that is, annuities that grow at a fixed rate and pay fixed benefits when the annuitant reaches a certain age. Another type of annuity in which rate of growth of the annuity values may vary according to the performance of the investment medium, and from which benefits may also vary, is the variable annuity.

Variable annuities provide annuitants the opportunity to experience large gains; they may, however, also produce a loss. Variable annuities are characterized by a variable rate of growth and a variable benefit payable to the annuitant.

Regulation as Securities

Under traditional, fixed annuity contracts, the insurance company assumes the investment risk. If investment performance is more than what is required to fund the contract's guarantees, the difference is added to the company's surplus. If investment performance is unfavorable, the insurance company, not the contract owner, bears the loss.

With all variable contracts, including variable life insurance and variable annuities, the investment risk is borne by the contract owner. This allows investment gains to be passed through to the contract owner, but it also means that investment losses will be passed through to the contract owner as well.

Buyers can usually choose from a variety of investment accounts, even including the company's (nonvariable) general account.

Because the contract owner bears the investment risk, the Securities and Exchange Commission (SEC), as well as some individual states, considers variable annuities to be securities rather than simple life insurance products. As a result, variable annuities and those who sell them are subject to federal securities regulations as well as to state insurance regulations.

Variable contracts must be registered with the SEC under the Securities Act of 1933. This means that, generally, the laws and rules that apply to securities also apply to variable annuities.

People who sell variable annuities must be dually licensed. First, they must be licensed by a state to sell life insurance. Second, they must be licensed as registered representatives of a member of the National Association of Securities Dealers (NASD). NASD registration requires passing an exam, either the Series 6 limited registration exam or the Series 7 general securities exam. Some states also require a separate state variable contract or variable annuities license in addition to the life license and NASD registration.

Accumulation Units

The money paid to an insurance company over the years by purchasers of variable annuities is accumulated in an account that is kept separate from all other fixed annuity and insurance sales. This separate account is used by the company to buy securities that it hopes will keep pace with the cost of living.

The variable annuity contract owner is actually buying *accumulation units* in the separate account. He or she is not buying shares of stock or other securities. The use of accumulation units is simply an accounting measure to determine a contract owner's interest in the separate account during the accumulation period, or purchase period, of a deferred variable annuity.

Not all of the purchase payments made by a contract owner go toward the purchase of accumulation units. Before units can be purchased, sales charges and taxes are deducted. Thus, the money used to buy accumulation units is the net purchase payment.

The number of units a net payment will buy depends on the value of an accumulation unit at that time. This value is determined periodically, usually daily. At the risk of oversimplification, the value of one accumulation unit is reached by dividing the value of the separate account by the number of accumulation units outstanding.

An annuitant can never end up with fewer accumulation units than he or she has purchased, although the value of each unit may become either larger or smaller. For example, assume that a net payment of $100 buys 100 accumulation units, and the next day the value of the portfolio held by the separate account increases so that accumulation units are worth $1.05 each. The annuitant still has only 100 units, but each is now worth $1.05 instead of the $1.00 that was paid. If the value of the portfolio had decreased, the accumulation units would be worth less each.

As the contract owner continues to buy accumulation units, these are added to those already purchased. The dollar value of all the units owned by the contract holder equals the number of units the contract holder owns times the value of one accumulation unit. For example, if Frank owns 2,000 units and the value of one accumulation unit equals $5, Frank's dollar interest in the separate account equals $10,000.

Annuity Units

When the time arrives for the annuitant to start receiving payments, another accounting device replaces the accumulation unit. This is the *annuity unit*, and it serves to determine the amount of each payment to the annuitant during the payout period.

Unlike the number of accumulation units, which increases with each payment into the separate account, the number of annuity units remains fixed. The first step in determining this fixed number is to find the dollar value of the accumulation account that is the contract holder's interest in the separate account. Recall that this is determined by multiplying the number of accumulation units by the value of each unit.

The second step in the process of finding the number of annuity units is to determine what the first monthly payment to the annuitant will be. Insurance company annuity tables—which take into account the annuitant's age and sex, the payout option chosen, and deductions for charges—give the monthly annuity payment per $1,000 applied.

For example, suppose that the annuitant transfers $50,000 from the accumulation account and the table shows a value of $5 per $1,000. The first monthly payment to the annuitant would be 50 × $5, or $250.

If the annuity involved were fixed instead of variable, the annuitant would receive that first month's value for the remainder of the contract. But with a variable annuity, this figure is converted into annuity units by dividing the first monthly payment by the value of an annuity unit at the time. If the first monthly payment is $250 and the value of an annuity unit is then $2.50, the annuitant will own 100 annuity units and, once established, this number will never change.

This number of annuity units remains fixed throughout the remainder of the contract, but the annuity payment will vary according to the value of an annuity unit. If the value of an annuity unit is $2.55 the next month, the annuitant in the preceding example would receive $255. If it is $2.45 the following month, the annuitant would receive $245.

Annuity Settlement Options

As is the case with life insurance, a number of settlement options are available for annuity contracts.

Life Annuities

Life annuities is a general payout category in which the payout is guaranteed for life. Life annuities may be contrasted with temporary annuities, discussed later.

Life Annuity—No Refund

Sometimes known as a *straight life annuity*, a *life annuity* pays a benefit for as long as the annuitant lives, and then it ends. Whether the annuitant lives past 100 or dies in 1 month, the annuity payments continue only until he or she dies. In other words, there is not a guarantee as to minimum benefits with a life annuity.

There is a risk to the annuitant that he or she might not live long enough after the annuity period begins to collect the full value of the annuity. If an annuitant dies shortly after benefits begin, the insurer keeps the balance of the unpaid benefits.

 This option will pay the highest amount of monthly income to the annuitant because it is based only on life expectancy with no further payments after the death of the annuitant. All other options will reduce the periodic income payments.

Guaranteed Minimum Payouts

Many people were not happy knowing that most or all of their investment would be lost if they were to die after receiving just a few payments. This caused insurance companies to start offering some alternatives that provided a minimum guaranteed payout.

Refund Life Annuity

The length of time for which income payments will be made to the annuitant under a *refund life annuity* contract is the same as that for a straight life annuity. Thus, under a refund life annuity, the annuitant will receive payments for as long as he or she lives.

The main difference between the refund and the life annuity is that a refund annuity guarantees that an amount at least equal to the purchase price of the contract will be paid. If the annuitant lives for quite some time after the annuity income payments begin, he or she could receive more in benefits than the contract cost. If death occurs before an amount equal to the purchase price has been paid, the annuitant's beneficiary receives the rest of the money in cash or installment payments.

Life Annuity with Period Certain

Another type of annuity is the *life annuity with period certain*, which calls for payments for a guaranteed minimum number of years—often 10, 15, or 20.

Most often, the period is 10 years because 10 years is approximately the average life expectancy of a male who retires at age 65. Obviously, the annuitant could outlive the minimum number of years specified in the contract, in which event the income payments continue until he or she dies.

Under a life annuity with period certain, income installments must be paid for the number of years guaranteed in the contract. Therefore, if the annuitant dies after payments have started, but before the guaranteed number of years (the "certain installments") have elapsed, the annuitant's beneficiary receives income payments until the remainder of the guaranteed (certain) period has elapsed. Thus, if Archie, the annuitant, retires at age 65 and selects life with 10 years certain and dies at age 70, his survivor will continue to receive the monthly annuity payments for the balance of the period certain, or 5 more years.

Joint Life and Survivorship and Joint Life Annuities

With a *joint life and survivorship* (or *last survivor*) annuity, there are more than one (usually two) annuitants, and both receive payments until one of them dies. A stated monthly amount is paid to the annuitant and upon the annuitant's death, the same or a lesser amount is paid for the lifetime of the survivor. The joint-survivor option is usually classified as a joint and 100% survivor, joint and two-thirds survivor, or joint and 50% survivor option.

For example, if the annuitant was receiving $1,000 monthly under a joint and 50% survivor option, the survivor would receive $500 (50% of $1,000) monthly upon the death of the annuitant.

The joint-survivor annuity option should be distinguished from a *joint life annuity*, which covers two or more annuitants and provides monthly income to each annuitant until one of them dies. Following the first annuitant's death, all income benefits cease. The joint life annuity can be viewed as a special case of the straight life annuity, with payments ending at the first death among the joint life annuitants.

Temporary Annuity Certain

As you know, under a life annuity with period certain, if the annuitant lives longer than the certain period stated in the contract, income payments continue for the lifetime of the annuitant. This is not the case with a *temporary annuity certain*, however. If the insured outlives the period of payments stipulated in the temporary annuity certain contract, payments stop at the end of the period.

Under a temporary annuity certain, the company guarantees that payments will be made for a specified number of years—often 10, 15, or 20 years. Because this income is guaranteed, if the annuitant dies before receiving payments for the specified number of years, the annuitant's beneficiary receives the payments for the remaining number of years.

Two-Tiered Annuities

A *two-tiered annuity* is one that has different values available for distribution at maturity depending on whether the value is taken in a lump sum before annuitization or left with the issuer for periodic payments.

These annuities offer relatively high rates, but only if the owner holds the contract for a certain number of years and then annuitizes it. If the annuity is surrendered at any point, interest credited to the contract is recalculated from the contract's inception using a lower tier of rates.

Although the higher tier of rates is designed to reward annuitization and to make the product more attractive than competing annuities, the lower tier of rates generally makes the contract very unattractive compared to other alternatives. This interest penalty applies under some contracts even if the annuity is surrendered due to the death of the owner.

A few states do not permit sales of two-tiered annuities because of the potential for misunderstanding on the part of consumers or lack of disclosure on the part of agents regarding the conditions that must be met in order for the owner to earn the higher tier of rates. Agents who sell two-tiered annuities must make sure that clients know how the product works and are prepared to commit themselves and their beneficiaries to the annuity for a lifetime.

Tax-Sheltered Annuities

To encourage public school systems and tax-exempt charitable, educational, and religious organizations to set aside funds for their employees' retirements, *tax-sheltered annuity plans (TSAs)* may be set up and the contributions excluded from the current taxable income of the employees. The plan must be established by the employer and contributions must be used to purchase annuity contracts or mutual fund shares.

Payments received from TSAs at retirement are generally fully taxable to the recipient as ordinary income. However, payments may be spread over a long period of time, and taxable income at retirement is usually lower, perhaps making the tax bracket lower, too.

Retirement Income Annuities

A *retirement income annuity* is an ordinary deferred annuity, but with an additional feature—a decreasing term life insurance rider that provides term life insurance with a face amount that decreases each year the policy is in force. The effect is that if the annuitant reaches retirement age—for example, 65—the decreasing term insurance death benefit expires and annuity payments begin providing retirement income. If, however, the annuitant dies before retirement, the decreasing term insurance death benefit is combined with the value of the annuity and then paid to the annuitant's beneficiary in any settlement option chosen.

Equity-Indexed Annuities

Equity-indexed annuities are generally considered to be fixed annuities because they offer a guaranteed minimum interest rate and a guarantee against loss of principal if held to term (as with other fixed annuities, surrender charges may reduce principal if the policy is surrendered early). However, with an equity-indexed annuity, interest crediting in excess of the minimum guaranteed rate is linked to the upward movement of a designated equity index, such as the Standard and Poor's 500. If the index moves upward, the interest rate is based on some portion of the increase. If the index moves downward, the equity-indexed annuity credits the guaranteed minimum rate.

Suppose Frank has an equity-indexed annuity with a guaranteed minimum interest rate of 6% and is linked to the Standard and Poor's 500 index. If that index should go up, Frank can expect his annuity interest rate to go up. But if that index should go down, the lowest annuity interest rate Frank can expect to receive would be 6%, the guaranteed minimum.

Market-Value Adjusted Annuities

Another fixed annuity product with a market-driven aspect is the *market-value adjusted (MVA) annuity*. Instead of having the annuity's interest rate linked to an index, as with an equity-indexed annuity, an MVA annuity's interest rate remains fixed. The market-value adjustment feature applies only if the contract is surrendered before the contract period expires. These contracts must disclose on the first page that the nonforfeiture values may increase or decrease based on the market-value formula specified in the contract. Otherwise, the annuity functions the same way a fixed annuity does.

If an MVA annuity owner decides to surrender his or her contract early, a surrender charge *and* a market-value adjustment will apply. If interest rates decreased during the contract period, the market-value adjustment will be positive and may add to the surrender value of the contract. However, if interest rates increased over that period, the market-value adjustment will be negative, which would increase the contract's surrender charge.

Suppose Martha owns a 10-year MVA annuity contract but decides to cash in the contract after the sixth year. By cashing it in early, Martha would be automatically subject to a surrender charge, and because interest rates rose by 2% since she purchased the contract, her market-value adjustment would be negative, forcing her to pay an even higher surrender charge.

Depending on whether the MVA annuity is registered, the market-value adjustment may apply only to interest earned under the contract. However, if the MVA annuity is registered, both principal and interest will be susceptible to a market-value adjustment. Because MVA annuities expose consumers to investment risk, they are classified as securities and people who sell them must be registered with the NASD.

Exam Prep Questions

1. Which of the following is a purpose of the annuity?

   ○ A. The creation of a fund at the death of an individual

   ○ B. The replacement of earnings upon the disability of an individual

   ○ C. The distribution of a lifetime income

   ○ D. Discounting of a principal sum back to its present value

2. An annuity might be called the flip side of

   ○ A. Compounding

   ○ B. Life insurance

   ○ C. Retirement planning

   ○ D. Social security

3. Annuities are a mechanism for transferring to an insurance company the risk of

   ○ A. Poor investment returns

   ○ B. Becoming uninsurable

   ○ C. Outliving financial resources

   ○ D. Outliving a spouse or child

4. An annuity that guarantees a minimum rate of return is

   ○ A. An immediate annuity

   ○ B. A deferred annuity

   ○ C. A variable annuity

   ○ D. A fixed annuity

5. Devon purchases an annuity that will pay a monthly income for the remainder of his life and then stop making payments. Devon has purchased

   ○ A. A fixed annuity

   ○ B. A straight life annuity

   ○ C. A variable annuity

   ○ D. Temporary annuity certain

6. Albert has purchased an annuity that will pay him a monthly income for the rest of his life. If Albert dies before the annuity has paid back as much as he put into it, the insurance company has agreed to pay the difference to Albert's daughter. Albert has purchased

   ○ A. A straight life annuity

   ○ B. A life annuity with period certain

   ○ C. A refund life annuity

   ○ D. A temporary annuity

7. Marcus purchases an annuity that offers a guaranteed minimum interest rate and a guarantee against loss of principal if the contract is held to term. However, if the NASDAQ moves upward, Marcus' annuity might end up accruing more than the guaranteed minimum interest rate. Marcus has purchased a(n)

- ○ A. Equity-indexed annuity
- ○ B. Market-value adjusted annuity
- ○ C. Market-value indexed annuity
- ○ D. Equity-adjusted annuity

8. Eric purchased an annuity with favorable rates. However, due to unforeseen circumstances, he needs to surrender the annuity. If the market has gone up, Eric will need to pay a higher surrender charge than if the market has gone down. Eric owns a(n)

- ○ A. Equity-indexed annuity
- ○ B. Market-value adjusted annuity
- ○ C. Market-value indexed annuity
- ○ D. Equity-adjusted annuity

9. Mikaela has an annuity for which she is the annuitant. Which of the following are definitely true based on this information?

- ○ A. Mikaela is the person who is paying into the annuity.
- ○ B. Annuity payments will be based, in part, on Mikaela's life expectancy.
- ○ C. Mikaela is the contract owner for the annuity.
- ○ D. Mikaela will be able to name a beneficiary to receive benefits after she dies.

10. Tracey is paying money into an annuity she hopes will support her retirement years. What period is her contract currently in?

- ○ A. The accumulation period
- ○ B. The nonforfeiture period
- ○ C. The payout period
- ○ D. The annuity period

11. Liz purchases an immediate annuity. What must be true about the annuity contract?

- ○ A. It must be a fixed annuity.
- ○ B. It must be a variable annuity.
- ○ C. It must be a deferred annuity.
- ○ D. It must be a single premium annuity.

12. Which of the following types of annuities are regulated as securities?

- ○ A. Fixed annuities
- ○ B. Flexible annuities
- ○ C. Variable annuities
- ○ D. Structured annuities

Exam Prep Answers

1. **C is correct.** The primary purpose of an annuity is to provide a lifetime income.

2. **B is correct.** Life insurance protects against premature death, and annuities protect against living too long.

3. **C is correct.** The possibility of outliving financial resources is one of the major motivations for buying an annuity that will provide lifetime income.

4. **D is correct.** This is an example of a fixed annuity.

5. **B is correct.** This is an example of a straight life annuity.

6. **C is correct.** This is an example of a refund life annuity.

7. **A is correct.** This is an example of an equity-indexed annuity.

8. **B is correct.** This is an example of a market-value adjusted annuity.

9. **B is correct.** Her benefit payments will be based on her life expectancy.

10. **A is correct.** The period of time during which a person pays into an annuity is known as the accumulation period.

11. **D is correct.** Immediate annuities are purchased with a single premium payment.

12. **C is correct.** Variable annuities have investment elements that are subject to securities regulation.

Group Life Insurance

Terms you need to understand:

✓ Policyowner
✓ Master policy
✓ Certificate of insurance

Concepts you need to master:

✓ Noncontributory plan
✓ Contributory plan
✓ Dependent coverage
✓ Conversion option

Social and economic changes due to industrialization of our society, the growth of large cities, and the growth of the union movement in the United States, have contributed to the development of group insurance. The influence and political strength of unionized workers have compelled employers to offer group insurance as an employee benefit. Group insurance is usually written as 1-year term insurance.

Legal Requirements

In keeping with the NAIC Model Group Life Insurance Bill, the legal requirements of group insurance are uniform throughout the majority of states and include the following six basic characteristics:

➤ All states define a "true" group as having at least 10 people covered under one master contract. Some states make allowance for even smaller groups.

➤ Coverage is generally available without individual medical examinations.

➤ The policy is issued to the employer, trust, union, or other association. Certificates of insurance are issued to the individual insured.

➤ The insurance cannot be obtained to benefit the employer, trust, union, or other association. It must be for the benefit of the covered employees or members and their dependents.

➤ Premiums are based on the experience of the group as a whole. Premium may be paid entirely by the policyowner, or it may be paid jointly by the policyowner and the insureds. The employer or association is always required to pay some portion of the premium. Insureds are, by law, not permitted to contribute 100% of the premium payments.

➤ Individuals covered under the plan are classified in such a way (usually by salary, position, or time on the job) that they do not choose the benefit levels.

If the premium is paid entirely by the policyowner (employer or association), it is a noncontributory plan and all eligible employees or members must be covered. If the premium is paid by both the policyowner and the insureds the plan is a contributory plan and at least 75% of all eligible employees or members must be covered.

Standard Provisions

Group insurance policies have special provisions unique to group insurance. Some of these provisions are the same as those found in policies of individual insurance. Most states have enacted or adopted the standard provisions found in the NAIC Model Group Life Insurance Bill. Group policies must contain provisions relating to the following:

➤ Grace period (usually 31 days)

➤ Incontestability (usually 1 or 2 years after the policy becomes effective; usually 2 years from the insured's effective date of coverage)

➤ Entire contract (the application must be attached to and made part of the contract)

➤ Representations (statements regarding the individual's health are representations, not warranties)

➤ Evidence of insurability (individual insurability must be proven if the employee or member joins the plan after the enrollment period)

➤ Misstatement of age (*premium is adjusted* to the correct age; under individual insurance *benefits are adjusted*)

➤ Facility of payment (allows payment of policy proceeds to a close relative or friend if no beneficiary is named, or living)

➤ Conversion (the right to convert to an individual policy when the insured's coverage is terminated because of termination of employment or the elimination of a class of insureds)

➤ Termination of master policy (the right to convert to an individual policy because the master policy has been terminated)

➤ Individual certificates (issued as evidence of coverage under a master policy)

In addition to the rights of conversion listed, an insured who dies after coverage has terminated but before the end of the 31-day conversion period will receive the group policy benefit.

Certificates of Insurance

In group insurance, the policy is evidence of a contract between the insurer and the employer or association (the policyowner). The policy is purchased for the benefit of the individuals who are covered under the policy, but is issued to the policyowner (the employer or sponsor). When an employee becomes covered by a group life plan, the employer, as the policyowner, retains the *master policy* itself. As proof of protection, the employee receives a form that certifies the coverage, the benefits under the plan, and the beneficiary's name.

Because it certifies or states all these things, we call this paper a *certificate of insurance*. The certificate shows two facts that are extremely important to the insured: the amount of the life insurance protection and the name of the beneficiary.

In addition, the certificate provides enough information so that insureds are aware of the benefits available to them and their rights and obligations.

The face page of the certificate has information on the coverage effective date, dependent coverage, and life insurance benefit amounts. The certificate covers such information as benefit amounts, benefit descriptions, age limits, notice of claim, proof of loss, and the insured's right to convert to individual coverage in the event of policy termination or employment termination.

Policy Forms

There are five main types of group life insurance being marketed to eligible groups: group term life, group permanent life, group creditor life, group paid-up life, and group survivor income benefit insurance. Group insurance is also written to include the dependents of the group members.

One disadvantage of group life insurance is that it is usually only temporary coverage, and an individual member of the group may lose that coverage when he or she leaves the group.

To lessen this disadvantage, group term policies must include provisions to provide for conversion to individual coverage. They may also include continuation of insurance provisions and waiver of premium provisions. Some employers continue group term insurance at reduced amounts for retired workers.

Dependent Coverage

In most cases, it's possible to include the dependents of employees who are insured under a group life plan. Dependents may be any of the following:

➤ The insured's spouse

➤ The insured's children

➤ The insured's dependent parents

➤ Any person for whom dependency can be proven

The insured's children can be stepchildren, foster children, or adopted children.

Dependent children must be under a specified age, usually age 19, or to age 21 if attending school full time. The law further requires that any other person dependent on the insured is eligible for coverage. Dependency is proven by the relationship to the insured, residency in the home, or the person being listed on the insured's income tax return as a dependent. A child may be a dependent beyond the ages of 19 or 21 if that child is permanently mentally or physically disabled prior to the specified age. Dependent coverage is not provided under credit life insurance.

Group Conversion Option

By law in most states, any employee covered by a group life insurance plan must be allowed to convert to an individual permanent life policy upon termination of employment. If an employee leaves the group, which normally happens when terminating employment, most states have laws that permit the departing employee to convert the coverage to an individual permanent life policy without evidence of insurability.

To summarize, here are the characteristics of conversion from group to permanent life insurance:

➤ No proof of insurability is required.

➤ Conversion must be to a whole life policy.

➤ Conversion must be applied for within 1 month of termination.

➤ Premiums for the new policy will be based upon the insured's attained age.

This conversion privilege may also be used if, for any reason, an employer discontinues group coverage. The same rules apply, except that application must be made within 1 month of the policy's cancellation rather than 1 month following the employee's termination.

The conversion period is usually 30 or 31 days, and coverage is automatically in force during that period. Coverage is often limited to $5,000 or $10,000 or the amount of coverage under the group policy, whichever is less.

FEGLI and SGLI

Federal Employees' Group Life Insurance (FEGLI), provides group life insurance automatically for federal employees unless they choose not to be included in the plan. Life insurance in the amount of 1 year's salary is customarily provided. Another 1 year's salary may be added but is contributory (the employee must pay that portion of the premium).

Servicemen's Group Life Insurance (SGLI), is automatically provided for members of the armed forces. The life insurance is provided on a group term life basis as soon as a member enters active duty. The maximum limit is now $200,000, with automatic full-time coverage also applicable to qualified reservists. Premiums are deducted from the service member's paycheck.

Both FEGLI and SGLI policies are underwritten by private insurers in very large group life insurance contracts.

Exam Prep Questions

1. According to the NAIC Model Group Life Insurance bill, a true group has at least
   - ○ A. 2 people
   - ○ B. 5 people
   - ○ C. 10 people
   - ○ D. 25 people

2. A contributory life insurance plan must cover
   - ○ A. At least 50% of the eligible employees
   - ○ B. At least 75% of the eligible employees
   - ○ C. At least 85% of the eligible employees
   - ○ D. All of the eligible employees

3. Doris dies 15 days after her group coverage is terminated and before she has the chance to convert her policy to permanent coverage. Doris's beneficiary will receive
   - ○ A. The full benefit under the group policy
   - ○ B. The full death benefit under an individual policy
   - ○ C. The death benefit minus unpaid premium under the group policy
   - ○ D. The death benefit minus unpaid premium under the individual policy

4. Which of the following would *not* qualify as a dependent for group insurance coverage?
   - ○ A. The insured's spouse
   - ○ B. The insured's parents, who live on their own and receive a small amount of financial support from the insured
   - ○ C. The insured's best friend, who lives with the insured and is listed as a dependent on the insured's tax return
   - ○ D. The insured's disabled 22-year-old daughter

5. Which of the following is true about conversion from group life insurance?
   - ○ A. Coverage must be converted to a term policy.
   - ○ B. Conversion must be applied for within 6 months of termination.
   - ○ C. Proof of insurability will be required.
   - ○ D. Premiums for the new policy will be based on the insured's attained age.

Exam Prep Answers

1. **C is correct.** A minimum of 10 people is usually the requirement.

2. **B is correct.** According to regulations, when employees contribute any part of the premium, at least 75% of the eligible employees must be covered.

3. **A is correct.** When a person dies during the conversion period, the full benefit is paid under the group policy.

4. **B is correct.** The parents would probably not qualify as dependents.

5. **D is correct.** Premiums for a converted policy are based on an insured's attained age at the time of conversion.

Social Security and Tax Considerations

Terms you need to understand:

✓ Social security
✓ Fully insured
✓ Currently insured
✓ Disability insured
✓ Primary insurance amount
✓ Total disability
✓ Dual benefit liability
✓ Quarter of coverage

Concepts you need to master:

✓ Covered workers
✓ Insured status
✓ Normal retirement age
✓ Retirement benefits
✓ Survivor benefits
✓ Disability benefits
✓ Maximum family benefit
✓ Retirement earnings limit

Social Security

Since the time of the Industrial Revolution most individuals and families have not been self-sufficient economic entities. Particularly since the Great Depression, society has wrestled with the problem of numbers of individuals being unable to care for themselves due to unemployment, disability or death of the family wage earner. The social security system was a political response to this issue.

Covered Workers

Most U.S. workers participate in social security, a benefit program run by the federal government. To some extent, social security competes with private insurance because it provides a basic level of benefits for death, disability, and retirement.

An automatic cost of living escalator is built into the program, which increases benefits each January to match the increase in inflation.

The Social Security Act covers a wide assortment of social insurance and public assistance (welfare) programs. What we refer to as social security is more properly called *Old Age Survivors and Disability Insurance (OASDI)*.

Types of Benefits

Generally speaking, OASDI provides the following categories of benefits:

➤ Monthly retirement benefits for retired workers at least 62 years old

➤ Monthly benefits for spouses of retired workers

➤ Monthly survivor benefits for the spouse and certain other survivors of deceased workers

➤ Monthly disability benefits for disabled workers and their dependents

➤ A modest lump-sum death benefit payable at a worker's death

Eligibility for Social Security

Generally, most workers must be covered under social security. This includes common law employers and employees, most self-employed persons, Armed Forces personnel, and employees of nonprofit organizations.

The main excluded worker groups are railroad workers and federal employees hired before 1984. Federal employees hired after 1984 are covered. Railroad workers contribute to their own railroad retirement system.

Employees of state and local governments are not covered unless the government entity has entered into an agreement with the Social Security Administration or does not have a retirement program. Generally, most government workers are covered.

Finally, there are certain types of family employment situations in which a family member may not be covered under social security. These include employment of a minor child (under age 18) by his or her parent, employment of a parent as a domestic in the home of the parent's child, and employment of a parent to do work not in the course of a son's or daughter's business.

Insured Status

A covered worker becomes qualified for social security benefits by attaining either fully insured, currently insured, or disability insured status. Insured status depends on how many quarters of coverage a worker has earned. The term quarters of coverage comes from the time when wages were reported to the government each quarter. Now, most employers report wages on an annual basis, but the terminology has stayed the same.

The amount of money needed to earn a quarter of coverage increases automatically each year with increases in the national average wage index. In 2002, for example, a worker earned one quarter of coverage for every $870 in earnings.

A worker may not earn credit for more than four quarters of coverage during any given year. So, for example, if Bill earned $3,500 in 2002 and Bob earned $35,000 in 2002, both of them would be credited with four quarters of coverage.

There is no requirement to work in different calendar quarters. For example, any worker who earned more than $3,480 during January 2002, would have earned four quarters of coverage ($870 × 4) for the year even if no work was performed for the remainder of the year.

Fully Insured

To achieve *fully insured* status, a worker must accumulate at least one quarter of coverage for each year after the person's 21st birthday and have a *minimum* of at least six quarters of coverage. This *birthday rule* enables young workers to achieve fully insured status within a relatively short time. The *maximum* requirement for fully insured status is 40 quarters of coverage, which gives the worker *permanent* status. Under the *40-quarter rule*, when a worker accumulates credit for 40 quarters of coverage, that person is fully insured for life and the status cannot be lost even if the person drops out of the work force.

Currently Insured

A worker who is not fully insured will still be *currently insured* if he or she has earned six credits within the last 13 calendar quarters. For example, a 35-year-old worker who did not have the 13 credits required to be fully insured would be currently insured as long as he or she had earned at least six credits within the last 3 years and 3 months.

Disability Insured

A special insured status, *disability insured*, is required if a worker is eligible for disability benefits under social security. This status requires that the worker be fully insured and have earned at least 20 quarters of coverage in the 40 calendar quarter periods ending with the calendar quarter in which the disability begins. This requirement is modified slightly if a covered worker is disabled prior to age 31.

The individual's insured status determines eligibility for social security benefits. A fully insured person and eligible dependents are entitled to all social security benefits. A worker who is only currently insured has limited benefits available. If a worker is only currently insured at death, social security benefits would be payable only to a dependent child in addition to the lump-sum death benefit of $255.

Primary Insurance Amount

Social security benefits are expressed as a percentage of the *primary insurance amount (PIA)*. The PIA for a worker is based on his or her average level of earnings and is updated and published annually in tables by the federal government. Most types of social security benefits are some percent of the PIA as set for the year for the worker's earnings level.

Normal Retirement Age

To receive full social security retirement benefits, a person must wait until the normal retirement age to begin receiving such benefits. If benefits are taken before this age, the monthly benefit amount is reduced.

The social security normal retirement age is 65 for workers born in 1937 or before; it increases gradually for workers born after that year until it reaches 67 for all workers born in 1960 and after.

Dual Benefit Eligibility

Often a person is eligible to receive more than one social security benefit. For example, a married individual who has reached age 65 may be eligible to receive a retirement benefit based on his or her own earnings and also a spousal benefit based on his or her spouse's earnings. In these cases, the person is entitled to receive only the larger of the two benefit amounts instead of both amounts.

Retirement Benefits

A worker receives 100% of his or her PIA as a retirement benefit if benefits are not taken until the normal retirement age. For each month earlier that the retirement benefit is taken, the monthly amount is reduced. At age 62—currently the earliest age at which retirement benefits may begin—the benefit is 80% of the PIA.

A worker's spouse is also eligible for a retirement benefit based on the worker's earnings. At age 65, this benefit is 50% of the PIA. The spouse can take a reduced benefit as early as age 62.

A retired worker's unmarried child is eligible for a benefit of 50% of the PIA if under 18, if under 19 and in high school, or at any age if disabled before 22.

A retired worker's spouse is eligible for a benefit of 50% of PIA at any age if caring for an unmarried, dependent child of the worker who is under 16 or was disabled before 22.

Survivor Benefits

When a worker dies, several members of his or her family may be eligible for benefits. The surviving spouse is eligible for a benefit at any age if caring for an unmarried child under 16 or a child who was disabled before age 22. This benefit is 75% of the deceased worker's PIA. When the youngest child reaches age 16, this benefit terminates.

However, the surviving spouse will be eligible for a benefit again when he or she reaches age 60. At this point, the benefit is 71.5% of the deceased worker's PIA. The spouse could delay the benefit until he or she reaches age 65 and receive 100% of the PIA. If the spouse is disabled, he or she can begin to receive the benefit as early as age 50.

The period during which the surviving spouse receives no social security benefits is sometimes referred to as the *blackout period*.

An unmarried child of a deceased worker is eligible for a benefit of 75% of the PIA if under 18, if under 19 and in high school, or at any age if disabled before 22.

A dependent parent age 62 or over who received at least half of his or her support from the deceased worker is eligible for a benefit of 82.5% of the PIA.

If both parents receive benefits, each gets 75% of the PIA.

A lump-sum death benefit of $255 is paid to the deceased worker's spouse or a dependent child.

Disability Benefits

Social security defines *total disability* as the inability to engage in any substantial gainful activity due to physical or mental disability, and the disability must be expected to last for at least 12 months or end in death. Substantial work activity means significant mental and/or physical duties for which a person is compensated.

This definition does not refer to the individual's occupation prior to disability or to the level of pre-disability compensation. A surgeon earning $200,000 annually may be disabled to the degree that he or she could no longer perform surgery. However, if this person could perform other meaningful work duties (bank employee, school teacher, salesperson, and so forth), he or she would probably not be eligible for disability benefits because they could not meet the social security definition of total disability.

The amount of the disability benefit is equal to the worker's PIA, which in essence is the same as the individual's monthly retirement benefit. Disability benefits are payable only for total disabilities. Disability benefits begin with the sixth month of disability. No benefit is paid for a partial disability. If the worker satisfies these conditions, there is still a 5-month waiting period before benefits begin.

The worker is entitled to a disability benefit of 100% of his or her PIA. If the worker's spouse is caring for an unmarried child under 16 or a disabled child under 22, he or she gets a benefit of 50% of PIA. Finally, each unmarried child is entitled to a benefit of 50% of PIA if under 18, if under 19 and still in high school, or if disabled before 22.

Maximum Family Benefit

When several members of a worker's family are entitled to receive benefits, the family may run up against an overall limitation on benefit payments called the *maximum family benefit*. Like the PIA, a maximum family benefit is established for each level of average earnings and is updated annually.

Earnings Limit

When a social security beneficiary reaches normal retirement age, there is no restriction on the amount he or she may earn from employment (or self-employment) without losing social security benefits. But beneficiaries under normal retirement age may earn only up to a certain amount without a reduction in benefits.

One earnings limit applies to the years prior to the year that beneficiaries reach their normal retirement age, and a higher limit applies for the year an individual reaches normal retirement age. The dollar amounts are indexed to inflation and change annually. For example, beneficiaries who had not reached normal retirement age in 2004 had their benefit reduced by $1 for every $1 earned above $11,640. Individuals who reached normal retirement age in 2004 had their benefits reduced by $1 for every $2 earned above $31,080 until the month that they actually reached their normal retirement age. After normal retirement age, no limits apply.

Social Security Payroll Taxes

Social security is a pay-as-you-go program. That is, the social security taxes collected from workers are not set aside in an account for each worker, but are used to pay benefits to current beneficiaries of the program. Put another way, when someone begins receiving benefits, he or she is not drawing on a fund of some specific amount that consists of his or her previous tax deposits plus earnings. Those benefits are financed by the taxes currently collected from covered workers.

 Social security benefits are financed by a payroll tax on employers, employees, and the self-employed. There is no social security tax on investment income (for example, interest, dividends) or any kind of income other than earnings from employment or self-employment.

The rate of tax is a flat amount set by Congress and adjusted upward from time to time. The tax rate for employers and employees is currently set at 6.2% (not counting the additional tax for Medicare). The self-employment tax rate is 12.4%—twice the employee rate, because self-employed individuals pay both the employee and the employer portion of the tax. The tax rate is multiplied by the relevant earnings figure to compute the social security tax.

If Clarice has $20,000 of earnings from her employer this year, she and her employer combined must pay in social security taxes on this income a total of $2,480 (.062 × 20,000 + .062 × 20,000).

Not all of a worker's earnings are necessarily subject to the social security tax. The law puts a cap on the maximum amount that is taxed each year; for 2004, the cap was $87,900. This is called the *maximum taxable wage base*. It is the same for employers, employees, and the self-employed. This wage base is indexed to inflation so that it rises each January.

Social security taxes may not be deducted in computing the federal income tax.

There is an additional payroll tax to help finance Medicare Part A (hospital insurance). The rate is 1.45% for both employers and employees and 2.9% for the self-employed. There is no cap on the amount of earned income subject to this Medicare tax.

Taxation of Social Security Benefits

A portion (up to 85%) of the social security benefit is includable in the worker's adjusted gross income for tax purposes. Various formulas apply depending on the level of adjusted gross income, whether the taxpayer is married or single, and if married, whether filing separate or joint returns.

Income Tax Treatment of Life Insurance

Various tax laws apply to life insurance premiums, proceeds, and benefit payment options.

Individual Life Insurance

Life insurance policies have traditionally been given favorable tax treatment. The two major tax advantages of life insurance are

➤ The annual earnings on the cash values generally accumulate on a tax-free basis (until they are distributed).

➤ The proceeds payable at the insured's death are generally income tax–free to the beneficiary.

Because of these tax advantages and the competitive returns life insurance policies have paid in recent years, they have sometimes been purchased as accumulation vehicles in addition to their traditional uses.

In order to deter policyowners from quickly accumulating large sums of money in their life insurance contracts and thus using them primarily as an investment vehicle, Congress created a definition of life insurance that all life insurance policies must meet in order to qualify for these tax advantages. To qualify, a policy must meet one of the two following tests:

➤ *Cash value accumulation test*—The cash surrender value of the policy may never exceed the net single premium that would be required to fund future benefits. *Example:* A 35-year-old male owns a $100,000 policy with a cash value of $9,000. In order to meet the cash value accumulation test, the net single premium for the same size policy at his age must be $9,000 or more.

➤ *Guideline premium and corridor test*—The corridor test relates to the amount of pure insurance in the contract, the relationship between the cash value and the death benefit at any point in time. The cash value of a life insurance policy must not account for more than a certain percentage of the total death benefit. *Example:* At age 40 or younger, the total death benefit cannot be less than 250% of the cash value. If a policy had $100,000 of cash value at the insured's age 40, it would have to provide a total death benefit of $250,000. The additional $150,000 of coverage required to produce that total death benefit is the insurance corridor. After age 40, the cash value ratio begins to scale down. At age 95, the cash value may equal the total death benefit.

The guideline premium test is met if the total premiums paid do not exceed the greater of the guideline single premium or the total of the guideline level premiums. The *guideline single premium* is the total premium payable at one time to fund the future benefits of the contract. The *guideline level premium* is the level annual amount payable over a period extending to at least the insured's 95th birthday to fund the future benefits of the contract.

If a contract fails to meet either the cash value or the guideline premium test, it will not qualify as life insurance. This may have the following serious tax consequences for the contract owner:

➤ The inside build-up of earnings in the policy may be taxable each year as income to the policyowner, to the extent these earnings, added to dividends received and the pure cost of insurance, exceed premiums paid.

➤ Only the pure insurance part of the death benefit proceeds (death benefit less the cash value) will be received income tax–free by the beneficiary.

The taxation rules explained here pertain to life insurance contracts that conform to the definition of life insurance in Section 7702 of the Internal Revenue Code.

Modified Endowment Contract

The tax consequences of a policy becoming a *modified endowment contract (MEC)* are serious, although not as serious as those listed earlier for a policy failing to meet the definition of life insurance. The penalties assessed against MECs affect primarily money taken out of the policy on the following basis:

➤ Money distributed from a MEC is considered to come first from earnings (excess of cash value over cost basis) and is taxed as ordinary income.

➤ If the policyowner is younger than 59 1/2 and is not disabled, these taxable distributions are considered to be premature and are subject to a 10% penalty tax in addition to the regular income tax.

Premiums

As a general rule, life insurance or annuity premiums paid by individuals are not deductible for federal income tax purposes.

Policy Proceeds

If the beneficiary of a life insurance policy receives the death proceeds in a lump sum, the entire amount of the payment is generally received income tax–free. It makes no difference whether the death benefit is the face amount alone or whether it includes additional benefits, such as double indemnity for accidental death.

Recall that death benefits, however, may be paid out in ways other than a lump sum. Regardless of what option is chosen, only a portion of each individual payment is taxable to the beneficiary as income. That portion of each payment that is principal, derived from the lump-sum death benefit, is received income tax–free.

In other words, the amount of the actual death benefit (equal to what would have been paid as a lump sum) is always paid to the beneficiary on an income tax–free basis. However, if the proceeds are held by the insurance company and paid out to the beneficiary in the form of an income stream, the proceeds will earn additional income that will form a part of each payment to the beneficiary. It is only this income element that is subject to income tax.

Accelerated Benefits

Accelerated, or *living*, benefits paid by a life insurance policy fall into the same category as a policy's death benefits. That is to say, accelerated benefits are received income tax–free so long as they are qualified. *Qualified* means the insured has been certified by a physician as having an illness or physical condition that can reasonably be expected to result in death 24 months or less after the date of the certification. Other stipulations may be applied, but the end result is that those who require access to these benefits may receive the money without having to pay income taxes on it.

Dividends and Surrender Values

Dividends paid to participating policyowners are generally not taxable as income. They are considered a return of premium. However, any interest earned on dividends is taxable. So the accumulation at interest dividend option explained earlier would incur income tax liability for the interest earned on the accumulated dividends.

Any dividend of a MEC that the insurer keeps to pay principal or interest on a policy loan is, just like the loan itself, considered to be money taken from the policy.

Generally speaking, when any proceeds are received from a surrendered or matured life insurance policy, the part of the proceeds, if any, that exceeds the cost of the policy is subject to ordinary federal income tax in the year received. *Cost* is equal to the total premiums paid (not including any costs for qualified additional benefits), less the sum of any amounts previously received under the contract that were not includable in gross income.

Suppose Olaf surrenders his whole life policy, and it has a cash value of $25,000. During the time he held the policy, Olaf paid $22,000 in premiums. As a result, $3,000 ($25,000 – $22,000) of the cash surrender value will be subject to federal income tax.

Annuity Payments

Like income payments made as a result of a settlement option in a life insurance policy, income payments made from an annuity are only partly subject to federal income taxation. Federal tax law holds that a fixed part of each annuity income payment is designated as a *return of capital*, and as such is nontaxable. The remainder of each annuity income payment is considered to be income and is taxable.

Determining how much of each payment is a return of capital and how much is income is outside the scope of this course. However, after it is determined that the capital has been fully recovered during the course of annuity payments, all of the annuity payment becomes taxable.

Cash Value Accumulation

As we've pointed out throughout this course, one of the most significant advantages of life insurance products is their capability of accumulating cash on a tax-deferred basis. Permanent life products, including variable and universal life products, may accumulate cash values that are not taxed unless and until withdrawn. The same is true of annuities, qualified retirement plans, and IRAs. All of a policyholder's current earnings are working for him or her, unreduced by a current tax liability.

Note, however, that annuities owned by corporations, for whatever purpose, do not accumulate cash on a tax-deferred basis. On the other hand, bank accounts, stocks, bonds, and other kinds of noninsurance investments pay interest or dividends that are taxed currently.

Group Life Insurance Proceeds

Proceeds from a group life policy, like those from an individual life policy, are not subject to federal income tax when received by the beneficiary as a lump-sum payment.

Premiums for group life insurance policies, whether paid by the employer entirely or shared by employer and employee, are not deductible by the employee. But a company can deduct such premium payments as a business expense.

When all or part of the premiums for group life insurance are paid by the employer, these contributions are generally not considered as income to the employees covered by the group life policy. However, this rule applies only to the first $50,000 of employer-provided coverage. The cost of coverage in excess of $50,000 will be taxed to the employee.

Doctrine of Economic Benefit

The *doctrine of economic benefit rule* appears from time to time with respect to life insurance products, especially those paid for by employers but which are designed to benefit employees. Briefly, this doctrine holds that if an employee receives property or benefit in lieu of income, and that property or benefit would have been taxable income were it received in cash, an economic benefit has been received and will be taxed accordingly.

Nonqualified plans, such as deferred compensation, that are funded with life insurance and aimed at certain key and/or highly compensated employees, may be affected by this rule. Qualified plans containing insurance on the life of the plan participant may also be affected. Care must be taken if those employees are to escape current taxation on such plans.

Federal Estate Tax

Federal estate taxes are imposed on estates that exceed certain amounts. Life insurance proceeds are includable in a deceased insured's gross estate if

➤ The proceeds are payable to the estate, either directly or indirectly.

➤ The deceased possessed any *incidents of ownership* in the policy at death (such as the rights to change the beneficiary, to assign the policy, or to borrow against the policy).

➤ The policy was assigned by the insured, other than for full and adequate consideration, within 3 years of death.

Charitable Uses of Life Insurance

There are two basic ways to make charitable gifts of life insurance, the first of which is to make an outright gift of a policy on the life of the donor. The value of the policy at the time of the gift is generally deductible, with certain restrictions. The charity (the donee) is the beneficiary. The donor may give the charity enough cash each year to pay the premium on the policy; if so, the cash gifts are generally deductible.

When this method of giving is used, it is important that the donee, the charity, be given all the rights of ownership. If the donor retains any control over the policy, the tax advantages (deductions) are lost.

In the second common method of making charitable gifts of life insurance, the donor can retain ownership of the policy, make the charity the beneficiary, and continue to pay the premiums. In this case, the premium payments are not tax-deductible. The amount of the proceeds will be included in the donor's estate, but will wash out as a charitable deduction. One advantage of this method is that the donor retains the right to change beneficiaries should this become necessary or desirable.

Other Gifts of Life Insurance

Gifts other than charitable gifts—including gifts of life insurance—are generally subject to *gift tax*. The giver of the gift pays this tax. Gift taxes prevent wealthy people from moving large amounts of assets to others in lower tax brackets—such as children or grandchildren—to avoid paying income taxes. However, the annual gift tax exclusion allows a certain amount of gifting to be done without incurring gift tax. For 2004, the annual gift tax exclusion is $11,000 per donee. That is, an individual can give any number of other individuals up to $11,000 each before gift tax is payable. An individual and his or her spouse may make joint gifts of up to $22,000 per donee without incurring gift tax. The annual gift tax exclusion may increase in later years due to inflation.

The most common method of making a gift of life insurance is to give a policy to the donee. If this gift involves the transfer of all the incidents of ownership from the donor to the donee, the gift will probably be considered a gift of a *present interest* and therefore qualify for the annual gift tax exclusion. Therefore, if the replacement value of the policy, which is usually about equal to the cash value, is $11,000 or less, ($22,000 or less for a joint gift by a donor and spouse), the entire policy can be given away without incurring gift tax.

The second most common method of making a gift of life insurance is to make a gift of the premiums on the insurance. An example of such a gift is when a new son-in-law takes out a life insurance policy and the father-in-law, the donor, gives the son-in-law the money to pay the premium. The policy belongs to the son-in-law, who is the donee of the amount of the premiums. As long as the amount of premium paid by the donor, plus all other gifts made during the same year to the same donee, is equal to or less than the annual gift tax exclusion, the donor should not incur any gift tax.

A donor (or donors) may continue to make gifts of insurance premiums up to the amount of the annual gift tax exclusion each year, as long as desired. The recipient of the gift does not have to pay income tax on the gift.

Transfer for Value Rules

Life insurance proceeds may not be exempt from income taxes if the benefit payment results from a *transfer for value*. If the benefits are transferred under a beneficiary designation to a person in exchange for valuable consideration (whether it be money, an exchange of policies, or a promise to perform services), the proceeds would be taxable as income. This section of the tax laws is designed to prevent a tax exemption for benefits that are purchased from another party, because the intent of the transaction would be to exchange something of value for tax-free income.

Taxation under the transfer of value rules *does not apply* to an assignment of benefits as collateral security, because a lender has every right to secure the interest in the unpaid balance of a loan. Nor does it apply to transfers between a policyholder and an insured, transfers to a partner of an insured, transfers to a corporation in which the insured is an officer or stockholder, or transfers of interest made as a gift (where no exchange of value occurs).

Section 1035 Policy Exchanges

Any gain on the exchange of property—such as insurance, endowment, or annuity policies—is generally taxable. However, the tax law recognizes that policyowners should be able to replace certain existing policies with new ones without incurring tax. Under Section 1035 of the Internal Revenue Code, no gain or loss is recognized on the exchange of the following:

➤ A life insurance contract for another life insurance contract or for an endowment or annuity contract

➤ An endowment contract for another endowment contract (provided the endowment contract that is received provides for regular payments beginning at a date not later than the date payments would have begun under the contract exchanged) or for an annuity contract

➤ An annuity contract for another annuity contract

Exchanges not coming within these three categories are taxable exchanges.

Business Insurance

The premiums paid by companies for life insurance policies used for business purposes are generally not deductible as business expenses, with the exception of group insurance. By the same token, the proceeds from life policies purchased for business purposes are received by the company income tax–free. However, if the business is subject to the *alternative minimum tax (AMT)*, that tax may apply to the death proceeds.

Exam Prep Questions

1. Which of the following people would not be eligible for benefits under social security?

   ○ A. Steve, 45, who loses his currently insured wife while still raising two young children.

   ○ B. Tina, 6, whose fully insured parent is killed in an auto accident.

   ○ C. Clarice, 60, whose fully insured son supported her.

   ○ D. Alice, 50, who is fully insured when she is disabled by cancer that is expected to kill her before she can return to work.

2. Disability benefits under social security require at least a

   ○ A. 3-month waiting period

   ○ B. 5-month waiting period

   ○ C. 7-month waiting period

   ○ D. 12-month waiting period

3. Which of the following policies would not meet Congress' definition of life insurance?

   ○ A. Tom, 35, owns a policy with a $100,000 death benefit and a $150,000 cash value.

   ○ B. Alice, 27, owns a policy with no cash value and a $2,000 single premium.

   ○ C. Calista owns a policy with a net single premium of $4,000 and a cash value of $2,500.

   ○ D. Ken, 96, owns a $250,000 policy with $250,000 cash value.

4. What happens if the contract fails to qualify as life insurance?

   ○ A. The entire death benefit will be taxed.

   ○ B. Only the cost basis part of the death benefit proceeds will be taxed.

   ○ C. The inside build-up earnings may be taxable each year as income to the policyowner if they exceed the cost basis of the policy.

   ○ D. The cost basis of the earnings may be taxable each year as income to the policyowner if it exceeds the inside build-up of the policy.

5. The penalties assessed against MECs affect primarily

   ○ A. The cost basis of the policy

   ○ B. Money put into the policy

   ○ C. Money taken out of the policy

   ○ D. The death benefits of the policy

6. As a general rule, for federal tax purposes,
   - ○ A. Neither life insurance nor annuity premiums are tax-deductible.
   - ○ B. Life insurance premiums are tax-deductible but annuity premiums are not.
   - ○ C. Annuity premiums are tax-deductible but life insurance premiums are not.
   - ○ D. Both life insurance and annuity premiums are tax-deductible.

7. Billy is receiving the proceeds of a life insurance policy as an income stream over a period of several years. What part of the money will be subject to tax?
   - ○ A. None of it, because it is life insurance proceeds.
   - ○ B. All of it, because it is being paid out in an income stream.
   - ○ C. Only the part that represents income earned on the original death benefit.
   - ○ D. Only the part that represents the original death benefit and not on the income earned on the original death benefit.

8. Carol is eligible for a retirement benefit based on her own earnings and also a benefit based on her late husband's earnings. Carol will receive
   - ○ A. Both benefits
   - ○ B. Only the benefit based on her own earnings
   - ○ C. Only the benefit based on her husband's earnings
   - ○ D. Only the larger benefit

9. Social security taxes are often shared between the employer and employee. What do self-employed people pay?
   - ○ A. Just the employee's portion of the tax
   - ○ B. Just the employer's potion of the tax
   - ○ C. Both the employer's portion and the employee's portion of the tax
   - ○ D. Neither the employer's portion nor the employee's portion of the tax

10. At what age can an individual who is fully insured start receiving retirement benefits?
   - ○ A. 60
   - ○ B. 62
   - ○ C. 65
   - ○ D. 67

Exam Prep Answers

1. **C is correct.** The fact that Clarice's son supported her does not entitle her to benefits.

2. **B is correct.** Disability benefits begin with the sixth month of disability. No benefits are paid for the first 5 months of disability.

3. **A is correct.** Under federal rules, if the cash value exceeds the face value the policy does not qualify as life insurance for tax purposes.

4. **C is correct.** The inside earnings may be taxable if they exceed the cost basis of the policy.

5. **C is correct.** Money taken out of the policy is taxed as ordinary income.

6. **A is correct.** For individuals, neither life insurance nor annuity premiums are tax-deductible.

7. **C is correct.** Only the interest earnings on the proceeds will be subject to tax.

8. **D is correct.** When dual benefits apply, only the larger benefit will be paid.

9. **C is correct.** Because there is no employer to match the required tax, a self-employed person pays double the amount paid by salaried employees.

10. **B is correct.** A person may elect to begin receiving social security retirement benefits at age 62, but the amount of the benefits will be lower than if elected at normal retirement age.

Retirement Plans

Terms you need to understand:

✓ Defined benefit plan
✓ Defined contribution plan
✓ Vesting
✓ Group deferred annuity
✓ Individual deferred annuity
✓ Profit-sharing plan
✓ Pension plan
✓ 401(k) plan
✓ Money purchase pension plan
✓ Target benefit pension plan
✓ Individual retirement account
✓ Roth IRA
✓ SIMPLE retirement plan
✓ Simplified employee pension
✓ Keogh plan
✓ Tax-deferred annuity

Concepts you need to master:

✓ Qualified plans
✓ Nonqualified plans
✓ Plan distributions
✓ Premature distribution
✓ Rollover
✓ Fiduciary responsibility

Qualified and Nonqualified Retirement Plans

People use many means to plan for retirement. Recognizing the necessity for working people to provide for their retirements, the government offers some significant tax benefits for certain kinds of retirement plans. These are called *qualified retirement plans*, and this chapter focuses on the plans that apply to businesses and their employees.

In order to be qualified, a retirement plan must meet certain requirements of the Internal Revenue Code with respect to participation, funding, benefits, vesting, and so forth. When qualified, a retirement plan offers significant tax advantages. If a plan qualifies, contributions made on behalf of participants to fund their retirement benefits are

➤ Tax-deductible to the business

➤ Generally not currently taxable to the employee

➤ Allowed to accumulate in the plan on a tax-deferred basis

➤ Taxed at the time of distribution to retirees under special, advantageous rules

Within the qualified category are two kinds of overall plans:

➤ A *defined benefit plan* offers benefits that are determined using a definite formula. Contributions to defined benefit plans must be made in amounts that fund the benefits promised to plan participants.

➤ A *defined contribution plan* focuses attention on the contributions made to the plan as opposed to the benefits the plan will pay out. At retirement, the amount in the plan participant's account is totaled and a distribution is made.

NOTE

Setting up and administering qualified plans is a complex, laborious task best left to those who specialize in such activity. There are numerous rules regarding eligibility, participation, the amount of contribution that can be made or benefit that can be paid. However, a life insurance agent who understands the basic aspects of the various qualified plans and how one or the other might meet the needs of a business client can do very well for himself or herself by selling qualified plans.

Vesting Rules

To be tax-qualified, retirement plans must satisfy the vesting rules included in the Internal Revenue Code. *Vesting* refers to the schedule an employer establishes that spells out the percentage ownership an employee has in the employer's contributions to the plan or the employee's accrued benefit. This percentage generally increases as the employee's length of service increases, until the employee owns 100% of his or her accrued benefit or the amount the employer has contributed to his or her account.

 Note that any employee contributions to a plan, whether mandatory or voluntary, must vest 100% immediately when made. In other words, employee contributions are always nonforfeitable.

The minimum vesting requirement consists of a choice between two acceptable schedules. Under one schedule, benefits must be 100% vested after 3 years of service. Under the other, vesting must begin after 2 years of service at an initial amount of 20% and increase in 20% increments so that the employee is 100% vested after 6 years of service.

Defined Benefits Plans

Defined benefit plans are designed to provide a specific benefit to an employee upon retirement. The amount of the benefit is usually dependent on length of service or highest salary earned or a combination of these. Deferred annuities are commonly used to fund defined benefit plans. These may be issued on a group or individual basis.

Group Deferred Annuity

With a *group deferred annuity*, the employer holds a master contract and certificates of participation are given to the persons covered by the plan. Specified amounts of deferred annuity are purchased each year to provide a specified retirement income to an employee.

Individual Deferred Annuity

Another means of funding a defined benefit plan is to take out *individual deferred annuities* on each plan participant. The premium rate is determined individually, based on attained age and sex. Premiums are level to retirement unless an employee's compensation changes and an increase in retirement benefits is warranted. In such an instance, an additional annuity contract is purchased to fund the increase in the retirement benefit level.

Defined Contribution Plans

Two of the most common defined contribution plans are profit-sharing and pension plans.

Profit-Sharing Plans

A qualified *profit-sharing plan* must provide a definite, predetermined formula for allocating among plan participants the profits contributed to the plan. However the *amount* of annual contributions, if any, is usually left to the discretion of the employer. When the employee retires or leaves under certain other circumstances, the contributions that have been allocated to that employee, plus all earnings on them, are distributed to the employee.

Pension Plans

Pension plan benefits are generally measured by and based on such factors as years of service and compensation received. The determination of the amount of plan contributions or benefits is *not* based on the employer's profits or left to the discretion of the employer.

A *money-purchase pension plan* requires the employer to make a fixed contribution to the plan each year, which is then allocated among the plan participant's accounts. At retirement an employee receives whatever benefit may be purchased with the money in his or her plan account.

A *target benefit pension plan* is a cross between a defined contribution and defined benefit plan. The target benefit plan works much like a money-purchase plan except that a target benefit is specified. The target benefit plan also looks like a defined benefit plan, but it's only a target and may or may not be reached.

401(k) Plans

When a profit-sharing or pension plan has been modified to provide a cash or deferred arrangement (CODA), the resulting plan is called a *401(k) plan* after the section of the Internal Revenue Code that authorizes it.

The term *CODA* refers to two different methods by which an employee can defer a portion of his or her pay into a 401(k) plan. In the classic case, the employee will be offered a cash bonus, all or part of which may be placed in, or deferred into, the plan on a before-tax basis. Alternately, the arrangement can take the form of a salary reduction agreement under which the employee elects to reduce his or her salary and place, or defer, the reduction portion

into the plan, also on a before-tax basis. With either method, plan participants can avoid immediate taxation of the diverted bonus or salary deferral
amount. Consequently, no income taxes are paid on these funds or their
earnings until they are withdrawn.

Individual Retirement Accounts and Annuities—IRAs

The government offers individual retirement accounts and annuities (IRAs)
so that people can plan for their own retirement. With an IRA, the amount
an individual contributes may be deductible, within limitations, from gross
income before taxable income is determined.

The contribution limit will increase in future years. Table 14.1 shows the
limits up to the year 2008.

Table 14.1 IRA Contribution Limits	
Year	Contribution Limit
2004	$3,000
2005	$4,000
2006	$4,000
2007	$4,000
2008	$5,000

In addition, individuals age 50 and over will be able to make catch-up contributions of an additional $500 per year in the years 2004–2005, and an
additional $1,000 per year beginning in 2006.

Whether or not an individual may make a *fully deductible* IRA contribution
depends on the answer to this question: Is the individual, or the individual's
spouse if filing jointly, covered by an employer-maintained retirement plan?

If the answer to this question is "No," the IRA contribution is fully
deductible up to the limit no matter what the adjusted gross income (AGI)
of the individual or couple may be. If a married worker's spouse does not
work, the married worker can contribute up to the limit to another IRA on
behalf of the spouse in addition to his or her own annual IRA contribution
for a total tax-deductible contribution of double the contribution limit per
year.

If the answer to this question is "Yes," the IRA contribution is fully deductible up to the limit (double the limit if also contributing to a spousal IRA) as long as *one* of the following holds true:

➤ The individual has an annual adjusted gross income of *less* than $45,000 (in 2004).

➤ A married couple filing jointly has an annual adjusted gross income of *less* than $65,000 (in 2004).

Married persons not covered by an employer-maintained retirement plan and who file separate returns are considered to be covered if their spouses are covered by such a plan unless they have lived apart from their spouses for the entire year.

These income limitations will increase in future years. In addition, partial deductions are permitted if the limitations are exceeded, but only up to a certain dollar amount. Table 14.2 shows the income limitations up to the year 2007.

Table 14.2 Income Limits For IRA Deductibility				
Year	**Single**		**Married**	**Filing Jointly**
	Full Deduction	**Partial Deduction**	**Full Deduction**	**Partial Deduction**
2004	Below $45,000	Up To $55,000	Below $65,000	Up To $75,000
2005	Below $50,000	Up To $60,000	Below $70,000	Up To $80,000
2006	Below $50,000	Up To $60,000	Below $75,000	Up To $85,000
2007	Below $50,000	Up To $60,000	Below $80,000	Up To $100,000

All earnings that accumulate in an IRA do so on a tax-deferred basis. That is, the interest earned on the contributions placed in an IRA are not taxed until withdrawn. This is also true for IRAs funded with nondeductible contributions.

Popular vehicles used to fund an IRA may include

➤ Mutual funds

➤ CDs or bank, savings and loan, or credit union accounts

➤ Bank trust accounts

➤ Fixed or variable flexible-premium annuities

Roth IRAs

Taxpayers also can make contributions to a new type of IRA, called either the *Roth IRA* (after the Senator who proposed it) or *IRA Plus*. But the *traditional* or regular IRA that we just looked at will continue to exist.

 The tax treatment of these two types of IRAs differs markedly. Traditional IRA contributions are deductible for some taxpayers. In addition, the earnings in traditional IRA accounts, which are tax-deferred as long as they remain in the account, are taxable when they are withdrawn. In contrast, contributions to Roth IRAs are not deductible. In addition to not being taxed while they remain in the account, the earnings in Roth IRAs may generally be withdrawn on a tax-free basis subject to certain restrictions.

To make tax-free withdrawals from a Roth IRA, the account owner must be at least age 59 1/2 and must have held the account for at least 5 years. Tax-free Roth IRA distributions may also be taken after 5 years in the event of the account owner's death or disability or, with a limit of $10,000, for the purchase of a first home.

Roth IRA contributions are subject to the same contribution limits that affect other IRAs. Each spouse can contribute up to the limit to an IRA (Roth or traditional) in any combination. If both spouses take advantage of this rule, the combined contribution could be as much as double the limit. Availability of Roth IRAs is phased out between $150,000 and $160,000 of AGI for married couples filing jointly and $95,000 and $110,000 of AGI for singles. Availability of the Roth IRA is not affected by participation in an employer-sponsored retirement plan.

Taxpayers with less than $100,000 of AGI, married or single, can convert existing traditional IRAs to Roth IRAs. This involves paying income tax on all deductible contributions and earnings.

Savings Incentive Match Plan for Employees (SIMPLE)

Certain small employers may establish a type of qualified retirement plan called a *Savings Incentive Match Plan for Employees (SIMPLE)*. To be eligible to establish a SIMPLE, a business must employ no more than 100 people who earned more than $5,000 the preceding year, and the business must have no other qualified plan.

A SIMPLE can take the form of either an employer-established IRA or a 401(k) plan. Under either format, employees may elect to make contributions of a percentage of their compensation up to a limit of $9,000 per year in 2004.

The limit is $10,000 in 2005, after which it will be indexed for inflation. In addition, individuals 50 and over will be eligible to make catch-up contributions according to the schedule shown in Table 14.3.

Table 14.3 Additional Catch-Up Contribution	
Year	**Amount of Catch-Up Contribution**
2004	$1,500
2005	$2,000
2006 and after	$2,500

These contributions are not included in the employees' taxable income, but they are subject to employment tax. Employers must contribute to the SIMPLE by one of the following:

➤ Match each employee's contribution on a dollar-for-dollar basis up to 3% of the employee's income.

➤ Contribute 2% of compensation to the account of each eligible employee who has earned at least $5,000 that year.

Under the IRA format, employers who elect to match contributions on a dollar-for-dollar basis may in some years reduce the matching percentage to as low as 1%, but may not reduce the matching percentage below 3% for more than 2 years in any 5-year period. The option to reduce the matching percentage is not available under the 401(k) format.

Employer contributions are deductible from the employer's income, excludable from the employee's income, and not subject to employment tax. Employees must be immediately 100% vested in all contributions. Distributions from SIMPLE IRAs are generally taxed like distributions from regular IRAs, except that a 25% penalty tax applies to withdrawals made from a SIMPLE within its first 2 years.

Simplified Employee Pensions (SEPs)

Simplified Employee Pensions (SEPs) are a cross between an IRA and a profit-sharing plan. Under a SEP, each eligible employee of an employer establishes an IRA. The employer then makes contributions to the employee's IRA according to a formula described in the SEP document. The maximum contribution that may be deducted by the employer is 25% of the total compensation paid to all participating employees.

KEOGH Plans

Self-employed persons may set up their own retirement plans, known as *Keogh plans*. Self-employed persons may be sole proprietors, partners in a business, farmers, or professionals such as doctors or lawyers. Other individuals who are employed by a company and covered under the company retirement plan may establish a Keogh plan provided they also are self-employed in some other capacity.

Contributions to a Keogh plan are not taxed as current income as long as they follow these guidelines:

➤ For a defined contribution Keogh plan, the contribution limit for a common-law employee is the lesser of $40,000 (indexed for inflation) or 100% of compensation.

➤ For a defined benefit Keogh plan, the contribution is limited to a sufficient amount, actuarially determined, to fund the maximum benefit allowable under the plan, but which cannot be more than $160,000 per year (indexed for inflation).

Tax-Deferred Annuity Arrangements—403(B) Arrangements

A *403(b) arrangement* (sometimes referred to as a *403(b) plan*) is an employer-sponsored arrangement available to employees of public school systems. Under this arrangement, the employee agrees to let the employer withhold a part of his or her salary. The employer then uses this deferred salary to purchase an annuity. The employee's current taxable income does not include the amount withheld to purchase the annuity. Employees may have only a certain amount of their salary withheld.

Plan Distributions

As a rule, funds from a qualified retirement plan or IRA may be distributed at any age when employment is terminated, the plan is terminated, or the employee retires. However, if the distribution is considered to be *premature distribution* (that is, made before age 59 1/2), a 10% penalty tax is usually applied to it. This penalty is in addition to the regular income tax due on the distribution.

The law also places limits on when distributions from a qualified plan or an IRA (with the exception of a Roth IRA) *must* begin. Distributions to all qualified plan participants or IRA holders must begin no later than April 1 of the year following the calendar year in which the participant reaches age 70 1/2. The minimum amount that must be distributed each year is set by regulation.

The penalty for failure to comply with this distribution requirement is a nondeductible excise tax equal to 50% of the amount by which the minimum amount required to be distributed exceeds the amount actually distributed.

Incidental Limitations

Certain limits are imposed by the IRS on the purchase of insurance as part of a qualified plan. These *incidental limitations* are designed to ensure that the death benefit of life insurance coverage purchased under a qualified plan be incidental to the other benefits provided by the plan. In a defined benefit plan, the face value cannot exceed 100 times the monthly pension benefit. With a defined contribution plan, when a ordinary life policy is used, 50% of the plan contribution is the limit. With universal life, the formula stipulates 25%.

Taxation of Plan Benefits

The only funds that escape taxation at distribution are those that have already been taxed. Distributions may be made in the form of annuity installments or, in the case of a defined contribution plan, in a lump sum. Those made in the form of installments may be made partially income tax–free. The portion of each payment that represents money that has already been taxed to the recipient, if any, is excluded from gross income. Distributions from a qualified retirement plan may also be triggered by the plan participant's death. Lump-sum distributions of plan benefits on a participant's death are considered *income in respect of a decedent* and are generally subject to income tax when received by the estate or other beneficiaries, less any amount the plan participant contributed using after-tax dollars.

Rollovers

A *rollover* occurs when money is taken out of an IRA and held in the owner's possession before it is transferred to a different IRA. Direct transfers of funds between IRAs are not considered rollovers. Rollovers between IRAs may be made only once within a 12-month period. From the date funds are withdrawn from the old IRA, the IRA owner has 60 days to make the deposit to the new IRA. Any funds not rolled over within that 60-day period become taxable to the extent they consist of deductible contributions and earnings on any contributions.

 For people changing jobs and receiving their vested interests in their former employer's qualified retirement plan, those funds will also become taxable unless rolled over into an IRA or another qualified plan within 60 days.

Amounts received from a qualified plan may also be transferred to another qualified plan with the consent of the individual's new employer. Any such rollover must be made directly or it will be subject to a 20% withholding rate. This is true even if the rollover occurs within the 60-day limit. To escape the withholding rate, the rollover must take place without the plan's funds ever being in the recipient's. If such control does occur and the 20% is withheld, the recipient must make up this amount out of other funds or the amount withheld will be subject to income taxation and, possibly, a penalty for premature distribution.

The Employee Retirement Income Security Act (ERISA)

The *Employee Retirement Income Security Act (ERISA)* was enacted to protect the interests of participants in employee benefit plans as well as the interests of the participants' beneficiaries.

Fiduciary Responsibility

ERISA mandates very detailed standards for fiduciaries and other parties-in-interest of employee welfare benefit plans, including group insurance plans. This means that anyone having control over plan management or plan assets of any kind must discharge that fiduciary duty solely in the interests of the plan participants and their beneficiaries.

Reporting and Disclosure

ERISA requires that certain information concerning any employee welfare benefit plan be made available to plan participants, their beneficiaries, the Department of Labor, and the IRS. The types of information that must be distributed include

➤ A summary plan description to each plan participant and the Department of Labor

➤ A summary of material modifications that details changes in any plan description to each plan participant and the Department of Labor

➤ An annual return/report (Form 5500 or one of its variations) submitted to the IRS

➤ A summary annual report to each plan participant

➤ Any terminal report to the IRS

In addition to monetary penalties, civil and criminal action may be taken against any plan administrator who willfully violates any of these requirements or who knowingly falsifies or conceals ERISA disclosure information.

Exam Prep Questions

1. Employer vesting schedules apply to
   - ○ A. All contributions made to qualified plans
   - ○ B. Only employee contributions made to qualified plans
   - ○ C. Only employer contributions made to qualified plans
   - ○ D. All contributions made to nonqualified plans

2. Who may contribute to an IRA?
   - ○ A. Anybody with earned income
   - ○ B. Only people who don't participate in company retirement plans
   - ○ C. Only people who earn less than certain specified amounts
   - ○ D. Only people who are self-employed

3. Who may not make fully deductible contributions to an IRA?
   - ○ A. Anybody with earned income above the specified income limits
   - ○ B. People who do not participate in company retirement plans
   - ○ C. People who do participate in company retirement plans and who earn less than specified amounts
   - ○ D. People who are not eligible for company retirement plans

4. Premature distribution from a qualified plan or an IRA can result in the amount being taxed as income plus a penalty tax of _____%.
   - ○ A. 5
   - ○ B. 10
   - ○ C. 15
   - ○ D. 25

5. A rollover from one IRA to another or from a qualified plan to an IRA must be accomplished within what time limit if the owner is to avoid an income tax liability on the amount rolled over?
   - ○ A. 10 days
   - ○ B. 30 days
   - ○ C. 60 days
   - ○ D. 90 days

6. At what age is an individual no longer subject to early withdrawal penalties under an IRA?
   - ○ A. 55
   - ○ B. 55 1/2
   - ○ C. 59
   - ○ D. 59 1/2

7. Which of the following organizations would be eligible to offer a 403(b) arrangement?
   - ○ A. A fire department
   - ○ B. A public school system
   - ○ C. Any small business
   - ○ D. Any corporation

8. Carmen owns a business that provides a retirement plan to its employees whereby the business makes contributions of up to 25% of the total compensation paid to all participating employees to IRA plans owned by the individual employees. Carmen's plan is most likely a
   - ○ A. SIMPLE plan
   - ○ B. Keogh plan
   - ○ C. 403(b) plan
   - ○ D. SEP

9. Delbert is self-employed, and sets up a retirement plan for himself. Delbert most likely sets up a
   - ○ A. SIMPLE plan
   - ○ B. Keogh plan
   - ○ C. 403(b) plan
   - ○ D. SEP

10. Kim is required to take a $2,000 minimum annual distribution from her IRA. She fails to comply and takes only a $1,000 distribution. Because of this failure, Kim will be subject to a
    - ○ A. Deductible excise tax of $1,000
    - ○ B. Nondeductible excise tax of $1,000
    - ○ C. Deductible excise tax of $500
    - ○ D. Nondeductible excise tax of $500

Exam Prep Answers

1. **C is correct.** All employee contributions are immediately 100% vested.

2. **A is correct.** Anyone with earned income may qualify for an IRA.

3. **A is correct.** If earned income exceeds a specified amount, limitations apply.

4. **B is correct.** There is a 10% penalty for premature distributions in addition to the normal tax rate.

5. **C is correct.** To avoid taxation the rollover must be completed within 60 days.

6. **D is correct.** After this age no early withdrawal penalties apply.

7. **B is correct.** A public school system is an example of an organization eligible for a 403(b) arrangement.

8. **D is correct.** This is an example of a SEP.

9. **B is correct.** Keogh plans are designed to provide retirement benefits for self-employed individuals

10. **D is correct.** A nondeductible excise tax equal to 50% of the difference between the amount withdrawn and the amount required applies.

Health Insurance Basics

Terms you need to understand:

- ✓ Principal sum
- ✓ Capital sum
- ✓ Surgicenters
- ✓ Urgent care centers
- ✓ Skilled nursing facilities
- ✓ Home health care
- ✓ Subscribers
- ✓ Health maintenance organization
- ✓ Service area
- ✓ Capitation fee
- ✓ Copayments
- ✓ Gatekeeper
- ✓ Primary care physician
- ✓ Preferred provider organization
- ✓ Exclusive provider organization
- ✓ Self-funding

Concepts you need to master:

- ✓ Types of health insurance policies
- ✓ Limited health insurance policies
- ✓ Determining health insurance needs
- ✓ Health care providers
- ✓ Managed care
- ✓ Reimbursement plans
- ✓ Service organizations
- ✓ Prepaid plans
- ✓ Fee-for-service plans
- ✓ Point-of-service plans
- ✓ Employer-administered plans
- ✓ Cafeteria plans
- ✓ Medical savings account
- ✓ Multiple employer trust
- ✓ Multiple employer welfare arrangement
- ✓ Blanket insurance policies
- ✓ Franchise insurance policies
- ✓ Government insurance programs

Health insurance provides payment of benefits for the loss of income and/or the medical expenses arising from illness or injury. Health insurance is often called *accident and sickness insurance* or *accident and health insurance*.

Types of Losses and Benefits

Let's first review some of the major categories of health insurance and consider their differences.

Loss of Income from Disability

Disability income insurance, also referred to as *loss of time insurance*, pays a weekly or monthly benefit for disabilities due to accident or sickness. The primary purpose of disability income coverage is to replace loss of personal income due to a disability. Disability income policies are issued on an individual basis or on a group basis through an employer-sponsored plan, labor union, or association.

Accidental Death and Dismemberment (AD&D)

Accidental death and dismemberment (AD&D) policies (or riders) pay the policy's *principal sum* for accidental death. The principal sum is similar in meaning to a policy's face amount. This same amount is paid if the insured suffers the actual severance of two arms, two legs, or the loss of vision in two eyes due to an accident. This amount is usually identified as the *capital sum* if the policy is paying an accidental dismemberment benefit.

AD&D benefits may be included as riders on life insurance policies, as part of disability income insurance, as part of health insurance, or as a separate policy (a type of limited coverage).

Medical Expense Benefits

Medical expense insurance, commonly referred to as *hospitalization insurance*, provides benefits for expenses incurred due to in-hospital medical treatment and surgery as well as certain outpatient expenses—such as doctor's visits, lab tests, and diagnostic services. Hospitalization insurance may be issued as an individual policy covering all family members or as a group insurance policy provided through an employer-sponsored program.

When medical expense coverage provided for proprietors and partners is paid for by the business, the premiums have traditionally been considered tax deductible to the business but includable as income to the individual. There is no limit to the amount of tax-free medical expense benefits the individual can receive, however.

Dental Expense Benefits

Dental expense benefits are generally sold as part of group health insurance coverage. Most insurers do not provide individual dental policies. Dental benefits are offered for preventive maintenance (cleanings and x-rays), repair (fillings, root canals, and so forth) and replacement of teeth.

Long-Term Care Insurance (LTC)

Long-term care (LTC) insurance pays for the care of persons with chronic diseases or disabilities and may include a wide range of health and social services provided under the supervision of medical professionals. LTC often covers *nursing home care, home-based care*, and *respite care* (full-time care provided to an impaired individual for a short period in order to give a rest, or respite, to a family member or friend who ordinarily provides that care at home).

Limited Health Exposures and Insurance Contracts

There are a variety of special health insurance policies providing limited coverage. To ensure that the insured has sufficient notice that the coverage is limited, every policy that provides limited coverage must, by law, state plainly on the first page of the policy: "THIS IS A LIMITED POLICY." The following is a list of the main types of limited health policies:

➤ *Travel accident insurance* provides coverage for death or injury resulting from accidents occurring while the insured is a fare-paying passenger on a common carrier.

➤ *Specified disease* or *dread disease insurance* provides a variety of benefits for only certain diseases, usually cancer or heart disease.

➤ *Hospital income insurance* pays a specified sum on a daily, weekly, or monthly basis while the insured is confined to a hospital. The amount of the benefit is not related to expenses incurred or to wages lost while the insured is hospitalized.

> *Accident only insurance* provides coverage for injury from accident and excludes sickness. Benefits may be paid for all or any of the following: death, disability, dismemberment, or hospital and medical expenses.

> *Credit insurance* is listed here because of the limited nature of its coverage. This policy is issued only to those who are in debt to a creditor. The coverage is limited to the total amount of the debtor's indebtedness.

> *Blanket insurance* is a form of group insurance. Often the individual's name is not known because the individuals come and go. Such groups include students, campers, passengers of a common carrier, volunteer groups, and sports teams. Unlike group insurance the individuals are automatically covered under the blanket policy, and they do not receive certificates of insurance.

Prescription Coverage

Prescription medication coverage is normally provided as an optional benefit under a group medical expense policy. The insured and eligible dependents are provided with a stated cost for any prescription medication required. This specific cost is usually $5–15 dollars per prescription. Thus, regardless of the cost of the medication, the insured pays only the stated amount, and the balance of the prescription cost is paid by the insurance company.

Determining Insurance Needs

Basically, the process of determining health insurance needs is similar to identifying an individual's life insurance requirements. The principal difference is the risk being insured—premature death or health insurance expenses.

The individual's and family's health insurance needs must be identified. These needs are then prioritized in terms of their importance to the family. Other forms of health insurance benefits should be reviewed with regard to this needs analysis:

> Workers compensation benefits for job-related disabilities

> Social security disability benefits

> Medicare, if the individual is eligible

> Work-related benefits through employer-sponsored plans

> Health coverage under any statutory plans

After the individual's total health insurance needs analysis has been completed, meaningful recommendations can be made as to the type and amounts of health insurance required.

Health Care Providers

Patients have traditionally been seen by physicians in office or hospital environments. Today physicians also see patients in a variety of settings including the following:

➤ *Surgicenters* provide a site for outpatient surgery where general anesthesia must be used, but a patient does not need to stay overnight.

➤ *Urgent care centers* see patients often without an appointment during the daytime, as well as evening and weekend hours.

➤ *Skilled nursing facilities* provide medical care for patients who no longer require hospitalization but cannot yet care for themselves at home.

➤ *Home health care* is also provided by nurses and others for patients ready to be at home but who cannot yet fully provide for all of their own needs.

The traditional broad health coverage provided by insurance plans provides little incentive for efficient, cost-effective health care delivery. *Managed care* imposes controls on the use of health care services, the providers of health care services, and the amount charged for these services, usually through health maintenance organizations (HMOs) or preferred provider organizations (PPOs) (discussed in the following sections).

Health Care Plans

The insurers of health care are not only the traditional stock and mutual companies, and Blue Cross and Blue Shield, but also the *health maintenance organizations (HMOs)* and PPOs formed by hospitals and physicians to deliver health care directly to enrollees in their plans.

Commercial Insurers

Commercial insurers are stock and mutual life insurers and sometimes casualty companies. Commercial insurers have traditionally provided coverage on a reimbursement basis but have also begun to embrace alternative approaches. *Reimbursement* plans pay benefits directly to the insured, who is responsible for paying the providers of medical services.

Commercial insurers offer both individual and group health insurance products. These products include basic medical expense coverage, major medical plans, comprehensive medical plans, disability income policies, and other types of health products.

Blue Cross and Blue Shield

Blue Cross and Blue Shield (the Blues) are different from traditional commercial insurers in the following important areas:

➤ The Blues provide the majority of their benefits on a *service* basis rather than on a reimbursement basis. This means that the insurer pays the provider directly for the medical treatment given the insured, instead of reimbursing the insured.

➤ The Blues have contractual relationships with the hospitals and doctors. As participating providers, the doctors and hospitals contractually agree to specific costs for the medical services provided to subscribers.

Corporate Structure

Blue Cross/Blue Shield organizations, which are often referred to as *service organizations*, are examples of *producers' cooperatives*. Physicians and hospitals that sponsor Blue Cross/Blue Shield plans provide the insurance, so are considered to be the producers in the cooperative.

Blue Cross traditionally has been a hospital service plan and Blue Shield a physicians service plan, but these distinctions are becoming blurred. In most states, Blue Cross and Blue Shield have merged, but each group still covers the expenses for which it was first developed: Blue Cross covers hospital expenses and Blue Shield covers medical and surgical expenses. In some states both Blue Cross and Blue Shield serve as hospital and physician service plans. With occasional exceptions, reimbursements for incurred expenses are made directly to the providers, not to the subscribers.

Enrollment and Premium Rates

Members of Blue Cross and Blue Shield are known as *subscribers*. Subscribers in either plan can transfer their membership from one Blues organization to another in other areas of town, or to other cities or states. Subscribers may also change their coverage from individual to family, from family to group, or any combination of change they need to make. When transfers or changes are made, the subscriber's coverage continues without interruption.

Blue Cross and Blue Shield plans are called *prepaid plans* because the plan subscribers pay a set fee, usually each month, for medical services covered under the plan.

Types of Coverage and Benefits

Blue Cross offers broad coverages and pays claims on a service basis. The plan covers hospital daily room and board, outpatient services for minor surgery or accidental injury, medical emergencies, diagnostic testing, physical therapy, kidney dialysis, chemotherapy, and in some cases preadmission testing.

Family plans may also include coverage for dependent handicapped children.

Maternity benefits are also made available the "same as for any other disability."

Blue Cross also has a supplemental coverage for catastrophic loss, which is similar to commercial major medical plans. This supplement has a deductible and an 80%/20% coinsurance feature.

Blue Shield offers prepaid medical coverage for physician services received by plan subscribers. Again, through the contractual arrangement with the providers, Blue Shield will normally pay the participating physician a predetermined amount for the specific service provided. Usually, this amount will be based on the usual, customary, and reasonable (UCR) fees charged by other physicians in the same geographical area for the same or similar medical procedures.

It is also possible to obtain dental coverage through Blue Cross/Blue Shield, which contracts with dental providers and pays fees on a service basis.

Blues and Managed Care

The Blues have also been strongly influenced by managed care. Many Blues subscribers are now covered by a Blues-affiliated HMO or PPO, or POS plan.

Special Requirements for Consolidated Plans

Jointly operated (consolidated) Blue Cross/Blue Shield plans are often so comprehensive that supplementing them with major medical coverage is not necessary. Plan provisions applying to consolidated Blue Cross/Blue Shield plans are similar to plan provisions applying to comprehensive major medical plans.

Health Maintenance Organizations (HMOs)

The number of HMOs has grown rapidly in response to increasing health care costs in recent decades.

History and Development

The purpose of HMOs is to manage health care and its costs through a program of prepaid care that emphasizes prevention and early treatment. This prepayment, which entitles the health care consumer to a wide range of services, is referred to as a *service-incurred* basis. In contrast, traditional health insurance coverage is handled on a *reimbursement basis*, with the insured or provider being reimbursed for all or part of medical expenses actually incurred.

The emphasis on prevention means HMOs cover preventive medicine, such as routine physical and well-child examinations and diagnostic screening paid for in advance. Theoretically, the HMOs' focus on prevention ultimately leads to reduced health care costs. At the same time, HMOs provide for hospital, surgical, and medical treatment when such services are needed.

One way HMOs differ from traditional health insurance providers is that HMOs have a dual function not shared by insurance companies. Under traditional arrangements, consumers receive the *health care* itself from one group, the medical profession—physicians, hospitals, therapists, and so forth—and the financial *coverage* comes from a separate entity—the insurance company. In contrast, an HMO provides both the health care services and the health care coverage.

These two functions are combined because the HMO is comprised of a group of medical practitioners who have contracted to provide specified services to HMO members at agreed-upon prices. In return, each consumer who is a member of the HMO agrees to pay the HMO a specified amount in advance to cover required hospital and medical services.

Federal Requirements

Although the emphasis on prevention and containing costs was a major factor in the development of HMOs, federal HMO laws further encouraged development by two primary means:

➤ Providing for government grants

➤ Requiring certain employers who provide health benefits to employees to offer enrollment in an HMO as an option

In order to receive government grants, HMOs must

➤ Maintain certain minimum financial requirements in terms of the net worth of the HMO and/or reserves to pay health claims.

➤ Provide a defined package of health services that includes routine preventive care.

➤ Require no more than nominal "use charges" or copayments (in addition to the prepaid amounts) for services actually rendered to individuals.

➤ Establish premiums on a community rating basis without considering actual usage of services by individuals.

When an HMO has met the minimum standards as well as other federal and state requirements, it is allowed to operate in a designated *service area*—often within a certain county or a specified distance surrounding the HMO facilities. Then, the federal law regarding employers comes into play.

The HMO Act of 1973 required employers with certain characteristics to offer HMO coverage by a federally qualified HMO as an alternative to an indemnity plan. Under this law, if the HMO operates in the service area of an employer that has 25 or more employees and that employer provides health care benefits, enrollment in the HMO must be offered as an alternative to traditional health insurance plans. This is often referred to as the *dual choice option* or *dual choice law*.

This requirement was repealed at the federal level in 1995, although some states still impose dual choice requirements. Federal law now simply requires that employers "not financially discriminate" in the amounts of employee contribution made toward HMO and indemnity plans. Employers are required to contribute equally to either type of health coverage for employees. However, the employer is never required to pay more for the HMO than it pays for any existing insurance plan already in place.

HMO Organization

There are a number of ways to analyze the organization of an HMO. The first concept we'll address is whether the HMO operates on a *for-profit* or a *not-for-profit* basis. Then we'll look at some other organizational variations.

Profit Versus Nonprofit

Usually, but not always, if the HMO is a *producers' cooperative* owned and operated by a group of physicians, the HMO is for-profit. If it is a *consumers' cooperative* where the doctors are salaried employees of the HMO, it is usually not-for-profit.

Typical Structures: Group Model

The basic structure of an HMO involves contractual agreements with a variety of health care providers and facilities to provide services to HMO subscribers. Within that structure, four models are used, one of which is the group model.

The *group model* is sometimes called the *medical group model* or the *group practice model*. Under this arrangement, the HMO contracts with an independent medical group that specializes in a variety of medical services to provide those services to HMO subscribers. Under the agreement, the HMO pays the medical group entity, not the individual service providers. The medical group itself chooses how to pay its individual physicians, all of whom remain independent of the HMO rather than becoming salaried employees.

Often, the HMO pays the group a *capitation fee*, which is a fixed amount paid monthly for each HMO member. Thus, the medical group can make a profit on those members for whom a fee is paid but who use few or no services. On the other hand, the medical group can lose money on frequent users.

Typical Structures: Staff Model

A second type of arrangement is the *staff model*, so named because the contracting physicians are paid employees working on the staff of the HMO. They generally operate in a clinic setting at the HMO's physical facilities. When hospital services are required, the staff doctors and HMO administration arrange for those services. In some cases, the HMO may even own and operate a hospital.

Typical Structures: Network Model

The *network model* operates much like the group model, except the HMO contracts with at least two, and more likely several, medical groups rather than just one. In addition, the HMO may make similar contractual arrangements with independent doctors to provide services in their individual offices. The purpose of a network is to increase accessibility to providers as a convenience for HMO subscribers who might otherwise be required to visit a facility far from their homes or workplaces.

Typical Structures: Individual Practice Association Model

The fourth and final model is one that gives HMO members the maximum freedom of choice of physicians and locations. The *Individual Practice Association (IPA) model* allows the HMO to contract separately with any combination of individual physicians, medical groups, or physicians' associations. Some HMOs, in fact, have been started by such groups.

In the IPA model, there is no separate HMO facility. Physicians operate out of their own private offices, and their HMO patients may be individuals the physicians were already attending.

Open and Closed Panel Types

Open and closed panels are yet another way to characterize HMOs. Physicians, hospitals, and other health care providers who have contracts with an HMO are referred to as the HMO's panel. An *open panel* means any and all providers who want to provide services for the HMO may do so as long as they agree to the HMO's requirements.

In contrast, a *closed panel* is a limited number of health care providers chosen by the HMO. HMO subscribers must receive their health care services from this closed panel of providers in order to have those services paid for on the prepaid plan.

Basic and Supplemental Services

The emphasis of HMOs is prevention, because the benefits offered are broader than those provided by commercial insurers or the Blues. HMO benefits are not limited to treatment resulting from illness or injury because they also include preventive health care measures such as routine physical examinations.

HMOs are required to provide for the following *basic health care services*:

➤ *Inpatient hospital and physician services* for a period of at least 90 days per calendar year for treatment of illness or injury. If inpatient treatment is for mental, emotional, or nervous disorders, including alcohol and drug rehabilitation and treatment, services may be limited to 30 days per calendar year. Treatment for alcohol and drug rehabilitation and treatment may be restricted to a 90-day lifetime limit. A partial list of the hospital services provided include room and board; maternity care; general nursing care; use of operating room and facilities; use of intensive care unit; x-rays, laboratory, and other diagnostic tests; drugs, medications, and anesthesia; physical, radiation, and inhalation therapy.

➤ *Outpatient medical services* when prescribed or supervised by a physician and rendered in a non-hospital–based health care facility (for example, physician's office, member's home, and so forth). Outpatient medical services include diagnostic services, treatment services, short term physical therapy and rehabilitation services, laboratory and x-ray services, and outpatient surgery.

➤ *Preventive health services* with the goal of protection against and early detection and minimization of the ill effects and causes of disease or disability. Specifically, this will include well-child care from birth, eye and ear examinations for children age 17 and under, periodic health evaluations, and immunizations.

➤ *In and out of area emergency services*, including medically necessary ambulance services, available on an inpatient or an outpatient basis 24 hours per day, 7 days per week.

Many HMOs may but are not required to provide one or more of the following supplemental health care services:

➤ Prescription drugs

➤ Nursing services

➤ Vision care

➤ Long-term care

➤ Dental care

➤ Mental heath care

➤ Home health care

➤ Substance abuse services

Consumers who want supplemental services may purchase them from the HMO only as an adjunct to the basic health care services the HMO offers.

Copayments

Members of an HMO may be charged only nominal amounts—*copayments*—for basic services in addition to the original monthly payment. In many cases, no additional payments are required for services. All of this is spelled out in a descriptive document, which is called either the *certificate of coverage* or the *evidence of coverage*.

On the other hand, HMOs are permitted to require copayments on supplemental services as well as charge an amount that is added to the monthly fee.

Exclusions and Limitations

HMOs may not exclude and limit benefits as readily as commercial insurers because the rationale of an HMO is to provide comprehensive health care coverage.

Some of the benefits an HMO may exclude from coverage, and often do, include

➤ Eye examinations and refractions for persons *over* age 17

➤ Eyeglasses or contact lenses resulting from an eye examination

➤ Dental services

➤ Prescription drugs (other than those administered in a hospital)

➤ Long-term physical therapy (more than 90 days)

➤ Out-of-area services (other than emergency services)

Important Features Of HMOs

Some features of HMOs are unique and do not apply to traditional forms of reimbursement insurance.

Gatekeeper System

HMOs often have a *gatekeeper system* under which the member must select a *primary care physician (PCP)*, who in turn provides or authorizes all care for the particular member. Any referrals, such as to specialists, must be made and authorized by the PCP. In emergency situations, the member's needs are covered, but generally the individual must notify the PCP as soon as possible if it wasn't possible to do so when the emergency arose.

Twenty-Four Hour Access

As a rule, members have 24-hour access to the HMO. Telephones are answered and referrals and authorizations are made 24 hours a day, 7 days a week. Nursing and medical staff, including PCPs, must be willing to respond during nonbusiness hours as well.

Open Enrollment

The term *open enrollment* can mean one of the following:

➤ In employer-sponsored group plans, a time period each year when employees may choose to enroll or remain enrolled in the HMO or to change health plans

➤ A time period each year when an HMO must advertise availability to the general public on an individual basis

In the first case, open enrollment allows employees who have not yet joined the HMO to do so if they wish. Those who are already HMO subscribers may at this time also choose to continue in the HMO or to change plans if another health care plan is available.

In the second case, open enrollment may be required by state law, permitting all who apply to join. During this period, which usually lasts 30 days, the HMO generally may not reject any applicant for health reasons. However, some laws permit the HMO to refuse enrollment to people who are hospitalized during the enrollment period or who have chronic illnesses or permanent injuries.

Nondiscrimination

When HMO coverage is offered to a group, the HMO may not refuse to cover an individual member of the group because of adverse preexisting health conditions, such as a history of heart trouble that predates enrollment in the HMO. This is different from traditional insurers, which generally have the option of refusing to cover certain group members and of excluding preexisting health conditions.

 HMOs are permitted to refuse coverage for individuals with preexisting conditions, except during open enrollment, as discussed previously.

Complaints

All HMOs are required to have a complaint system, often called a *grievance procedure*, to resolve written complaints by members. The HMO is required to provide forms for written complaints, including the address and telephone number of where complaints should be directed. Additionally, on providing the necessary forms for a complaint to a member, the HMO must notify the member of any time limits applying to a complaint. Complaints must be resolved within 180 days of being filed with the HMO (with a few exceptions).

Prohibited Practices

HMOs are prohibited from excluding a member's preexisting conditions from coverage and from unfairly discriminating against a member based on age, sex, health status, race, color, creed, national origin, or marital status. HMOs are also prohibited from terminating a member's coverage for reasons other than nonpayment of premiums or copayments, fraud or deception in the member's use of services, a violation of the terms of the contract, failure to meet or continue to meet eligibility requirements prescribed by the HMO, or a termination of the group contract under which the member was covered.

Quality Assurance

Because HMOs provide service benefits rather than reimbursement benefits, they are required to follow guidelines prescribed by the insurance department to assure quality service to members. These guidelines specify the requirements for reasonable hours of operation and after-hours emergency health care and standards to ensure that sufficient personnel will be available to attend to members' needs. The guidelines also require adequate arrangements to provide inpatient hospital services for basic health care and a requirement that the services of specialists be provided as a basic health care service.

Open-Ended Plans

An *open-ended HMO* (also known as a *leaky HMO* and *point-of-service HMO*) is a hybrid arrangement whereby participants may use non-HMO providers at any time and receive indemnity benefits that are subject to higher deductible and coinsurance amounts. The out-of-pocket cost to the participant (and probably the employer, too) is higher, but the arrangement allows participants to remain in control in choosing a health care provider.

Open-Access HMOs

Dissatisfaction with the gatekeeper mechanism, delays in receiving care, and problems in obtaining referrals have led many health plans to offer open access. An *open-access HMO* allows members to receive care from network specialists without first going through a primary care physician (gatekeeper) and receiving a referral. Alternatively, a *point-of-service (POS)* plan allows members to seek the care of a specialist outside the HMO provider network.

Because the plan does not control the outside provider, POS plans tend to be more expensive than open-access HMOs.

Preferred Provider Organizations (PPOs)

Other efforts to reduce medical costs have resulted in *preferred provider organizations (PPOs)*, arrangements under which a selected group of independent hospitals and medical practitioners in a certain area, such as a state, agree to provide a range of services at a prearranged cost.

The organizers and the providers agree upon medical service charges that are generally less than the providers would charge patients not associated with the PPO. The providers are paid on a fee-for-service basis. Providers are willing to enter into this arrangement in return for guaranteed payment from the PPO and a potential increase in the number of patients.

The people who will receive services choose a preferred provider from a list the PPO distributes. As a general rule, the users have more choices among doctors and hospitals under a PPO than under an HMO arrangement.

However, some recent HMO structures offer similar arrangements. PPOs fall somewhere between commercial insurers, where the user has unlimited choice of practitioners, and HMOs, where the user might be severely restricted.

 Keep in mind that a PPO agrees to pay its full benefits only when a preferred provider is used. If an individual uses a nonpreferred facility, the PPO usually pays a reduced amount (perhaps 80%) and the individual must pay the balance.

Recognizing that emergencies may require treatment in other than preferred facilities or by providers who have not agreed to the PPO arrangement, PPO plans will generally pay in full for emergency treatment regardless of where and by whom it is performed.

Point-of-Service Plans

Point-of-service plans (POS) are a form of managed care, in which the insured is given a choice of receiving care in-network or out-of-network. In-network means receiving care through a particular network of doctors and hospitals participating in the plan and all care is coordinated by the insured PCP. This includes referrals to specialists and arrangements for hospitalization, which must all be approved by the PCP. In-network coverage is the highest level of coverage within the plan, which means the plan will pay more for medical services and the insured won't have to submit claim forms. Out-of-network coverage applies when the insured receives care for a provider who does not participate in the plan's network and the care is not coordinated by the primary care physician.

 When the insured receives out-of-network care, he or she will usually pay more of the cost than if it had been in-network care (emergencies excepted). Out-of-network care also means that the insured will have to submit claim forms in order to receive benefits.

Exclusive Provider Organizations (EPOs)

Exclusive provider organizations are a type of PPO in which individual members use particular preferred providers, instead of having a choice of a variety of preferred providers. Providers are not paid a salary, but are paid on a fee-for-service basis.

EPOs are characterized by a primary physician who monitors care and makes referrals to a network of providers (the gatekeeper concept), strong utilization management, experience rating, and simplified claims processing. EPOs can serve as an alternative to or companion to HMOs and PPOs.

Emerging Variations

Today there are many variations of managed health care providers, including *physician hospital organizations (PHOs)*, *practice management organizations (PMOs)*, and *provider sponsored networks (PSNs)* .

The principal differences between these organizations are the parties to the contracts and their basic structure and organization. For example, with the PHO, the physicians and hospitals contract directly with employers to provide health care services. Most of these arrangements are funded through capitation fees much like HMOs.

Multiple Option Plans

A *multiple option plan* is an integrated health plan that may include services of an HMO, PPO, EPO, and/or indemnity plan, all of which are administered by a single vendor (usually an insurance company).

Employer-Administered Plans

Some employers have reduced costs for health care benefits by self-insuring or offering new options that have become available due to changes in tax laws.

Self-Funding

With a self-funded plan an employer, not an insurance company, provides the funds to make claim payments for company employees and their dependents. In the event that claims are higher than predicted, a self-funded health insurance plan can be backed-up by a stop-loss contract. A stop-loss contract is designed to limit the employer's liability for claims.

There are two variations of this coverage. Specific stop-loss coverage begins to apply after an individual's medical expenses exceed a predetermined threshold, such as $5,000. Aggregate stop-loss coverage applies when the employer's liability for group insurance claims exceeds a specified amount. The insurer pays all claims after the specified amount is reached.

An employer self-funded plan may be an indemnity program that reimburses covered employees for medical care they have received. Or, the employer may provide benefits through the service plan offered under an HMO, or through an insurer's PPO network.

An insurer may also be used for a self-funded employer under an *administrative services only (ASO)* contract. Under the *ASO contractual agreement* the insurer provides claim forms, administers claims, and makes payments to health care providers, but the employer still provides the funds to make claims payments.

Advantages of Self-Insurance

Self-insurance has four major advantages:

➤ The company can save money if actual losses are less than those predicted.

➤ The expense of carrying insurance may be reduced because of the elimination of administrative costs, agent commissions, brokerage fees, and premium tax.

➤ Because the company has assumed the entire risk, there may be a greater effort on its part to seek ways to reduce claims and encourage employees to actively participate in wellness programs and improved lifestyles.

➤ The company has use of the money that would normally be held by the insurance company.

Disadvantages of Self-Insurance

The following are the main disadvantages of self-insurance:

➤ Actual losses may be more than predicted.

➤ Expenses could be higher than expected if additional personnel have to be hired to administer claims, manage risk, or offer employee information.

➤ Income taxes could be higher because the company will not be able to take premiums paid as a deduction; only the claims paid and operating expenses may be taken as a tax deduction.

➤ Contracts are usually not regulated by the insurance department, and therefore the department cannot assist consumers with problems.

➤ Contracts are not subject to mandated benefits laws.

501(c)(9) Trusts

Section 501(c)(9) of the Internal Revenue Code provides for the establishment of voluntary employees' beneficiary associations or *501(c)(9) trusts* that are funding vehicles for the employee benefits that are offered to members.

Some employers may prefer to establish a 501(c)(9) trust for some of the tax advantages it provides. Under a regular self-funded plan, contributions to the plan cannot be deducted until benefits are distributed. But contributions to 501(c)(9) trusts are deducted immediately. Accumulated earnings on 501(c)(9) assets are also tax-deductible, unlike earnings on funds in a regular self-insured plan.

Maintaining a 501(c)(9) trust can be quite costly though, and administration of the plan must be exceptional to make it worthwhile to the employer. High losses under the plan may negate any tax advantages a 501(c)(9) trust offers.

Small Employers

Small employers (usually defined as those with fewer than 25 or 50 employees) have been especially hard hit by increases in health care insurance premiums.

Because many group plans are *experience rated*, small employers see an immediate premium increase whenever claims are particularly high. If the average age of the participants is particularly high, or if claims experience is high, or if there has been even one long or catastrophic illness in a small employer plan, it can have a devastating effect, making health insurance unaffordable for the whole group.

Several states have acted to ensure that health insurance coverages are available at a reasonable cost and under reasonable conditions for small employers, including imposing these requirements:

➤ Standard benefit plans that must be offered to small employers

➤ Maximum waiting periods for preexisting conditions

➤ No exclusion from coverage for particular individuals or medical conditions

➤ Cancellation or nonrenewal of small employer plans only for nonpayment of premium, fraud, misrepresentation, or noncompliance with plan provisions

Cafeteria Plans

A *cafeteria plan* could be defined as a plan in which employees select health benefits from a variety of coverage options, based on their individual and family needs. Cafeteria plans tend to be more complex (and more expensive) than traditional plans, especially with regard to plan administration, and usually make the most sense for larger employers. Benefits are elected in advance of the year in which they will be used. Taxation of cafeteria plans is regulated by Section 125 of the Internal Revenue Code.

Multiple Employer Trusts (METs)

Multiple employer trusts (METs) provide health insurance benefits to small businesses through a series of trusts usually established based on specific industries such as manufacturing, sales and service, real estate, and so forth. Generally, states may require a minimum of five to ten participants for a group to be eligible for group benefits. METs typically have no such requirements and in reality a group of one could be eligible for group benefits.

METs are formed by insurers or third-party administrators who are called *sponsors*. The sponsor develops the plan, sets the underwriting rules, and administers the plan. To help prevent the possibility of adverse selection, the underwriter must make sure that the sponsor's underwriting rules are adequate and that he or she adheres to them. This is necessary because an employer with only two, three, or five employees could elect to join a MET because they know of the poor health condition of one of the employees. The underwriting standards must be able to prevent this from happening.

If state law allows, METs may be noninsured. The trustee has charge of the funds, and the policies and all financial activities occur through the trust.

As with a traditional group insurance plan, a master policy is issued to a trustee who is operating under a trust agreement. The master contract has its own policy effective date and renewal dates that the insurer may use for changing rates on the MET's entire block of business. Each individual employer under the MET has its own effective dates and anniversary dates.

Rates are generally changed on the employer's anniversary date, but usually not more than once in 12 months.

Multiple Employer Welfare Arrangements (MEWAs)

Multiple Employer Welfare Arrangements (MEWAs) are employer funds and trusts providing health care benefits (among other benefits) to employees of two or more employers.

MEWAs need to obtain a Certificate of Authority in order to transact insurance business and must be fully insured by a licensed insurer. MEWAs have recently been used to dupe employers and producers in fraudulent insurance schemes. Before representing a MEWA, agents and brokers should check with the department of insurance and make sure that the entity is properly licensed to do business in his or her state.

Other Forms of Group Insurance

In addition to traditional forms of individual and group health insurance, there are some variations known as blanket or franchise policies.

Blanket Policies

Many types of groups, such as the students of a single school or a group of campers, are indefinite in number and composition and are constantly changing. These characteristics prevent qualification for group insurance under the usual terms.

However, groups such as these can have health coverage at group rates under a *blanket policy*. Because no employer/employee relationship is involved, the members of such groups are not usually interested in covering themselves for loss of income resulting from their activities as a group. Instead, they usually want only hospital, medical, and surgical coverages.

Blanket policies may be either contributory or noncontributory.

Franchise Policies

An arrangement that allows very small groups to have some of the benefits of group insurance, especially the lower cost, is called *franchise insurance*.

Franchise insurance works much like group insurance, but there is no master policy. Instead, each member of the group receives an individual insurance policy. This allows group members to make some coverage choices, but they are required to provide health information on their applications, just as they would for individual policies.

Like true group coverage, franchise insurance offers hospital, surgical, medical, and disability income coverage. Plans may be contributory or noncontributory. One premium is paid for the whole group.

One example of franchise insurance is coverage sold by mail to groups such as the members of a certain association or holders of certain credit cards. Purchasers receive individual policies at group rates.

Government Health Insurance

Both the federal and state government offer statutory health insurance programs. On the federal level, social security provides disability income benefits and administers the medicare program. On the state level, all states have workers compensation laws and medicaid or some similar form of state-subsidized health care.

Social security benefits were covered in an earlier chapter. In this chapter, we will look at workers compensation, medicare, and medicaid.

Workers Compensation

Most states require employers to provide workers compensation benefits for their employees. Workers compensation is designed to help the person who suffers from loss of income due to injury or sickness that occurs as a result of his or her occupation.

Eligibility

In order to be *eligible* for workers compensation benefits the disabled worker must

➤ Work in an occupation that is covered by workers compensation

➤ Have had an accident or sickness that is work-related

Benefits

Workers compensation laws provide for the payment of four types of benefits:

➤ Medical benefits

➤ Income benefits

➤ Death benefits

➤ Rehabilitation benefits

Medical benefits are provided without limit. An injured or diseased employee is entitled to receive all necessary medical and surgical treatment to cure or relieve the condition. Certain maximums or limits may apply to a type of care or a particular medical item, but overall benefits are unlimited.

Income *benefits* are paid to employees who suffer work-related disabilities.

An *elimination period* applies before benefits for loss of wages begin. If the disability continues beyond a certain period, retroactive benefits will be paid for the initial waiting period. A disability may be total (making employment impossible) or partial (resulting in a reduced ability to work). Either type of disability may be temporary or permanent. For *permanent total disability or temporary total disability*, the benefit is 66 2/3% of weekly wages, subject to minimum and maximum weekly limits. However, for permanent total disability, the dollar maximum and the benefit period are greater (benefits for permanent total disability often continue for life, but benefits for a temporary total disability are limited). People with *partial disabilities* are able to perform some work, so the laws provide a benefit equal to a percentage of the wage loss (difference between earnings before and after the accident). In addition to benefits for lost wages, the state provides scheduled benefits for specific *permanent partial disabilities*, such as loss of limbs, sight, or hearing.

Usually these benefits are paid in addition to any other income benefits. *Death benefits* provide two types of payments. Up to a certain dollar amount is provided as a burial allowance, and the state also provides weekly income payments for a surviving spouse and/or children. Weekly benefits are 66 2/3% of the deceased worker's wages, subject to minimum and maximum dollar amounts, a maximum time limit, and an aggregate payment limit. Surviving children generally receive benefits until a certain age.

Rehabilitation benefits are now recognized as a valuable tool for reducing workers compensation costs and returning disabled employees to their jobs as soon as possible. Rehabilitation may include therapy; vocational training; devices such as wheelchairs; and the costs of travel, lodging, and living expenses while being rehabilitated.

Medicaid

Medicaid provides health care benefits for the financially needy. It is basically a state program with some federal financial support. Medicaid is designed to provide increased assistance to those who are unable to pay for their medical needs. For those persons aged 65 or over, medicaid principally supplements medicare for those who cannot pay the expenses not covered by medicare. For those not eligible for medicare, it provides medical assistance for certain categories of people who are medically needy—the blind, the disabled, families with dependent children, or medically needy children under age 21.

Medicaid is a federal-state program. The federal government encourages states to increase medical assistance to the indigent, regardless of age, by paying one-half of the administration cost of state medical assistance programs and 50%–80% of the fees to the providers of services to the needy. The actual federal matching proposition varies inversely with the state average per capita income; therefore, the poorer states receive the larger federal grants.

Generally, medicaid helps to pay for medical services for which the patient cannot pay. Thus, medicaid will cover such services as hospitalizations, physician's services, diagnostic testing, pregnancies, and so forth.

In addition, medicaid also serves as a supplement to medicare in some situations. For example, medicare currently offers extremely limited coverage for nursing home care. Often medicaid will supplement these limited benefits by paying for nursing home expenses. Other health care expenses not completely covered by medicare may be paid for by medicaid.

TRICARE

The Department of Defense operates one of the largest health care systems in the United States, covering more than 8 million active duty and retired military personnel and their families. In response to increasing health care costs and the closing of many military hospitals, the Pentagon has revised and renamed its health care program. Formerly called CHAMPUS (Civilian Health and Medical Program of the Uniformed Services), the new TRICARE program provides care for all seven of the uniformed services, and incorporates many of the managed care options found in private health care plans. A choice of three health care plans is offered:

➤ *TRICARE Prime* offers HMO-style care provided through a primary care manager. All nonemergency care is received at military hospitals and clinics, or through the TRICARE network of contracted civilian care providers (TRICARE Prime is the least expensive to the enrollee).

➤ *TRICARE Extra* offers health care through a network of civilian hospitals and clinics that have agreed to charge an approved rate for medical treatments and procedures.

➤ *TRICARE Standard*, which is essentially the same as the old CHAMPUS program, allows enrollees the flexibility of using civilian doctors for all outpatient care, with partial reimbursement by the government (TRICARE Standard is the most expensive to the enrollee).

Several military organizations also offer TRICARE Supplements, which, like medicare supplements, are insurance plans that cover the deductibles and copayment charges imposed by the TRICARE health plan.

Exam Prep Questions

1. The Albuquerque HMO's contracting physicians are paid employees working on the staff of the HMO, operating in a clinic setting at the HMO's physical facilities. The Albuquerque HMO operates as a(n)
   - ○ A. Staff model HMO
   - ○ B. Network model HMO
   - ○ C. Group model HMO
   - ○ D. Individual Practice Association Model HMO

2. Star HMO contracts with 14 medical groups to increase accessibility to providers as a convenience for subscribers. Each of the medical groups is paid on a capitation basis to provide services to Star's subscribers. The Star HMO operates as a(n)
   - ○ A. Staff model HMO
   - ○ B. Network model HMO
   - ○ C. Group model HMO
   - ○ D. Individual Practice Association Model HMO

3. The Provider's Choice HMO was started by a group of individual physicians who each operate out of their own offices. The physicians are paid on a fee-for-service basis with the fees negotiated in advance. Provider's Choice HMO operates as a(n)
   - ○ A. Staff model HMO
   - ○ B. Network model HMO
   - ○ C. Group model HMO
   - ○ D. Individual Practice Association Model HMO

4. Gwyneth's HMO requires that she receive health care services from a specified, limited number of health care providers chosen by the HMO. Gwyneth's HMO is
   - ○ A. Open-panel
   - ○ B. Closed-panel
   - ○ C. Choice-panel
   - ○ D. Guarded-panel

5. All of the following are examples of managed care plans except
   - ○ A. Health maintenance organizations
   - ○ B. Preferred provider organizations
   - ○ C. Indemnity arrangements
   - ○ D. Point-of-service plans

6. A method of payment in which a provider is paid a specific fee monthly for each subscriber is known as
   - ○ A. Indemnity
   - ○ B. Fee-for-service
   - ○ C. Managed care
   - ○ D. Capitation

7. Calvin is hit by a car while traveling out of state. When the bill for his emergency services arrives, Calvin's HMO will probably
   - ○ A. Pay for the services, even though they were incurred out-of-network, because emergency coverage is a basic health care service.
   - ○ B. Deny the claim, because the services were out of network.
   - ○ C. Pay the claim only if the HMO had an affiliation agreement with the facility where the services were provided.
   - ○ D. Pay the claim if the HMO had an affiliation agreement with the facility where the services were provided, or there is no affiliated facility within 50 miles.

8. The Gargantuan Garage company funds its own claims, but it uses another company to make sure the plan is run correctly, acting as a liaison between the insurer and the employer. This arrangement is probably a
   - ○ A. Cafeteria plan
   - ○ B. Health Maintenance Organization
   - ○ C. Multiple employer trust
   - ○ D. Third-party administrator

9. Julia has a policy that will pay any expenses that she incurs due to in-hospital medical treatment, as well as some of the expenses she incurs on an outpatient basis. Julia probably has a
   - ○ A. Disability income policy
   - ○ B. Medical expense insurance policy
   - ○ C. Long-term care policy
   - ○ D. Hospital income insurance policy

10. George has a policy that will provide him an income if he is disabled from illness or injury and recuperating at home. George probably has a
    - ○ A. Disability income policy
    - ○ B. Medical expense insurance policy
    - ○ C. Long-term care policy
    - ○ D. Hospital income insurance policy

Exam Prep Answers

1. **A is correct.** This is an example of a staff model.

2. **B is correct.** This is an example of a network model.

3. **D is correct.** This is an example of an individual practice association model.

4. **B is correct.** This is an example of a closed-panel HMO structure.

5. C is correct. Traditional insurance plans are indemnity arrangements and not a form of managed care.

6. **D is correct.** A capitation fee is a fixed amount paid to the provider for each patient.

7. **A is correct.** Emergency coverage is provided even when received out of state and out of network.

8. **D is correct.** The garage is using a third-party administrator.

9. **B is correct.** This is an example of a medical expense policy.

10. **A is correct.** This is an example of a disability income policy.

Health Insurance Policy Underwriting, Issuance, and Delivery

Terms you need to understand:

✓ Premium
✓ Earned premium
✓ Unearned premium
✓ Initial premium
✓ Policy effective date
✓ Policy term
✓ Policy fee

Concepts you need to master:

✓ Premium modes
✓ Policy delivery
✓ Servicing a policy
✓ Policy replacement
✓ Fiduciary responsibilities

Underwriting Objectives

Health insurance underwriting is the process of selection, classification, and rating of risks. Most companies offering health policies have a variety of policies available, and underwriting standards for each policy are usually established.

Low-limit policies with limited coverages do not require the underwriting that broad-coverage policies with high limits do; the greater the company's exposure, the more careful the underwriter has to be. Underwriting is generally more restrictive for individual than for group policies. The underwriter's principal functions are to review applications to eliminate those that do not meet underwriting standards, thus reducing *adverse selection*, and to *classify risks* to establish benefits and corresponding premium.

Certain underwriting factors for health insurance may be more or less important than for the underwriting of life insurance. For example, an individual with a serious back ailment presents a major risk for the health insurance underwriter because of the danger of such a chronic condition creating several expensive claim situations. However, for the life insurance underwriter, this same condition may be of little significance because a bad back is not likely to affect the individual's mortality.

Premium Payments

You should understand the definitions of premium, earned premium, and unearned premium, as well as the concept of premium payment modes.

Definition of Premium

The *premium* is a sum of money the insured pays the insurer in exchange for or in consideration of the benefits or indemnities provided in the policy.

Earned and Unearned Premium

Premium payment frequency varies, but regardless of frequency, the insured is always paying for the upcoming period. That is, insurance premiums are paid in advance.

Suppose Kathryn's health insurance premium is $500 per year, which she pays in full on January 1. Because the $500 covers an entire year, the insurer earns the premium as the time passes, having both *earned* and *unearned* premium on hand during the policy term. By March 31 of the year, the insurer has provided protection for 3 full months, so approximately 25% of the premium represents the amount paid for the period for which protection has been provided and $125 would be the *earned premium* at that time. The remaining $375 of premium Kathryn has paid is, as of March 31, called the *unearned premium*.

Payment Modes

In the insurance industry, *mode of premium payment* refers to the *frequency* with which premiums are paid. Payments may be made

➤ Annually—once a year

➤ Semiannually—twice a year

➤ Quarterly—once every 3 months

➤ Monthly—once a month

➤ Weekly—once a week

Of these five modes, the least-used frequency for individual policies is weekly.

You probably know that in group health plans employers often deduct the employees' shares weekly, but it is likely that the employer actually sends the premium to the insurer less frequently.

Insurers generally calculate premiums on an annual basis. If the insured wants to pay by any of the other modes, the premium increases slightly as the frequency increases. The increases allow the insurer to recoup both the additional billing and handling costs and the lost interest the insurer could have earned by having the full annual premium to invest all at once. So, for example, a monthly premium mode results in a premium that is somewhat higher than a semiannual mode. An annual premium mode results in a premium that is somewhat lower than a quarterly mode.

Initial Premium

The *initial premium*, as the name implies, is the first premium the applicant pays in order to place the policy into effect. A health insurance policy goes into force when the initial premium has been paid and the policy has been delivered to the insured, unless the initial premium was paid with the application and a conditional receipt was issued. When the initial premium is paid with the application and the applicant satisfies all the conditions of the conditional receipt, coverage takes effect as if the policy had already been issued.

A producer should always try to obtain the initial premium with an app and submit the entire package for underwriting. This affords faster protection to applicants, and applicants are less likely to change their minds about purchasing policies when they have money invested in them.

The important thing to remember is that coverage never applies until the insured has paid for it. If the initial premium does not accompany the application, the premium must be collected at policy delivery along with a signed statement that the insured continues to be in good health. The policy is then effective as of the date stated in the policy.

Policy Effective Date

Although it is generally true that a policy is effective when the initial premium has been paid and the policy delivered (or under the conditions of a conditional receipt), there is a better way for a producer to respond when asked when a particular policy takes effect.

The best approach is to state that the policy takes effect on the date specified in the policy as the effective date. Remember that accident coverages usually take effect immediately when the policy is issued, and sickness coverages may require a probationary period. Therefore, different coverages under the same policy might have different effective dates.

Policy Term

When a health insurance policy becomes effective, it will stay in force for the period for which the premium has been paid, unless the insurer or the insured cancels it. In other words, the policy will stay in force for a specified period or *term*.

The length of the term is governed by the length of time for which coverage is purchased by the premium payment. If a policy calls for annual premium payment, for example, 1 year is the term of the policy. If premiums are paid semiannually, the term extends for each 6-month period for which the premium is paid.

Policy Fee

When a policy is issued, some companies charge a *policy fee*, which is generally a flat amount that helps defray expenses such as acquisition costs, producer commissions, administration, and maintenance of the policy. There are two different ways a policy fee might be handled.

Exam Prep Questions

1. When a health insurance policy becomes effective, unless it is canceled, it will stay in force
   - ○ A. For 1 year
   - ○ B. For 6 months
   - ○ C. The length of the term
   - ○ D. Indefinitely

2. Legally, the policy is considered delivered in all of the following situations except:
   - ○ A. When the policy is approved by the company
   - ○ B. When the policy is mailed to the policyowner
   - ○ C. When the policy is turned over to the policyowner
   - ○ D. When the policy is turned over to someone acting on behalf of the policyowner

3. An insurer might require personal delivery
   - ○ A. To ensure the policy goes to the right person
   - ○ B. For verification of the continued good health of the insured at the time of delivery
   - ○ C. To ensure the correct policy is delivered
   - ○ D. To verify information listed on the application

4. No loss-no gain legislation
   - ○ A. Requires a replacing policy to have exactly the same premium as the policy it replaces
   - ○ B. Requires a replacing policy to have exactly the same limits of coverage as the policy it replaces
   - ○ C. Requires a replacing policy to continue to pay claims ongoing under the policy it replaces
   - ○ D. Requires a replacing policy to continue to use the same producer to manage the policy as the policy it replaces

5. A statement that assures benefits provided under the old policy will continue under the new policy is
   - ○ A. A transfer of benefits statement
   - ○ B. A continuation of benefits statement
   - ○ C. A preexisting conditions coverage statement
   - ○ D. A replacement statement

6. Restrictions applying to the replacement of Medicare supplement policies

   ○ A. Are often less restrictive than regulations applying to the replacement of other policies

   ○ B. Are generally the same as regulations applying to the replacement of other policies

   ○ C. Are often more restrictive than regulations applying to the replacement of other policies

   ○ D. Are prohibited entirely by federal law

7. Ally pays for her health insurance monthly. Her identical twin Georgia has the same policy, but pays annually. Which of them probably pays more for the policy?

   ○ A. Ally probably pays more.

   ○ B. Georgia probably pays more.

   ○ C. They probably pay the same.

   ○ D. It is not possible to determine from the information provided.

8. Health insurance coverage never applies until

   ○ A. The policy is delivered.

   ○ B. An underwriting decision is made.

   ○ C. The application is reviewed by underwriting.

   ○ D. The insured has paid for the policy.

Exam Prep Answers

1. **C is correct.** The policy will stay in force for the length of the term for which a premium has been paid.

2. **A is correct.** Underwriting approval does not constitute delivery.

3. **B is correct.** If a verification of good health is required, the agent will have to personally deliver the policy.

4. **C is correct.** To avoid gaps in coverage the new policy has to cover claims that would have been covered by the previous policy.

5. **A is correct.** This is the term used for the document that assures that the same benefits will continue.

6. **C is correct.** Requirements related to replacing Medicare supplement policies are more restrictive in order to protect senior citizens.

7. **A is correct.** Ally will pay more because the insurance company does not have the use of her entire annual premium in advance.

8. **D is correct.** Health insurance will not take effect until the insured has paid the premium.

Health Insurance Policy Provisions

Terms you need to understand:

- ✓ Entire contract
- ✓ Incontestability
- ✓ Grace period
- ✓ Reinstatement
- ✓ Notice of claim
- ✓ Claim forms
- ✓ Proof of loss
- ✓ Payment of claims
- ✓ Legal actions
- ✓ Pro rata return
- ✓ Short-rate return
- ✓ Policy face
- ✓ Free look
- ✓ Insuring clause
- ✓ Consideration clause
- ✓ Exclusion
- ✓ Reduction
- ✓ Preexisting condition

Concepts you need to master:

- ✓ Mandatory provisions
- ✓ Optional provisions
- ✓ Change of occupation
- ✓ Misstatement of age
- ✓ Other insurance
- ✓ Relation of earnings to insurance
- ✓ Unpaid premium
- ✓ Policy cancellation
- ✓ Flat cancellation
- ✓ Nonoccupational coverage
- ✓ Case management provisions
- ✓ Waiver of premium

Because both state insurance laws and insurance policies vary greatly, an attempt has been made to make health insurance policies conform to certain standard regulations. To accomplish this, all states have adopted the Uniform Individual Accident and Sickness Policy Provisions Law. Nearly every state has modified the law to some extent, but all have adopted it in principle.

The law includes *12 mandatory provisions* that must be included in individual health insurance policies and *11 optional provisions*. Each of the mandatory provisions must be included in each policy, usually in a section of the policy entitled "Mandatory or Required Provisions." Insurance companies need not use the exact wording of the provisions, but any variations must be *at least as favorable to the insured* as the original statutory wording.

This chapter presents each provision exactly as it appears in the law, followed by a short discussion of the content. Because the provision language is somewhat stilted "legalese," don't be surprised if you have to read a provision more than once.

Mandatory Provisions

The following is a review of the mandatory, or required, health insurance provisions.

Required Provision 1: Entire Contract; Changes

Here is the exact wording of the provision:

> This policy, including the endorsements and the attached papers, if any, constitutes the entire contract of insurance. No change in this policy shall be valid until approved by an executive officer of the insurer and unless such approval be endorsed hereon or attached hereto. No agent has authority to change this policy or to waive any of its provisions.

This provision defines an entire contract as:

➤ The insurance policy

➤ Endorsements, if any

➤ Attachments, if any

Nothing else is part of the contract.

Required Provision 2: Time Limit on Certain Defenses; Incontestability

(a) After two years from the date of issue of this policy, no misstatements, except fraudulent misstatements, made by the applicant in the application for such policy shall be used to void the policy or to deny a claim for loss incurred or disability (as defined in the policy) commencing after the expiration of such two-year period.

(b) No claim for loss incurred or disability (as defined in the policy) commencing after two years from the date of issue of this policy shall be reduced or denied on the ground that a disease or physical condition, not excluded from coverage by name or specific description effective on the date of loss, had existed prior to the effective date of coverage of this policy.

Unless the insured has made a fraudulent misstatement, the policy cannot be voided or claims denied after 2 years (3 years in some states).

After 2 years, preexisting conditions cannot affect the policy's benefits. An insurer may specifically exclude coverage for a certain condition if it is named in the policy when it is written.

Required Provision 3: Grace Period

A grace period of...days (the period varies according to premium payment frequency: seven days for weekly-premium policies; 10 days for monthly-premium policies; 31 days for all other policies) will be granted for the payment of each premium falling due after the first premium, during which grace period the policy shall continue in force.

A policy that contains a cancellation provision may add the following at the end of the above provision: "subject to the right of the insurer to cancel in accordance with the cancellation provision hereof."

A policy in which the insurer reserves the right to refuse any renewal shall have the following at the beginning of the above provision: "unless not less than five days prior to the premium due date the insurer has delivered to the insured, or has mailed to the last address as shown by the records of the insurer, written notice of its intention not to renew this policy beyond the period for which the premium has been accepted."

Insurers must allow the insured a period of grace for premium payment. This is a specified time following the premium due date during which coverage remains intact. During a grace period, the company continues coverage in full force and will accept the premium from the policyowner just as if it were not late.

If a policy is cancelable, the grace period is subject to the policy's cancellation provision. In an optionally renewable policy the company has decided not to renew, the company must follow certain steps to avoid having the grace period affect its right not to renew. The insurer is required to mail written notice of its intention not to renew to the insured's last known address at least 5 days before the premium due date.

Required Provision 4: Reinstatement

Before you read this provision, let's cover some information not specifically mentioned in the provision itself. The insured, unlike the insurer, may cancel a policy at any time. In addition, the insured can simply refuse or fail to pay the premium when it is next due. When this occurs, we say that the policy has lapsed. Whether the policy is canceled by the insurer or the insured or it lapses, the end result is the same—the coverage terminates.

Because this provision is quite long, we'll cover it in two parts. Here is the first portion:

> If any renewal premium be not paid within the time granted the insured for payment, a subsequent acceptance of premium by the insurer or by any agent duly authorized by the insurer to accept such premium, without requiring in connection therewith an application for reinstatement, shall reinstate the policy; provided, however, that if the insurer or such agent requires an application for reinstatement and issues a conditional receipt for the premium tendered, the policy will be reinstated upon approval of such application by the insurer or, lacking such approval, upon the 45th day following the date of such conditional receipt unless the insurer has previously notified the insured in writing of its disapproval of such application.

A lapsed policy is reinstated when either the company or the company's agent accepts subsequent premiums unless an application for reinstatement is required. In that case, a conditional receipt would be issued to the insured and the insurer has 45 days to notify the applicant of a denial or the policy is automatically reinstated.

> The reinstated policy shall cover only loss resulting from such accidental injury as may be sustained after the date of reinstatement and loss due to such sickness as may begin more than 10 days after such

date. In all other respects the insured and insurer shall have the same rights thereunder as they had under the policy immediately before the due date of the defaulted premium, subject to any provisions endorsed hereon or attached hereto in connection with the reinstatement. Any premium accepted in connection with the reinstatement shall be applied to a period for which premium has not been previously paid, but not to any period more than 60 days prior to the date of reinstatement The last sentence of the above may be omitted from policies guaranteed renewable to age 50, or if issued after age 54, guaranteed renewable for at least five years.

When the policy is reinstated, there is a 10-day waiting period for sickness coverage but no waiting period for accident coverage.

Otherwise, both the insurer and the insured have all the same rights each had the day before the policy lapsed, subject to any endorsements or riders attached at the time of reinstatement.

Required Provision 5: Notice of Claim

This lengthy provision is also presented in two parts. Here is the first portion:

Written notice of claim must be given to the insurer within 20 days after occurrence or commencement of any loss covered by the policy, or as soon thereafter as is reasonably possible. Notice given by or in behalf of the insured or the beneficiary to the insurer at . . . . (insert the location of such office as the insurer may designate for the purpose), or to any authorized agent of the insurer, with information sufficient to identify the insured, shall be deemed notice to the insurer.

If reasonably possible, the insured must give written notice of claim to the insurer or agent within 20 days after a loss.

Here is the remainder of Required Uniform Provision 5. Policies providing loss-of-time benefits payable for at least 2 years may insert the following between the first and second sentences of the above provision:

Subject to the qualifications set forth below, if the insured suffers loss of time on account of disability for which indemnity may be payable for at least two years, he or she shall, at least once in every six months after having given notice of claim, give to the insurer notice of continuance of said disability, except in the event of legal incapacity. The period of six months following any filing of proof by the insured or any payment by the insurer on account of such claim or any denial of liability in whole or in part by the insurer shall be excluded in applying this provision. Delay in the giving of such notice shall not impair the insured's right to any indemnity which would otherwise have accrued during the period of six months preceding the date on which such notice is actually given.

The essence of this provision is that if the policy provides disability income for an extended period, the insurer can require that the insured provide, every 6 months, written notice that the claim is continuing. This provision does not apply when the insured suffers a legal incapacity.

Required Provision 6: Claim Forms

The insurer, upon receipt of a notice of claim, will furnish to the claimant such forms as are usually furnished by it for filing proofs of loss. If such forms are not furnished within 15 days after the giving of such notice, the claimant shall be deemed to have complied with the requirements of this policy as to proof of loss upon submitting, within the time fixed in the policy for filing proofs of loss, written proof covering the occurrence, the character and the extent of the loss for which claim is made.

Insureds should be given forms to provide proof of loss within 15 days. If the insurer fails to do so, however, the insured must file his or her own written proof of loss.

Required Provision 7: Proof of Loss

Written proof of loss must be furnished to the insurer at its said office in case of claim for loss for which this policy provides any periodic payment contingent upon continuing loss within 90 days after the termination of the period for which the insurer is liable, and in case of claims for any other loss within 90 days after the date of such loss. Failure to furnish such proof within the time required shall not invalidate nor reduce any claim if it was not reasonably possible to give such proof within such time, provided such proof is furnished as soon as reasonably possible and in no event, except in the absence of legal capacity, later than one year

NOTE

Normally, written proofs of loss must be furnished within 90 days after the date of loss. But when the claim involves periodic payments because of a continuing loss, proofs must be furnished within 90 days after the end of the period for which the company is liable.

If it was not reasonably possible for the insured to provide proofs of loss within the time required, the claim is not invalidated. Still, unless the insured suffers legal incapacity, proofs of loss must be furnished no later than 1 year from the date they were otherwise due.

Required Provision 8: Time of Payment of Claims

> Indemnities payable under this policy for any loss other than loss for which this policy provides any periodic payment will be paid immediately upon receipt of due written proof of such loss. Subject to due written proof of loss, all accrued indemnities for loss for which this policy provides periodic payment will be paid...(insert period for payment, which must not be less frequently than monthly) and any balance remaining unpaid upon the termination of liability will be paid immediately upon receipt of due written proof.

According to this provision, except for claims involving periodic payments over a specified time span, the insurer must make the payment immediately after receiving proof of loss. Payment of periodic indemnities (for disability, for instance) must be made at least monthly.

Required Provision 9: Payment of Claims

This long provision actually contains both a required portion and two optional paragraphs. Here is the required section:

> Indemnity for loss of life will be payable in accordance with the beneficiary designation and the provisions respecting such payment which may be prescribed herein and effective at the time of payment. If no such designation or provision is then effective, such indemnity shall be payable to the estate of the insured. Any other accrued indemnities unpaid at the insured's death may, at the option of the insurer, be paid either to such beneficiary or to such estate. All other indemnities will be payable to the insured.

This *required* portion of the provision states that

➤ Death benefits will be paid to the named beneficiary.

➤ If there is no beneficiary designated, the company will pay the benefit to the insured's estate.

➤ If the insured was receiving monthly indemnities under the policy and some accrued benefits remain at the time of death, the company may pay these accruals to either the beneficiary or the insured's estate.

➤ While the insured is alive, all other benefits are paid to the insured unless otherwise specifically designated in the policy.

Here is the first of the two optional paragraphs that are included in Required Provision 9:

> If any indemnity of this policy shall be payable to the estate of the insured, or to an insured or beneficiary who is a minor or otherwise not competent to give a valid release, the insurer may pay such indemnity, up to an amount not exceeding $...(insert an amount which shall not exceed $1,000), to any relative by blood or connection by marriage of the insured or beneficiary who is deemed by the insurer to be equitably entitled thereto. Any payment made by the insurer in good faith pursuant to this provision shall fully discharge the insurer to the extent of such payment.

This first optional paragraph is often called the *facility of payment clause* because it makes claim payment easier under the circumstances described. It stipulates the following:

➤ If the insured or the beneficiary cannot legally release the company from further liability, as when the insured or beneficiary is a minor or is legally incapacitated, the company may pay the benefits to any relative by blood or marriage who is deemed to be entitled to the money.

➤ The amount paid to this person cannot exceed $1,000.

If a claim is paid under this provision, the payment absolves the company of further liability.

Here is the second of the optional paragraphs that may be included with Required Provision 9:

> Subject to any written direction of the insured in the application or otherwise, all or a portion of any indemnities provided by this policy on account of hospital, nursing, medical or surgical services may, at the insurer's option, and unless the insured requests otherwise in writing not later than the time of filing proofs of such loss, be paid directly to the hospital or person rendering such services but it is not required that the service be rendered by a particular hospital or person.

According to this second optional paragraph, unless the insured specifically directs otherwise, the company may pay benefits to a hospital or person rendering medical or surgical services. However, the company may not require that the insured enter a specific hospital or see a particular doctor.

Required Provision 10: Physical Examination and Autopsy

The insurer at its own expense shall have the right and opportunity to examine the person of the insured when and as often as it may reasonably require during the pendency of a claim hereunder and to make an autopsy in case of death where it is not forbidden by law.

While the insured is alive and receiving benefits, the insurer may require that he or she submit to a physical examination.

If an insured has died, apparently accidentally, the insurer may have an autopsy performed to determine the exact cause of death.

Required Provision 11: Legal Actions

No action at law or in equity shall be brought to recover on this policy prior to the expiration of 60 days after written proof of loss has been furnished in accordance with the requirements of this policy. No such action shall be brought after the expiration of three years after the time written proof of loss is required to be furnished.

This provision prohibits the insured from suing the insurer within less than 60 days or more than 3 years after filing a written proof of loss.

Required Provision 12: Change of Beneficiary

Unless the insured makes an irrevocable designation of beneficiary, the right to change of beneficiary is reserved to the insured and the consent of the beneficiary or beneficiaries shall not be requisite to surrender or assignment of this policy or to any change of beneficiary or beneficiaries, or to any other changes in this policy.

The policyowner, who is usually the insured, may name a beneficiary either revocably, which means that the insured can change the beneficiary later, or irrevocably, which means the beneficiary designation may not be changed. In other words, the right to change the beneficiary or dispose of the policy or its benefits in any manner one chooses is reserved to the insured unless he or she has named an irrevocable beneficiary.

Suppose Ben has named his wife the irrevocable beneficiary of the accidental death benefit of his health insurance policy. Now he wants to obtain a large loan and the lender agrees to make the loan if Ben will assign any payments under his policy to the lender. Ben may assign the policy only with his wife's permission.

Optional Policy Provisions

The optional provisions are not required to be included in the policy, but if the subject of any of them is contained in the policy, it must be worded in accordance with the wording of the appropriate optional provision.

Optional Provision 1: Change of Occupation

Here is the first optional provision:

> If the insured be injured or contract sickness after having changed his or her occupation to one classified by the insurer as more hazardous than that stated in this policy, or while doing for compensation anything pertaining to an occupation so classified, the insurer will pay only such portion of the indemnities provided in this policy as the premium paid would have purchased at the rates and within limits fixed by the insurer for a more hazardous occupation. If the insured changes an occupation to one classified by the insurer as less hazardous than that stated in this policy, the insurer, upon receipt of proof of such change of occupation, will reduce the premium rate accordingly, and will return the excess pro rata unearned premium from the date of change of occupation or from the policy anniversary date immediately preceding receipt of such proof, whichever is the more recent.

> In applying this provision, the classification of occupational risk and the premium rates shall be such as have been last filed by the insurer prior to the occurrence of the loss for which the insurer is liable, or prior to date of proof of change in occupation with the state official having supervision of insurance in the state where the insured resided at the time this policy was issued; but if such filing was not required, then the classification of occupational risk and the premium rates shall be those last made effective by the insurer in such state prior to the occurrence of the loss or prior to the date of proof of change in occupation.

This provision relieves the insurer from paying benefits not anticipated when the premium was established. If an insured's occupation is more hazardous than the insurer knew, and resulted in injury or illness, the insurer might be required to pay a larger benefit than the premium warrants.

When calculating how much of the extra premium to return, the company uses the more recent of

➤ The date the occupation changed

➤ The policy anniversary date immediately preceding receipt of the proof of change

Optional Provision 2: Misstatement of Age

If the age of the insured has been misstated, all amounts payable under this policy shall be such as the premium paid would have purchased at the correct age.

When an insured is younger, a premium dollar buys a certain amount of insurance. As the insured ages, the same premium dollar buys less insurance. This provision is similar to the previous provision regarding a more hazardous occupation. If the insured has misstated his or her age on the application, the company may adjust benefits to the amount the premiums paid would have bought had the insured's correct age been known.

 Whether the insured misstated his or her age intentionally or unintentionally, the company adjusts benefits accordingly.

Optional Provision 3: Other Insurance in This Insurer

If an accident or sickness policy or policies previously issued by the insurer to the insured be in force concurrently herewith, making the aggregate indemnity for…(insert type of coverage or coverages) in excess of $…(insert maximum limit of indemnity or indemnities) the excess insurance shall be void and all premiums paid for such excess shall be returned to the insured or to the estate.

Or, insurance effective at any one time on the insured under a like policy or policies in this insurer is limited to one such policy elected by the insured, his or her beneficiary or estate, as the case may be, and the insurer will return all premiums paid for all other such policies.

This provision deals with insurance of the same type with the same insurer. If an individual has so much insurance that it is more profitable to see a doctor, enter a hospital, or stay home from work, there might be some temptation to do just that rather than to have a quick recovery. Such an individual is *overinsured*—a situation insurers try to avoid.

This optional provision allows an insurer to control overinsurance through its own policies. The company can establish maximum amounts payable to any one insured for certain coverages—disability income insurance being the most common—so no matter how many policies an insured has with this particular company, there is a limit on the amount of benefits that will be paid.

Either of the two provisions may be included in the policy. If the insurer chooses the first paragraph, it is the insurer's responsibility to decide on the maximum indemnity that will be paid and the type of coverage to which the provision applies. If the insurer uses the second paragraph, coverage is limited to one policy as selected by the insured, the beneficiary, or the administrator of the insured's estate.

Optional Provisions 4 and 5: Insurance with Other Insurers

Although the previous optional provision concerned overinsurance with the same insurer, the next two deal with other insurers. Because they are closely related, they are presented together.

Provision 4

> If there be other valid coverage, not with this insurer, providing benefits for the same loss on a provision of service basis or on a expense-incurred basis and of which this insurer has not been given written notice prior to the occurrence or commencement of loss, the only liability under any expense-incurred coverage of this policy shall be for such proportion of the loss as the amount which would otherwise have been payable hereunder plus the total of the like amounts under all such other valid coverages for the same loss, and for the return of such portion of the premiums paid as shall exceed the pro rata portion of the amount so determined.

For the purpose of applying this provision when other coverage is on a provision of service basis, the "like amount" of such other coverage shall be taken as the amount that the services rendered would have cost in the absence of such coverage.

Provision 5

> If there be other valid coverage, not with this insurer, providing benefits for the same loss on other than an expense-incurred basis

and of which the insurer has not been given written notice prior to the occurrence or commencement of loss, the only liability of such benefits under this policy shall be for such proportion of the indemnities of which the insurer had notice (including the indemnities under this policy) bear to the total amount of all like indemnities for such loss, and for the return of such portion of the premium paid as shall exceed the pro rate portion for the indemnities thus determined.

The essence of Optional Provisions 4 and 5 is this: If an insured has two or more policies from *different* companies that cover the same expenses, and if the insurers were not notified that the other coverage existed, each insurer will pay a *proportionate share* of any claim. Each company must also refund a proportionate share of the excess premiums on a pro rata basis.

The law allows an insurer to include a definition of *other valid coverage* to cover more than just another insurer's individual health policy. This allows other benefit sources such as automobile coverage medical payments, union welfare plans, or Blue Cross/Blue Shield benefits to be taken into account.

Optional Provision 6: Relation of Earnings to Insurance—Average Earnings Clause

This provision specifically concerns loss of time, or disability income, coverage:

> If the total monthly amount of loss of time benefits promised for the same loss under all valid loss of time coverage upon the insured, whether payable on a weekly or monthly basis, shall exceed the monthly earnings of the insured at the time disability commenced, or the average monthly earnings for the period of two years immediately preceding a disability for which claim is made, whichever is greater, the insurer will be liable only for such proportionate amount of such benefits under this policy as the amount of such monthly earnings or such average monthly earnings of the insured bears to the total amount of monthly benefits for the same loss under all such coverage upon the insured at the time such disability commences, and for the return of such part of the premiums paid during such two years as shall exceed the pro rata amount of the premiums for the benefits actually paid hereunder; but this shall not operate to reduce the total monthly amount of benefits payable under all such coverage upon the insured below the sum of $200 or the sum of the monthly benefits specified in such coverages,

whichever is the lesser, nor shall it operate to reduce benefits other than those payable for loss of time.

 This optional provision is also designed to prevent overinsurance malingering—remaining disabled in order to collect insurance. The provision specifically addresses the relationship between what the insured actually has been earning on the job and the amount of insurance available by failing to return to work.

The insurer may define "all valid loss of time coverage" to take into account other benefit sources such as workers compensation, union welfare plans, or employee benefit payments.

Because this provision allows for computation of the insured's average earnings over the course of two years, it is often called the *average earnings clause*.

Optional Provision 7: Unpaid Premium

Upon the payment of a claim under this policy, any premium then due and unpaid or covered by any note or written order may be deducted therefrom.

This simple optional provision enables an insurer to deduct premiums that are due or past due as part of settling a claim.

Optional Provision 8: Cancellation

Let's break this optional provision into two parts. Here is the first part:

The insurer may cancel this policy at any time by written notice delivered to the insured or mailed to the last address as shown by the records of the insurer, stating when, not less than five days thereafter, such cancellation shall be effective; and after the policy has been continued beyond its original term the insured may cancel this policy at any time by written notice delivered or mailed to the insurer, effective upon receipt or on such later date as may be specified in such notice.

Although this provision may not be used in noncancelable policies, in policies that may be canceled, the insurer may do so by delivering (usually by mail) written notice to the insured's last known address. Cancellation is effective no fewer than 5 days after the date of notice.

In the event of cancellation, the insurer will return promptly the unearned portion of any premium paid. If the insured cancels, the earned premium shall be computed by the use of the short rate table last filed with the state official having supervision of insurance in the state where the insured resided when the policy was issued. If the insurer cancels, the earned premium shall be computed pro rata. Cancellation shall be without prejudice to any claim originating prior to the effective date of cancellation.

When the *insurance company* cancels, the portion of the premium dollar the insurer has already earned is kept by the insurer and the entire unearned portion is returned to the insured. This is a *pro rata return*.

When the *insured* cancels, the insurance company is allowed to retain a portion of premium over and above that which it has earned. The insurer keeps earned premium and a portion of unearned premium, returning the balance of unearned premium to the insured. This is a *short-rate return*.

A *flat cancellation* means that a policy is canceled as of its effective date. Usually this means that no premium is charged. For example, when an insured returns a policy during a *free-look period*, any premium payment will be fully refunded.

Optional Provision 9: Conformity with State Statutes

Any provision of this policy which, on its effective date, is in conflict with the statutes of the state in which the insured resides on such date is hereby amended to conform to minimum requirements of such statutes.

Although this provision is usually optional, some states insist that it be included in all policies. Not only does the provision help insurers avoid issuing policies that conflict with existing state laws, it can also prevent reissuing policies that are in conflict with any ruling enacted during the time a policy is being or is about to be issued.

The provision applies to the laws of the insured's state of residence.

Optional Provision 10: Illegal Occupation

The insurer shall not be liable for any loss to which a contributing cause was the insured's commission of or attempt to commit a felony or to which a contributing cause was the insured's being engaged in an illegal occupation.

Suppose Dan's policy contains this provision. Dan's application stated that he is the proprietor of a small newsstand. After Dan was severely beaten one night by someone who apparently was trying to rob him, he applied for benefits under the hospital and medical provisions of his policy. Upon investigating the incident, police discover that Dan was using his newsstand simply as a front. His real employment is fencing stolen goods, and the beating he suffered was the result of a quarrel with other criminals. Because Dan was engaged in an illegal occupation that contributed to his injury, the insurer will not pay his claim.

Optional Provision 11: Narcotics

> The insurer shall not be liable for any loss sustained or contracted in consequence of the insured's being under the influence of any narcotic unless administered on the advice of a physician.

Injuries or death resulting while the insured is under the influence of either alcohol or narcotics are commonly excluded.

Other Health Insurance Provisions

There are a few other policy provisions or concepts you should be aware of that relate to health insurance but are not part of the required or optional provisions specified by law.

The Policy Face

The *face* of the policy is a standard printed form containing the name of the insurance company and providing enough information to give the insured a capsule summary of what type of policy and what type of coverage is provided by the contract. The policy face identifies the insured and states the term of the policy (when it goes into effect and when coverage expires). The policy face also states how the policy can be renewed.

The policy face usually gives a brief statement of the type or types of benefits. However, it is essential to examine the benefit provisions within the body of the contract to obtain a complete understanding of the coverage provided.

Free Look

As mentioned previously, many states require that health policies contain a free-look provision, allowing individuals to look over the policy for a specified period with the right to refuse it. Usually, this is a 10-day trial period, and in some states, may be a 15- or 20-day period, beginning on the day the individual receives the policy. If the individual decides to return the policy by the end of the trial period, he or she receives a full refund of the prepaid premium.

If the individual cancels during the trial period, the insurance company is not liable for any claims originating during that period.

Insuring Clause

The *insuring clause* is usually the initial policy clause. In general, it represents the insurer's promise to pay under the conditions stipulated in the policy.

The insuring clause performs these functions:

➤ Describes the general scope of coverage

➤ Provides any definitions required

➤ Sets forth the conditions under which benefits will be paid

Consideration Clause

In health insurance, the insurance company exchanges the promises in the policy for a two-part consideration from the insured. A health insurance contract is valid only if the insured provides consideration in the form of both of the following:

➤ The full minimum premium required

➤ The statements made in the application

Policy Continuation

A number of policy provisions may affect policy continuation.

Optionally and Conditionally Renewable Policies

To remain in force, health policies must be renewed periodically; that is, the coverage remains in force only for the length of time for which premiums have been paid.

A policyowner has the option of canceling a policy at any time by so notifying the insurer, as well as allowing it to lapse at a premium due date by not paying the premium.

When the insurer has the option to refuse to renew, the policy may be one of two types:

> Optionally renewable, which means the insurer may elect not to renew for *any reason* or for no reason, but may exercise that right only on the premium due date.

> Conditionally renewable, which means the insurer may elect not to renew only *under conditions specified* in the policy.

To protect the insured when a valid claim is being paid or is eligible for payment at the time the premium is due, the claim will be paid even if the insurer elects not to renew the policy.

Cancelable Policies

With a *cancelable* policy, the insurer may cancel coverage at any time, provided it returns any unearned premiums to the insured.

Guaranteed Renewable Policies

In some policies, the insurer relinquishes its rights to cancel at any time and to refuse renewal at a premium due date. This type of policy is called *guaranteed renewable*, and it includes several important features:

> Renewal is guaranteed as long as the insured pays the premium.

> The insurer may not cancel unless the insured fails to pay the premium.

> Premiums may not be increased on an individual basis.

> Premiums may be increased on the basis of an entire classification, such as occupation.

> The guarantee to renew ends at a specified age.

Nonpayment of premium is the only reason an insurer may cancel or refuse to renew a guaranteed renewable policy. Furthermore, the insurer is not permitted to increase the premiums based on the individual insured's experience. It may, however, increase the premiums on a class basis. One common classification, for example, is by occupational groups.

Noncancelable Policies

The terms *noncancelable* and *noncancelable and guaranteed renewable* are often used interchangeably to describe a noncancelable policy. There is one important difference, however. With a guaranteed renewable policy, the insurer may increase the premiums by classifications. With a noncancelable policy, however, the insurer may never increase the premiums. Other features of noncancelable policies are the same as for guaranteed renewable policies.

Term Policies

Coverage that extends only for a specified length of time is called *term insurance*. A term health policy cannot be renewed at all. When it expires, the insured must purchase another policy. Flight insurance is a well-known example of term accident insurance.

Benefit Payment Clause

Health insurance benefits are paid differently depending on the type of policy. How benefits will be paid is set out in the policy's *benefits provision*.

Typically, benefits are paid in the form of

➤ Periodic income under disability policies

➤ Lump-sum reimbursements for expenses incurred under hospital, medical, surgical, and major medical policies

➤ Lump-sum indemnity payments for death or dismemberment under accidental death and dismemberment policies

Preexisting Conditions

By definition, a preexisting condition is any condition for which the insured sought treatment or advice prior to the effective date of the policy. Further, a preexisting condition can also be defined as any symptom that would cause a reasonable and prudent person to seek diagnosis and medical treatment.

Preexisting conditions may be covered by the insurer if they are indicated on the application. The insurer will then review the medical information and, depending on the condition, may elect to cover the problem or exclude it.

Nonoccupational Coverage

Many insurance companies won't assume the risk of covering people such as steeplejacks for the hazards involved in their occupations. To provide these individuals with general accident and sickness and/or disability income coverage, some companies issue policies that contain a provision excluding job-related injuries.

Case Management Provisions

In order to control the costs associated with medical care, many insurers are instituting provisions to reduce costs while giving the insured options for health care. These provisions are variously called *case management, managed care, claims control, cost containment,* or similar terms.

The *second surgical opinion* is a provision that can be included in policies that offer surgical expense benefits. This coverage allows the insured to consult a doctor, other than the attending physician, to determine alternative methods of treatment. Although the use of this provision is sometimes optional, it is more often mandatory for certain procedures, such as tonsillectomy, cataract surgery, coronary bypass, mastectomy, and varicose veins.

One cost control mechanism being used by insurers and employers is *utilization review*. Utilization review consists of an evaluation of the appropriateness, necessity, and quality of health care, and may include preadmission certification and concurrent review.

Under the *precertification provision* (also known as *precertification authorization* or *prospective review*), the physician can submit claim information prior to providing treatment to know in advance whether the procedure is covered under the insured's plan and at what rate it will be paid. This provision allows the insurance company to evaluate the appropriateness of the procedure and the length of the hospital stay.

Under the *concurrent review* process, the insurer will monitor the insured's hospital stay to make sure that everything is proceeding according to schedule and that the insured will be released from the hospital as planned.

Ambulatory outpatient care is the alternative to the costly inpatient diagnostic testing and treatment. Today, ambulatory care is best known to operate in hospital outpatient departments. However, this care can be provided by special ambulatory care health centers, group medical services, hospital emergency rooms, multispecialty group medical practices, and health care corporations.

Exam Prep Questions

1. The grace period varies according to
   - ○ A. Premium payment frequency
   - ○ B. Premium payment amount
   - ○ C. Method of premium payment
   - ○ D. Type of policy

2. Mike allows his policy to lapse and then applies for reinstatement using the company's required application. The company does not inform Mike either that the policy has been accepted or that the policy is being rejected. At what point can Mike consider the policy reinstated?
   - ○ A. Not until the insurer notifies him that it has been reinstated
   - ○ B. As soon as the application has been submitted
   - ○ C. After 45 days
   - ○ D. After 90 days

3. The maximum time during which suit can be filed is
   - ○ A. 1 year after written proof of loss is furnished
   - ○ B. 2 years after written proof of loss is furnished
   - ○ C. 3 years after written proof of loss is furnished
   - ○ D. 4 years after written proof of loss is furnished

4. Which of the following is not a required provision under the Uniform Provisions Model Act?
   - ○ A. Grace period
   - ○ B. Change of occupation
   - ○ C. Time of payment of claims
   - ○ D. Proof of loss

5. Which of the following is an optional provision under the Uniform Provisions Model Act?
   - ○ A. Cancellation
   - ○ B. Physical examination and autopsy
   - ○ C. Legal actions
   - ○ D. Reinstatement

6. Cindy has a claim for $2,000, and a past due premium of $200. The insurer will
   - ○ A. Refuse to pay the claim until the past due premium is paid.
   - ○ B. Pay the claim minus the past due premium.
   - ○ C. Pay the claim and forgive the past due premium.
   - ○ D. Pay the claim and bill Cindy for the past due premium.

7. If Lois cancels her health insurance policy, the insurer will
   - ○ A. Issue a pro rata refund of all of the unearned premium.
   - ○ B. Issue a pro rata refund of most of the unearned premium.
   - ○ C. Issue a short-rate refund of all of the unearned premium.
   - ○ D. Issue a short-rate refund of most of the unearned premium.

8. Carmen gets her health insurance policy on May 1, and on May 3 she decides she doesn't want it and returns it to the company. On May 6, she is hit by a car. The company
   - ○ A. Will pay any resulting claim, because she was injured within the 10-day free-look period.
   - ○ B. Will pay any resulting claim only if the premium has not yet been returned to Carmen.
   - ○ C. Will pay any resulting claim minus the amount of the returned premium.
   - ○ D. Will only return any premium Carmen has paid and not any resulting claim.

9. CeeCee's policy is guaranteed renewable. Which of the following may the insurer not do?
   - ○ A. Refuse to renew the policy if CeeCee fails to pay the premium.
   - ○ B. Increase the premiums on all members of CeeCee's class.
   - ○ C. Increase the premiums on CeeCee's policy only.
   - ○ D. Refuse to renew the policy after CeeCee reaches a specified age.

10. George has a noncancelable policy. Which of the following may the insurer do?
   - ○ A. Cancel the policy if George fails to pay premiums.
   - ○ B. Increase the premiums on all members of George's class.
   - ○ C. Increase the premiums on George's policy only.
   - ○ D. Cancel the policy if the insurer chooses to no longer do business in George's state.

Exam Prep Answers

1. **A is correct.** The grace period depends on how frequently premiums are paid.

2. **C is correct.** The policy provisions state that reinstatement may be assumed after 45 days if there has been no notification to the contrary.

3. **C is correct.** The limit on filing suit is 3 years.

4. **B is correct.** Change of occupation is an optional, not a required, provision.

5. **A is correct.** A cancellation provision is an optional policy feature.

6. **B is correct.** The insurer has the right to deduct past due premiums from any claim settlements.

7. **D is correct.** It is standard procedure when an insured cancels for the insurer to issue a short-rate refund and retain a portion of the unearned premium to cover its expenses.

8. **D is correct.** Carmen canceled the contract by returning it, and the fact that she later had an accident and regretted her decision has no legal weight.

9. **C is correct.** The insurer is not permitted to increase the premium for an individual policy.

10. **A is correct.** For all types of insurance, the insurer is permitted to cancel a policy for nonpayment of premium.

Disability Income Insurance

Terms you need to understand:

- ✓ Probationary period
- ✓ Elimination period
- ✓ Benefit period
- ✓ Total disability
- ✓ Presumptive disability
- ✓ Partial disability
- ✓ Residual disability
- ✓ Recurrent disability
- ✓ Permanent disability
- ✓ Temporary disability
- ✓ Accidental injury
- ✓ Sickness
- ✓ Short-term disability
- ✓ Long-term disability
- ✓ Rehabilitation benefit
- ✓ Future increase option
- ✓ Cost of living benefit
- ✓ Social security rider
- ✓ Social insurance supplement
- ✓ Additional monthly benefit rider
- ✓ Hospital confinement rider
- ✓ Impairment rider
- ✓ Nondisabling injury rider
- ✓ Waiver of premium rider
- ✓ Accidental death and dismemberment rider

Concepts you need to master:

- ✓ Own occupation
- ✓ Any occupation
- ✓ Lump-sum benefit
- ✓ Lifetime benefits
- ✓ Business overhead expense
- ✓ Key person disability insurance
- ✓ Disability buy-sell insurance
- ✓ Disability reducing term insurance

Disability is often called "the living death." Earning power, in a sense, dies while life goes on—expenses continue and may even increase.

Disability income insurance is available to continue a portion of earnings while an insured is disabled. Disability income insurance, sometimes referred to as *loss of time coverage*, is designed to protect an individual's most important asset—the ability to earn an income.

Financial Planning Considerations

A family's future is at stake when the ability to work is in peril. Here are some practical considerations in determining disability income needs:

➤ Establish the *minimum income* that would be required if income stops because of disability.

➤ Consider the need for *retirement plan maintenance* if the individual has such a plan that would be disrupted in the event of long-term disability.

➤ After establishing the insured's total needs, allow for any benefits that would be provided by *social security and workers compensation*.

➤ Include enough *long-term disability coverage* for both occupational and nonoccupational sickness or injury as well as short-term disability coverage to provide income during the social security waiting period or to supplement workers compensation.

Alternatives to Disability Income Insurance

The following are options people might consider if they develop a disability:

➤ *Using savings*—According to one source, if an individual saved 5% of his or her income each year, 6 months of total disability could wipe out 10 years of savings; savings that might have been designated for another purpose such as retirement or children's education.

➤ *Borrowing*—The problem is, who is going to lend money to someone who can't work?

➤ *Depending on spouse's income*—If two incomes were needed before, one income might be insufficient.

➤ *Liquidating assets*—Can the individual get a fair market price when forced to liquidate? By their very nature, disabilities are unexpected and the market might be down for the stocks, real estate, or other asset to be liquidated.

Definitions and Benefits

Disability income insurance can be defined as a contract that normally pays a monthly benefit, following the elimination period, for total disability due to accident or sickness. Disability benefits may also be paid for partial or residual disability as well as total disability.

NOTE

An understanding of each of these terms is important because as a producer, you must be able to explain to the insured how this policy will work if he or she becomes disabled. Benefits will be paid in accordance with the policy's terms and conditions.

Probationary Period

A *probationary* or *qualification period* may be found in some disability income policies. It is a time period that begins when a policy goes into effect. During this period, no benefits will be paid under the policy. The period is often 15 or 30 days, or even 60 days for long-term policies. This probationary period generally applies to sickness, but not to accidents. Its major purpose is to relieve the insurance company from paying benefits for *preexisting conditions*—health problems that existed prior to the policy's inception.

Elimination Period

An *elimination period* is the period of time an insured person must be disabled before benefits begin. The elimination period may be thought of as a time deductible rather a dollar deductible, because benefits are not payable for the elimination period.

The elimination period may be 30, 60, 90, or 180 days, or longer depending on the period elected by the insured. The longer the elimination period, the smaller the insurance premium, because the insured is willing to go without benefits for a longer period of time and the insurer will not have to pay for short-term claims.

Benefit Period

After the elimination period has been satisfied and monthly disability bene-fits begin, they will be paid for a specific period of time, provided the insured remains totally disabled. This period of time is known as the *benefit period*.

Typical benefit periods are 1 year, 2 years, 5 years, and to age 65.

Defining Total Disability

Because the major purpose of disability income policies is to provide income when the insured is totally disabled and unable to work, the meaning of total disability is important.

 Total disability is always defined in the policy, and different companies may use dif-ferent definitions. These definitions are based on work activity, and insurers look at work activity in terms of two dimensions: the insured's own occupation and any occupation the insured may be qualified to perform.

Own Occupation

The first way total disability might be defined concerns the occupation in which the particular individual is normally engaged. In this case, *total disabil-ity* is defined as the insured's inability to perform any or all of the duties of his or her *own occupation*.

Any Occupation

An alternative and more restrictive definition of total disability is the insured's inability to perform the duties of *any occupation* for which he or she is reasonably qualified by education, training, or experience.

The term *own occupation*, which is less restrictive and therefore more favor-able to the insured, is more commonly used than the term *any occupation*. Long-term policies generally use both definitions to cover different periods during the insured's disability. The term *own occupation* is generally used for the initial period of disability, which might extend from 2–5 years as stated in the policy. The term *any occupation* applies to disability continuing beyond the initial period.

Loss of Earnings

Some policies use a two-tier definition that refers to the insured's own occu-pation during an initial period of disability and then shifts to any occupation.

These policies usually define total disability as the inability to perform the duties of the insured's own occupation for a period of 2–5 years, and thereafter the inability to perform the duties of any occupation for which the insured is suited by reason of education, training, experience, or prior economic status. This is known as the *loss of earnings test* for disability.

Injury Versus Sickness

Total disability is occasionally further defined in terms of its cause. Some policies may cover only—or cover differently—disability caused by accidental injury, and some may cover only disability caused by sickness.

Occupational Versus Nonoccupational

Although short-term policies often cover only nonoccupational disability, most long-term plans cover both *occupational* and *nonoccupational* sickness and accidents. When occupational benefits are provided, they are often reduced by benefits received from workers compensation and social security.

Medically Defined

Some older policies also require that in addition to meeting the definition of total disability, the insured must also be confined to the house and under the treatment of a doctor. This is called *medically defined disability*.

Presumptive Disability

Many disability income policies have a classification called *presumptive disability*, which automatically qualifies the insured for total disability regardless of whether he or she can work. Conditions that are generally considered to be presumptive disabilities are

➤ Loss of use of any two limbs

➤ Total and permanent blindness

➤ Loss of speech and hearing

Presumptive disability may also be determined using a loss of earnings test. The insured's level of earnings prior to disability is compared to his or her level of earnings after disability. If post-disability earnings fall below pre-disability earnings by a given percentage, the insured is considered totally disabled.

Partial Disability

Some people may suffer only a *partial disability*. This means the person

➤ Cannot perform every duty of his or her occupation

➤ Can perform one or more important duties of the occupation

Partial disability is generally not a factor in sickness disability. The insured usually either is or is not sick enough to stay off the job. The usual partial disability indemnity is 50% of the monthly or weekly indemnity for total disability.

Residual Disability

Many recent policies have replaced the partial disability provision with a *residual disability* provision. A residual disability benefit is usually a percentage of the total disability benefit as defined in the policy.

Earnings during partial disability must be at least a stated percentage less than earnings prior to disability—20% less, for example. The percentage of reduction in earnings is multiplied by the normal benefit to determine the residual benefit. If the normal benefits were $1,000 per month, and the insured had a 20% reduction in earnings, the residual benefit would be $200—20% × $1,000.

Recurrent Disability

When a second period of disability arises due to the same or a related cause of a prior disability, the second event is called a *recurrent disability*.

Most disability income policies stipulate that if the insured returns to work for a specified period of time after the original disability, a recurrence must be handled as a new claim for a new period of disability requiring a new elimination period, rather than as a continuation of a prior claim. Usually, the specified period is 90 days, although some insurers permit 6 months.

Permanent Disability

A *permanent disability* is one that reduces or eliminates the insured's ability to work for the rest of his or her life. Permanent disability results from any injury from which the insured is not expected to recover, such as loss of sight or one or more limbs.

Temporary Disability

A *temporary disability* occurs when an insured is unable to work while recovering from an illness or injury, but is expected to fully recover from that illness or injury.

Confining Versus Nonconfining Disability

Some policies may include a provision that differentiates between disabilities in still another way—whether the disability is confining or nonconfining.

A total, *confining disability* refers to a condition that requires the individual to stay indoors, perhaps in the hospital or at home except for visits to the doctor.

A total, *nonconfining disability* refers to a condition that disables but does not require the individual to remain confined indoors.

Accidental Means

Of the different terms used to define *accident*, the two that will be discussed here are accidental bodily injury and accidental means.

A policy that includes the *accidental means* wording is more restrictive than one that refers simply to *accidental bodily injury*.

For example, Mary is carrying a heavy bag of groceries and strains her back. This accident would be defined as accidental bodily injury because Mary did not intentionally strain her back. However, although the injury was caused by accident it could not be defined as accidental means because the cause of the accident was foreseeable. The term *accidental bodily injury* encompasses almost all but self-inflicted injuries, subject to any other events the policy excludes. Accidental means, on the other hand, involves a more literal interpretation of accident—an event that is completely unforeseen and unintended.

Definition of Sickness

Sickness or illness may not be defined in any manner that is more restrictive than "sickness or disease that first manifests itself after the effective date of the policy." If a policy provides nonoccupational coverage only, the definition of sickness may exclude work-related disabilities.

Types of Disability Benefits

There are some significant differences between short-term and long-term disability policies.

Short-Term Disability

Most group short-term policies provide for short elimination periods (usual-ly 30 days or less) and short benefit periods. The benefit period is normally for 6 months but not longer than 1 year. The benefit amount is limited to a percentage of compensation, such as 60% or 70%.

One of the rationales for *short-term disability* has been that the worker pre-sumably is eligible for social security disability benefits after the 5-month social security waiting period.

Long-Term Disability (LTD)

Long-term disability (LTD) policies provide for longer elimination and bene-fit periods than short-term policies. Typically, the elimination period will be 90 days or 6 months with benefits provided for 2 or 5 years or to age 65. Most often LTD policies provide benefits to age 65. The amount of the long-term benefit is limited to a percentage of the worker's compensation, such as 60% or 70%. Like short-term policies, LTD coverage may be occu-pational or nonoccupational.

Additionally, LTD policies usually provide for *integration* of plan benefits with other disability income benefits payable to the insured. The LTD ben-efit may be offset by any of the following:

➤ Any benefits provided by another formal employer plan

➤ Benefits payable under workers compensation or any similar statutory program

➤ Any benefits payable under social security

Lump-Sum Benefits

Lump-sum payments under disability policies were once paid more often than they are today. It is more common for disability income benefits to be received in the form of installment payments.

Disability Exclusions

Common exclusions found in disability income policies are losses arising from war, military service, attempted suicide, overseas residence, aviation under certain circumstances (pilot or crew of aircraft), and losses that result when an insured is injured while committing a felony.

Optional Disability Income Policy Benefits and Riders

This section reviews common optional benefits that may be added to disability policies.

Rehabilitation Benefit

Because of disability, the insured may not be able to return to his or her normal occupation but still be able to work at some kind of job. The *rehabilitation benefit* facilitates vocational training to prepare the insured for a new occupation.

The rehabilitation benefit applies when the insured is totally disabled and receiving benefits. If the insured chooses to participate in a vocational rehabilitation program approved by the insurer, total disability benefits will continue as long as the insured actively participates in the training program and remains totally disabled.

Future Increase Option

The *future increase option* may also be referred to as the *guaranteed insurability option* or *guaranteed purchase option* because it enables the insured to purchase additional disability income protection, regardless of his or her insurability, at specified future dates. However, the rate for this additional coverage will be at the insured's attained age at the time of purchase, not the age when the policy was originally issued.

This benefit has some limitations. The insured will be able to purchase only a specified predetermined amount of disability income insurance at each option date. The insured's earned income also must warrant additional coverage. Another limitation is the number of option dates on which the insured may purchase additional coverage. Usually, these option dates will be every 2 or 3 years from ages 25 to 40—or even to age 50. These dates may be arbitrarily selected by the insurer or they may coincide with the insured's birthdays, marriage, and the birth of children.

Cost of Living Benefit

To protect against inflation, most insurers will offer an optional *cost of living benefit*.

Under the provisions of this option, the insured's monthly disability benefit (total or residual) will be automatically increased after the insured is on claim (receiving disability income benefits). Typically, this increase will occur after the insured is on claim for 12 months and each 12-month period thereafter as long as the insured remains on claim.

Lifetime Benefits

The *lifetime benefits* option extends the benefit period from age 65 to lifetime. This extension may apply to accident only benefits or to accident and sickness benefits. Normally, if the total disability is due to an accident and it occurs prior to age 65, benefits will be paid for the lifetime of the insured provided he or she remains totally disabled.

Most companies will place some time limitations for the lifetime sickness benefit. That is, the disabling sickness must begin prior to a specified age, such as 50, 55, or 60. A policy providing lifetime sickness benefits may stipulate that if the sickness begins at age 55 or earlier, 100% of the total disability benefit will be provided for the lifetime of the insured. However, if the disability begins after age 55, but before age 65, a reduced benefit will be paid for life.

Social Security Rider

The Social Security Administration defines total disability as the inability to perform any substantial gainful work that may exist in the national economy. In addition, the disability must be expected to last at least 12 months or end in death. As a result, many disabled people do not qualify for social security disability benefits. Even when social security benefits are payable, there is a 5-month waiting period and benefits do not begin until the 6th month of disability. When a social security rider is added to an individual's disability income policy, an additional monthly benefit is payable during the waiting period.

The rider may enable continued benefits after social security benefits begin. There are two different methods by which this type of rider may provide benefits:

➤ *All or nothing rider*—Under this approach, the insured will be paid a benefit only if social security pays nothing. Conversely, if social security provides any benefit, the rider pays nothing.

➤ *Offset rider*—Under this approach, the benefit provided by the rider will be reduced, or offset, by the amount of any benefit provided by social security.

Social Insurance Supplements

Some insurers offer social insurance supplements that are designed to fill gaps left by various government benefit programs. The concept is similar to the social security rider, except that this coverage may also mesh with workers compensation benefits and benefits provided by state disability funds.

Additional Monthly Benefit (AMB) Riders

Most insurers offer short-term riders to provide additional benefits during the first 6 months or 12 months of a claim. Some companies may call these *social security riders* because the benefit is payable during the social security waiting period, although the rider itself may not even refer to social security benefits. More commonly, the term *additional monthly benefit (AMB) rider* is used.

Hospital Confinement Rider

This optional benefit results in the elimination period being waived when the insured is hospitalized as an inpatient. The payment of any disability benefits usually requires satisfying the elimination period. The *hospital confinement benefit* pays the regular total disability benefit during the elimination period when the insured is hospitalized.

The factor that triggers the payment of the benefit is any period of hospitalization during the elimination period. Benefits will be paid for only as long as the insured is hospitalized.

Impairment Rider

When an applicant for insurance has an existing medical problem or chronic condition, an insurer might attach an *impairment rider* to the standard policy. This rider excludes coverage for a specific ailment or condition that would otherwise be covered. Because the condition currently exists, the insurance company would be unlikely to take the risk, so it would normally refuse coverage.

Nondisabling Injury Rider

The *nondisabling injury rider* benefit does not pay a disability benefit but rather provides for the payment of medical expenses incurred due to injury that does not result in total disability.

Waiver of Premium (with Disability Income)

The *waiver of premium rider* specifies that in the event of disability, premiums will be waived retroactively to the beginning of the disability. The definition is usually *permanent and total disability*. However, a few companies have gone to a definition in terms of occupation.

Accidental Death and Dismemberment (AD&D)

Accidental death policies or riders include a death benefit that is payable in the event of death resulting from accidental bodily injury. A companion coverage is provided for loss of limbs or sight, often called *dismemberment coverage*.

A schedule is made a part of the policy that lists various dismemberments and losses of sight for which a specified sum will be paid to the insured. In policies with weekly disability income benefits, the sum payable is usually expressed as a multiple of the weekly indemnity. In policies without weekly disability income benefits, the sums payable are usually expressed as percentages of the death benefit limit or sometimes as percentages of a limit in the policy known as the *capital sum*. The capital sum might be $20,000, and the death benefit is usually the same amount ($20,000).

If the policy has a disability income feature, when a dismemberment sum is paid, the disability income payments stop. In some cases the insured might be disabled for a while, and during the disability suffer one of the losses listed previously. In that event, the insured would be paid disability income up to the time of the loss of limb or sight only.

Other Provisions

Although disability income policies do not typically accumulate cash value or have a life insurance component, it is possible to purchase riders to the policy that provide benefits similar to life insurance policies. Thus, an *annual renewable term* life insurance feature may be attached to a disability income policy, providing a death benefit as well as disability income coverage.

Similarly, a *return of premium rider* may be attached to a disability income policy. This rider provides for the return of a percentage of premiums paid (usually 80%) during a specific term period (usually every 10 years) minus the claims paid during the term period. The refund is made every 10 years and at age 65 or as of the date of death.

Business Uses of Disability Income Insurance

The application and use of disability income coverage is not confined to individuals but also is very relevant in business situations.

Business Overhead Expense (BOE)

The *business overhead expense (BOE)* policy is designed for the small business owner. Its purpose is to cover certain overhead expenses, which continue when the business owner is disabled. Most insurers will limit the BOE policy to those businesses that are relatively small.

The policy will indemnify the business (not the owner) for such business expenses as rent, taxes, insurance premiums, utility bills, employees' compensation (not the owner's salary), and so forth. By covering these expenses when the owner is disabled, the business is able to keep its doors open and continue to operate.

Generally, BOE policies will have elimination periods of usually 15 or 30 days and benefit periods of 1 or 2 years. The benefit amount will be determined by the average eligible overhead expenses of the business. BOE premiums are tax-deductible to the business. The disability benefits received are thus taxable to the business. However, these taxable benefits are then used to pay tax-deductible business expenses.

Key Person Disability Insurance

This type of coverage pays a monthly benefit to a business to cover expenses for additional help or outside services when an essential person is disabled. The key person could be a partner or working stockholder of the business. The key person could also be a management person who is personally responsible for some very important functions, such as a sales manager.

The key person's economic value to the business is determined in terms of the potential loss of business income that could occur as well as the expense of hiring and training a replacement for the key person. The key person's value then becomes the disability benefit that will be paid to the business. The benefit amount may be paid in a lump sum or in monthly installments.

The business is the owner and premium payor of the policy. Benefits are received by the business tax-free because the premium paid is not tax-deductible.

Disability Buy-Sell Insurance

Every business owner needs to plan for the buyout of the owner's business interest in the event of disability. Naturally, this disability provision should be funded with *buy-sell disability income* insurance.

One of the critical considerations with reference to the disability buy-sell policy is the elimination period. After the elimination period is satisfied, benefits will begin to be made to the business for the purpose of buying out the interest of the disabled owner or partner. Generally, after the buyout begins it cannot be stopped. The elimination period for disability buy-sell insurance will normally be 1 or 2 years. The buy-sell agreement will specify the value or a method of determining the value of the owner's business interest. The benefits may be paid in a lump sum or in monthly installments. If the policy provides a monthly benefit, usually the benefit period will not exceed 5 years.

Usually, the business is the owner and premium payor for the policy or policies. The premiums are not deductible but the benefits are received by the business tax-free.

Disability Reducing Term Insurance

To protect the financial obligation and the assets that could be lost in case of default on a loan due to disability, the business can purchase a *disability reducing term policy*, which provides a monthly benefit in the case of total disability sufficient to cover the monthly financial obligation until it is satisfied (the end of the loan repayment period). The business purchases and owns the policy, the business owner is the insured, and the business is the beneficiary of the monthly benefit. Premiums are not tax-deductible to the business, but benefits are received tax-free. *Reducing term* refers to the fact that the full monthly benefit is payable only for the remaining term of indebtedness or obligation.

Exam Prep Questions

1. The longer the benefit period
   - ○ A. The higher the policy's premium will be
   - ○ B. The lower the policy's premium will be
   - ○ C. The higher the policy's benefits will be
   - ○ D. The lower the policy's benefits will be

2. Which definition of total disability is more favorable to the insured?
   - ○ A. Own occupation.
   - ○ B. Any occupation.
   - ○ C. They are the same in terms of benefits to the insured.
   - ○ D. There is no way to determine from the information provided.

3. Which of the following statements is not true about partial disability?
   - ○ A. The person is not able to perform every duty of his or her prior occupation.
   - ○ B. The person is able to perform one or more important duties of his or her occupation.
   - ○ C. Sickness disability is more likely than accident disability to be partial.
   - ○ D. An insured might receive both total and partial disability benefits as the result of a single accident.

4. Brandon injures his back working at a warehouse. Six months later, he is well enough to go back to work lifting boxes. Two weeks into working, however, he strains his back again and has to go back on bed rest. This is an example of a
   - ○ A. Redundant disability
   - ○ B. Residual disability
   - ○ C. Recurrent disability
   - ○ D. Reduced disability

5. Lee is helping a friend move his pool table when he strains his back, causing a disability. The insurer declines coverage, saying the injury was not accidental under the terms of Lee's policy. Lee's policy must include
   - ○ A. An accidental bodily injury definition of accidental
   - ○ B. An accidental means definition of accidental
   - ○ C. A confining definition of accidental
   - ○ D. A nonconfining definition of accidental

6. Most often, LTD policies provide benefits
   - ○ A. For 2 years
   - ○ B. For 5 years
   - ○ C. To age 60
   - ○ D. To age 65

7. Which of the following statements is not true regarding the future increase option rider?

○ A. The rate for additional coverage will be at the insured's attained age at the time of purchase.

○ B. The rider guarantees the ability to increase coverage to a predetermined limit, regardless of change in the insured's income.

○ C. The rider generally limits the number of option dates on which the insured may purchase additional coverage.

○ D. The rider usually limits the amount of additional coverage available at each option date.

8. Full disability benefits will generally be paid for the lifetime of the insured if total disability due to sickness begins at age

○ A. 45 or earlier

○ B. 50 or earlier

○ C. 55 or earlier

○ D. 65 or earlier

9. Which of the following statements is true regarding social security disability benefits?

○ A. For benefits to be paid, the disability must be permanent and expected to end in death.

○ B. For benefits to be paid, the disability must prevent the individual from being able to perform any substantial gainful work existing in the national economy.

○ C. Most of the people who apply for disability under social security are able to get benefits.

○ D. Social security provides a fairly liberal definition of total disability to keep individuals able to spend and support the national economy.

10. The benefit that pays the regular total disability benefit during the elimination period when the insured is hospitalized is known as the

○ A. Hospital confinement rider

○ B. Rehabilitation benefit

○ C. Nondisabling injury rider

○ D. Offset rider

Exam Prep Answers

1. **A is correct.** If an insured selects a long benefit period the insurer will have to charge more premium because it is assuming more risk.

2. **A is correct.** The inability to perform the duties of one's own occupation may provide benefits not provided by a policy that pays only for the inability to work in any occupation.

3. **C is correct.** Many forms of sickness do not result in total disability.

4. **C is correct.** When a disabling injury is related to an earlier injury, it is an example of a recurrent disability.

5. **B is correct.** This is an example of an accidental means definition of disability.

6. **D is correct.** Most LTD policies do provide benefits until age 65.

7. **B is correct.** An increase in the amount of benefits must be warranted by an increase in the insured's income.

8. **C is correct.** Full lifetime benefits are usually provided if the disability begins at age 55 or earlier. At later ages, percentage reductions in the benefits apply.

9. **B is correct.** Benefits are provided only if the individual is prevented from performing any gainful work.

10. **A is correct.** This is an example of a hospital confinement rider.

Medical Expense Insurance

Terms you need to understand:

✓ Hospital expense benefits
✓ Room and board benefit
✓ Miscellaneous medical benefits
✓ Surgical expense benefits
✓ Regular medical expense benefits
✓ Emergency accident benefits
✓ Hospice care
✓ Home health care
✓ Coinsurance
✓ Stop-loss limit
✓ Inside limits

Concepts you need to master:

✓ Basic medical insurance
✓ Major medical insurance
✓ Comprehensive major medical insurance
✓ Supplemental major medical insurance
✓ Restoration of benefits

Medical expense insurance provides benefits for medical care. Contracts may provide for payment of medical expenses incurred on a *reimbursement basis* (by paying benefits to the policyowner), on a *service basis* (by paying those who provide the services directly), or on a *reimbursement basis* (as a contract providing an indemnity by paying a set amount regardless of the amount charged for medical expenses). Medical expense or hospitalization insurance may be written on an individual basis or on a group basis. Benefits provided cover the individual and eligible dependents.

Although there are many types of benefits available, medical expense insurance can generally be categorized as basic medical expense insurance, major medical insurance, comprehensive medical insurance, and special policies. It should be noted that these products have largely been replaced by managed care alternatives and are not sold as standalone coverages any longer. These types of plans have been modified and replaced in response to changes in the health care field relative to cost containment and market competition. However, an understanding of basic medical, hospital, and surgical plans can serve as a foundation for understanding the hybrid plans currently being marketed.

Basic Medical Expense

Basic coverages provided by an individual medical expense policy include *hospital expense*, *surgical expense*, and *medical expense*. These three basic coverages may be sold together or separately. Frequently this is written as *first dollar* coverage, which means it does not have a deductible.

Hospital Expense Benefits

As the name implies, hospital expense coverage provides benefits for expenses incurred during hospitalization. Hospital indemnities are usually classified into two broad groups:

➤ Room and board, including nursing care and special diets

➤ Miscellaneous medical expenses, including x-rays, lab fees, medications, medical supplies, and operating and treatment rooms

In some cases, surgical benefits may be included for certain types of surgery and associated costs.

Room and Board Benefit

Hospital expense coverage provides benefits for daily hospital room and board and miscellaneous hospital expenses (not including telephone and television) while the insured person is confined to the hospital. The policy may provide for a certain dollar amount for the daily hospital room and board benefit, although the trend is toward coverage of not more than the semi-private room rate unless a private room is medically necessary.

 The room and board benefit may be paid on either an indemnity basis or a reimbursement basis, depending on the particular policy.

When room and board (R&B) are covered on an indemnity basis, the insurer pays a specified, preestablished amount per day, as shown in a schedule in the policy, for a stated maximum number of days. Indemnity policies are sometimes called *dollar amount plans*. R&B rates will vary by geographical location. Typically, the maximum number of days is from 90 up to 365.

More commonly, room and board expenses are paid on a reimbursement basis.

This is also referred to as an *expenses-incurred basis*. Under this arrangement, the policy will pay in one of two ways: the actual charges for a semiprivate room, or a percentage of the actual charges with no specific dollar limit. A maximum number of days will still be specified.

Some room and board benefits include intensive care, which may be paid in full or in part. Hospital plans with this provision generally provide for a maximum intensive care benefit of some multiple of the room and board maximum—usually two or three times.

Miscellaneous Medical Expenses Benefit

Benefits for *miscellaneous medical expenses* are generally stated as a limit separate from the room and board benefits. Usually, the limit is expressed as some multiple of the per-day limit for room and board for each period of hospital confinement.

Surgical Expense Benefits

Surgical expense policies pay surgeons' fees and related costs incurred when the insured has an operation. Related costs might include fees for an assistant surgeon, an anesthesiologist, and even the operating room when it is not covered as a miscellaneous medical item.

Scheduled Plan

Basic surgical coverage is often included in the same policy as basic hospital and medical expense. Benefit amounts are included in a schedule that lists major commonly performed operations and benefits payable for each. The fact that a particular type of surgery is not listed in the schedule does not mean that no benefit is available to cover it. Instead, insurers indemnify on the basis of the *absolute value* and the *relative value* of each surgical procedure.

For example, suppose the insurer has determined that the prevailing value or cost of a certain type of surgery is $4,000, as indicated in the schedule that accompanies the policy. This is the *absolute value* of that procedure. Another procedure, not listed in the schedule, might be relatively less complicated; let's say the company has determined that it is only 50% as complex as the $4,000 procedure. Therefore, its *relative value* is $2,000, and that is the benefit that will be paid for the unscheduled, less complicated procedure.

In some cases, the schedule itself may be referred to in terms of the maximum benefit paid for the most costly procedure, with all other surgical benefits paid as a percentage of that maximum. For example, under a $10,000 schedule, that amount might be paid for open-heart surgery. A less complex procedure, say, a tonsillectomy, might trigger a benefit equal to 10% of that, or $1,000.

Nonscheduled Plan

When surgical benefits (and sometimes other benefits) are not listed by a specific dollar amount in a schedule, a policy will pay on the basis of what is considered *usual, customary, and reasonable (UCR)* in a certain geographical area. This type of indemnity is more often found in the major medical and comprehensive policies discussed later in this chapter.

Under this type of arrangement, the definition of UCR is based on the amount physicians in the area usually charge for the same or similar procedures.

Regular Medical Expense Benefits

Another category, regular medical expense benefits, is sometimes called *physicians' nonsurgical expense*. Remember that some states refer to this particular category as basic medical expense. Coverage is for nonsurgical services a physician provides. Sometimes, it is quite narrowly applied to physician visits to patients confined in the hospital. If so, the benefit will usually pay for

➤ A specified maximum number of visits per day

➤ A specified maximum dollar amount per visit

➤ A specified maximum number of days coverage applies

In other policies, the benefit might be for nonsurgical services a physician performs whether the patient is in the hospital or not. Again there are limits, such as $25 per visit for up to 50 visits a year.

Other Medical Expense Benefits

In addition to the hospital, surgical, and medical benefits, there are other benefits that might be included, that may be added at the insured's option, or for which separate policies might be written. Different insurers may include different options as part of their standard policies, so each policy must be considered individually. Some coverage options are

➤ Maternity

➤ Prescription drugs

➤ Convalescent/nursing home

➤ Dread disease

➤ Emergency first-aid

➤ Outpatient treatment

➤ Home health care

➤ Dental

➤ Mental infirmity

➤ Private duty nursing

➤ Hospice care

➤ Vision

We discuss the most common options here, and in Chapter 20, "Special Types of Medical Expense Policies," you'll learn about those that are more typically written as separate policies.

In-Hospital Physician Visits

Frequently, a basic medical expense policy will include a daily benefit for expenses incurred when the insured's physician visits him or her in the hospital. This benefit is limited to a dollar amount, such as $25 or $30 per day. This amount would be paid for any charges made by the doctor for visiting the patient.

Maternity Benefits

Some policies provide *maternity benefits* subject to certain conditions and limitations—the most usual of which is a 10-month waiting period designed to prevent purchase of health insurance solely to cover pregnancy and childbirth expenses. You should be aware, however, that group policies for employee groups of 15 or more are required by law to provide maternity benefits on the same basis as nonmaternity benefits. Thus, under a group plan with 15 or more employees, a 10-month waiting period would not apply unless nonmaternity benefits also required a 10-month waiting period.

Pregnancy may not be subject to a waiting period if the worker has already met the waiting period required by the group coverage of a previous employer.

Aside from group plans as described earlier, many policies exclude maternity benefits but make them available at extra cost. Often, a maternity benefit is a lump sum paid for normal childbirth. The actual amount might be

➤ Usual, customary, and reasonable charges

➤ A specified amount

➤ A multiple of the daily hospital benefit

The benefit generally includes routine newborn care while the mother is hospitalized.

Other benefits that might be available under the same maternity coverage, but scheduled at amounts different from the benefit for normal childbirth, include

➤ Cesarean deliveries

➤ Natural abortions

➤ Elective abortions

Emergency First-Aid Coverage

An accident may require immediate first aid on the scene. When a medical professional who happens upon an accident provides first-aid service, he or she might bill the insured. Sometimes, such treatment must be performed without the insured's knowledge or assent.

Some policies offer coverage for such contingencies by including emergency first-aid coverage for treatment expenses incurred within a very short time after an accident. This length of time is specified in the policy.

Emergency Accident Benefits

A basic plan may include a specific benefit for expenses incurred due to an accident when the insured is taken to the emergency room of a hospital as an outpatient. The benefit is to cover the cost of treatment in the emergency room, including physician expenses, x-rays, stitches, and so forth.

Mental Infirmity

Although some policies exclude coverage for *mental infirmities*, more now include this coverage. Typically, the benefits are lower than for physical infirmities, usually a stated percentage of the benefit paid for other types of medical care. Alternatively, a policy might specify a particular dollar amount for mental infirmity that is different from the amount for physical infirmity.

Hospice Care

Most states require that any hospitalization policy (individual or group) include benefits for *hospice care* expenses. The hospice is a facility designed to control pain and suffering of terminally ill patients until their death. It does not treat diseases nor does it attempt to cure. In addition, the hospice also provides counseling for the patient and the family of the terminally ill. Expenses covered include R&B, medication, outpatient services, and expenses.

Home Health Care

Home health care is usually an optional benefit that provides for reimbursement of expenses incurred by the insured for the services of a visiting nurse, a therapist, or some other support-type person who, because of a medical necessity, visits the insured in his or her home and provides necessary medical services.

Outpatient Care

Outpatient care refers to expenses incurred by the insured for doctor's office visits and out-of-the-hospital diagnostic services such as lab work and x-rays. Often a basic medical expense policy covers only in-hospital expenses (inpatient), whereby treatment is provided to the patient who has been assigned a room and a bed and is staying in the hospital for some period of time. Basic plans may add coverage for certain medical services provided to the insured as an outpatient.

Common Exclusions and Limitations

Both disability income and medical expense policies exclude or limit coverage for certain types of injuries and illnesses. The exclusions and limitations below are representative of common items a policy might list. Many policies will, in fact, include benefits for all or part of some in the following list. It is important for you to be aware of your own state laws and your company's policies regarding each specific item. Common exclusions are

➤ Preexisting conditions (note, however, that some states have *no loss-no gain laws* that require a replacing health insurance policy to cover any conditions for which there are ongoing claims under existing coverage, thus overriding the preexisting conditions exclusion in the replacing policy)

➤ Hernia

➤ Self-inflicted injuries

➤ Suicide

➤ War or acts of war resulting in death or injury, whether or not war is officially declared

➤ Military duty, usually a suspension of the policy that ends when the insured is released from such duty

➤ Noncommercial air travel, which is any air travel other than as a scheduled airline passenger

➤ Injury while committing a felony

➤ Injury, illness, or death while under the influence of intoxicants or narcotics

➤ Cosmetic surgery, except for surgery required as the result of an accidental injury or a congenital defect

➤ Dental expense, although some policies will cover such expenses resulting from accidental injury

➤ Vision correction, such as eye exams and eyeglasses

➤ Care provided in a government facility, normally paid by the Veterans Administration or by workers compensation

➤ Sexually transmitted diseases

➤ Experimental procedures

➤ Organ transplants

➤ Infertility services

➤ Alcohol and/or drug abuse treatment

Major Medical Insurance

When basic benefits are purchased piecemeal, the total benefits provided can be substantially less than the actual expenses incurred. Providing more complete coverage with fewer gaps, *major medical insurance* covers a much broader range of medical expenses with generally higher individual benefits and policy maximums.

These more extensive health policies are divided roughly into two groups:

➤ *Comprehensive* major medical expense, in which the more traditional basic coverages and essentially any other type of medical expense are combined into a single comprehensive policy

➤ *Supplemental* major medical expense, in which coverage begins with a traditional basic policy, which pays first, and the major medical coverage is added to pick up expenses not covered by the basic policy

Comprehensive Major Medical Benefits

Comprehensive major medical benefits provide the most complete coverage. Let's take a look at some of the features.

Deductibles

There are essentially two types of *comprehensive major medical* plans—one with first dollar coverage and one without.

 First dollar coverage means that as soon as covered medical expenses are incurred, the policy begins to pay. Policies with first dollar coverage effectively have a deductible of zero. Without first dollar coverage, the insured must pay a specified deductible amount first, and when that amount of expenses incurred has been paid by the insured, the policy starts reimbursing. Deductibles are generally an important feature of major medical policies.

Coinsurance

Coinsurance means that the insurer and the insured share any expenses above the deductible amount. The insurer always carries the bulk of the expense, usually paying 80% of covered expenses. Other proportions, such as 75%/25%, may be used, so it is important to read the policy. In some areas, coinsurance is referred to as *percentage participation*.

In some policies, certain types of medical expenses are not subject to the deductible, although others are. It is not uncommon for no deductible to apply to initial hospital and/or surgical expenses up to a specified amount—

for example, the first $5,000 of such expenses. In this case, the insured would pay no deductible—in essence getting first dollar coverage on the first $5,000 of hospital and surgical expenses—but would be required to pay the deductible before major medical covered any additional expenses. Then, the insurer and the insured would share in remaining expenses at 80%/20% or whatever percentage applies.

Stop-Loss Limit And Maximum Benefits

More major medical policies include a *stop-loss limit*, which is a dollar amount beyond which the insured no longer participates in payment of the expenses. The stop-loss limit is sometimes known as the *out-of-pocket limit*. After the insured's total coinsurance and deductible payments reach that amount, the insurer picks up the entire cost of remaining expenses, up to a stated *maximum benefit*. Currently, the lifetime maximum limits on health policies might range from $100,000 to $1,000,000 and some policies even have unlimited benefits.

Just as the maximum benefit varies considerably, so does the amount of the stop-loss limit.

Supplemental Major Medical Benefits

When major medical benefits are provided through a *supplemental policy*, the major medical portion supplements a basic policy that includes hospital, surgical, and medical coverage with an additional policy covering the broader range of medical expenses.

 Generally the basic plan will pay covered medical expenses with no deductible, up to the policy limit. Above that limit, the supplemental policy operates identically to a comprehensive policy that provides no other first dollar coverage. That is, after the basic policy limits are exhausted, the insured must pay a deductible, after which the major medical coverage begins. Because the deductible comes between the basic policy and the major medical policy, it is often called a *corridor deductible*.

Like the comprehensive major medical policy, a supplemental plan is likely to include a stop-loss limit and a maximum benefit limit.

Covered Expenses

Major medical policies, whether supplemental or comprehensive, cover a wide range of medical expenses. The precise services covered may vary somewhat from policy to policy, but many of the following will be included in most major medical plans:

➤ Hospital inpatient room and board, including intensive and cardiac care

➤ Hospital medical and surgical services and supplies

➤ Physicians' diagnostic, medical, and surgical services

➤ Other medical practitioners' services

➤ Nursing services, including private duty service outside a hospital

➤ Anesthesia and anesthetist services

➤ Outpatient services

➤ Ambulance service to and from a hospital

➤ X-rays and other diagnostic and laboratory tests

➤ Radiologic and other types of therapy

➤ Prescription drugs

➤ Blood and blood plasma

➤ Oxygen and its administration

➤ Dental services resulting from injury to natural teeth

➤ Convalescent nursing home care

➤ Home health care services

➤ Prosthetic devices when initially purchased

➤ Casts, splints, trusses, braces, and crutches

➤ Rental of durable equipment, such as hospital-type beds and wheelchairs

Expenses that are excluded from major medical policies generally parallel the exclusions listed previously in this unit.

Other Major Medical Concepts

The following sections review some variations you might find in major medical policies.

Deductible Features

There are a number of ways deductibles might be handled in major medical policies. Some policies include a *per-cause*—injury or sickness—*deductible*, and others have an *all-cause deductible*, which is also referred to as a *cumulative* or *calendar year deductible*.

With a per-cause deductible, the insured pays one deductible for all expenses incurred for the same injury or illness. The benefit period for each cause begins when the deductible for that particular injury or illness has been satisfied and may run for 1 or 2 years. With an all-cause deductible, expenses for any number of different or the same type of illness or accidents are accumulated to meet the deductible during a single calendar year. After enough expenses have been paid by the insured to meet the stated deductible, all other covered charges are paid during the remainder of the calendar year.

Under this latter deductible arrangement, usually a *carryover provision* permits expenses incurred during the last 3 months of the calendar year to be carried over into the new year if needed to satisfy the deductible for the next year. Policies that cover entire families usually have a *family deductible* rather than individual deductibles.

Another deductible provision that can be advantageous to families is the *common injury or illness provision*. Under this provision, only one deductible must be paid when two or more members of the same family are injured in a common accident or become ill concurrently from the same sickness.

Benefit Periods and Inside Limits

The time during which benefits are paid, known as *benefit periods*, are generally tied to the deductible and to any *inside* or *internal limits* included in the major medical policy.

When a deductible must be paid, the benefit period might begin either on the first day of the accident or illness or on the date the insured has satisfied the deductible (if later than the date of the event) and may extend for up to 2 years. In other cases, the benefit period ceases at the end of the calendar year and begins anew with the new deductible.

Inside or internal limits are benefit limitations placed on specified coverages in a major medical policy. For example, the policy might limit both the room and board benefit and the number of days benefits will be paid. In this case, the benefit period for hospital room and board would be whatever number of days is specified. Other examples of internal limits might be restrictions placed on convalescent care days, mental health care, x-rays per claim, and similar items.

Restoration of Benefits

The *restoration* or *reinstatement* of plan benefits is not so important as in the past when maximums were much lower. However, some policies in force today carry fairly low maximums, and most major medical policies still include a provision that allows restoration of the maximum to the original level.

For example, a lifetime level might be $100,000. An insured with a severe injury or illness could easily use up half or more of that in a single year, leaving only $50,000 for the rest of his or her life. Generally, a policy allows the maximum to be restored after a certain amount of benefits are used, though sometimes the insured must prove he or she is once again insurable.

Many policies have an automatic reinstatement provision that restores a specified number of dollars each January 1, or after a given period of time elapses, without requiring the insured to prove insurability.

Medical Expense Limitations

Reimbursement-type medical expense policies frequently include limitations on the benefits to be provided for the following:

➤ Rehabilitation and skilled nursing/extended care facilities care

➤ Home health care

➤ Hospice care

➤ Ambulance services

➤ Outpatient treatment

➤ Medical equipment and supplies

➤ Reconstructive cosmetic surgery

➤ Treatment of AIDS

➤ Infertility and sterilization

➤ Maternity/complications of pregnancy/well-baby care

➤ Psychiatric conditions

➤ Substance abuse

➤ Organ transplants

➤ Preexisting conditions

➤ Reimbursement for non-physician services

Mental or Emotional Disorders

Lifetime benefit amounts are limited for outpatient treatment of these disorders.

For example, a major medical policy may have a lifetime maximum of $1 million, but the policy may limit coverage for outpatient treatment of mental or emotional disorders to a lifetime benefit of $25,000. In addition, frequently there may be a limitation with regard to the number of outpatient psychiatric visits per calendar year (such as a maximum of 26 visits per year) and/or the benefit amount paid per visit (such as a maximum benefit of $50 per visit or coverage for no more than 50% of the actual charges). These limits would not apply to inpatient treatment of mental or emotional disorders. (*Note:* New federal laws have removed these limitations for group coverage.)

Maternity

As previously discussed, maternity benefits are often optional. When elected, the amount of the maternity benefit is often limited because of the high cost of a maternity claim and the corresponding high premium charged for the benefit.

For example, a maternity benefit may be limited to a total benefit of $1,000 regardless of the actual expenses incurred. Usually, the only time additional benefits are paid is if there are certain complications during the pregnancy or at the time of delivery. A very liberal maternity benefit (and a costly one) would be that maternity is treated as any other illness and thus a full range of benefits would be payable.

Substance Abuse

Outpatient treatment for drug or alcohol problems is usually limited in much the same way that coverage for nervous or emotional disorders is limited. Usually, if the insured is hospitalized as an inpatient for treatment of the substance abuse problem, regular medical expense benefits would be payable.

Chiropractic Services

The treatment rendered by a chiropractor is normally a covered expense subject to a limitation with regard to total benefits (for example, $10,000 lifetime) or a limitation with regard to the number of visits that will be covered in a given year and/or the amount that may be paid per visit.

Preexisting Conditions

Generally, a preexisting condition is any condition for which the insured sought treatment or advice prior to the effective date of coverage. Many policies contain a preexisting conditions limitation that excludes coverage for unspecified conditions for a period of time (usually 6 months). If an insurer wants to permanently exclude a preexisting condition, it usually has to specify the condition by name in the issued policy. Depending on the severity of the condition, it may be permanently excluded or temporarily excluded (for example, for the first 12 months following the effective date of coverage).

Seldom is a preexisting condition covered by means of limited benefit amounts. Generally, it is either excluded or covered in full as any other condition.

Benefits for Other Practitioners

In past years, coverage was often limited to treatment rendered by a physician. In effect, this eliminated coverage for treatments rendered by chiropractors, midwives, and other nontraditional healers.

In recent years, it has become recognized that many alternative providers who are subject to state licensing and/or standards of conduct imposed by professional organizations are qualified health care providers. Use of alternative providers can help minimize health care costs and reduce the demand on hospitals and doctors. Under current laws in many states, policies must provide benefits for services given by various providers if benefits would be payable for the same services when given by a physician, as long as the providers are properly qualified and are acting within the scope of their profession. Such providers generally include the following;

➤ Chiropractors

➤ Optometrists

➤ Opticians

➤ Psychologists

➤ Podiatrists

➤ Clinical social workers

➤ Dentists

➤ Physical therapists

➤ Professional counselors

Medical Expense Exclusions

Medical expense policies contain many exclusions that are found in all health and disability policies: preexisting conditions, war, intentionally self-inflicted injuries, and active military duty. Medical expense policies also commonly exclude

➤ Workers compensation

➤ Government plans (care in government facilities)

➤ Well-baby care

➤ Cosmetic surgery

➤ Dental care

➤ Eyeglasses

➤ Hearing aids

➤ Custodial care

➤ Routine physicals and medical care

Workers compensation and other government plans are excluded to prevent overpayment of claims or over-insurance. If an injured employee will have his claim taken care of by workers compensation because the injury was work-related, individual or group medical expense plans will not pay the same claim. The same concept applies if, for example, an individual's medical care is to be provided by a veterans administration facility.

Some plans exclude well-baby care because the purpose of medical expense coverage is to indemnify an individual who sustains a loss due to an accident or an illness. If a newborn baby is normal and healthy (a well baby) following delivery, no benefits would be paid for any hospital claim while the child is in the hospital's nursery pending discharge of the mother. If the newborn has a medical problem following birth, normal benefits would be paid.

Cosmetic surgery is usually excluded unless the reason for the surgery is a medical necessity, such as an accident or a disease that disfigures a person. Cosmetic surgery is viewed as voluntary and thus not covered.

Routine dental care is usually excluded with individual medical expense policies but is frequently offered as an optional benefit under a group contract. Again, if a person is injured, such as in an automobile accident, and needs dental surgery for repair of damaged teeth, this type of care would normally be covered.

Eyeglasses and hearing aids are normally excluded unless there is a medical reason for acquiring these devices, such as injury that causes loss of hearing or vision. Reduced hearing or vision due to age and similar factors would not be covered.

Custodial care is care provided to assist the individual in the activities of daily living, which does not contribute to the improvement of a medical condition and which can be performed by a person who does not have medical training. Routine physicals, preemployment physicals, or preschool physicals are normally excluded from coverage. Routine medical care such as immunizations is usually excluded. On the other hand, if an insured is injured and requires a tetanus shot as a result of an accident, the immunization would be covered. It should be noted that some insurers offer coverage for routine physicals and medical care because it is generally recognized that these preventive health care measures benefit the insured and the insurer. A routine physical exam could result in a potential major medical problem being diagnosed before it develops into a very large claim for the insurer.

Optional Features and Benefits

A variety of optional benefits are available as additions to health insurance policies or as separate plans.

Prescription Drugs

The prescription drug benefit is most often found in group health insurance policies. Some individual health insurance policies offer this benefit as a rider.

Different policies offer different prescription card benefits. For example, some policies will cover birth control pills as part of the benefit, and in other policies they are specifically excluded. Usually prescription drug coverage requires a small deductible of typically $5 to $15.

A prescription drug benefit generally works one of two ways. Either insureds can be reimbursed for their prescription drug expenses using standard claim forms, or a prescription drug card can be issued. A prescription drug card allows prescriptions to be paid for by paying only the deductible with each prescription purchase. The pharmacy bills the insurer issuing the card directly for the prescription.

Vision Care

Vision care includes eye examinations (refractions) and eyeglasses. Although not a very common benefit, it occasionally is offered as an optional benefit under group health insurance. Generally, this option will pay a specific amount or the entire cost of an annual eye examination. It normally also covers all or part of the cost of prescribed eyeglasses once in every 2-year period.

Hospital Indemnity Rider

A hospital indemnity benefit provides for the payment of a daily benefit for each day that the insured is hospitalized as an inpatient. Available amounts are usually $50 to $100 per day or possibly slightly higher. Benefit periods are usually 1 or 2 years.

Nursing/Convalescent Home

Under this benefit, a daily maximum amount is paid for each day the insured is confined to a nursing or convalescent home after a hospital stay. Benefits are paid generally for as short as 1 month or up to 1 year.

Organ Transplants

More and more insurers are offering this coverage as it becomes less experimental and more commonplace. To provide coverage, many insurers require that a transplant must be performed only for life-threatening situations. Some of the more commonly covered transplants include bone marrow and kidney.

Exam Prep Questions

1. Carmen falls and breaks her leg, incurring $2,000 in medical expenses. Her policy pays the entire amount. Carmen has a
   - ○ A. Hospital expense policy
   - ○ B. Surgical expense policy
   - ○ C. Medical expense policy
   - ○ D. Policy with first dollar coverage

2. A combination of basic medical expense coverage and major medical expense coverage is
   - ○ A. A basic medical expense policy
   - ○ B. A major medical expense policy
   - ○ C. A comprehensive medical expense policy
   - ○ D. A supplemental medical expense policy

3. A type of policy covering doctor visits while the insured is in the hospital is
   - ○ A. A basic medical expense policy
   - ○ B. A major medical expense policy
   - ○ C. A comprehensive medical expense policy
   - ○ D. A supplemental medical expense policy

4. Maternity benefits must be provided on the same basis as nonmaternity benefits
   - ○ A. In all cases
   - ○ B. Only if the insurer chooses to do so
   - ○ C. If the policy covers an employee group of 15 or more people
   - ○ D. If the policy provides disability income coverage

5. Among individual policies that include coverage for mental infirmities, the benefit will generally be
   - ○ A. Lower than the benefit for physical infirmities
   - ○ B. Higher than the benefit for physical infirmities
   - ○ C. Unlimited
   - ○ D. The same as the benefit for physical infirmities

6. A hospice
   - ○ A. Treats diseases only, not accident-related medical issues
   - ○ B. Controls pain and suffering and treats illness
   - ○ C. Alleviates pain and suffering among terminally ill patients until their death, but does not attempt to cure
   - ○ D. Works with medical professionals when they become ill, to provide treatment in a private setting away from lay patients

7. The dollar limit beyond which the insurer no longer participates in payment of expenses is the
   - ○ A. Deductible
   - ○ B. Coinsurance
   - ○ C. Stop-loss limit
   - ○ D. Maximum benefit

8. The expenses that must be incurred before major medical benefits begin to be paid is the
   - ○ A. Deductible
   - ○ B. Coinsurance
   - ○ C. Stop-loss limit
   - ○ D. Maximum benefit

9. A deductible that runs between the first dollar coverage of a basic policy and the comprehensive coverage of a supplemental policy is known as a
   - ○ A. Stop-loss deductible
   - ○ B. Capitated deductible
   - ○ C. Corridor deductible
   - ○ D. Limited deductible

10. Which of the following would be most likely to be covered under a medical expense policy?
    - ○ A. Gertrude steps on a rusty nail and requires a tetanus shot.
    - ○ B. Carmelita decides to get a flu shot this year.
    - ○ C. Gary goes to the doctor each year for an annual checkup.
    - ○ D. Earl requires some help getting dressed in the morning.

Exam Prep Answers

1. **D is correct.** This is an example of first dollar coverage.

2. **D is correct.** This is an example of supplemental major medical coverage.

3. **A is correct.** This is an example of basic medical expense coverage.

4. **C is correct.** This is a requirement in most states.

5. **A is correct.** Many policies place limitations on treatment of mental illness, including lower limits.

6. **C is correct.** This is an example of a hospice environment.

7. **D is correct.** When the maximum benefit amount has been paid, the insurer has no further obligations.

8. **A is correct.** This is an example of a deductible.

9. **C is correct.** This is an example of a corridor deductible.

10. **A is correct.** This is the type of accident that is almost always covered. The other answer choices reflect situations for which coverage may be limited or excluded.

Special Types of Medical Expense Policies

Terms you need to understand:

✓ Prepaid dental plan
✓ Dread disease
✓ Provider contracts
✓ Service area

Concepts you need to master:

✓ Dental care insurance
✓ Limited policies
✓ Travel accident insurance
✓ Credit insurance

In this chapter you review several special types of health insurance plans that are designed for very specific and limited insurance needs:

➤ Dental care policies

➤ Limited policies, including dread disease, travel accident, hospital income, vision care, and long-term care

➤ Credit insurance policies

Dental Care Insurance

Occasionally, dental insurance is part of a health benefits package with a single deductible called an *integrated deductible*, applying to both medical and dental coverage. More often, dental coverage and dental claims are handled separately, with a separate deductible for health insurance coverage and for dental insurance coverage.

Traditional Dental Coverage

Some dental policies are *scheduled* policies —that is, benefits are limited to specified maximums per procedure, with first dollar coverage. Most, however, are *comprehensive* policies that work much the same way as comprehensive medical expense coverage.

In addition to deductibles, coinsurance and maximums may also affect the level of benefits payable under a dental plan. Coinsurance percentages may apply to reimbursements that are either the *reasonable and customary (R & C)* type or the scheduled type. A plan based on R & C will apply coinsurance percentages to the dentist's usual and customary fee, provided it is reasonable.

This type of plan is also known as *usual, customary, and reasonable (UCR)* or *usual and prevailing (U & P)*. A plan that is scheduled will apply coinsurance percentages to a schedule or list of fixed-dollar amounts for each covered benefit. Scheduled benefits are generally lower than R & C allowances.

NOTE | Comprehensive dental plans usually provide routine dental care services without deductibles or coinsurance to encourage preventive dental care. Generally there is a specified maximum dollar amount payable per year, and sometimes, per family member covered. There may also be a lifetime maximum per individual.

Nonroutine dental care includes the following:

➤ *Restorative*—Repairing or restoring dental work that has been damaged in some way

➤ *Oral surgery*—Surgery performed in the oral cavity (for example, the removal of wisdom teeth)

➤ *Endodontics*—Treatment of the pulp (the soft tissue substance located in the center of each tooth)

➤ *Periodontics*—Treatment of the supporting structures of the teeth

➤ *Prosthodontics*—Artificial replacements

➤ *Pediatric dentistry*—Patient management and preventive and restorative techniques particularly suited to children and adolescents

➤ *Oral pathology*—Microscopic analysis of tissue biopsy material for diagnosis of oral diseases including oral cancer

➤ *Orthodontics*—Correction of irregularities of the teeth (most commonly, braces)

For nonroutine treatments, a comprehensive policy pays a percentage, such as 80%, of the reasonable and customary charges. The patient pays an annual deductible and whatever expense remains.

Policies that provide for orthodontic care generally have separate limits and deductibles for orthodontia. The coinsurance percentage is likely to be 50%.

Benefits may be on a fixed prepaid basis rather than a fee-for-service plan in which the plan participant is reimbursed. Such plans often provide 100% coverage for

➤ Routine visits to the dentist

➤ Protective fluoride treatments

➤ Diagnostic x-rays

➤ Dental exams and diagnosis

➤ Local anesthetics

➤ Teeth cleanings (usually once every 6 months)

➤ Preventive care

Exclusions and Limitations

The following are examples of common exclusions and limitations:

➤ The *cosmetic exclusion* stipulates that benefits are not payable for dental work that is not necessary for sound dental health.

➤ The *missing tooth provision* excludes coverage for teeth that are missing at the time coverage becomes effective.

➤ The *five-year replacement exclusion* does not allow replacement of prosthetic appliances (such as retainers or spacers) for five years after a benefit is paid.

➤ The *vertical dimension, splinting, and restoring occlusion exclusion* limits liability for exotic and highly optional procedures.

➤ Expenses for *oral hygiene instructions* and *plaque control programs* are often limited or excluded.

➤ Some plans offer members coverage up to a certain amount for emergency dental treatment required when *outside the service area*.

Minimizing Adverse Selection

Because the nature of dental coverage is quite different from medical coverage, the underwriting of dental coverage requires a few special considerations. Three circumstances make dental coverage unique:

➤ Patients have wider choices in treatment options. For instance, a patient can choose bridgework that is fixed or removable and inlays that are gold or non-gold.

➤ A person who needs dental work can often postpone treatment until an insurance plan becomes effective, causing the insurer to be liable for larger benefits than it would otherwise expect to pay.

➤ Many dental expenses are cosmetic; therefore, underwriting must often limit benefits for cosmetic procedures.

In order to offset these factors, a new program of dental insurance will often include provisions to minimize adverse selection:

➤ A reduced maximum annual benefit

➤ A lower coinsurance percentage for expenses that are optional

➤ A graduated coinsurance factor that begins at 60% and increases each plan year

> ➤ An advance approval requirement for treatment plans that exceed a certain minimum, usually $200

> ➤ A provision that bases the benefit on the least costly treatment option

> ➤ A longer eligibility period before an employee's coverage is effective

> ➤ A limited benefit for late entrants

Prepaid Dental Plans

In a prepaid dental plan, a corporation, partnership, or other entity, in return for a prepayment, provides or arranges for the provision of dental care services to enrollees or subscribers.

Prepaid dental plans operate in much the same way as health maintenance organizations. They offer services based on capitation, or fixed per member per month payments where the provider assumes the full risk for the cost of contracted services without regard to the type, value, or frequency of the services provided.

Dentist Access to Membership

A prepaid dental plan provides that any licensed dentist may participate as a provider in the plan.

Member Choice of Provider

Subscribers must have the right to select any participating dentist as a provider. If a prepaid dental plan would restrict an enrollee's ability to receive services from a class of providers, the limitations must be described in the evidence of coverage and in all solicitation documents.

Provider Contracts

The prepaid plan may contract with licensed dentists to provide dental care to subscribers in a specific service area or geographic location. In an *open panel* system, dentists render services to both prepaid dental plan subscribers and to nonmembers. In a *closed panel* system, services are provided only to subscribers to the prepaid dental plan.

Under the *precertification* or *prior authorization* requirement, when the enrollee's dentist prescribes any course of treatment expected to exceed a specific amount (such as $200), the treatment must be outlined on a precertification form and submitted to the insurer for review and approval before it may be undertaken.

Evidence of Coverage

All enrollees must be issued an evidence of coverage describing the dental services covered, limitations on those services (including deductibles and copayments), how to obtain services and information, and methods for resolving complaints.

Complaint Procedure

The complaint system must establish reasonable procedures for resolving written complaints from both enrollees and providers. Copies of complaints and responses must be maintained for 3 years.

Quality Assurance Program

Prepaid dental plans must have a quality assurance program to evaluate the quality of care given to enrollees, and provide ways to correct deficiencies in provider or organizational performance.

 Because dental coverage is usually available only on a group basis, most plans do not include a conversion privilege. Members cannot convert to individual insurance when their membership in the group ends or the group plan is terminated.

Limited Policies

In this section, you look at a series of policies, each of which covers only a limited, specified risk. Collectively, they are called *limited policies*.

Dread Disease

Dread disease policies can be purchased to cover specific diseases as named in the policy, such as heart disease or cancer. Generally, these policies cover illnesses that do not occur frequently, but incur significant costs when they do occur. Because of the low frequency of the disease covered, these policies are often fairly inexpensive in comparison to full health coverage.

Travel Accident Insurance

Travel accident insurance may be offered as a benefit of either an individual or a group accidental death and dismemberment policy. Benefits are limited to losses caused by accidents while traveling, usually by common carriers such as airlines or bus lines.

Hospital Income (Indemnity) Insurance

A policy that pays a specific amount of insurance for each day an individual is hospitalized is called *hospital income* or *hospital indemnity* coverage. These policies pay an indemnity directly to the insured, not to the hospital. They are not intended to cover expenses for hospitalization, but to provide a flow of income that begins when the insured is confined to the hospital and ends on the final day of hospitalization.

Limitations may apply. Some hospital indemnity policies include an elimination period, in which case coverage does not begin on the first day of confinement.

Limits also may be placed on benefits paid for preexisting conditions. Usually, the amount of insurance available is indicated as a monthly amount for a specified number of months.

Vision Care Insurance

Basic, comprehensive and major medical policies cover disease and injury to eyes, but not eye exams, eyeglasses, or contact lenses. To close this gap, insurers may offer *vision care* policies, which usually cover

➤ Eye examinations

➤ Cost of lenses and frames

➤ Cost of contact lenses

➤ Other corrective items

Limitations normally apply. For example, the policy may pay for only one eye exam and one set of lenses per year. Common exclusions are

➤ Replacement frames or lenses required because of loss or breakage

➤ Sunglasses and safety glasses

➤ Medical and surgical costs of the type covered by basic and major medical policies

Prescription Drug Policies

Prescription drug policies can be described as discount plans for members. Very often an individual health policy does not cover prescription drugs. For an annual fee or premium, an individual can join a plan that provides discounts of one degree or another for doctor-prescribed drugs. Prescription drug plans operate with a network of pharmacies that members must use in order to receive benefits. Sometimes a mail order service may be provided for drugs used on a regular basis. Plan members receive cards that must be presented to the pharmacy when a prescription is filled, and they are responsible for a copayment. Usually generic drugs are dispensed. Some drugs may be excluded, such as fertility drugs, vitamins, experimental drugs, or drugs covered by other programs.

A dispensing limit such as 34 days worth or 100 units, whichever is larger, is included. Premiums are guaranteed for 1 year. Individual and family coverage is generally available.

Credit Insurance

Credit health insurance covers a debtor, with the creditor receiving the benefits to pay off the debt if the debtor is disabled or dies accidentally. *Individual credit health insurance* is handled essentially the same way as any other individual health insurance policy. The policyowner is the debtor and he or she names the creditor as the recipient of the policy's benefits.

The most common type of credit health insurance is *group coverage* sold as a master policy to a creditor that acquires many new debtors each year. For example, an auto dealership that provides financing for the vehicles it sells might have a group credit policy to cover all clients who finance their cars through the dealership.

In most states, a creditor must have a minimum number of debtors per year, often 100, before it qualifies for group credit insurance. Group credit health insurance has many of the same features as any other group coverage. No evidence of insurability is required. Group credit coverage is nearly always contributory, and a high percentage—usually 75%—of those to whom it is offered must want the coverage.

The accidental death benefit or monthly disability payment may not exceed the total amount of indebtedness at any given point. Some lending institutions have their own or affiliated insurance companies. However, a debtor is not required to carry insurance through the company suggested by the creditor. In some states, and under certain conditions, a creditor can insist that the debtor have some type of insurance to help secure the loan. Even so, the debtor, not the creditor, has the option of selecting the insurer.

Notice of Proposed Insurance

When the loan is closed, the creditor must give the debtor a *notice of proposed insurance* informing the debtor that he or she is covered by a plan. Even if the creditor pays the full cost of the coverage, the debtor must be notified. Creditors are not permitted to place insurance on debtors without telling them about it. Later, a Certificate of Insurance is prepared by the insurer and forwarded to the debtor. The Certificate of Insurance must be delivered within *30 days* of the date the indebtedness is incurred.

Sometimes, coverage might be terminated because the debtor pays off the loan early or because of refinancing. Any such termination requires the insurance company to refund unearned premiums.

Credit Life: A Corollary Coverage

Credit health insurance covers death only when it is accidental. If a debtor dies a natural death, credit health insurance policy does not apply.

Credit life insurance, on the other hand, pays death benefits whether death occurs accidentally or by natural causes. Keep this distinction between credit health and credit life insurance in mind.

Credit life insurance, which may be either individual or group coverage, names the creditor as the beneficiary of the policy. The proceeds or face amount of the policy may not exceed the indebtedness at the time of death. A credit life policy intended to cancel a given indebtedness is usually decreasing term life insurance. This means that the policy is in force for the period of indebtedness, and the face amount of the policy equals the amount owed at any given time.

Exam Prep Questions

1. Comprehensive dental policies
   - ○ A. Limit benefits to specified maximums per procedure
   - ○ B. Work much the same way as comprehensive medical expense coverage
   - ○ C. Never require deductibles
   - ○ D. Seldom require coinsurance

2. Which of the following is not likely to be considered nonroutine dental care?
   - ○ A. Treatment of the soft tissue substance located in the center of each tooth
   - ○ B. Microscopic analysis of tissue biopsy material for diagnosis of oral diseases, including oral cancer
   - ○ C. Annual checkups and cleaning of teeth, including x-rays to check the health of the teeth
   - ○ D. Repairing or restoring dental work that has been damaged in some way

3. For nonroutine treatments, a comprehensive dental policy generally pays
   - ○ A. The full amount
   - ○ B. A percentage of the reasonable and customary charges from the first dollar
   - ○ C. A percentage of the reasonable and customary charges after a deductible
   - ○ D. Nothing

4. The main difference between a prepaid dental plan and a comprehensive dental plan is that
   - ○ A. Comprehensive dental plans pay based on reasonable and customary charges, and prepaid dental plans pay on a capitation basis.
   - ○ B. Comprehensive dental plans pay on a capitation basis, and prepaid dental plans pay based on reasonable and customary charges.
   - ○ C. Comprehensive dental plans cover routine services, but prepaid dental plans do not.
   - ○ D. Comprehensive dental plans do not cover routine services that are covered by prepaid dental plans.

5. Hospital indemnity insurance pays
   - ○ A. Medical costs only while the insured is confined to the hospital
   - ○ B. Supplemental costs, such as television or phone charges, while the insured is confined to the hospital
   - ○ C. An income for each day the insured is confined to the hospital
   - ○ D. An income for each month the insured spends partially confined to the hospital

6. Vision care insurance is generally needed to cover all of the following except

   ○ A. Injury to the eye

   ○ B. Eye examinations

   ○ C. Costs of contact lenses

   ○ D. Costs of prescription lenses

7. Prescription drug policies generally exclude

   ○ A. Any narcotic substance

   ○ B. Any drugs not covered by other programs

   ○ C. Experimental drugs

   ○ D. Drugs for ongoing medical conditions

8. Credit health insurance covers

   ○ A. A creditor

   ○ B. A debtor

   ○ C. Either a creditor or a debtor

   ○ D. Neither a creditor nor a debtor

9. The amount of coverage available under a credit insurance policy is generally limited to

   ○ A. The total amount of indebtedness at any given point

   ○ B. The total amount of the loan covered

   ○ C. The amount the policy is written for

   ○ D. No limit

10. The creditor must notify the debtor that he or she may be covered by the group insurance plan

   ○ A. Only if the debtor is to be charged the full premium for the insurance

   ○ B. If the debtor is to be charged more than half the premium amount

   ○ C. Even if the creditor pays the full cost of the coverage

   ○ D. If the creditor chooses to make the disclosure

Exam Prep Answers

1. **B is correct.** Comprehensive dental policies are designed much like comprehensive medical policies.

2. **C is correct.** Annual checkups are routine.

3. **C is correct.** This is typically how the policy operates.

4. **A is correct.** Prepaid plans pay on a capitation basis.

5. **C is correct.** These policies pay a daily income during confinement.

6. **A is correct.** Vision care insurance covers routine examinations and maintenance. Accidental injuries are covered by regular forms of health insurance.

7. **C is correct.** Experimental drugs are typically excluded.

8. **B is correct.** Credit health insurance covers the debtor although the benefits are paid to the creditor.

9. **A is correct.** By law, the amount of insurance at any given time may not exceed the outstanding debt.

10. **C is correct.** This is true even if the creditor pays all of the premium.

Group Health Insurance

Terms you need to understand:

✓ Conversion privilege
✓ Qualifying event
✓ Qualified beneficiary

Concepts you need to master:

✓ Types of group health insurance
✓ Dependent coverage
✓ Coordination of benefits
✓ Portability of coverage

Most people have at least a superficial acquaintance with *group insurance* because the most common type of group coverage is provided through employment. Many employers make health insurance available to their employees—either by paying the premiums for the employees, by sharing in premium payment, or by deducting the premiums from employees' paychecks.

Group Health Insurance Policy Types

Group health plans may include any of the several types of insurance we discussed earlier, so this section will serve as a review of those individual coverages. Group plans need not include all coverages, but most will include at least two or more. In addition, disability income coverage may be offered under a group arrangement, but it is usually offered separately from hospital, medical, and surgical coverage.

The first possible group coverage pays benefits for lost earnings resulting from accident or sickness disability and is commonly called *disability income insurance*.

Another common type of group coverage deals with accidental loss of life and accidental loss of one or more limbs or of eyesight. Recall that accidental loss of life is referred to as *accidental death* and accidental loss of one or more limbs or of eyesight is known as *dismemberment*.

Still another type of group coverage is *hospital expense*. These policies can pay for hospital expenses, whether treatment is on an inpatient or resident basis—the insured is admitted to the hospital—or outpatient basis—the insured is not admitted for an overnight stay, but is treated and released the same day. The fees of an attending physician during hospital treatment may also be covered.

Some group policies cover only surgical expenses. Although fairly unusual today, such policies do exist. Group health policies frequently provide coverage for medical expenses involving physician or nursing services, but no surgical expense.

Group Coverage Provisions

Several provisions apply solely or primarily to group policies:

➤ Describe who is eligible for the group plan

➤ Describe when individuals become eligible for the plan

➤ Specify the minimum number of individuals and the minimum participation by eligible people required to sustain the plan

➤ Specify the amounts of insurance to which individual group members are entitled

➤ Describe the responsibilities of the master policyowner

As was mentioned previously, not all members of a group are necessarily eligible for coverage under a group plan. Often, an employee becomes eligible for coverage after working with a company for a given period of time, commonly 90 days. The employee is then eligible to apply for coverage during the eligibility period, usually 31 days, within which no medical examination will be required. Any such qualifications or limitations must be indicated in the policy.

Conversion Privilege

The *conversion privilege* allows the insured to convert his or her group coverage to individual coverage *without evidence of insurability*. This privilege goes into effect only when the insured is no longer eligible for group coverage because

➤ The insured's employment is terminated.

➤ The insured becomes ineligible for coverage because the class he or she was insured under is no longer eligible for coverage. (For example, to save expenses, a company that formerly provided coverage for all employees working not less than 20 hours per week might now provide coverage only to the class of employees who do not work less than 40 hours per week.)

➤ The insured's dependent child reaches the age specified in the policy as the age of terminating dependent coverage.

The insured has 31 days from the time of ineligibility to convert to the new plan of insurance. The new plan of insurance is an individual plan, normally a hospitalization policy, which will not provide the same benefits that the group plan did.

Usually, the group medical expense benefits are more liberal than the converted policy's benefits. Often, those who elect to exercise this conversion privilege, do so because frequently they may have insurability problems. To limit adverse selection against the company, the insurer typically offers this conversion plan with reduced or limited benefits.

Dependent Coverage

Life or health insurance benefits may be extended to the primary insured's dependents. Dependents may be any of the following individuals:

➤ The insured's spouse

➤ The insured's children

➤ The insured's dependent parents

➤ Any other person who is dependent upon the insured

The insured's children can be stepchildren, foster children or adopted children. Dependent children must be under a specified age (usually age 19, or 21 if attending school full time). The law further requires that any other person dependent on the insured is eligible for coverage. Such dependency is proved by the relationship to the insured, residency in the home, or the person being listed on the insured's income tax return as a dependent.

A child may be a dependent beyond the ages of 19 or 21 if that child is permanently mentally or physically disabled prior to the specified age.

A dependent child also may be offered coverage beyond the limiting age of 19 if he or she is a full-time college student in an accredited college. Usually, dependent coverage for a student will be extended until age 21 or even to age 25.

Coordination of Benefits Provision

Many working couples have employment-provided group coverage, and each is covered as a dependent by the other's plan. To address this situation, a special provision is required by law in most states. The *Coordination of Benefits Provision* is designed to give insureds as much coverage as possible while eliminating overinsurance. The insurer covering the employee who has the claim is called the *primary insurer*. The primary company must pay as much of the claim as the policy limits permit. The secondary company will pay whatever the primary company will not pay, up to its own limits. When a working couple is doubly covered by group insurance, any children they support will also be doubly covered. Before June of 1985, the usual way to coordinate benefits for children was to make the father's group plan primary, and the mother's plan secondary.

This sex-based procedure is being phased out. Instead, the birth months and days of the parents are often used to decide which plan is primary. The plan of the parent whose birthday comes *first during the year* is primary. The other parent's plan is secondary. If parents are separated or divorced, the plan of the parent with custody is primary, barring any other legal arrangements.

Records and Clerical Errors

The Records provision contains information as to whether the insurer or the policyholder will maintain records on the insureds. It provides for the policyholder to furnish the insurance company with necessary information to determine premiums and administer coverage.

If there is an error or omission in the administration of a group policy, the person's insurance is considered to be what it would be if there had been no error or omission.

Federal and State Regulations Affecting Group Policies

A number of federal regulations enacted over the past 20 years affect group life and health insurance policies. These are known by the acronyms COBRA, OBRA, TEFRA, and ERISA. The health reform package HIPAA passed in 1996 also has major implications for group health insurance policies.

Health Insurance Portability and Accountability Act (HIPAA)

The Health Insurance Portability and Accountability Act (HIPAA), legislation that took effect July 1, 1997, ensures portability of group insurance coverage and includes various mandated benefits that affect small employers, the self-employed, pregnant women, and the mentally ill.

Portability

The new law makes it easier for individuals to change jobs and still maintain continuous health coverage. Employers now must make full health care coverage available immediately to newly hired employees who were previously covered at another job (the individual must have had coverage for at least 18 months). Prior to this change, coverage for preexisting conditions could be delayed for 6 months to 1 year, and new hires were subject to a waiting period before being eligible for health insurance. If the worker goes without health insurance for more than 63 days between jobs, the waiting period can be reinstated.

An individual with group health insurance who leaves to become self-employed also cannot be denied coverage (although the premium charged may be higher).

Group plans cannot impose more than a 12-month preexisting conditions exclusion for a person who sought medical advice, diagnosis, or treatment within the previous 6 months. However, this exclusion cannot be applied in the case of newborns, adopted children, or pregnancies existing on the effective date of coverage.

Mandated Benefits

The new law guarantees coverage for a 48-hour hospital stay for new mothers and their babies after a regular delivery (96 hours for a cesarean section birth). It also expands coverage for mental illness by requiring similar coverage for treatment of mental and physical conditions. The law eliminates the special limitations included in many policies, such as lifetime spending limits and annual limits applied only to mental health coverage.

Small employers (those with 2–50 employees) now cannot be denied group health insurance coverage because one or more employees are in poor health.

Continuation of Benefits (COBRA)

The Consolidated Omnibus Budget Reconciliation Act (COBRA) is a federal law that requires employers with 20 or more employees to provide for a continuation of benefits under the employer's group health insurance plan for former employees and their families. Coverage may be continued for 18–36 months.

Employees and other qualified family members, who would otherwise lose their coverage because of a qualifying event are allowed by COBRA to continue their coverage at their own expense at specified group rates. COBRA specifies the rates, coverage, qualifying events, qualifying beneficiaries, notification of eligibility procedures, and time of payment requirements for the continuation of insurance.

Below are the terms and concepts most important to the understanding of COBRA and its limitations.

Qualifying Event

A *qualifying event* is an occurrence that triggers an insured's protection under COBRA. Qualifying events include the death of a covered employee, termination or reduction of work hours of a covered employee, medicare eligibility for the covered employee, divorce or legal separation of the covered employee from the covered employee's spouse, the termination of a child's dependent status under the terms of the group insurance plan, and the bankruptcy of the employer. Termination of employment is not a qualifying event if it is the result of gross misconduct by the covered employee.

Qualified Beneficiary

A *qualified beneficiary* is any individual covered under an employer-maintained group health plan on the day before a qualifying event, including children born or adopted during the 18-month coverage period.

Notification Statements

Employers are obligated to provide notification statements to individuals eligible for COBRA continuation.

In addition to notifying current employees, the company must also notify new employees when they are informed of other employee benefits. Initial notification made to the spouse of an employee, or to his or her dependents, must be made in writing and sent to the last known address of the spouse or dependent. Following the notification of eligibility for continuation of benefits an individual has 60 days in which to elect such continuation.

Duration of Coverage

The maximum period of coverage continuation for termination of employment or a reduction in hours of employment is *18 months*. For all other qualifying events the maximum period of coverage continuation is *36 months*. There are also certain *disqualifying events* that can result in a termination of coverage before the time periods specified previously. The dates of these events are as follows:

➤ The first day for which timely payment is not made

➤ The date the employer ceases to maintain any group health plan

➤ The first date on which the individual is covered by another group plan (even if coverage is less)

➤ The date the individual becomes eligible for medicare

It should be remembered that COBRA deals with *continuation* of the exact same group coverage that the employee had as a covered employee. This distinction is important so as not to confuse this provision with the conversion of group coverage to a lesser amount of insurance as part of an individual plan.

Not only is the type of coverage the same that the insured had while employed, the premium is also the same except now the terminated employee will pay the entire premium to the employer for the privilege of continuing the group benefits. To cover any administrative expense that the employer may incur, the terminated individual may also pay an additional amount each month not to exceed 2% of the premium. It should also be noted that only the health benefits can be continued under COBRA. Any group life insurance under the plan may not be continued. It can of course be converted.

Recent amendments to COBRA require the continuation of coverage if a preexisting condition limitation is included in the new group health coverage. However, the new group health coverage is primary and the continuation coverage is secondary.

Plan Termination
In most states, if an employer discontinues its group insurance plan, employees must have the opportunity to convert to individual insurance without a medical exam or other evidence of insurability.

Omnibus Budget Reconciliation Act (OBRA)

The Omnibus Budget Reconciliation Act of 1989 (OBRA) extended the minimum COBRA continuation of coverage period from 18–29 months for qualified beneficiaries disabled at the time of termination or reduction in hours.

The disability must meet the social security definition of disability, and the covered employee's termination must not have been for gross misconduct.

Changes to COBRA in 1996 permit individuals who become disabled during the first 60 days of the 18-month coverage period to extend their coverage to 29 months to extend coverage until the person would become eligible for medicare (the 5-month waiting period plus 24 months of eligibility for social security disability benefits).

Under OBRA 1989, an employer may terminate COBRA coverage because of coverage under another health plan, provided the other plan does not limit or exclude benefits for a beneficiary's preexisting conditions.

OBRA 1989 also clarifies that COBRA coverage may be terminated only because of medicare entitlement, not merely eligibility. Before terminating COBRA coverage for beneficiaries at age 65, an employer must first be certain that the individual has actually enrolled under medicare. Thirty-six months of COBRA coverage must be provided for the spouse and dependent children of a covered employee whose group insurance terminates because of entitlement to medicare.

Tax Equity and Fiscal Responsibility Act (TEFRA)

The Tax Equity and Fiscal Responsibility Act of 1982 (TEFRA) is intended to prevent group term life insurance plans (usually always part of group health insurance programs) from discriminating in favor of key employees. *Key employees* include officers, the top 10 interest-holders in the employer, individuals owning 5% or more of the employer, or owning more than 1% who are compensated annually at $150,000 or more.

TEFRA amends the Social Security Act to make medicare secondary to group health plans. TEFRA applies to employers of 20 or more employees, and to active employees and their spouses between ages 65 and 69. TEFRA also amends the Age Discrimination in Employment Act (ADEA) to require employers to offer these employees and their dependents the same coverage available to younger employees.

Employee Retirement Income Security Act (ERISA)

The Employee Retirement Income Security Act of 1974 (ERISA) was intended to accomplish pension equality, but it also protects group insurance plan participants.

ERISA includes stringent reporting and disclosure requirements for establishing and maintaining group health insurance and other qualified plans. Summary plan descriptions must be filed with the Department of Labor, and an annual financial report must be filed with the IRS. For other qualified plans, legal documentation of the trust agreement, plan instrument, plan description, plan amendments, claim and benefit denials, enrollment forms, certificates of participation, annual statements, plan funding, and administrative records must be maintained.

Age Discrimination in Employment Act (ADEA)

The Age Discrimination in Employment Act (ADEA) applies to employers with 20 or more employees and is directed toward employees who are age 40 or older. Generally speaking, this act prohibits compulsory retirement, except for those in executive or high policymaking positions. Employee benefits, which in the past usually ceased or were severely limited when an employee turned 65, must be continued for older workers, although some reductions in benefits may be allowed. Some states have laws that are even stricter with regard to retirement and benefits.

The Americans with Disabilities Act (ADA)

The Americans with Disabilities Act (ADA) makes it unlawful for employers with 15 or more employees to discriminate on the basis of disability against a qualified individual with respect to any term, condition, or privilege of employment. Employees with disabilities must be given equal access to whatever health insurance coverage the employer provides to other employees, although certain coverage limitations may be acceptable for mental and nervous conditions, as opposed to physical conditions, as long as such limitations apply to employees without disabilities as well those with disabilities.

Among other things, the law forbids exclusion or limitation of benefits for

➤ Specific disabilities such as deafness or AIDS

➤ Individually distinct groups of afflictions, such as cancer, muscular dystrophy, or kidney disease

➤ Disability in general

Pregnancy Discrimination

Women affected by pregnancy, childbirth, or related medical conditions must be treated the same for employment-related purposes as persons who are not affected in the same way but are in similar positions. This includes receiving benefits under an employee benefit plan, such as group health insurance. Although the federal law applies only to employers who have 15 or more employees, various state laws may affect employers with fewer than 15 mployees.

State Regulation

Many states have some form of mandated group health benefits. These commonly include required coverage for adopted or newborn children, continued coverage for handicapped dependents, coverage for treatment of alcoholism or drug abuse, and coverage for mammograms and Pap smears.

Some state statutes mandate continuation of coverage for individuals whose group insurance has terminated. Most often, COBRA satisfies the state continuation of coverage requirements. In instances where the state requirements are more generous than COBRA, the employer must follow the more generous plan.

Extension of benefits is similar to continuation of coverage. In this case, benefits that began to be paid while a health insurance policy was in force continue, or are extended, after the insurance contract is terminated. Some states require group policies to provide extension of benefits for a covered member who is totally disabled at the time of policy discontinuance.

States often regulate the marketing and advertising of accident and health insurance policies to assure truthful and full disclosure of pertinent information when selling these policies. As a rule, the insurer is held responsible for the content of advertisements of its policies. Advertisements cannot be misleading, obscure, or use deceptive illustrations, and must clearly outline all policy coverages as well as exclusions or limitations on coverage (such as preexisting condition limitations).

Exam Prep Questions

1. Which of the following is not part of the qualification process for legal dependency?

   ○ A. Relationship to the insured

   ○ B. Residency in the home

   ○ C. Eligibility for insurance

   ○ D. Listing on the insured's tax return as a dependent

2. When both parents have employer-provided group coverage, the children are covered under

   ○ A. The father's plan

   ○ B. The mother's plan

   ○ C. The plan of the parent whose birthday falls closest to the child's birthday

   ○ D. The plan of the parent whose birthday falls closest to the start of the calendar year

3. Under the coordination of benefits rule, the primary company pays

   ○ A. If there is no other coverage

   ○ B. As if there were no other coverage

   ○ C. Whatever the other coverage does not pay, up to the policy limits

   ○ D. Only if the other coverage refuses the claim

4. Carla enrolls in group insurance when she is eligible under her employer's plan. Because of an administrative error, her enrollment form is never sent to the company. When she later has a claim, the insurer will

   ○ A. Deny the claim, because it has no record of her policy.

   ○ B. Force the employer to pay the claim, because it was the employer's error.

   ○ C. Pay the claim only if the insurer is proven to have made an error.

   ○ D. Accept the enrollment form and all of the past due premium and pay the medical claim.

5. What is the federal law that requires employers with more than 20 employees to include in their group insurance plan a continuation of benefits provision for all eligible employees?

   ○ A. COBRA

   ○ B. OBRA

   ○ C. ERISA

   ○ D. TEFRA

6. What is the federal law that extends the minimum continuation of coverage period from 18–29 months for qualified beneficiaries disabled at the time of termination or reduction in hours?

- ○ A. COBRA
- ○ B. OBRA
- ○ C. ERISA
- ○ D. TEFRA

7. Which of the following provisions is not a part of HIPAA?

- ○ A. Employers must make full health care coverage available immediately to newly hired employees who were previously covered for at least 18 months.
- ○ B. New mothers and their babies must be allowed to stay in the hospital for at least 48 hours following a regular delivery.
- ○ C. Small employers may not be denied group health insurance coverage because one or more employees is in poor health.
- ○ D. Annual limits and lifetime spending limits may no longer apply to mental health coverage.

8. Which of the following is considered a disqualifying event under COBRA?

- ○ A. The employer ceases to maintain any group health plan.
- ○ B. The employee is no longer eligible for the group health plan due to a change in the covered classes.
- ○ C. The employee voluntarily leaves employment with the employer.
- ○ D. The employee's employment is terminated by the employer.

9. Under OBRA, an employer may terminate COBRA coverage because of coverage under another health plan

- ○ A. As soon as the coverage is in force
- ○ B. As long as the other health plan does not limit benefits for the insured's preexisting conditions
- ○ C. As long as the other health plan limits benefits for the insured's preexisting conditions
- ○ D. Only if the premiums for the new plan are paid entirely by the insured's new employer

10. The Age Discrimination in Employment Act applies to employees who are

- ○ A. 40 or older
- ○ B. 45 or older
- ○ C. 50 or older
- ○ D. 55 or older

Exam Prep Answers

1. **C is correct.** Dependency may be proved by family relationship, residence in the home, or qualification as a dependent on the insured's tax returns.

2. **D is correct.** This is an example of how the birthday rule applies.

3. **B is correct.** Under the COB rule the primary policy will pay as if there were no other coverage.

4. **D is correct.** Administrative errors will not negate a claim.

5. **A is correct.** COBRA is the law that makes continuation of benefits available.

6. **B is correct.** OBRA extends the continuation period for qualified beneficiaries.

7. **D is correct.** HIPAA does not alter limits for mental health benefits.

8. **A is correct.** If the employer terminates all group coverages there are no remaining rights under COBRA.

9. **B is correct.** This is a protection included in the law.

10. **A is correct.** The provisions apply to employees who are age 40 or older.

Social Health Insurance

Terms you need to understand:

- ✓ Medicare
- ✓ Medicare Part A
- ✓ Inpatient hospital care
- ✓ Skilled nursing facility care
- ✓ Home health care
- ✓ Hospice care
- ✓ Medicare Part B
- ✓ Medicaid

Concepts you need to master:

- ✓ Medicare supplement insurance
- ✓ Standardized medicare supplement benefits
- ✓ Core medicare supplement benefits
- ✓ Optional medicare supplement benefits
- ✓ Workers compensation

The term *social health insurance* refers to health coverage subsidized and implemented through government administration of tax money and social programs. We will look at four areas:

➤ Medicare and associated private coverages

➤ Medicaid

➤ Social security

➤ Workers compensation

Medicare

Medicare is a federal program administered by the Health Care Financing Administration (HCFA). To make medicare benefit payments, the U.S. government contracts with selected private insurance companies. The insurance companies that handle claims for hospital, skilled nursing facility, home health agency, and hospice services are called *intermediaries*. The insurance companies that handle claims for physician services are called *carriers*.

Enrollment

Medicare benefits are divided into two parts:

➤ Part A, Hospital Insurance

➤ Part B, Supplementary Medical Insurance

Enrollment in Part A is automatic for individuals entitled to social security benefits. These persons are eligible for Part A benefits as of the first day of the month in which they reach age 65.

Enrollment in Part B is voluntary and requires payment of a monthly premium. When individuals become eligible for Part A, they will be enrolled and their premium payment established for Part B coverage unless they sign a form indicating they do not want the Part B coverage.

If individuals enroll before the month in which they reach age 65, Part B coverage begins as of the first day of the month when they are 65, just as it does for Part A. If enrollment takes place later, coverage also begins later.

People who choose not to enroll in Part B during their initial enrollment period may do so later. A *general enrollment period* occurs each year from January 1 through March 31. When enrollment occurs during this period, coverage always begins on the following July 1.

Benefits Under Medicare Part A

Part A provides coverage for four different kinds of care:

➤ Inpatient hospital care

➤ Skilled nursing facility care

➤ Home health care

➤ Hospice care

The services covered under each of these arrangements are subject to certain limitations.

Inpatient Hospital Care

Medicare's *inpatient hospital care* benefit helps pay the reasonable charges that result from hospitalization in a semiprivate room for medically necessary care. This includes meals, regular nursing services, special care units, drugs taken in the hospital, tests, medical supplies, operating room, and many other supplies and services.

For each benefit period, medicare pays the full cost of up to 60 days of inpatient hospital care, after the patient pays a deductible, which changes annually. From the 61st through 90th days of hospitalization, medicare pays all but a specified coinsurance amount per day. This figure also changes annually.

For a stay longer than 90 days, the patient may draw upon 60 lifetime reserve days. The patient's daily copayment amount increases substantially when these reserve days are used.

A benefit period begins upon admission and ends 60 days after hospital discharge. A readmission during this 60 days is considered part of the same benefit period; a readmission after the 60 days run out is the beginning of a new benefit period.

Skilled Nursing Facility Care

Medicare will share the cost of *skilled nursing facility (SNF) care* for up to 100 days in each benefit period. The patient must pay a specified dollar amount (coinsurance) for the 21st through 100th days of confinement. This amount changes annually. Medicare pays all reasonable charges for the first 20 days.

Medicare defines the skilled nursing facility benefit quite narrowly. The patient must be receiving medically necessary services provided by a highly skilled staff in a medicare-approved facility, following a prior hospital stay of at least 3 days. The care must be of a type that can be performed only by or under the supervision of licensed nursing personnel, and only as the result of a doctor's orders.

Any type of intermediate or custodial, as opposed to skilled, nursing care is not covered.

Home Health Care

If a patient is confined at home, the *home health care benefit* provides for certain services performed by a participating home health agency. This is a public or private agency that provides skilled nursing or therapeutic services in the home. Eligible expenses include

➤ Intermittent part-time nursing care

➤ Physical, occupational, or speech therapy

➤ Home health aides

➤ Medical social services

➤ Medical supplies

➤ 80% of certain durable medical equipment, such as wheelchairs or hospital beds

No benefits will be paid for housekeeping services, meal preparation or delivery, shopping, full-time nursing care, blood transfusions, drugs, or biologicals.

The home health care benefit pays for an unlimited number of home visits as medically necessary, provided they are *intermittent*, rather than constant or full-time. Note that this is *not* the same benefit that is found in long-term care policies.

Hospice Care

A hospice is organized primarily for the purpose of providing support services to terminally ill patients and their families. For terminally ill patients, the *hospice care benefit* provides inpatient and outpatient hospice care. Payments are made for pain relief and symptom management, but not for curative or other types of treatment.

It is possible for medicare to cover hospice care for an unlimited period of time as long as a physician certifies need. Medicare pays virtually all costs for hospice treatment, with no deductible.

Only two services require copayments:

➤ Prescription drugs, for which patients must pay 5% or $5 per prescription, whichever is less

➤ Respite care, for which patients must pay 5% of the medicare-approved rate up to a specified dollar amount, which changes annually

The *respite care* benefit covers temporary care in a hospice for a patient who is normally cared for in the home. The respite is for the usual caregivers and may last no more than 5 consecutive days.

What Part A Does Not Cover

Hospital insurance under medicare does not cover

➤ Private duty nursing

➤ Charges for a private room, unless medically necessary

➤ Conveniences, such as a telephone or television in an insured's room

➤ The first three pints of blood received during a calendar year (unless replaced by a blood plan)

Benefits Under Medicare Part B

Medicare Part B provides coverage for three general kinds of medical services:

➤ Doctors' services

➤ Home health care (if not covered by Part A)

➤ Outpatient medical services and supplies

Common Deductible and Copayment

Medicare Part B requires cost-sharing by the patient. There is an annual deductible and a coinsurance percentage that applies to all Part B covered services, across the board. This contrasts with Part A, where each benefit provided has its own unique copayment requirements for the patient.

Under Part B, a patient is always responsible for these copayments:

➤ An annual deductible amount

➤ 20% of all reasonable charges for covered, medically necessary services

➤ The first three pints of blood

Medicare determines what is a reasonable charge for a particular service. If the actual charge is more than that, the patient must pay the difference, unless the doctor or supplier agrees to accept *assignment. Assignment* means that the doctor or supplier will accept medicare's approved amounts as full payment and cannot legally bill the patient for anything above that amount. Doctors and suppliers are not required to accept assignment, but many will.

If medicare decides that an expense is medically unnecessary, the patient must pay the entire cost.

Doctors' Services

Part B covers most physicians', surgeons', and osteopaths' services and supplies furnished as part of such services. The following are some of the specific services:

➤ Medical and surgical services, including anesthesia

➤ Office visits, house calls, and hospital calls

➤ Radiological and pathological services provided by a physician

➤ Medical supplies furnished as part of a physician's professional services

➤ Second opinions before surgery

➤ Diagnostic tests that are part of the patient's treatment

➤ X-rays

➤ Services of the doctor's office nurse

➤ Physical, occupational, and speech therapy services

➤ Blood transfusions

➤ Drugs and biologicals that cannot be self-administered.

Specifically *excluded* from Part B coverage are physicians' services for

➤ Routine physical exams

➤ Routine foot care, treatment of flat feet, and treatment for subluxations of the foot

➤ Eye exams, fitting of eyeglasses, or contact lenses

➤ Hearing exams, fitting of hearing aids

➤ Most types of dental care

➤ Most immunizations

➤ Cosmetic surgery (unless needed to repair an accidental injury or to correct a malformed body part)

Home Health Care Services

For persons who participate in Part B but not Part A, Part B pays the full cost of medically necessary home health visits for patients requiring home nursing care. The patient pays no deductible or coinsurance, except for 20% of the cost of durable medical equipment, provided under the home health care benefit (for example, wheelchairs, hospital beds).

Outpatient Medical Services and Supplies

Medicare Part B will help pay for certain services received as an outpatient from a medicare-certified hospital for the diagnosis or treatment of an illness or injury.

The following is a relatively comprehensive list of some of the outpatient medical services and supplies covered under medicare Part B:

➤ Outpatient clinic services

➤ Emergency room services

➤ X-rays, whether for therapy or diagnosis billed by the hospital

➤ Medically necessary ambulance services

➤ Purchase or rental of durable medical equipment used in the patient's home

➤ Artificial limbs and eyes

➤ Artificial replacements for internal organs (for example, colostomy bags and supplies)

➤ Braces for neck, back, or limbs

➤ Casts, splints, and surgical dressings

➤ Blood transfusions (after the first three pints) furnished to an outpatient

➤ Outpatient physical, occupational, and speech therapy provided in a therapist's office, as an outpatient, or in the patient's home

➤ Drugs and biologicals that cannot be self-administered

➤ Mammograms, Pap smears, and colon-rectal screenings

➤ Diabetes glucose monitoring and education

➤ Flu shots

The following are outpatient services not covered by Part B:

➤ Routine physical exams

> ➤ Eye exams, fitting of eyeglasses or contact lenses

> ➤ Hearing exams, fitting of hearing aids

> ➤ Most immunizations

> ➤ Routine foot care

What Part B Does Not Cover

Medical insurance under medicare does not cover

> ➤ Private duty nursing

> ➤ Skilled nursing home care costs over 100 days per benefit period

> ➤ Intermediate nursing home care

> ➤ Physician charges above medicare's approved amount

> ➤ Most outpatient prescription drugs

> ➤ Care received outside the United States (limited coverage for Canada and Mexico)

> ➤ Custodial care received in the home

> ➤ Dental care, routine physicals and immunizations, cosmetic surgery, eyeglasses, hearing aids, orthopedic shoes, acupuncture expenses

> ➤ Expenses incurred due to war or act of war

Claims and Appeals

If a doctor has not accepted a medicare assignment, the doctor sends the bill directly to the patient. The patient fills out a medicare claim form and attaches itemized bills from the doctor. Upon receiving the claim, the carrier will send a form called *Explanation of Medicare Benefits*. This form shows which services are covered and the amounts approved for each service.

If medicare claims are denied, there is an appeal process a patient can go through. Within 6 months of the receipt of the Explanation of Medicare Benefits form, the patient must file a written request for review. The carrier will check for miscalculations or other clerical errors. If the carrier, after review, declines to make a change, an appeal can be made (if the amount disputed is $100 or more) to the social security office. The patient must appear in person to attend a hearing and present evidence, such as a doctor's letter, to support his or her point. A written notice of the decision will be sent after the hearing.

Medicare Supplement Insurance

Even after medicare pays its share of medical costs, the patient may still owe the following large amounts:

➤ Deductibles

➤ Coinsurance

➤ Noncovered services

➤ Actual charges by service providers in excess of the approved amount that medicare will pay

A medicare supplement insurance policy can help cover the costs not paid by medicare. This may also be referred to as a *Medigap policy.*

Standardized Medicare Supplement Benefits

Under federal law, only 10 standardized types of medicare supplement policies may be offered.

 Every medicare supplement policy must offer a basic core of benefits. Each of the 10 forms also may provide a number of additional benefits.

Core Benefits

These must be included in any medicare supplement policy:

➤ Part A copayments for the 61st through 90th day of hospitalization

➤ Part A copayments for the 60 lifetime reserve days

➤ All charges for 365 days of hospitalization after all Part A inpatient hospital and lifetime reserve days are used up

➤ Blood deductible (first three pints)

➤ Part B copayments on medicare-approved charges for physicians' and medical services

Optional Benefits

Table 22.1 shows optional benefits that may be included in a medicare supplement policy in addition to the core benefits.

Table 22.1 Medicare Optional Benefits	
Benefit	**Description**
Part A Deductible	Pays the inpatient hospital deductible for each benefit period.
Skilled Nursing Facility Care	Covers the Part A copayments for the 21st through the 100th day of skilled nursing facility care.
Foreign Travel Emergency	Pays 80% of the charges for emergency care given in a foreign hospital that would have been covered by medicare had the treatment been given in the U.S.
Part B Deductible	Covers the calendar-year deductible for physicians' and medical services regardless of hospitalization.
Part B Excess Charges	Pays charges for physicians' and medical services that exceed the medicare-approved amount. Coverage may be obtained for 80% or 100% of these charges.
At-Home Recovery	Pays for a care provider to give assistance with ADLs while a beneficiary qualifies for medicare home health care benefits and for up to 8 weeks following the last medicare-approved home health care visit.
Preventive Care	Pays for an annual flu shot, an annual physical, and any screening tests or preventive measures deemed appropriate by a physician.
Prescription Drugs	Pays 50% of an outpatient's prescription drug charges after a $250 deductible. The basic drug benefit has a yearly limit of $1,250; the extended drug benefit has a yearly limit of $3,000. (Starting January 1, 2006, when prescription drugs begin to be covered by medicare, this benefit will no longer be available.)

Standardized Policy Forms

Insurance companies are not free to offer these benefits in any combination they wish. The NAIC model regulation outlines 10 medicare supplement plans, designated by the letters A through J, containing various combinations of the benefits that may be offered. Some states also allow new and innovative additional benefits to be offered.

Other Standard Provisions

The following is a list of other provisions that may apply:

➤ No Medigap policy may duplicate benefits provided by medicare.

➤ Benefits under Medigap policies must automatically change to coincide with changes in medicare deductibles and copayments. Premiums may be modified accordingly.

➤ After a Medigap policy has been in force for 6 months, benefits may not be denied or limited on the basis of preexisting conditions. *Preexisting condition* may not be defined more restrictively than a condition for which medical advice or treatment was given by a physician within 6 months before the policy was in force.

➤ Except for an exclusion regarding preexisting conditions (just described), no Medigap policy may contain limitations or exclusions on coverage that are more restrictive than those of medicare.

➤ Losses resulting from sickness may not be treated differently than losses resulting from accidents.

➤ The definition of *accident* may not employ an accidental means test.

➤ Medigap policies must be at least guaranteed renewable. Issuers may not cancel or not renew a policy solely on the ground of an individual's health status. Issuers may not cancel or not renew a policy for any reason other than nonpayment of premium or material misrepresentation.

➤ Except for nonpayment of premium, coverage may not be terminated on a spouse solely because the issuer has reason to terminate coverage on an insured.

➤ If a Medigap policy is terminated while a loss is continuing, benefits must still be paid for that loss, subject to the continuing total disability of the insured and the policy's limits on the benefit period and maximum amount.

➤ If a group Medigap policy is replaced by another group Medigap policy, the new policy must cover all persons covered by the old policy. The new policy may not deny or limit any benefits on the basis of preexisting conditions that would not have been denied or limited under the old policy.

➤ If a group Medigap policy is terminated and not replaced, insureds must be given the choice of converting to an individual policy that offers the same benefits as the group policy or another standardized plan.

> ➤ If a person insured under a group Medigap policy terminates membership in the group, the person must be given the choice of converting to an individual standardized plan unless the group policyholder offers the person continuation of benefits under the group plan.

> ➤ If a Medigap insured begins receiving medicaid, the insured may, within 90 days, request a suspension of premiums and benefits under the policy for up to 2 years and get an appropriate refund of premium. Coverage must be automatically reinstated if the insured loses medicaid and notifies the issuer within 90 days.

Medicare SELECT

Medicare SELECT is another version of the standard Medigap policies we have been discussing. It offers the same 10 plans with the same coverage.

The only difference between Medicare SELECT and standard Medigap insurance is that Medicare SELECT is operated on a preferred provider basis. Each insurer has a list of doctors and hospitals from which the insured must make his or her choice for treatment in order to receive benefits. As a result of this requirement, Medicare SELECT policies generally have lower premiums than standard Medigap policies.

Medicare+Choice

A number of options to the traditional medicare program have been introduced under the heading of *Medicare+Choice*, which is sometimes referred to as *Medicare Part C*.

All of these options are designed to fill medicare gaps that must be paid by the medicare beneficiary.

Fee-for-Service Plans

A new fee-for-service system under Medicare+Choice, called *private fee-for-service plans*, combines some of the advantages of regular medicare coverage with those of private insurance. Under this option, medicare beneficiaries can buy plans from insurance companies that include both medicare-covered services *and* other medicare supplement coverage. The insurance companies are paid by medicare to cover the individuals using this option. Beneficiaries continue to pay medicare Part B premiums directly to medicare, but an additional premium is paid to the insurance company. Premiums are not limited by the government and medicare's payment to the insurance company for individuals participating in this option probably will not meet the total cost of the coverage. In effect, the individual and medicare share the cost of coverage under the Medicare+Choice fee-for-service option.

In return, this option will provide all medicare-covered care from any provider.

There may be additional benefits to cover medicare gaps, such as prescription costs and preventive services.

Health Maintenance Organizations (HMOs)

Medicare beneficiaries can receive health care through a medicare-contracting *health maintenance organization (HMO),* if one is available in their geographic area. Medicare prepays a monthly amount for each beneficiary. In return, the HMO must deliver all medically necessary medicare-covered treatment. A number of extras may be included, such as preventive or routine care not normally provided by medicare. Depending on the plan, beneficiaries may pay the HMO a fixed monthly premium. Beneficiaries continue to pay the medicare Part B premium directly to medicare. Copayments may be required for some services, but there are no medicare deductibles or coinsurance. Like many HMOs, this Medicare+Choice option may not pay for services delivered by physicians outside the HMO's network.

Preferred Provider Organizations (PPOs)

A *preferred provider organization (PPO)* is a network of providers who contract to provide services at prenegotiated rates. Participants in this option may go outside the network for services if they're willing to pay more. This option pays a higher percentage of costs when participants use its preferred providers and a lower percentage if they go outside the network to a non-preferred provider.

Medicare prepays a monthly amount to the PPO on behalf of each participant.

Participants may also pay a fixed monthly premium. Medicare Part B premiums must continue to be paid directly to medicare. Although participants do not pay medicare deductibles or coinsurance, the PPO may have its own deductibles and/or coinsurance. In return the PPO delivers all medically necessary medicare-covered care to participants.

Provider-Sponsored Organizations (PSOs)

Under Medicare+Choice, physicians and hospitals are allowed to create their own organizations to contract with medicare the same way HMOs and PPOs do. These *provider-sponsored organizations (PSOs)* are owned and operated by the providers themselves. PSOs work much like HMOs.

Medicare managed care plans may be either *risk plans* or *cost plans*. Plans with risk contracts have *lock-in requirements*. This means that plan participants generally are locked into receiving all covered care from the doctors, hospitals, and other health care providers that are affiliated with the plan. If plan participants go outside the plan for services, neither the plan nor medicare will pay, and participants will have to foot the entire bill—with the possible exception of emergency services.

Plans with cost contracts do not have lock-in requirements. Plan participants can go to health providers affiliated with the plan or go outside the plan. If they go outside the plan, the plan will not pay, but medicare will pay its share. Participants are responsible for medicare's coinsurance, deductible, and other charges.

Medicare and Employer Coverage

Many individuals continue working beyond the age of 65 or have spouses who are working. In such cases, medicare beneficiaries may be covered by their own or their spouse's employer group health plan. When this occurs, medicare may be the secondary payer to any group health plan provided by an employer with 20 or more employees. This means that the group health plan pays first on hospital and medical bills. If the plan does not pay all of the expenses incurred, medicare may pay secondary benefits for medicare-covered services to supplement the amount paid by the group health plan.

Note that employers with 20 or more employees must offer the same health benefits to employees who are age 65 or older, and to their spouses who are age 65 or older, as they offer to younger employees and spouses. The older employee has the option of rejecting such group health coverage, in which case medicare becomes the primary payer for medicare-covered health services.

Medicare may also be a secondary payer to employer-provided group health coverage for certain individuals under age 65 who are entitled to medicare based on their disability. To be the primary payer, the group health plan must generally be that of an employer or employee organization that covers the employees of at least one employer with 100 or more employees. Such plans are known as *large group health plans (LGHPs)*. An LGHP may not treat disabled employees differently than other employees because of their disability.

Medicaid

Medicaid is a welfare health care program for indigent persons. It was established by the federal government but is administered by the states. The eligibility requirements for medicaid vary somewhat state-by-state. Generally speaking, to be eligible for medicaid, a person must either qualify for *Aid for Families with Dependent Children* (also known as *public assistance* or *welfare*) or *Supplemental Security Income*, an assistance program under social security for indigent persons who are age 65 or over, blind, or disabled.

For those who do qualify, Medicaid covers most health care costs, including hospital and doctor bills and nursing home care.

Financial Tests

Each state establishes its own limit on the income and financial resources that a medicaid recipient may have and still qualify for medicaid. The recipient must *spend down* or exhaust his or her income and resources to a minimal amount before medicaid becomes available.

The recipient—an individual, a couple, or a family—is permitted to retain a small amount of monthly income plus certain assets (or what the law refers to as *resources*). The recipient is allowed to keep his or her home. Within important limits, the recipient may also be able to keep some personal property.

Spousal Impoverishment Rule

In the case of a married couple where one spouse requires nursing home care, the law provides that the spouse who is not institutionalized is permitted to keep a portion of the couple's resources, as determined by state and federal guidelines.

Medicare Cost Assistance

Medicaid is required by law to pay certain medicare costs of indigent medicare patients:

➤ Medicare deductibles

➤ Part B premium

➤ Medicare copayments

➤ Part A premiums (when required)

Social Security Disability

Social security disability benefits are a type of social health insurance. They are available to people who meet these requirements:

➤ Totally and permanently disabled for at least 5 months

➤ Expected to be disabled for 12 months or longer, or the disability will end in death

➤ Fully insured and disability insured as defined under social security regulations

Benefits available are equal to 100% of the individual's *primary insurance amount (PIA)*, which is the amount the person would normally receive as a retirement benefit. After being entitled to disability benefits for 2 years, an individual may also receive medicare benefits.

Benefit amounts are based on the PIA as follows:

➤ A disabled worker receives a benefit equal to 100% of his or her PIA.

➤ A spouse caring for an unmarried child of the worker who is under age 16 or was disabled before age 22 also receives a benefit, equal to 50% of the worker's PIA.

➤ Each unmarried child under age 18 (19 if in high school) or disabled before age 22 receives a benefit equal to 50% of the worker's PIA.

The total dollar amount a family may receive is capped by a *Maximum Family Benefit* amount that is also based on the worker's average earnings. If the total amount a family is eligible for would exceed the Maximum Family Benefit, the disabled worker receives the full amount he or she is eligible for, but dependents' benefits are scaled back proportionately until the total amount equals the Maximum Family Benefit.

 Social security disability payments will generally continue as long as the recipient cannot engage in any substantial gainful activity. This is essentially the same as the *any occupation* definition discussed in a previous chapter.

TRICARE

TRICARE is a regionally managed health care program for active duty and retired members of the military uniformed services and their families, as well as survivors who are not eligible for medicare. Participants choose among three health care options: TRICARE Standard, a fee-for-service plan; TRI-CARE Extra, a preferred provider plan; and TRICARE Prime, for those who seek care at Military Treatment Facilities (MTFs).

Workers Compensation

Workers compensation is also a form of social insurance. Although the benefits are not provided directly by the government, the benefits are mandated by law.

Types of Benefits

All state workers compensation laws incorporate four categories of benefits:

➤ Disability (loss of income) benefits

➤ Medical benefits

➤ Survivor (death) benefits

➤ Rehabilitation benefits

Compensable Injuries

In order to be considered *compensable* as interpreted in workers compensation law, an injury must meet three basic criteria:

➤ It must be accidental.

➤ It must arise out of the individual's employment.

➤ It must arise in the course of the individual's employment.

Occupational Diseases

In order to be classified as an *occupational disease* under a workers compensation law, the disease must meet these requirements:

➤ Arise out of employment

➤ Be due to causes or conditions characteristic of and peculiar to the particular trade, occupation, process, or employment

The requirement of peculiarity to a particular employment means workers compensation coverage does not apply for any ordinary diseases to which the general public is exposed.

Types of Disability

Four types of disability are defined under workers compensation law:

➤ Permanent total

➤ Permanent partial

➤ Temporary total

➤ Temporary partial

Compulsory and Elective Compensation Laws

State workers compensation laws are either compulsory or elective, with the majority being compulsory. This means the employer must accept and comply with all the provisions of the law. If the state law is elective, however, the employer and employee both have the option of accepting or rejecting the law.

Some state workers compensation laws are deemed compulsory for specific types of work, and elective for still other types. However, if an employer chooses not to be subject to a state's elective workers compensation law, the employer is denied any rights provided under its law, and loses use of most pro-employer law defenses as well.

Both compulsory and elective states often exclude two classifications of employees from required coverage:

➤ Farm workers

➤ Domestic servants

Extraterritorial Provisions

Most state workers compensation laws contain an *extraterritorial provision*. This means that a worker who is employed in a particular state is covered under that state's workers compensation law, even while temporarily working in another state.

Second Injury Funds

Second injury funds have been established in almost every state to promote the hiring of previously injured or physically handicapped workers. These funds provide that if a handicapped employee is injured a second time, the employer will be charged only for the loss accrued by that specific second injury, not for the total disability.

Exam Prep Questions

1. Carla is 67 and eligible for social security and medicare. When she comes out of retirement to work at a large corporation which provides health benefits

   ○ A. Her private benefits become secondary to medicare benefits.
   ○ B. Her medicare benefits become secondary to her private benefits.
   ○ C. The employer is not required to offer her private benefits.
   ○ D. She will cease to be eligible for medicare benefits.

2. Medicare Part A covers all of the following except

   ○ A. Charges for a private room
   ○ B. Skilled nursing facility care
   ○ C. Home health care
   ○ D. Hospice care

3. For each benefit period, medicare will pay the full cost of up to

   ○ A. 30 days of hospital care
   ○ B. 60 days of hospital care
   ○ C. 90 days of hospital care
   ○ D. 365 days of hospital care

4. Medicare will pay the entire cost for skilled nursing facility care for the first

   ○ A. 20 days
   ○ B. 80 days
   ○ C. 100 days
   ○ D. 0 days

5. Medicare Part A provides coverage for all of the following kinds of care except

   ○ A. Private duty nursing
   ○ B. Skilled nursing facility care
   ○ C. Home health care
   ○ D. Hospice care

6. Medicare Part B provides coverage for all of the following kinds of care except

   ○ A. Skilled nursing facility care not covered by Part A
   ○ B. Doctor's services
   ○ C. Home health care not covered by Part A
   ○ D. Outpatient medical services and supplies

7. Which of the following statements about medicare supplement plans is false?

- ○ A. Benefits must automatically change to coincide with changes in medicare deductibles and copayments.
- ○ B. Losses resulting from sickness may not be treated differently than losses resulting from accidents.
- ○ C. The definition of *accident* may employ an accidental means test.
- ○ D. Policies must be at least guaranteed renewable.

8. In order to be compensable as interpreted in workers compensation law, an injury must meet all of the following criteria except

- ○ A. It must be accidental.
- ○ B. It must arise out of the individual's employment.
- ○ C. It must arise in the course of the individual's employment.
- ○ D. It must be unforeseeable.

9. Juanita is employed in California. She takes a business trip to Colorado to demonstrate some techniques to workers in another facility and is injured in the process. Her worker's compensation benefits will be paid according to the laws of

- ○ A. California
- ○ B. Colorado
- ○ C. Whichever state would provide the greater benefit
- ○ D. Whichever state would provide the lesser benefit

10. Medicare supplement policies are also known as

- ○ A. Medicare policies
- ○ B. Medigap policies
- ○ C. Medicaid policies
- ○ D. Medicare+Choice policies

Exam Prep Answers

1. **B is correct.** Her medicare benefits will become secondary to her private benefits.
2. **A is correct.** Medicare does not pay for private room and board charges.
3. **B is correct.** The limit is 60 days of hospital care.
4. **A is correct.** Medicare will pay this cost for the first 20 days.
5. **A is correct.** Coverage for private duty nursing is not provided.
6. **A is correct.** This service is not covered by Part B.
7. **C is correct.** Use of an accidental means test is prohibited.
8. **D is correct.** This is not a requirement.
9. **A is correct.** The benefits of her home state will apply.
10. **B is correct.** Medigap is a common term used to refer to medicare supplement policies.

Long-Term Care

Terms you need to understand:

✓ Skilled nursing care
✓ Intermediate care
✓ Custodial care
✓ Home health care
✓ Adult day care
✓ Hospice care
✓ Respite care
✓ Elimination period

Concepts you need to master:

✓ Long-term care
✓ Suitable purchasers
✓ Benefit trigger
✓ Activities of daily living
✓ Cognitive impairment

Better medical care means many individuals are living into their 80s, 90s, and beyond. Unfortunately, although life expectancy has increased, many older individuals have serious health problems that keep them from living on their own or completely caring for themselves. Long-term care pays for the kind of care needed by individuals who have chronic illnesses or disabilities.

It often covers the cost of nursing home care, and also provides coverage for home-based care—visiting nurses, chore services, and respite care for daily caregivers who need time away from these difficult duties. Such coverage becomes important when one considers that the annual cost for nursing home confinement can reach $40,000.

Many people believe medicare or medicare supplement policies will pay for this care if they need it. Medicare will cover nursing home care if it is part of the treatment for a covered injury or illness, but care needed because of aging is not covered by medicare or medicare supplements. Medicare and supplementary insurance pay for skilled nursing care, but the coverage is extremely limited (the care must immediately follow a period of hospital confinement, and no benefits are provided after the 100th day). Medicaid does pay for nursing home care, but provides coverage only for needy families. Sadly, many people must pay for their own nursing home care and eventually turn to medicaid when their life savings are gone.

History of LTC Coverage

The earliest long-term care (LTC) policies were relatively more restrictive than the current generation of plans, often requiring prior hospitalization and a level of service greater than mere custodial care. Many covered care in a nursing facility only, rather than also providing coverage for services in the home of the individual or in an adult day care center. Most excluded Alzheimer's and dementia—two common illnesses of the elderly and the reason many older persons require such care.

Some long-term care policies were so closely tied to medicare's restrictions that they paid little that medicare did not already pay. During the early development period, policies often had so many restrictions that few insureds qualified for payment of benefits.

LTC policies are still evolving. However, with attention to the problem of long-term care firmly focused, legislators and the insurance industry have begun to come to grips with the far-reaching ramifications of health services for an older population. With the federal government responding to consumer interests in long-term care coverages, the National Association of Insurance Commissioners (NAIC) developed a model to help state legislatures in an effort to keep regulation on a state level. More than half of the states currently use the NAIC or a similar model. Key issues include

➤ A benefit period of at least one year

➤ Strict restrictions on cancellation, specifically prohibiting cancellation due to the insured's aging; most policies now guarantee renewability

➤ Standards for covering preexisting conditions

➤ A free-look period

➤ Prohibition of exclusions for Alzheimer's disease

Another factor in the evolution and increasing availability of LTC policies is that consumers, too, are more aware of the following:

➤ Medicare does not cover long-term care (much to the surprise of most of the population, who at one time believed medicare did cover most nursing home care).

➤ One in four people are likely to spend at least some time in a nursing home after age 65, increasing to about a third if they live to age 85.

➤ The average cost for nursing home confinement is currently about $3,300 per month and can be as high as $5,000 per month, depending on location and level of care. These costs are likely to continue growing.

The increased knowledgeability of insurance buyers has played a part in the development and refinement of LTC policies. In addition, law changes have clarified the tax status of long-term care policies, which are now treated like accident and health policies taxwise. Proceeds of *qualified* long-term care policies are generally received income tax–free, and premiums may be deductible as a medical expense, within certain limitations. Federal law now determines what constitutes a qualified long-term care policy eligible for these tax advantages. The law spells out when benefits must be paid and what options must be offered to prospects for long-term care insurance.

Insurers are not required to offer, and consumers are not required to purchase, qualified long-term care policies. Nonqualified policies may offer benefits that are more attractive or easier to obtain than qualified policies and may be more desirable to certain consumers even if the nonqualified policies do not offer the tax advantages of qualified policies.

Suitable Purchasers

LTC insurance enables the senior citizen to maintain his or her independence. With adequate coverage, the individual does not have to rely on friends or family to provide custodial needs or necessary funds to help defray the costs of a nursing home stay.

Protection of personal assets may well be the most important reason for purchasing LTC insurance. Possibly, the question isn't "Can I afford to buy LTC insurance?" but rather, "Can I afford not to purchase LTC insurance?"

When an individual has substantial financial assets (and retirement income), the possibility that LTC expenses could mean a significant reduction in the person's assets and standard of living is a real threat. Thus, the purchase of LTC insurance to protect one's personal financial resources may well be a wise financial decision.

Paying periodic premiums is a more efficient and manageable way to provide for future LTC costs than having to rely on personal savings. LTC insurance provides that a person's financial resources need not be liquidated either to pay for nursing home expenses or to spend down to satisfy medicaid eligibility.

For example, an individual with no dependents and few financial responsibilities may have little need for life insurance. Likewise, a person without substantial assets at risk may have little need to purchase LTC insurance.

If a senior citizen's sole source of income is a relatively small pension and his or her financial assets are minimal, this person may already be eligible for medicaid reimbursement of LTC expenses. Also, because of the individual's low income and limited financial resources, LTC insurance premiums may be unaffordable.

For example, Joe and Irene Brown are both 67 years old. Their only source of income is social security and a small pension ($200 monthly). They rent an apartment in a senior citizen complex, have a very small amount of life insurance (enough for burial) and usually maintain a savings account balance of no more than $1,000. They have no other assets other than personal possessions and an automobile. Are Mr. and Mrs. Brown prospects for LTC insurance?

Probably not. First of all, it's doubtful that they could afford the premiums based on their relatively small retirement income. Secondly, they have no assets of any consequence to protect. They do not own a home or a large savings account or have other investments. In essence, they probably are already eligible for medicaid benefits should they be forced into a nursing home.

Probability of Needing Care

In 1980, there were 25 million Americans 65 and older. By the turn of the century, the over-65 population exceeded 35 million, and it is estimated that by the year 2030 there will be more than 64 million Americans age 65 and over.

In addition, life expectancy is increasing in the United States. In 1980, life expectancy for males, 65 years old, was about 78, and for females, 81. By the year 2000, life expectancy for males became age 81, and for females, 86. These retirees will face a greater potential need for long-term medical care, simply because of longer life expectancy.

At age 65, the likelihood of a nursing home confinement is about 1 in 3. The odds increase as age increases. An individual 75 years of age has a 2 to 1 chance of confinement in a nursing home. In 1990, there were approximately 7 million Americans, 65 or older, who needed long-term care. This figure increased to more than 9 million by the year 2000 and will exceed 20 million by 2050.

Options Other than Insurance

What are the available options for the senior citizen facing a stay in a nursing home? Following are some of the alternatives:

➤ Using personal assets

➤ Dependency on relatives

➤ Dependency on government programs

Dependency on friends and relatives for custodial type care may not be practical due to changing socioeconomic trends in today's society. Today's family is no longer a cohesive unit but rather a fragmented group, with family members living great distances from each other.

The medicare program is not designed to provide custodial care. It will cover a limited amount of rehabilitative care in a skilled nursing facility approved by medicare. Because medicare will pay for only rehabilitative services, it requires prior hospitalization before admission to the skilled nursing facility. Another avenue is medicaid, which requires the individual to prove financial need.

This normally requires the individual to get rid of financial resources and spend down to a poverty level to obtain medicaid eligibility. The Health

Care Financing Administration reports that about one-half of all medicaid spending goes to people who had financial resources when they entered a nursing home but reached the poverty level while in the nursing home.

Rating Factors

One way LTC policies differ from other health plans concerns how risks are rated. Whereas people afflicted with heart disease or diabetes, for example, would be rated as substandard risks under most health insurance plans, LTC policies, because of their focus on aging people, use a different means of classification. The key for LTC policies is whether an individual can perform the *activities of daily living (ADL)*, and if so, with what degree of proficiency.

ADL include such things as dressing, bathing, eating, walking, and similar activities to care for oneself. Thus, an individual who has a heart disease, but is still able to perform ADL, is a standard risk under LTC policies. For example, Corey, who is age 60, has had several strokes during the past 5 years but is completely capable of performing the activities of daily living.

Under a major medical policy, it is likely that Corey would be classed as a substandard risk. But under an LTC policy, Corey would be classified as a standard risk.

Types of Benefits

An LTC policymight include one or more of the following three types of long-term care:

➤ *Skilled nursing care* is nursing and rehabilitative care that is required daily and can be performed only by skilled medical practitioners on a doctor's orders.

➤ *Intermediate care* is nursing and rehabilitative care that is required occasionally and can be performed only by skilled medical practitioners on a doctor's orders.

➤ *Custodial or residential care* is help in performing ADL and can be performed by someone without medical skills or training, but still must be based on a doctor's orders.

Custodial or residential care is the type of LTC most elderly people will require at some time in their later years, and is also the type that is not covered by medicare.

Other important types of LTC include

➤*Home health care* refers to services performed from time to time in the individual's home. It may include skilled nursing, various types of therapy, help with ADL, and help with housework.

➤*Adult day care* provides company, supervision, social, and recreational support during the day for people who live at home and need assistance. This service is especially useful for those who are being cared for by relatives who work during the day.

Common Provisions

Now that you understand some of the terms and concepts involved in long-term care policies, let's look at provisions that are commonly included in these coverages. You might also want to glance back at the NAIC model requirements for comparison purposes.

Currently, most LTC policies include provisions or options to include those described in the following sections.

Eligibility

Eligibility specifies the youngest and oldest ages at which LTC policies may be purchased. Most minimum ages are in the 50–60 years range, but more recent policies may include a much lower minimum age, including some as low as age 18. Upper age limits at which policies may be purchased range from age 69–89.

Renewability

Virtually all of the current generation of LTC policies are guaranteed renewable and cannot be canceled except for nonpayment of premium. The insurer cannot cancel the policy but does reserve the right to increase premiums in accordance with the policy provisions. If the premiums are to be increased, they will be changed on the policy anniversary and the increased premium will be for an entire class of insureds, not just a single individual.

Some LTC policies are noncancelable, which means the insured has the right to continue the coverage by timely payment of premiums, and the insurer has no right to make any change in policy provisions, cannot decline to renew, and cannot change the premium rate at renewal for any reason.

Premiums

Similar to life insurance, premiums are generally based on when an individual purchases this insurance. The younger the individual is at the time of purchase, the lower the premium. In addition, premiums will fluctuate according to the elimination and benefit periods selected: the longer the elimination period, the lower the premium; the longer the benefit period, the higher the premium. Finally, premium variations may result from underwriting considerations.

Underwriters consider risk factors, including an applicant's current ability to perform ADL. The premium will be higher if an applicant needs assistant with an ADL at the time of application than it would if the applicant did not need such assistance.

Waiver of Premium

Nearly all LTC policies include a waiver of premium provision that takes effect after the insured has been confined for a specified period of time. Ninety days is the usual period, but it is as long as 180 days in some policies. A few policies have no such provision, which means the insured will be required to continue premium payments no matter how long he or she is receiving care.

When waiver of premium applies, premium payment generally resumes when the care ceases.

Prior Hospitalization

Formerly, most nursing home policies required a hospital stay prior to confinement to a nursing home in order for benefits to be paid. This is no longer the case.

Care Level

Care level refers to whether the policy pays only if skilled nursing, intermediate, or custodial care, as specified in the policy, is required at the time the individual enters the nursing home. This is extremely important, because some policies pay only if intermediate or skilled care is involved, whereas custodial care, which is the most common type required by elders, may not be included. The best policies are those that will pay regardless of the level of care.

Hospice Care

Hospice care is often offered as an optional benefit under LTC policies. The primary focus of hospice care is pain control, comfort, and counseling for the terminally ill patient and the patient's family. A hospice is simply a facility whose purpose is to help terminally ill patients die with dignity and with as little suffering as possible. Typically, the expenses incurred in a hospice will be room and board and medication for pain.

Respite Care

Respite care is normally associated with hospice care. With this benefit, the patient is admitted to a nursing home for needed care for a short period of time, or the LTC policy will cover the cost of replacing for a short period (a day or weekend perhaps) the primary caregiver, usually a family member, who is looking after an elderly person in the home.

Home Health Care

Most LTC policies now cover home health care as an alternative to nursing home care. Home health care is provided in the individual's home and must begin within a prescribed period of time following a nursing home stay. Usually, the home health care benefit under the policy will be 60% of the regular daily nursing home benefit. Home health care is an extension of intermediate custodial care. The patient is in need of some health care, but is able to generally function without the need to be confined to a nursing home. Home health care might include physical therapy and some custodial care, such as meal preparations.

Adult Day Care

LTC policies also increasingly make provision for adult day care to allow the primary care giver who works the opportunity to tend to his or her employment responsibilities. The day care may be provided in the home or in an adult day care facility. Adult day care is basically social and health care services for functionally impaired adults. This benefit provides reimbursement for expenses pertaining to an adult day care center, such as a neighborhood recreational center, a community center, and so forth. Typically adult day care includes transportation to and from a day care center, and a variety of health, social, and related activities. This care usually also includes meals and certain medical services. Specialized care for Alzheimers victims is usually included in adult day care benefits.

Professional Care Advisor

Coverage may be provided for the services of a care coordinator to help design the most appropriate plan of treatment.

Benefit Amount

The prospective insured may be offered a choice of the maximum daily benefit amount for a nursing home stay or covered home health care. Naturally, higher daily benefits mean higher annual premiums.

Most LTC policies provide a daily benefit during confinement. Traditionally, this benefit has been provided as a maximum daily amount (reimbursement for charges up to the stated limit, but not more than the daily limit). Benefit amounts range from $50 per day up to $150 or $200 per day. However, some insurers provide coverage on an expense-incurred basis (full reimbursement for the actual charges incurred). The maximum policy benefit may be calculated by multiplying the daily benefit by the number of days in the benefit period.

To illustrate these points, let's use the example of Kim who has an LTC policy with a 30-day elimination period, a daily benefit of $75 per day, and a 2-year benefit period. Her maximum policy benefit would be $54,750 ($75 a day × 730 days). If Kim is confined to a nursing home for a total of 7 months, her benefit calculation would be as follows:

➤ First 30 days: no benefit paid (elimination period)

➤ Next 6 months: $75 per day (assumes 30-day month)

➤ $75 × 180 = $13,500

If Kim's actual charges were more than $75 per day, the additional amount would have to be paid by her.

Most policies specify the dollar amount per day that will be paid for skilled nursing care. Some policies may include sublimits for special types of care or services (such as home health care or adult day care). The benefit for home health care or adult day care is usually a fixed percentage of the specified daily benefit, usually 50%. In addition, there may be a deductible amount that must be satisfied before the policy begins to pay.

Benefit Periods

LTC policies vary as to the maximum period for which benefits will be paid, usually from 3–5 years. Some policies offer unlimited benefit periods.

Some policies may contain both a benefit period per stay plus a lifetime maximum benefit period. The benefit period may also end when a maximum amount has been paid out.

Exclusions

Each policy should be read carefully to determine what is excluded. A major stride in current policies is that most now cover Alzheimer's disease and organic-based mental illness, both of which formerly were often excluded.

However, some exclusions remain. Among these are war and acts of war, alcohol or drug dependency, self-inflicted injuries, mental illness and nervous disorders without a demonstrable organic cause, and treatment provided without cost to the insured (such as that received in a veteran's hospital).

Preexisting Conditions

Most—but not all—LTC policies do not cover conditions that existed during the 6 months before the policy's effective date. A few policies have no such exclusion.

Elimination Period

Similar to a disability income policy, no LTC benefits will be paid until the elimination period is satisfied. Most long-term care policies provide for a period of time, usually expressed in days or months at the beginning of a confinement in a long-term care facility, during which no benefits are payable.

The elimination period could be defined as a *time deductible*. The elimination period could be 30 days or longer. Thus, after the insured is confined to a nursing home for a period of 30 days, LTC benefits would begin.

The longer the waiting period, the lower the premium, all other facts being equal. The waiting period can be viewed as the deductible in an LTC policy.

Benefit Triggers

In order to qualify for LTC benefits, certain benefit triggers must be activated.

Activities of Daily Living (ADL)

ADL are functions or activities that are performed by individuals without assistance, thus allowing personal independence in everyday living. These functions are used as measurement standards to determine the level of personal functioning capacity. Examples of ADL include

➤ *Mobility* (or *transferring*)—The ability to walk

➤ *Dressing*—Being able to adequately clothe one's self

➤ *Personal hygiene*—Being able to go to and from the toilet and remain continent

➤ *Eating*—Being able to take in food

➤ Bathing

An individual who cannot accommodate these needs will need some type of care.

> Some LTC policies base eligibility for nursing home benefits on the inability to perform some of the activities of daily living in lieu of sickness or injury. These contracts do not require prior hospitalization nor that the insured be admitted to a nursing facility as a result of sickness or injury. Federal standards that determine whether an LTC policy is tax-qualified also base eligibility on ADL.

Cognitive Impairment

This means a deficiency in the ability to think, perceive, reason, or remember, which results in the inability of individuals to take care of themselves without the assistance or supervision of another person. LTC policies may base eligibility for nursing home benefits on cognitive impairment.

Medical Necessity

An LTC policy by definition provides coverage only for *medically necessary* diagnostic, therapeutic, rehabilitative, maintenance, or personal care services.

Qualified Plans

A qualified long-term care policy must stipulate that the insured be incapable of performing at least two of the ADL without assistance for at least 90 days in order to qualify for benefits. The cognitively impaired must require substantial supervision. A physician must certify that the insured is chronically ill and provide a plan of care. A long-term care policy will not be qualified if it does not conform to these standards.

Remember, however, that *nonqualified* long-term care policies do not *have* to conform to these federal standards. A nonqualified policy, for example, might require that the insured need assistance with only one ADL and with no stipulated time period in order to be eligible for policy benefits. The prospective insured's concern over qualification for benefits must be weighed against tax consequences when considering qualified versus nonqualified long-term care policies.

Regulation

Just as with medicare supplement insurance, long-term care policies are heavily regulated by the state insurance departments. States frequently regulate minimum standards, renewability, the insured's right to return the policy, replacement, marketing standards, and the appropriateness of recommending the purchase of LTC insurance. As with medicare supplement insurance, frequently the delivery of a buyers guide and outline of coverage is mandatory.

Federal law allows the sale of long-term care coverage that "substantially" duplicates that provided under medicare or medicaid (but not multiple policies) to medicare beneficiaries, provided the company discloses the duplication and the policy pays without regard to other benefits.

Emerging LTC Issues

Long-term care insurance is still in an evolutionary state. There are literally hundreds of individual contracts, which have not been standardized like medicare supplement policies. Some emerging issues in the LTC field include inflation protection and nonforfeiture provisions. New federal standards that determine whether an LTC policy is tax-qualified require consumer protections, such as the offer of inflation protection and nonforfeiture provisions, as well as imposing additional disclosure requirements.

Inflation Protection

Many states require that insurers offer optional inflation protection at the time of policy purchase. The feature must either increase benefit levels annually or cover a specific percentage of actual or reasonable charges, or allow the insured to periodically increase benefit levels without needing to provide evidence of continued insurability.

Nonforfeiture Provisions

Nonforfeiture provisions protect the policyholder from forfeiting all policy values or benefits when the policyowner stops paying premiums and lapses the policy for any reason. Standard nonforfeiture options may include cash surrender value (a lump sum payable upon policy surrender), reduced paid up insurance (a reduced daily benefit payable for the policy's benefit period with no further premium payments required), or extended term insurance (a limited extension of coverage for the full amount of policy benefits, without further premium payments required). Nonforfeiture provisions are not commonly included in LTC policies but are beginning to appear in some contracts.

Marketing LTC Coverage

In addition to individual LTC policies, a growing number of insurers offer group LTC plans with provisions similar to those mentioned previously. A third marketing device involves attaching an LTC rider to a life insurance policy called an *accelerated benefits rider* or a *living benefits rider*.

Accelerated benefits may be available to insureds who are chronically ill and need money for long-term care. Such riders are subject to the same rules as individual long-term care policies, especially with respect to benefit triggers.

They may also be designed to cover home health care as well as nursing home care. Adding an accelerated benefits rider to a life policy costs money in the form of additional premium.

How much may be paid by such a rider varies from policy to policy. Some limit benefits to 50% or 75% of the policy's face value. Others place an absolute ceiling on the amount paid out—for example, $250,000. All, however, take into consideration any outstanding loans against the policy. Payments are ordinarily made to the insured on some kind of periodic basis. Naturally, any accelerated benefits paid out are subtracted from the death benefit paid to the beneficiary when the insured dies.

Exam Prep Questions

1. Early long-term care policies were
   - ○ A. More restrictive than current policies
   - ○ B. Less restrictive than current policies
   - ○ C. The same as current policies
   - ○ D. Prohibited by law

2. Which of the following individuals is most likely to be rated a substandard risk under an LTC policy?
   - ○ A Gerald, who lives alone and has no trouble taking care of himself, but who has been diagnosed with an inoperable brain aneurysm that, if it bursts, would almost certainly kill him immediately
   - ○ B. Ken, who is on medication to bring down his blood pressure, but who gets around and takes care of himself easily
   - ○ C. Brenda, whose diabetes is under control
   - ○ D. Garrison, who has been diagnosed with early-stage Alzheimer's disease

3. Which of the following is the type of care most people will require at some time during their later years?
   - ○ A. Inpatient hospital care
   - ○ B. Skilled nursing care
   - ○ C. Custodial care
   - ○ D. Intermediate care

4. Virtually all of the current LTC policies are guaranteed renewable. This means that
   - ○ A. The insurer cannot cancel the policy but does reserve the right to increase policy premiums on specified classes of policies.
   - ○ B. The insurer cannot cancel the policy but does reserve the right to increase policy premiums on individual policies.
   - ○ C. The insurer cannot cancel the policy or increase policy premiums on specified classes of policies.
   - ○ D. The insurer cannot cancel the policy or increase policy premiums on individual policies.

5. When waiver of premium applies
   - ○ A. The premium is waived immediately upon disability.
   - ○ B. The premium payment is suspended permanently after it is invoked.
   - ○ C. The premium payment generally resumes when care ceases.
   - ○ D. The premium payment is waived only if disability is considered permanent and total.

6. Typically, the expenses incurred in a hospice will be

   ○ A. Surgical and room and board

   ○ B. Room and board and physical therapy

   ○ C. Surgical and physical therapy

   ○ D. Room and board and medication for pain

7. The elimination period may be thought of as

   ○ A. A dollar amount deductible

   ○ B. A time deductible

   ○ C. A dollar amount copayment

   ○ D. A time copayment

8. Which of the following is not considered an activity of daily living for the purposes of qualifying a person for LTC benefits?

   ○ A. Transferring

   ○ B. Dressing

   ○ C. Bathing

   ○ D. Working

9. Nursing home care is generally covered by

   ○ A. Medicare

   ○ B. Medicare supplements

   ○ C. Long-term care policies

   ○ D. All of the above

10. Which of the following individuals would be least likely to be a good candidate for an LTC policy?

   ○ A. George, whose law practice has allowed him to fund a generous retirement fund for himself and his wife

   ○ B. Nina, a single mother whose financial struggles raising her children have left her with few assets and no independent retirement savings

   ○ C. Carla, whose 25 years of civil service have provided a generous retirement, but who worries about the legacy she will leave her children

   ○ D. Darrell, whose inherited estate has provided him with over $6 million in net worth

Exam Prep Answers

1. **A is correct.** Early long-term policies were more restrictive than current policies.

2. **D is correct.** Garrison's preexisting condition would make him a substandard risk.

3. **A is correct.** With advancing age many people will require inpatient hospital care.

4. **A is correct.** The insurer cannot cancel the policy but may increase premiums on a class basis.

5. **C is correct.** Premiums would resume when the disability ends.

6. **D is correct.** A hospice does not provide surgical or therapy services.

7. **B is correct.** The elimination period relates to a period of time.

8. **D is correct.** Obviously if someone is able to work they do not need LTC benefits.

9. **C is correct.** LTC coverage is designed to cover nursing home care. Medicare and medicare supplements provide almost no coverage for nursing home care.

10. **B is correct.** Nina would probably qualify for medicaid and does not need LTC insurance.

Health Insurance and Taxation

Terms you need to understand:

✓ Payroll tax
✓ Current wage base
✓ Medical savings accounts

Concepts you need to master:

✓ Individually owned policies
✓ Group policies
✓ Chronically ill

Social Security Disability Benefits

Social security disability benefits are financed through a *payroll tax*. The tax rate is applied to an employee's gross wages (up to the *current wage base*) and an appropriate amount is deducted from the employee's wages each pay period. A like amount is contributed by the employer. Self-employeds must pay 100% of the combined employee/employer tax rate.

Tax Treatment of Social Security Contributions

Although employers may take a tax deduction for contributions on behalf of their employees as a routine and necessary cost of doing business, employees are not entitled to a deduction for their share of the social security tax.

Social security benefits are generally received free of income tax. However, federal income taxes are imposed on some benefits if the taxpayer has a substantial amount of additional income.

 The specifics of the calculations are not important at this stage of your training. However, it is important to understand that social security benefits may not be entirely free from federal income taxes.

Health Insurance

To understand how health insurance is taxed, we need to organize coverage into the following groups:

➤ Individually owned

➤ Group

➤ Sole proprietors and partners

➤ Business

Individual Policies

The premiums for *individually owned* accident, health, disability, or long-term care (LTC) policies generally are *not* deductible to the individual taxpayer. However, if the taxpayer's medical expenses exceed 7.5% of his or her adjusted gross income during a taxable year, any medical expenses, including premiums for accident and health insurance (but *not* disability insurance), incurred above the 7.5% threshold can be deducted. For long-term care insurance, there is an annual dollar limit for deductions. This limit is based on the taxpayer's age.

Benefits paid by individually owned accident, health, disability, or long-term care policies generally are received income tax–free by the taxpayer provided the benefits do not exceed actual expenses.

Congress has determined that individual long-term care insurance policies be treated taxwise the same as accident and health policies, as long as such policies are qualified according to federal law. Individual premiums may be deductible if the 7.5% of adjusted gross income threshold is exceeded.

 All qualified long-term care policy benefits are received income tax–free so long as they do not exceed actual expenses.

As for nonqualified long-term care policy premiums and benefits, their precise status is not clear. Until Congress or the IRS clarifies that status, however, it would be wise to treat nonqualified policies as if they did *not* have the tax advantages of qualified policies.

Group Policies

The premiums paid by a company for *group accident, health* and *dental coverage* for its employees are generally deductible by the company as a business expense. The premiums are not taxed to the employees. The benefits are received by the employees income tax–free to the extent the benefits do not exceed actual expenses.

The premiums paid by a company for *group disability insurance* for its employees are generally deductible by the company as a business expense. The premiums are not taxed to the employees, but the benefits are taxable. However, if an employee pays all or part of the premiums for group disability coverage, he or she may not deduct these premiums; the benefits will be received income tax–free to the extent that the employee paid the premiums.

However, disability benefits are subject to social security tax (FICA) and federal unemployment tax (FUTA) for the first 6 calendar months following the last month the employee was on the job.

Group accidental death and dismemberment coverage premiums may be deducted as a business expense by companies. The premiums are not taxable to the employees and the benefits are received income tax–free.

Qualified group long-term care insurance, like individually owned long-term care policies, are treated the same as other group health policies, and companies offering this coverage may deduct any premiums paid as a business expense. The employee is not taxed on these premiums and the benefits are tax-exempt.

Companies offering group long-term care coverage can deduct any premiums paid as a business expense. The employee is not taxed on these premiums, and the benefits are tax-exempt. However, these tax advantages do not apply to group long-term care coverage provided through a Section 125 cafeteria plan, and expenses for long-term care services cannot be reimbursed under flexible spending arrangements.

Sole Proprietors and Partnerships

Self-employed persons are allowed to deduct the amount they pay for health insurance (including qualified long-term care insurance). To claim this deduction, however, self-employed persons

➤ Must show a net profit for the year

➤ Cannot claim the deduction for any month in which they were eligible to participate in a health plan subsidized by their employer or by the employer of their spouse

Payments of premiums by a *partnership* for a partner's health and accident insurance is generally deductible by the partnership.

Business Policies

The premiums paid for business overhead expense insurance are deductible as a business expense whether the business is a sole proprietorship, partnership, or corporation. The proceeds of business overhead expense insurance, however, are taxable.

The premiums paid for a disability policy that is used to fund a buy-sell agreement are not deductible, nor are the proceeds taxable. Similarly, the premiums paid for a key employee disability policy are not deductible, nor are the proceeds taxable.

Disability Insurance

Premiums paid by the insured for individually owned disability income insurance are not tax-deductible. However, benefits paid in this type of situation are tax-free to the insured.

In situations where the business is providing disability income coverage for its employees, the *premium paid by the business* is tax-deductible as a business expense. This is true whether the coverage is provided by a group policy or individual contracts. Naturally, the benefits received by the employees would then be taxable as income.

In situations where the business is providing disability income coverage to protect itself (key person, disability buy-sell insurance), premiums paid by the business are not tax-deductible as a business expense. The basic premise is that either the premium or the benefit will be taxed. If the premium is not deductible to the business, the benefits will be received tax-free. If the premium is deductible, the benefits are taxable as is the case with the BOE policy.

Medicare Supplement and Long-Term Care Insurance

Individual Medicare supplement insurance premiums are considered deductible medical expenses to the extent that the combination of premiums paid plus other nonreimbursed medical expenses exceeds 7.5% of adjusted gross income. Benefits are considered reimbursements for medical expenses already incurred and are therefore received tax-free. Premiums paid by an employer for group Medicare supplement insurance is tax-deductible to the employer, and benefits are received tax-free.

The Health Insurance Portability and Accountability Act of 1996 provided that premiums paid for individually owned long-term care insurance are tax-deductible to the extent that combined premiums and nonreimbursed medical expenses exceed 7.5 of adjusted gross income. This tax deductibility is subject to age-related limits ranging from $200 per year for taxpayers under age 40 up to $2,500 per year for taxpayers age 71 and older (these limits are subject to annual indexing after 1997).

Premiums for group LTC insurance paid by employers are deductible as a business expense, but the coverage cannot be part of a cafeteria plan or flexible spending account. Benefits are received tax-free up to specified limits ($190 per day for per diem benefits in 1999, indexed annually).

LTC policies issued on or after January 1, 1997, must meet federal standards for tax-qualified status. LTC policies issued before that date are grandfathered and are automatically tax qualified.

The federal standards establish new eligibility requirements. The individual must be certified by a licensed health care professional to be chronically ill, with a condition that is expected to last at least 90 days, and must have a plan of care. *Chronically ill* means that the individual

➤ Is unable without substantial help from another person to perform at least two of five (or six) Activities of Daily Living (ADLs) for at least 90 days. The ADLs include bathing, dressing, toiletting, transferring, eating, and continence. It is up to the state legislatures to determine whether to include five or all six of the ADLs.

➤ Needs substantial supervision because of a cognitive impairment (for example, Alzheimer's disease).

The individual must be recertified as chronically ill on an annual basis. The new federal standards also establish consumer protection standards, such as guaranteed renewability, the option to add inflation protection and nonforfeiture benefits (but not in the form of cash surrender values), and the option to impose new disclosure requirements.

Exam Prep Questions

1. Medicare Part A hospital insurance is primarily funded by
   - ○ A. General tax revenue
   - ○ B. Premiums from beneficiaries
   - ○ C. State government taxes
   - ○ D. Social security payroll taxes

2. Social security taxes are paid by employees with
   - ○ A. Pre-tax dollars
   - ○ B. Tax-deductible dollars
   - ○ C. After-tax dollars
   - ○ D. Tax-deferred dollars

3. Premiums for individually owned health policies may be deductible if the taxpayer's medical expenses exceed
   - ○ A. 5% of his or her adjusted gross income during the taxable year
   - ○ B. 5% of his or her adjusted net income during the taxable year
   - ○ C. 7.5% of his or her adjusted gross income during the taxable year
   - ○ D. 7.5% of his or her adjusted net income during the taxable year

4. The premiums paid by a company for group health for its employees are
   - ○ A. Not tax-deductible to either the company or the business
   - ○ B. Tax-deductible by the company and not considered taxable income to the employees
   - ○ C. Tax-deductible by the company and considered taxable income to the employees
   - ○ D. Tax-deductible to the employees and the company

5. Benefits paid by individually owned accident, health, disability, or long-term care policies generally are
   - ○ A. Received income tax–free by the taxpayer, provided benefits do not exceed actual expenses
   - ○ B. Received income tax–free by the taxpayer even if benefits exceed actual expenses
   - ○ C. Received partially tax-free by the taxpayer, provided benefits do not exceed actual expenses
   - ○ D. Taxed on receipt by the taxpayer

6. Qualified group long-term care coverage
   - ○ A. Is deductible by both the company and the employee
   - ○ B. Is not deductible by either the company or the employee
   - ○ C. Is deductible by the company but not the employee
   - ○ D. Is deductible by the employee but not the company

7. Individual disability insurance premiums
   - ○ A. Are deductible to the insured, and the benefits are received tax-free
   - ○ B. Are not deductible to the insured, but the benefits are received tax-free
   - ○ C. Are deductible to the insured, but the benefits are taxed
   - ○ D. Are not deductible to the insured, and the benefits are taxed

8. An individual who is considered chronically ill must be recertified as such
   - ○ A. Every month
   - ○ B. Every 6 months
   - ○ C. Annually
   - ○ D. Every 2 years

Exam Prep Answers

1. **D is correct.** Medicare Part A is funded by payroll taxes.

2. **C is correct.** Social security taxes are paid by employees with after-tax dollars.

3. **C is correct.** Premiums may be deducted if total medical expenses exceed 7.5% of adjusted gross income.

4. **B is correct.** Company-paid premiums are tax-deductible for the employer.

5. **A is correct.** These benefits are generally received tax-free.

6. **C is correct.** These premiums are deductible by the employer as a normal business expense.

7. **B is correct.** The premiums are not deductible, but the benefits are received tax-free.

8. **C is correct.** This is an annual requirement.

Practice Exam 1

1. In the medical insurance field, the term coinsurance means that an insured person
   - O A. Has coverage under two or more policies
   - O B. Has to pay a portion of covered expenses
   - O C. Is covered in full, after paying the deductible amount
   - O D. Has coverage under his or her own policy and under the spouse's policy

2. The principal purpose of the Medicaid program is to assist in providing medical care to persons who are
   - O A. Not covered by Medicare
   - O B. Over the age of 65
   - O C. Unable to afford the medical care they need
   - O D. Not covered by any individual insurance plan

3. Because an insurer writes the policy language and the insured has little or no control over the content, any ambiguity in the wording is usually resolved in favor of the insured. Because the design and wording of a policy are in the hands of the insurer, insurance policies are said to be
   - O A. Unilateral contracts
   - O B. Contracts of indemnity
   - O C. Aleatory contracts
   - O D. Contracts of adhesion

4. Suppose an insurance contract contains inconsistent or contradictory provisions. Various parts of the contract are printed, typewritten, and handwritten. In seeking to determine the original intent, a court is likely to rely on

- O A. The handwritten material first, then the typewritten, and then the printed
- O B. The typewritten material first, then the printed, and then the handwritten
- O C. The printed material first, then the typewritten, and then the handwritten
- O D. All parts of the contract, giving equal importance to each

5. All of the following are true about Medicare supplement policies except

- O A. The policies are subject to approval by state insurance departments.
- O B. They supplement Medicare by paying toward deductibles and copayments.
- O C. They may cover some services not covered by Medicare.
- O D. They are sold by state and federal government agencies.

6. A group major medical policyholder that provides benefits on a self-funding basis may limit its total liability for claims by purchasing

- O A. Supplementary coverage
- O B. A stop-loss contract
- O C. Coinsurance
- O D. A deductible

7. One technique that helps to control health care costs is a requirement for

- O A. Preexisting conditions
- O B. Second surgical opinions
- O C. Waiver of premiums
- O D. Optional benefit riders

8. All of the following are true about insurance except

- O A. Insurance is a mechanism for handling speculative risk.
- O B. Insurance transfers risk from one party to a group.
- O C. It is a social device for spreading loss over a large number of people.
- O D. A large uncertain loss is traded for a small certain loss.

9. Members covered by a group health insurance plan receive a document that summarizes the benefits and the important policy provisions. This document is known as a

- O A. Master policy
- O B. Member's policy
- O C. Coordination of benefits
- O D. Certificate

10. All of the following are true about group health insurance except
- A. It has fewer limitations on benefits than individual insurance.
- B. All participants are insured under a single master contract.
- C. All members of the insured group must be covered.
- D. It is rated on a group basis.

11. A type of insurance that provides a death benefit and benefits for a permanent loss of sight or limbs is known as
- A. Medical expense insurance
- B. Disability income insurance
- C. Life insurance with coinsurance
- D. Accidental death and dismemberment insurance

12. In health insurance policies, a preexisting condition is one that
- A. An insurer puts forth as a prerequisite to acceptance of the risk
- B. An applicant suspects already exists when completing the application
- C. An applicant received medical advice or treatment for prior to applying
- D. An insurer requires the applicant to agree to before it issues a policy

13. A self-funded health care plan may be a practical alternative to insurance for an employer if
- A. Claim costs are fairly predictable.
- B. Claim costs are generally unpredictable.
- C. The employer cannot afford to buy insurance.
- D. The employer is engaged in a high-risk industry.

14. It is illegal for an agent to pay, allow, give, offer, or promise to a prospective insurance buyer any return of premiums, any special favor or advantage, or anything of value not specified in the insurance contract, as an inducement to buy insurance. This illegal practice is known as
- A. Twisting
- B. Rebating
- C. Coercion
- D. Defamation

15. Small employers, who might not otherwise qualify for a group health insurance plan, may be able to obtain similar low-cost benefits for their employees by joining a
- A. Health care service organization
- B. Health maintenance organization
- C. Preferred provider organization
- D. Multiple employer trust

16. Blue Cross and Blue Shield are
    - A. Health maintenance organizations
    - B. Prepaid health care service organizations
    - C. Administrative service organizations
    - D. Preferred provider organizations

17. All of the following are common characteristics of disability income insurance except
    - A. The policies do not have any exclusions.
    - B. Each contract defines the disabilities it covers.
    - C. Benefits are usually paid in periodic installments.
    - D. Disabilities caused by accidental injury or illness are covered.

18. A residual disability benefit provides an income benefit if an insured
    - A. Has exhausted all partial disability benefits
    - B. Has exhausted all temporary disability benefits
    - C. Returns to work and cannot earn as much as earned before the disability
    - D. Is receiving no other benefits during a waiting period

19. All of the following are true about a coordination of benefits provision in group health insurance policies except
    - A. It establishes which plan pays first.
    - B. It is designed to prevent overcompensation for incurred losses.
    - C. It coordinates benefits under all available group and individual policies.
    - D. It limits benefits when insurance is provided under more than one plan.

20. All of the following are true about dependent coverage under a group health insurance policy except
    - A. Generally, eligible children must be under a specified age.
    - B. All dependents must be related to the insured by blood or marriage.
    - C. The insured worker's parents may qualify as dependents.
    - D. Disabled children may be covered beyond the limiting age.

21. In the administration of a group health insurance plan, if there is a clerical error concerning the information about an insured, that person's coverage and benefits
    - A. Could be reduced
    - B. Could be delayed
    - C. Could be terminated
    - D. Will not be affected

22. For employer-paid (noncontributory) group health insurance, the percentage of eligible group members that must be covered is
    - ○ A. 50%
    - ○ B. 65%
    - ○ C. 75%
    - ○ D. 100%

23. Which of the following terms means that an insurance contract is dependent on an uncertain outcome?
    - ○ A. Valued
    - ○ B. Aleatory
    - ○ C. Unilateral
    - ○ D. Adhesion

24. One of the reasons why many group disability insurance policies are written on a nonoccupational basis is that
    - ○ A. Occupational coverage is too expensive.
    - ○ B. Health insurance can no longer be written on an occupational basis.
    - ○ C. Occupational coverage is provided by workers compensation.
    - ○ D. Few occupational risks exist because of health and safety regulations.

25. A disability that prevents a person from performing one or more of the regular duties of that person's job and that is a condition that will last for the remainder of the person's life, is a
    - ○ A. Permanent partial disability
    - ○ B. Permanent total disability
    - ○ C. Temporary partial disability
    - ○ D. Temporary total disability

26. Under contract law, the payment of money in exchange for a service would be known as
    - ○ A. An offer
    - ○ B. Agreement
    - ○ C. Consideration
    - ○ D. Implied authority

27. What is the name of a health care delivery system providing prepaid doctor and hospital care, emphasizing preventive care, and charging a fixed periodic fee to its enrolled members?
    - ○ A. Preferred provider organization
    - ○ B. Administrative services organization
    - ○ C. Health care service organization
    - ○ D. Health maintenance organization

28. What is the name of a health care delivery system involving private insurers who contract with doctors and hospitals to provide services at set prices and that allows insureds to choose among designated doctors and hospitals when medical treatment and care is needed?
    - ○ A. Preferred provider organization
    - ○ B. Administrative services organization
    - ○ C. Health care service organization
    - ○ D. Health maintenance organization

29. The part of a health insurance policy that states the kind of benefits provided and the circumstances under which they will be paid is/are the
    - ○ A. Definitions
    - ○ B. Conditions
    - ○ C. Benefit clause
    - ○ D. Face of the policy

30. In health insurance policies, the purpose of a grace period is to give a policyholder extra time to
    - ○ A. Pay a premium after the due date.
    - ○ B. Submit a proof of loss to an insurer.
    - ○ C. Appear for a medical exam to justify a claim.
    - ○ D. Make application for reinstatement of a policy.

31. Each of the following is a significant consideration in the underwriting of individual health insurance risks except
    - ○ A. Occupation
    - ○ B. Age of applicant
    - ○ C. Physical condition
    - ○ D. Geographic location

32. Which definition of total disability would be the most restrictive for an insured claiming benefits?
    - ○ A. The inability to perform the duties of any occupation
    - ○ B. The inability to perform all the duties of the insured's regular occupation
    - ○ C. The inability to perform some of the duties of the insured's regular occupation
    - ○ D. The inability to perform any one of the duties of the insured's regular occupation

33. In health insurance policies, a waiver of premium provision keeps the coverage in force without premium payments
    - ○ A. Whenever an insured is unable to work
    - ○ B. During the time an insured is confined in a hospital
    - ○ C. Following an accidental injury, but not during sickness
    - ○ D. After an insured has become totally disabled as defined in the policy

34. Social security disability benefits begin after a waiting period. Generally, benefits begin with the
    ○ A. 3rd month of disability
    ○ B. 6th month of disability
    ○ C. 9th month of disability
    ○ D. 18th month of disability

35. Disability income policies often do not begin paying benefits immediately when an insured person becomes disabled. Usually, the disability must continue for a period of time before benefits begin. This period is known as the
    ○ A. Trial period
    ○ B. Probationary period
    ○ C. Elimination period
    ○ D. Verification period

36. Eligibility for social security disability benefits depends on having earned the required work credits, which are accumulated in units of time. During each calendar year, a full-time worker may earn up to
    ○ A. Three work credits
    ○ B. Four work credits
    ○ C. Six work credits
    ○ D. Twelve work credits

37. Workers compensation programs provide each of the following types of benefits except
    ○ A. Death benefits
    ○ B. Medical benefits
    ○ C. Disability benefits
    ○ D. Retirement benefits

38. All of the following are true about a presumptive disability except
    ○ A. Such a condition is considered to be total and permanent.
    ○ B. Examinations to verify the loss will be required only every 2 years.
    ○ C. Loss of two limbs qualifies as a presumptive disability.
    ○ D. Loss of sight qualifies as a presumptive disability.

39. Not all disabilities are covered by social security disability benefits. To be covered, a disability must be serious enough to be expected to be fatal or to last at least
    ○ A. 6 months
    ○ B. 12 months
    ○ C. 18 months
    ○ D. 24 months

40. An agent's obligation to act in an insurance applicant's or insured's best interest, based on the faith and trust placed on the agent by members of the insurance-buying public, is known as
    - ○ A. A presumption of agency
    - ○ B. The warranty of the agent
    - ○ C. A fiduciary duty
    - ○ D. The duty owed to a principal

41. Health insurance policies have a consideration clause, which states that the insurance is provided in consideration of what?
    - ○ A. Payment of a conditional premium
    - ○ B. Statements made by the applicant to the agent
    - ○ C. The representations made in the completed, signed application
    - ○ D. Payment of the first premium and completion of the application

42. Under the Uniform Policy Provisions Law, a required provision concerning notice of claim obligates a policyholder to give the insurer or its agent notice of a claim within
    - ○ A. 20 days of a loss, or as soon as reasonably possible
    - ○ B. 30 days of a loss, or as soon as reasonably possible
    - ○ C. 60 days of a loss, or as soon as reasonably possible
    - ○ D. 90 days of a loss, or as soon as reasonably possible

43. Under the Uniform Policy Provisions Law, a required provision concerning proof of loss obligates a policyholder to file a written proof of loss within
    - ○ A. 20 days after a loss
    - ○ B. 30 days after a loss
    - ○ C. 60 days after a loss
    - ○ D. 90 days after a loss

44. Restrictions are usually placed on the amount of insurance that agents can write on their own property or interests, or those of their immediate families, their employers, and certain business relationships. This type of insurance is known as
    - ○ A. Admitted business
    - ○ B. Controlled business
    - ○ C. Authorized business
    - ○ D. Unauthorized business

45. When a party appears to have given up a particular right by acts or by inaction that another party has relied on, the legal basis for asserting the original right may have been lost. This is known as the legal doctrine of
    - ○ A. Waiver
    - ○ B. Warranty
    - ○ C. Estoppel
    - ○ D. Condition precedent

46. Under a provision known as time payment of claims in a health insurance policy, after receiving proof of loss, all benefits other than those that are paid in periodic installments are supposed to be paid
    - ○ A. Within 30 days
    - ○ B. Within 60 days
    - ○ C. Immediately
    - ○ D. At the end of the month

47. A health insurance policy has lapsed because of nonpayment of premium. If the policy does not require an application for reinstatement, the policy must be reinstated on
    - ○ A. Acceptance of the overdue premium by the agent
    - ○ B. Acceptance of the overdue premium by the insurer
    - ○ C. Receipt by the agent of a written request for reinstatement
    - ○ D. Receipt by the insurer of a written request for reinstatement

48. If a health insurance policy has lapsed and it is later reinstated, the reinstated policy will cover only sickness that begins
    - ○ A. After the date of reinstatement
    - ○ B. At least 10 days after the date of reinstatement
    - ○ C. At least 20 days after the date of reinstatement
    - ○ D. At least 30 days after the date of reinstatement

49. Individual health insurance policies may include a provision concerning unpaid premiums. When the provision applies, if a premium payment is overdue when a claim for benefits is made
    - ○ A. Coverage is suspended until the premium is paid.
    - ○ B. The insurer may pay the claim and then cancel the policy.
    - ○ C. A written demand for premium payment will be sent to the insured.
    - ○ D. The insurer may deduct the overdue premium from the benefits

50. Which of the following is not covered under Medicare hospital insurance benefits (Part A)?
    - ○ A. Physician's services
    - ○ B. Semiprivate room and board
    - ○ C. Home health care
    - ○ D. Skilled nursing facility care

26

Answer Key 1

1. B	**21.** D	**41.** D
2. C	**22.** D	**42.** A
3. D	**23.** B	**43.** D
4. A	**24.** C	**44.** B
5. D	**25.** A	**45.** C
6. B	**26.** C	**46.** C
7. B	**27.** D	**47.** B
8. A	**28.** A	**48.** B
9. D	**29.** C	**49.** D
10. C	**30.** A	**50.** A
11. D	**31.** D	
12. C	**32.** A	
13. A	**33.** D	
14. B	**34.** B	
15. D	**35.** C	
16. B	**36.** B	
17. A	**37.** D	
18. C	**38.** B	
19. C	**39.** B	
20. B	**40.** C	

1. **Answer B is correct.** The term coinsurance means the insured will have to pay a portion of the covered expenses. Usually the insured pays 20% and the insurance company pays 80% within a given range.

2. **Answer C is correct.** Medicaid is a joint federal-state program designed to provide health care to people who are unable to afford health insurance.

3. **Answer D is correct.** Because the insurer drafts the language of the contract, the insured simply adheres to the terms.

4. **Answer A is correct.** Any handwritten material will be considered first because it probably reflects last minute revisions of the terms. After that the typewritten material will be considered and then the printed material.

5. **Answer D is correct.** Medicare supplement policies may not be sold by any state or federal government agencies.

6. **Answer B is correct.** The term for this type of agreement that caps obligations is stop-loss.

7. **Answer B is correct.** Second surgical opinions are often recommended before expensive surgical procedures are performed because they may help to avoid unnecessary treatments and costs.

8. **Answer A is correct.** Speculative risks may not be covered by insurance policies. Insurance is used only to cover pure risks.

9. **Answer D is correct.** Members covered by group insurance plans receive certificates of insurance that summarize the benefits.

10. **Answer C is correct.** Under contributory group plans, only 75% of the eligible members must be covered.

11. **Answer D is correct.** This is an example of accidental death and dismemberment insurance.

12. **Answer C is correct.** A preexisting condition is one for which an applicant received medical advice or treatment prior to applying for coverage.

13. **Answer A is correct.** Self-funding may be a realistic alternative to traditional insurance if claim costs are predictable.

14. **Answer B is correct.** This is an example of rebating.

15. **Answer D is correct.** A multiple employer trust allows small employers to join together in order to obtain health care benefits for their employees at a reasonable cost.

16. **Answer B is correct.** Blue Cross and Blue Shield are examples of prepaid health care service organizations.

17. **Answer A is correct.** All insurance policies have exclusions.

18. **Answer C is correct.** A policy that provides an income benefit if an insured returns to work and cannot earn as much as earned before the disability is an example of a residual disability benefit.

19. **Answer C is correct.** Coordination of benefit provisions applies only to group insurance plans. Any benefits under individual policies are not affected.

20. **Answer B is correct.** Adopted children and other dependents may be eligible for coverage.

21. **Answer D is correct.** Coverage will not be affected by a clerical error.

22. **Answer D is correct.** When an employer pays all of the group health insurance premium, the plan is noncontributory and it is required to cover all eligible group members.

23. **Answer B is correct.** An aleatory contract is one that depends on chance or an uncertain outcome. This is the case with insurance because a loss may or may not occur.

24. **Answer C is correct.** Because work-related injuries are covered by workers compensation, most group health insurance plans are written on a nonoccupational basis to cover only injuries or illnesses that are not work-related.

25. **Answer A is correct.** This is an example of a permanent partial disability. It is permanent because the person will not recover, and it is partial because it does not prevent the person from performing any work at all.

26. **Answer C is correct.** To form a valid contract, each party must give some form of consideration to the other. With insurance, the consideration the insured gives is the premium payment and the consideration the insurer gives is the promise to pay if a loss occurs.

27. **Answer D is correct.** This is an example of a health maintenance organization (HMO).

28. **Answer A is correct.** This is an example of a preferred provider organization (PPO).

29. **Answer C is correct.** The part of a health insurance policy that states the kind of benefits provided and the circumstances under which they will be paid is the benefit clause.

30. **Answer A is correct.** In health insurance policies, the purpose of a grace period is to give a policyholder extra time to pay a premium after the due date.

31. **Answer D is correct.** An applicant's occupation, age, and physical condition are important factors in the underwriting of a risk. The geographic location of the applicant is not relevant.

32. **Answer A is correct.** The inability to perform the duties of any occupation is the most restrictive because a person who could perform any work at all would not be entitled to benefits.

33. **Answer D is correct.** The waiver of premium provision keeps the coverage in force without premium payments if the insured has become totally disabled as defined in the policy.

34. **Answer B is correct.** Social security disability benefits begin after a waiting period of 5 months. Benefits begin with the 6th month of disability.

35. **Answer C is correct.** This is an example of an elimination period.

36. **Answer B is correct.** Under the social security program, a person may earn up to four work credits in any calendar year based on the amount of income earned.

37. **Answer D is correct.** Workers compensation programs provide death benefits, medical benefits, and disability benefits. They do not provide retirement benefits.

38. **Answer B is correct.** After a presumptive disability has been medically verified, no further examinations are required to verify the loss.

39. **Answer B is correct.** To be covered under social security, a disability must be serious enough to be expected to be fatal or to last at least 12 months.

40. **Answer C is correct.** An agent's duty to act in the best interest of insurance applicants or insureds is known as a fiduciary duty.

41. **Answer D is correct.** The clause states that the insurance is provided in consideration of payment of the first premium and completion of the application.

42. **Answer A is correct.** The provision requires a policyholder to give the insurer or its agent notice of a claim within 20 days of a loss, or as soon as reasonably possible.

43. **Answer D is correct.** Generally, a policyholder is required to file a written proof of loss within 90 days.

44. **Answer B is correct.** Insurance coverage on an agent's own property or interests, or those of the agent's family members or an employer, are known as controlled business and the amount of such business that may be written is limited by law.

45. **Answer C is correct.** Estoppel is a legal term that means a party has given up a right by previous acts or inactions on which another party has relied.

46. **Answer C is correct.** Generally, all claims other than those for periodic installments should be paid immediately after the insurer has received proof of loss.

47. **Answer B is correct.** If a policy does not require an application for reinstatement, the policy must be reinstated upon acceptance of the overdue premium by the insurer.

48. **Answer B is correct.** If a health insurance policy has lapsed and it is later reinstated, the reinstated policy will cover only sickness that begins at least 10 days after the date of reinstatement. This provision exists because a person who becomes sick might be motivated to rein-

state coverage only to claim benefits. Accidents are covered immediately because accidents cannot be anticipated.

49. **Answer D is correct.** This is a standard provision in almost all life and health insurance policies. The insurer always has the right to deduct overdue premiums from any benefits paid.

50. **Answer A is correct.** Under Medicare, physician's services are covered under Part B.

Practice Exam 2

1. All of the following are true about term life insurance except
   - ○ A. Term insurance is temporary insurance.
   - ○ B. Term insurance is one of the most expensive forms of protection.
   - ○ C. There is no cash value when a term policy expires.
   - ○ D. Term insurance policies are written for a specified number of years.

2 Not all risks are insurable. Certain characteristics must be present for a particular risk to be considered an insurable risk. Which of the following characteristics might make a risk uninsurable?
   - ○ A. If a loss occured, it would result in an economic hardship.
   - ○ B. The risk of loss can be defined in terms of a specific number of dollars.
   - ○ C. Expected loss can be predicted due to a large number of exposure units.
   - ○ D. The risk of loss exists because of a catastrophic exposure.

3. All of the following are true about group life insurance except
   - ○ A. It may be written to include dependent coverage.
   - ○ B. Each individual insured receives an insurance policy.
   - ○ C. Coverage is usually available without medical exams.
   - ○ D. Group policy provisions include a grace period.

4. Which of the following is not a characteristic of a whole life continuous premium policy (also known as straight life)?
   - ○ A. The premiums are paid only until the insured reaches age 70.
   - ○ B. The policy builds a cash surrender value.
   - ○ C. The face amount is a constant amount of protection.
   - ○ D. The policy requires level premium payments.

5. An insurance policy is a legal contract. Each of the following elements is necessary for formation of a valid contract except
   - A. Consideration
   - B. Competent parties
   - C. Signatures of each party
   - D. Agreement

6. If a life insurance policy loan is made and the insured person dies before it is repaid, the beneficiary will receive
   - A. The cash value, minus the outstanding loan amount
   - B. The death benefit, minus the outstanding loan amount
   - C. The full face value of the policy
   - D. Nothing

7. Which of the following is not a common life insurance nonforfeiture option?
   - A. Taking a full refund of all premiums paid
   - B. Requesting the cash surrender value
   - C. Converting to a lesser amount of paid-up insurance
   - D. Converting to an equal amount of extended term insurance

8. Which of the following is not one of the available methods for dealing with an exposure to risk?
   - A. Avoid the risk.
   - B. Retain the risk.
   - C. Ascertain the risk.
   - D. Transfer the risk.

9. Under a group life insurance conversion privilege, an employee who terminates membership in the insured group is allowed to
   - A. Continue to participate in the group plan by taking over premium payment
   - B. Continue to participate in the group plan until covered elsewhere
   - C. Convert to an individual policy if evidence of insurability is given
   - D. Convert to an individual policy without evidence of insurability

10. A type of life insurance that is usually written for small amounts, and that requires frequent premium payments collected by the agent, is called
   - A. Group life insurance
   - B. Key executive life insurance
   - C. Industrial life insurance
   - D. Credit life insurance

11. The law of large numbers states that
    - ○ A. Predictions become more accurate as the number of units being considered increases.
    - ○ B. Large losses are easier to predict than small losses.
    - ○ C. Small losses are the most predictable.
    - ○ D. All losses are equally predictable.

12. The cash surrender value of a whole life insurance policy will equal the face amount of coverage
    - ○ A. On the insured's 65th birthday
    - ○ B. If the insured lives to be age 100
    - ○ C. On the date final payment is made under any limited payment plan
    - ○ D. On any date that total premiums paid exceed the amount of insurance

13. The social security program provides all of the following types of benefits except
    - ○ A. Survivors benefits
    - ○ B. Disability benefits
    - ○ C. Deferred compensation benefits
    - ○ D. Retirement income benefits

14. Which of the following does not apply to credit life insurance?
    - ○ A. Benefits are paid directly to the insured or beneficiary.
    - ○ B. Coverage is usually provided by term insurance.
    - ○ C. The outstanding debt is paid if the debtor dies.
    - ○ D. Premium payments are usually added to the loan payments.

15. One approach to determining life insurance needs is to calculate the human life value of the person to be insured. Which of the following is not a factor in determining a person's remaining human life value?
    - ○ A. Years remaining to retirement
    - ○ B. Annual income
    - ○ C. Annual expenses
    - ○ D. Property owned

16. Misrepresenting an insurance policy, or making incomplete comparisons of policies, for the purpose of inducing someone to change or replace an existing insurance policy is an illegal practice known as
    - ○ A. Defamation
    - ○ B. Coercion
    - ○ C. Twisting
    - ○ D. Rebating

17. In the rating of a life insurance policy, a preferred risk is an applicant who has
    - ○ A. Provided evidence of insurability
    - ○ B. Never been turned down when applying for life insurance
    - ○ C. A low-risk occupation and follows a healthy lifestyle
    - ○ D. The financial ability to make the premium payments

18. Life insurance companies are required to establish a variety of reserves for record-keeping purposes. These accounting measurements are actually
    - ○ A. A measure of net worth
    - ○ B. Liabilities
    - ○ C. Assets
    - ○ D. Contingency funds and surplus

19. When a group life insurance plan is written on a contributory basis, the group plan must insure at least
    - ○ A. 90% of the eligible group members
    - ○ B. 75% of the eligible group members
    - ○ C. 65% of the eligible group members
    - ○ D. 50% of the eligible group members

20. In the famous South-Eastern Underwriters' case, the Supreme Court held that insurance
    - ○ A. Should be regulated by the individual states
    - ○ B. Was exempt from the federal antitrust laws
    - ○ C. Transacted across state lines was not interstate commerce
    - ○ D. Transacted across state lines was interstate commerce

21. All of the following are true about variable annuities except
    - ○ A. Insurance companies cannot sell this type of annuity.
    - ○ B. The annuity premium is invested in securities.
    - ○ C. Installments will fluctuate with the market value of securities.
    - ○ D. The payout is not guaranteed to be a fixed number of dollars.

22. When a life insurance policy lapses or is surrendered prior to maturity, any built-up cash value may be used to buy a lesser amount of the same type of insurance. When this is done, the new policy would be known as
    - ○ A. Additional insurance
    - ○ B. Convertible insurance
    - ○ C. Paid-up insurance
    - ○ D. Extended insurance

23. The owner of a life insurance policy does not have to be the insured person. A policyowner is the person responsible for paying the premium and has a number of legal rights. A policyowner has all of the following rights except

   ○ A. The owner may designate or change a beneficiary.
   ○ B. The owner may change the person who is insured.
   ○ C. The owner may select settlement options.
   ○ D. The owner may assign or transfer the policy to a new owner.

24. All of the following are true about reinstatement of a life insurance policy except

   ○ A. Evidence of insurability is usually required.
   ○ B. All overdue premiums, plus interest, must be paid.
   ○ C. The policy will be rated at the insured's current age.
   ○ D. Reinstatement must be made within a specified period of time.

25. The authority of an insurance agent, which is spelled out in the written words of the agency contract between the agent and insurer, is

   ○ A. Express authority
   ○ B. Apparent authority
   ○ C. Implied authority
   ○ D. Presumed authority

26. All of the following are true about annuities except

   ○ A. They may be used to provide a lifetime income.
   ○ B. They may be used to provide income for a fixed period.
   ○ C. They are used to systematically liquidate a principal sum.
   ○ D. They have all the same characteristics as life insurance.

27. All of the following are true about a life insurance settlement option known as life income except

   ○ A. When the payee dies, all benefit payments end.
   ○ B. The option may be used to provide retirement income.
   ○ C. Total benefits may not exceed the principal amount plus interest.
   ○ D. The older the payee when payments begin, the larger the payments.

28. A life insurance policy that provides whole life insurance for the breadwinner plus minimal amounts of term life insurance for a spouse and each dependent child is often referred to as a

   ○ A. Family maintenance policy
   ○ B. Family protection policy
   ○ C. Family income policy
   ○ D. Family split-life policy

29. A contingent beneficiary designated in a life insurance policy is a person who will receive benefits if
   - ○ A. The insured dies because of a contingent cause specified in the policy.
   - ○ B. The insured dies when there is no surviving primary beneficiary.
   - ○ C. The primary beneficiary dies after the insured, before receiving payment.
   - ○ D. The only primary beneficiary designated is a minor.

30. On a life insurance policy, a waiver of premium clause or rider is a provision that suspends the premium payments
   - ○ A. While a premium loan is in effect
   - ○ B. On the date the insured reaches normal retirement age
   - ○ C. If the insured is unable to pay premiums because of economic hardship
   - ○ D. During total disability, usually lasting at least 6 months

31. Each of the following is a typical characteristic of group life insurance except
   - ○ A. The master policy cannot be terminated.
   - ○ B. The plan has a conversion privilege.
   - ○ C. The plan has a grace period.
   - ○ D. Individual certificates are issued.

32. All of the following are true about the group life insurance conversion option except
   - ○ A. The option is available on termination of employment.
   - ○ B. Evidence of insurability is not required for conversion.
   - ○ C. Conversion permits the insured to continue to be covered by the group policy.
   - ○ D. The option must be exercised during a specified period of time.

33. Adverse selection exists when
   - ○ A. A beneficiary selects a settlement option that is likely to pay more than the principal.
   - ○ B. An underwriter carefully screens out poor risks by charging higher premiums or declining applications.
   - ○ C. A disproportionate number of people who have a high risk of loss apply for insurance.
   - ○ D. Insurance companies order inspection reports to supplement applications.

34. For any given amount of annuity, which method of disposition of the funds would provide the greatest level of periodic income payments to the payee?
   - ○ A. Life annuity
   - ○ B. Life annuity refund
   - ○ C. Life annuity, period certain
   - ○ D. Installment refund annuity

35. All of the following are true about variable annuities except
    - ○ A. Payouts are made in units, not fixed dollar amounts.
    - ○ B. Annuity income varies with the market value of securities.
    - ○ C. Variable annuities are regulated by the S.E.C.
    - ○ D. Inflation has no effect on the value of the annuity payouts.

36. In life insurance, a return of premium rider is
    - ○ A. Decreasing term insurance added to an underlying policy
    - ○ B. Increasing term insurance added to an underlying policy
    - ○ C. A guarantee that premiums will be returned if the insured commits suicide
    - ○ D. A guarantee that if the policy is surrendered, premiums will be returned

37. All of the following are true of the double indemnity provision found in life insurance policies except
    - ○ A. It provides for payment of double the face amount.
    - ○ B. It applies only if death occurs within 90 days of injury.
    - ○ C. It applies to death by accident or unexpected illness.
    - ○ D. It is a relatively inexpensive additional benefit.

38. A type of life insurance that periodically allows the insured to change the face amount of the policy or the amount of the premium is
    - ○ A. Universal life insurance
    - ○ B. Variable life insurance
    - ○ C. Adjustable life insurance
    - ○ D. Multiple protection life insurance

39. Which of the following is not generally a feature of term life insurance policies?
    - ○ A. It is convertible.
    - ○ B. It offers permanent protection.
    - ○ C. It offers pure protection.
    - ○ D. It is renewable.

40. The distinguishing characteristic of variable life insurance is that
    - ○ A. The policyowner bears the investment risk.
    - ○ B. The amount of the premium increases annually.
    - ○ C. The policy is not subject to regulation.
    - ○ D. The insured can request changes in the face amount.

41. In the field of estate planning, arrangements are often made to dispose of business interests, provide for survivors, and to minimize tax consequences. One technique, an inter vivos transfer, means
    - A. Provisions for settling the estate are written into a will.
    - B. Properties or rights are transferred while the estate owner is living.
    - C. Annuities will be used to create special trust funds.
    - D. All insurance proceeds will be paid to the estate.

42. A person who dies without leaving a will has died
    - A. Innocuously
    - B. Testamentary
    - C. Inter vivos
    - D. Intestate

43. In order to become eligible for social security retirement benefits, a worker must
    - A. Not have a private pension plan
    - B. Have dependents who are not disabled
    - C. Have earned the required work credits
    - D. Not be eligible for Medicare

44. If an irrevocable beneficiary designation has been made on a life insurance policy, the designation
    - A. Can never be changed
    - B. Cannot be changed during the remainder of the policy year
    - C. Cannot be changed for at least 5 years
    - D. Can be changed only with consent of the beneficiary.

45. An insured has purchased a $100,000 whole life insurance policy. After a period of years, the cash value of the policy has grown to $42,000. If the insured dies at this time, the beneficiary will receive
    - A. $142,000
    - B. $100,000
    - C. $58,000
    - D. $42,000

46. A person who wants to accumulate a specific number of dollars that would be available at a given age, while having insurance protection prior to reaching that age, should consider buying
    - A. Level term insurance
    - B. Endowment insurance
    - C. Convertible insurance
    - D. Limited payment whole life insurance

47. Life insurance settlement options were developed in order to
    - ○ A. Give insureds and beneficiaries alternative ways of receiving benefits
    - ○ B. Reduce the number of lawsuits over life insurance settlements
    - ○ C. Give insurance companies more control over settlements
    - ○ D. Simplify the administration of estates

48. When life insurance is written on a participating basis, dividend options may be selected by the
    - ○ A. Insured person
    - ○ B. Insurance company
    - ○ C. Policyowner
    - ○ D. Beneficiary

49. Each of the following is true about taxes and life insurance except
    - ○ A. Dividends paid to a policyholder are subject to income taxes.
    - ○ B. Proceeds paid to an estate are subject to estate taxes.
    - ○ C. Premiums paid for individual life insurance are not tax-deductible.
    - ○ D. On surrender of a policy any cash value received in excess of the premiums paid is taxable as current income.

50. A Keogh plan is
    - ○ A. A low-cost type of group insurance
    - ○ B. A business continuation plan used by partnerships
    - ○ C. A type of pension plan used by corporations
    - ○ D. A retirement plan for self-employed persons

Answer Key 2

1. B	**21.** A	**41.** B
2. D	**22.** C	**42.** D
3. B	**23.** B	**43.** C
4. A	**24.** C	**44.** D
5. C	**25.** A	**45.** B
6. B	**26.** D	**46.** B
7. A	**27.** C	**47.** A
8. C	**28.** B	**48.** C
9. D	**29.** B	**49.** A
10. C	**30.** D	**50.** D
11. A	**31.** A	
12. B	**32.** C	
13. C	**33.** C	
14. A	**34.** A	
15. D	**35.** D	
16. C	**36.** B	
17. C	**37.** C	
18. B	**38.** C	
19. B	**39.** B	
20. D	**40.** A	

1. **Answer B is correct.** Term insurance provides the most amount of protection for a given amount of premium dollars. But it is not permanent insurance and has no other features, such as cash value or nonforfeiture values.

2. **Answer D is correct.** Catastrophic exposures are generally not insurable.

3. **Answer B is correct.** A single master policy is issued to the group policyowner, such as an employer or labor union. Individual insureds or members receive certificates of insurance that summarize the benefits and rights under the contract.

4. **Answer A is correct.** Straight life policies are designed to provide coverage until age 100, and premium payments continue until that age or an earlier death or termination of coverage.

5. **Answer C is correct.** Consideration, competent parties, and offer and agreement are required to form a legal contract. Signatures of the parties are not required, because oral contracts are binding.

6. **Answer B is correct.** In such cases the insurer will pay the death benefit minus any outstanding loan amount and interest on the loan.

7. **Answer A is correct.** Receiving a full refund of all premiums paid is not a nonforfeiture option.

8. **Answer C is correct.** Common risk management methods include avoiding, retaining, reducing, or transferring a risk. Ascertaining a risk is simply a process of evaluating a risk before a decision is made about how to deal with it.

9. **Answer D is correct.** When a conversion privilege applies, an employee who loses coverage may convert to an individual policy without having to provide evidence of insurability.

10. **Answer C is correct.** Small amounts of insurance with frequent premium payments that are collected by the agent are features of industrial life insurance.

11. **Answer A is correct.** According to the law of large numbers, predictions become more accurate as the number of units being considered increases.

12. **Answer B is correct.** A whole life policy will mature and the cash value will equal the face amount when the insured reaches age 100.

13. **Answer C is correct.** Social security provides survivor, disability, and retirement benefits. Deferred compensation is a special type of employer benefit designed for company executives.

14. **Answer A is correct.** If the insured dies, benefits are paid to the creditor to extinguish the loan and are not paid to a beneficiary.

15. **Answer D is correct.** Annual income and expenses and years remaining until retirement are factors. The amount of any property owned is not.

16. **Answer C is correct.** Misrepresenting insurance policy provisions or making incomplete comparisons of policies for the purpose of inducing someone to change or replace an existing insurance policy is an illegal practice known as twisting.

17. **Answer C is correct.** A person who has a low-risk occupation and follows a healthy lifestyle is an example of a preferred risk.

18. **Answer B is correct.** Reserves are accounting measurements of an insurer's liabilities to its policyholders.

19. **Answer B is correct.** Under state law, when covered employees under a group life insurance policy contribute any part of the premium, the policy must insure at least 75% of the eligible group members.

20. **Answer D is correct.** In the South-Eastern Underwriters' case the Supreme Court held that insurance transacted across state lines was interstate commerce.

21. **Answer A is correct.** Insurance companies commonly sell variable annuities.

22. **Answer C is correct.** Paid-up insurance is the term used to describe a new policy when cash value is used to buy a lesser amount of the same type of insurance upon lapse or surrender.

23. **Answer B is correct.** The owner of a policy does not have the right to change the person who is insured.

24. **Answer C is correct.** Upon reinstatement, when all overdue premiums, policy loans, and interest are paid, the policy is reinstated with all its original values and the rates are still based on the insured's age on the original issue date.

25. **Answer A is correct.** Express authority is the authority spelled out in the written agency contract.

26. **Answer D is correct.** Annuity contracts are not the same as life insurance and have some unique characteristics.

27. **Answer C is correct.** Because a lifetime income is guaranteed, the benefits could exceed the principal plus interest if the insured lives long enough.

28. **Answer B is correct.** This is an example of a family protection policy.

29. **Answer B is correct.** A contingent beneficiary will receive the proceeds if the insured dies when there is no surviving primary beneficiary.

30. **Answer D is correct.** A waiver of premium clause or rider is a provision that suspends the premium payments during total disability, usually lasting at least 6 months. A waiver of premium provision is designed to suspend the premium payments in the event of total disability.

31. **Answer A is correct.** The group policyowner always has the right to terminate the contract.

32. **Answer C is correct.** The right of conversion allows an insured to switch to an individual policy, not to remain covered under the group plan.

33. **Answer C is correct.** This is a classic definition of adverse selection, which exists when a disproportionate number of people who have a high risk of loss apply for insurance.

34. **Answer A is correct.** The life annuity with no other provisions provides the greatest level of periodic income payments because it is based only on the life expectancy of the annuitant. All other features, such as refund options or payment period certain, reduce the payment because the insurer has to set aside some money for these contingencies.

35. **Answer D is correct.** Because the funds supporting variable annuities are invested in securities, inflation does affect the ultimate payouts.

36. **Answer B is correct.** Increasing term insurance is needed to cover the growing premium payments over time.

37. **Answer C is correct.** Double indemnity applies only in cases of death by accident.

38. **Answer C is correct.** This is an example of adjustable life insurance.

39. **Answer B is correct.** Although term life insurance provides pure protection and may be convertible and renewable, it does not provide permanent protection.

40. **Answer A is correct.** With variable life insurance the amount of insurance does change automatically.

41. **Answer B is correct.** An inter vivos transfer occurs when properties or rights are transferred while the estate owner is still living.

42. **Answer D is correct.** Intestate is the term that applies when a person dies without leaving a will.

43. **Answer C is correct.** Eligibility for social security benefits depends on work credits. It does not matter whether a person has dependents, a private pension plan, or is eligible for Medicare.

44. **Answer D is correct.** When an irrevocable beneficiary designation has been made on a life insurance policy, the designation may be changed with consent of the beneficiary, but not otherwise.

45. **Answer B is correct.** A whole life policy pays the face value on death at any time, regardless of the amount of cash value.

46. **Answer B is correct.** An endowment is the type of contract that guarantees a specific value at a given time or age while providing insurance protection prior to that time.

47. **Answer A is correct.** Life insurance settlement options were developed in order to give insureds and beneficiaries alternative ways of receiving benefits.

48. **Answer C is correct.** It is the policyowner, who may not be the insured, who has the right to select dividend options or any other options available under the policy.

49. **Answer A is correct.** Dividends paid to a policyholder are subject to income taxes.

50. **Answer D is correct.** Keogh plans were designed specifically to provide retirement accounts for self-employed individuals.

What's on the CD-ROM

The CD features practice questions over each of the chapters in this book (and in the *Life/Health Concepts* course available from BISYS Education Services, on which this book is based), as well as some practice questions over the state insurance law topics that will be covered on your exam (state law questions are not provided for California, Florida, Georgia, Oklahoma, or Wisconsin). The CD also includes a 50-question exam simulator test that randomly combines questions from all of the chapters in this book and the state insurance law topics, giving you some practice at answering these questions in a format similar to the one you'll experience on your state insurance licensing qualification exam.

Review Questions and Exam Simulator

The review questions for the various chapters and the state insurance law topics are under separate links so that you can study particular areas in turn. After you answer each review question, you will be told whether your answer was correct, and you will be given feedback on why the answer was right or wrong. In contrast, when you go to the exam simulator, you will not be told after each question whether you answered correctly or be given feedback on your answer. When you finish all 50 questions on the exam simulator, you will be given a percentage score to see how well you did on the exam as a whole. Each time you take the exam simulator, a different set of questions will be chosen from the chapter and state law review questions, and they will be presented in a different randomized order so that you can use the exam simulator up to three times to test your comprehension of the material without simply learning the test.

These questions are the default settings for each type of quiz/exam, but you have other options. When you access each quiz/exam, you will be given the option (by clicking the Change Settings button) of changing the setting on each quiz/exam so that you can turn off feedback altogether, see feedback for all questions after you complete the entire quiz/exam, see feedback after the quiz/exam only for those questions you answered incorrectly, or see feedback after each question only for those questions you answered incorrectly. The Change Settings options enables you to tailor the feedback to practice questions and exam simulator to your preferences.

Installing the CD

To install the CD-ROM, follow these instructions:

1. Close all applications before beginning the installation.

2. Insert the CD in your CD drive.

3. The installation program will start automatically. Click Next.

4. To indicate your consent to the licensing agreement, click Yes.

5. Click Next to copy the installation program to the Bisys CBT folder under the Program Files folder on your computer's hard drive.

6. Click Next to add the BISYS Education Services icon to your Program Folder.

7. The installation program will then copy all the Exam Simulator files to your computer's hard drive (this may take a few minutes). Click Finish to complete the installation process; the installation program will automatically restart your computer when you do so (if you do not click Finish at this point, you have to restart your computer later to complete the installation process).

8. To start your Exam Simulator, click the Start button, and then select Programs, BISYS Education Services. Click Preview Edition— Life/Health Exam Cram Review.

9. Press Begin, New User.

10. Fill in the information as required and choose a password. Then click Create Account.

11. Type the two-letter postal abbreviation of the state for which you will be taking the licensing exam and click Begin.

You are now ready to use the Exam Simulator program. Click Exams and you can either take exams with their default settings described previously or change the settings as you want.

Need to Know More?

This appendix includes several resources that will help in your preparation for the Life and Health Insurance licensing exam. The primary resource is the *Life/Health Concepts* course, on which this book is based. In preparing for your insurance licensing exam, it is essential that you supplement your review of the general insurance concepts presented here with careful study of the state insurance law topics that will also appear on your licensing exam and that vary from state to state. Study materials for the state insurance law topics on the insurance licensing exam for your state can be obtained by purchasing *Life/Health Concepts* as a licensing training package, which includes an insurance law digest of the relevant laws in your particular state.

We've also included references to some in-depth resources that contain more detailed information on insurance-related topics than you'll need for your licensing exam, but that you might find useful for professional development or for continuing education credit as you progress in your insurance career.

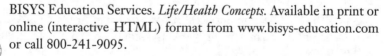
BISYS Education Services. *Life/Health Concepts*. Available in print or online (interactive HTML) format from www.bisys-education.com or call 800-241-9095.

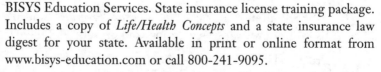
BISYS Education Services. State insurance license training package. Includes a copy of *Life/Health Concepts* and a state insurance law digest for your state. Available in print or online format from www.bisys-education.com or call 800-241-9095.

BISYS Education Services. *Principles of Life Insurance*. Available in print or online (interactive HTML) format from www.bisys-education.com or call 800-241-9095.

BISYS Education Services. *Introduction to Life Insurance*. Available in print or online (interactive HTML) format from www.bisys-education.com or call 800-241-9095.

BISYS Education Services. *Needs Analysis*. Available in print or online (interactive HTML) format from www.bisys-education.com or call 800-241-9095.

BISYS Education Services. *Life Insurance Policy Comparison & Underwriting*. Available in print or online format from www.bisys-education.com or call 800-241-9095.

BISYS Education Services. *Annuity Concepts*. Available in print or online (interactive HTML) format from www.bisys-education.com or call 800-241-9095.

BISYS Education Services. *Individual Retirement Accounts*. Available in print or online (interactive HTML) format from www.bisys-education.com or call 800-241-9095.

BISYS Education Services. *Introduction to Advanced Markets*. Available in print or online (interactive HTML) format from www.bisys-education.com or call 800-241-9095.

BISYS Education Services. *Disability Income Insurance*. Available in print or online format from www.bisys-education.com or call 800-241-9095.

BISYS Education Services. *Suitability Standards for Long-Term Care*. Available in print or online format from www.bisys-education.com or call 800-241-9095.

BISYS Education Services. *Medicare & Medigap Insurance*. Available in print or online (interactive HTML) format from www.bisys-education.com or call 800-241-9095.

BISYS Education Services. *Exam Simulator*. Available in CD-ROM or online format from www.bisys-education.com or call 800-241-9095.

BISYS Education Services. *Audio Review Program*. Available in CD-ROM from www.bisys-education.com or call 800-241-9095.

Prentice-Hall. *Life and Health Insurance*. Available in print from http://vig.prenhall.com.

Kluwer Academic Publishers. *Handbook of Insurance*. Available in print from www.wkap.nl.

Kluwer Academic Publishers. *Changes in the Life Insurance Industry.* Available in print from www.wkap.nl.

McGraw-Hill/Irwin. *The Financial Services Revolution.* Available in print from www.bn.com.

Harcourt Legal and Professional Publishing. *Evaluating the Life Insurance Decision.* Available in print from www.bn.com.

Aspen Publishers. *The Health Insurance Answer Book.* Available in print from www.aspenpublishers.com.

Washburn School of Law. *Washlaw Legal Research on the Web.* Available online at www.washlaw.edu.

Insurance Information Institute. *Glossary of Insurance Terms.* Available online at www.iii.org/media/glossary.

National Association of Insurance and Financial Advisors. *Advisor Today.* Available online at www.naifa.org.

Pfingsten Publishing LLC. *Life Insurance Selling.* Available online at www.lifeinsuranceselling.com.

Glossary

A

Absolute Assignment
Assignment by a policyowner of all control and rights in the policy to a third party.

Accelerated Benefits
Riders on life insurance policies that allow the life insurance policy's death benefits to be used to offset expenses incurred in a convalescent or nursing home facility.

Accidental Death and Dismemberment
A policy or a provision in a disability income policy that pays either a specified amount or a multiple of the weekly disability benefit if the insured dies, loses his or her sight, or loses two limbs as the result of an accident.

Accidental Means
Wording in certain accident policies that restricts recovery to loss for bodily injury that is both unexpected and unintended.

Acquisition Cost
Expenses incurred by an insurer that are directly related to putting the business on the books of the company. The largest portion of this cost is usually the agent's or sales representative's commission or bonus.

Activities of Daily Living (ADL)
Everyday living functions and activities performed by individuals without assistance. These functions include mobility, bathing, dressing, personal hygiene, and eating.

Additional Monthly Benefit
Riders added to disability income policies to provide additional benefits during the first year of a claim while the insured is waiting for social security benefits to begin.

Adhesion

Term used to describe certain contracts. Insurance policies are contracts of adhesion because the terms are drawn up by the insurer and the insured simply "adheres." For this reason ambiguous provisions are often interpreted by courts in favor of the insured.

Administrative Services Only (ASO)

An arrangement with an insurance company to administer a self-insured fund or multiple employer trust. The insurer provides only its services, not insurance coverage.

Admitted or Authorized Company

An insurance company authorized and licensed to do business in a given state.

Adverse Selection

Selection against the insurer in terms of insuring more poor risks than good or average risks; the tendency of more poor risks to buy and maintain insurance than good risks.

Agency

The power vested in an insurance agent so that the actions of the agent are taken to be the actions of the principal, the insurer in this case.

Aleatory

A contract in which the number of dollars to be given up by each party is not equal. Insurance contracts are of this type because the policyholder pays a premium and may collect nothing from the insurer or may collect a great deal more than the amount of the premium if a loss occurs.

Alien Company or Insurer

An insurer organized and domiciled in a country other than the United States.

Annual (or Yearly) Renewable Term

Term life insurance that may be renewed annually without evidence of insurability until some stated age.

Annuitant

One who receives an annuity payout.

Annuity Certain

An annuity that pays income for a fixed number of years regardless of whether the insured lives or dies.

Apparent Authority

Authority of an agent that is created when the agent oversteps actual authority, and when inaction by the insurer does nothing to counter the public impression that such authority exists.

Assessment Company, Society, or Insurer

An insurer who retains the right to assess policyholders additional amounts if premiums are insufficient for operations.

Assignment

(1) Transfer of rights in a policy to an individual or entity other than the policyowner. (2) Under medicare, agreement by the health care provider to accept medicare's approved amounts as full payment.

Authorized Company

See *Admitted or Authorized Company*.

Automatic Premium Loan Provision

In life insurance, an optional provision that allows the insurer to use, automatically, whatever portion of the cash value is needed to pay premiums as they fall due.

B

Beneficiary

A person who may become eligible to receive, or is receiving, benefits under an insurance plan other than as an insured.

Beneficiary, Contingent

A secondary beneficiary designated to receive the proceeds of a policy if the primary beneficiary does not survive the insured.

Beneficiary, Irrevocable

A named beneficiary whose status as beneficiary cannot be changed without his or her permission.

Blanket Policy

A health insurance contract that covers all of a class of persons who are not individually identified.

Blue Cross and Blue Shield

Service organizations providing hospital and medical expense coverages under which payments are made directly to the health care providers rather than to the individual. Blue Cross pays hospital expenses; Blue Shield pays physicians' and other medical expenses.

Broker

An individual who procures insurance or the renewal or continuance of insurance on behalf of prospective insureds.

Business Overhead Expense Insurance

A type of business disability income insurance designed to pay for continuing overhead while an owner or other key person is disabled.

C

Capital Conservation
A life insurance calculation method that factors in only interest earned on principal to generate income for a policyowner after benefits are distributed. Also called *capital retention*.

Capital Liquidation
A life insurance calculation method that factors in both interest and principal to generate income for a policyowner after benefits are distributed. Also called *capital utilization*.

Capitation
A system, under Health Maintenance Organization (HMO) forms of health benefits, whereby physicians receive a monthly payment from the HMO for every member of the HMO without regard to actual services the physician provides.

Cash Refund Annuity
A form of annuity contract that provides if at the death of the annuitant installments paid out have not totaled the amount of the premium paid for the annuity, the difference will be paid to a designated beneficiary in a lump sum.

Churning
An illegal practice wherein insurance agents unnecessarily replace existing life insurance for the purpose of earning additional (higher) first-year commissions.

Coinsurance
In health insurance, an arrangement whereby the insurer and the insured share payment of covered losses in agreed proportions, often 80% for the insurer and 20% for the insured. Also called *percentage participation*.

Cold Lead Advertising
An illegal method of marketing insurance policies (often associated with medicare supplement policies) that fails to disclose in a conspicuous manner that a purpose of the method of marketing is solicitation of insurance or other similar coverage, and that further contact will be made by an insurance agent or insurer.

Collateral Assignment
Assignment of a life or health insurance policy as security for a loan or debt, with the creditor to receive the proceeds or values to the extent of the interest assigned.

Commingling
An illegal practice that occurs when a producer mixes personal funds with the insured's or insurer's funds.

Commission
The portion of the premium stipulated in the agency contract to be retained by the agent as compensation for sales, service, and distribution of insurance policies.

Commissioner of Insurance

The title of the head of most state insurance departments. In some states, the title *Director* or *Superintendent of Insurance* is used instead.

Common Disaster Provision

A provision that can be included in a life insurance contract providing that the primary beneficiary must outlive the insured for a specified period of time in order to receive the proceeds. If not, the contingent beneficiary receives the proceeds.

Concealment

The withholding, by an applicant for insurance, of facts that materially affect an insurance risk or loss.

Conditional Receipt

A receipt that provides that if the premium accompanies the application, the coverage is in force from the date of application (whether the policy has yet been issued or not), provided the insurer would have issued the coverage on the basis of facts as revealed by the application and other usual sources of underwriting information.

Consideration

The exchange of values on which a contract is based. In insurance, the consideration offered by the insured is usually the premium and the statements contained in the application. The consideration offered by the insurer is the promise to pay in accordance with the terms of the contract.

Contestable Clause

A provision in an insurance policy setting forth the conditions under which, or the period of time during which, the insurer may contest or void the policy. After that time has lapsed, normally 2 years, the policy cannot be contested.

Contingent Beneficiary

Person or persons named to receive benefits if the primary beneficiary is not alive at the time the insured dies.

Controlled Business

Life insurance coverage written on the producer's own life, and on the lives of persons such as the producer's relatives and business associates. Many states limit the amount of controlled business that may be written, and if the premium or commissions on controlled business exceed a given percentage (usually 50%) of all business, the producer's license may be suspended, revoked, or not renewed.

Conversion Privilege

The right of group policyholders or their dependents, if their group coverage should end, to convert to an individual policy without evidence of insurability.

Convertible Term Insurance

A term policy that can be converted to a permanent type of coverage without proof of insurability.

Coordination of Benefits

The method of determining which company pays as primary insurer and which company pays as secondary or excess insurer when a working couple or their dependents have a claim covered by more than one group insurance contract.

Copayment or Copay

Under medicare, any amount, other than deductibles, that the recipient must pay for medicare to pay the greater share. In an HMO, it is any nominal use charge the subscriber is required to pay for services in addition to the prepaid amounts. Also called *coinsurance*.

Cost of Living Adjustment (COLA) Rider

A rider that may be attached to policies adjusting the benefits based upon a formula tied to inflationary or deflationary trends.

Custodial Care

Care that is primarily for meeting personal needs such as help in the activities of daily living (bathing, dressing, eating, and so forth). It can be provided by someone without professional medical skills or training but must be according to doctor's orders. See also *Activities of Daily Living (ADL)*.

D

Decreasing Term Insurance

Term insurance for which the initial amount gradually decreases until the expiration date of the policy, at which time it reaches zero.

Deductible

The portion of an insured's loss to be borne by the insured before any recovery may be made from the insurer.

Defamation

Under insurance law an unfair trade practice involving false, maliciously critical or derogatory statements intended to injure a person engaged in the insurance business.

Deferred Annuity

An annuity on which payments to the annuitant are delayed until a specified future date.

Deferred Compensation Plan

A nonqualified arrangement in which compensation is deferred until the employee retires.

Defined Benefit Plan

A qualified retirement plan that offers predetermined benefits to plan participants.

Defined Contribution Plan

A qualified retirement plan that is based on contributions to the plan.

Dividend

The return of part of the premium paid for a participating policy.

Domestic Company

An insurer formed under the laws of the state in which the insurance is written.

Double Indemnity

Payment of twice the basic benefit in event of loss resulting from specified causes or under specified circumstances.

E

Elimination Period

A period of time between the onset of a disability and the date benefits begin. Also known as *waiting period*.

Endorsement

Technically, a change made directly on the policy form by writing, printing, stamping, or typing and approved by an executive officer of the insurer. In general use, also may refer to a change made by means of a form attached to the policy.

Entire Contract Clause

A provision in an insurance contract stating that the entire agreement between the insured and the insurer is contained in the contract, including the application if it is attached, declarations, insuring agreements, exclusions, conditions, and endorsements.

Errors and Omissions (E&O) Liability

Liability a producer assumes, by the fact of doing business, for errors or omissions he or she may commit in recommending, providing, continuing, or failing to provide or continue the insurance coverage clients require. Producers can protect themselves by purchasing E&O liability coverage.

Estoppel

The legal principle that holds that anyone whose words or actions have caused a waiver of a right or privilege cannot later reclaim the waived right or privilege if a third party has relied on it.

Executor

A person named in a will to settle an estate.

Explanation of Benefits (EOB)

The statement sent to a participant in a health plan listing services, amounts paid by the plan, and total amount billed to the patient.

Express Authority

Authority of an agent that is specifically granted by the insurer in the agency contract or agreement.

Extended Term Option

In life insurance, a nonforfeiture option under which the insured uses the policy's cash value accumulation to purchase 1-year renewable term insurance in an amount equal to the original policy face amount.

F

Fair Credit Reporting Act

Federal act that provides consumer protection in transactions, including insurance transactions, wherein the consumer's credit rating is examined, which might result in a positive or negative effect on the outcome of the transaction.

Family Income Policy

A policy that pays an income up to some future date designated in the policy to the beneficiary after the death of the insured. The period of payment is measured from the date of the inception of the contract, and at the end of the income period the face amount of the policy is paid to the beneficiary. If the insured lives beyond the income period, only the face amount is payable in the event of the insured's death.

Family Maintenance Policy

A policy that pays an income to the beneficiary starting after the death of the insured and continuing for a stated period of time. At the end of the income period, the face amount of the policy is paid to the beneficiary.

Family Plan Policy

An all-family plan, usually with permanent insurance on the father's life, with mother and children automatically covered for lesser amounts, usually term, all paid by a single premium.

Fee-for-Service

A payment system for health care in which the provider is paid for each service given.

Fiduciary

A person holding the funds or property of another in a position of trust, and who is obligated to act in a prudent and ethical manner. Examples are attorney, bank trustee, or executor of an estate.

Fixed Amount Option

A settlement option under which the beneficiary receives a fixed amount for an unspecified period of time. Payments continue until the principal and interest are depleted.

Fixed Annuity

An annuity that provides that the annuitant will receive a fixed payment during the period of the annuity.

Fixed Period Option

A settlement option under which the beneficiary receives a regular income for a specified period of time.

Flexible Premium Annuity

An annuity that allows the contract owner the option of whether to pay the annuity premiums following the establishment of the annuity. Commonly used in conjunction with an Individual Retirement Account (IRA).

Foreign Company

An insurer organized under the laws of a state other than the one where the insurance is written.

Fraternal Benefit Societies

Social organizations that act as insurers providing insurance benefits for their members. The societies are nonprofit and are typically organized into series of lodges; an individual must be a member in order to buy coverage.

Free-Look Provision

A policy provision that permits the proposed policyowner to review the policy for a specified number of days and, if desired, return it to the insurer for a full premium refund.

G

Gatekeeper System

Under a Health Maintenance Organization (HMO) arrangement, a system requiring members of the HMO to select a primary care physician who in turn provides or authorizes all care for that particular member.

General Account

An investment portfolio used by the insurer for investment of premium income. This portfolio generally consists of safe, conservative, guaranteed investments, such as real estate and mortgages.

General Agent

A company representative in a given territory, entrusted with the task of supervising the company's business within that territory. A general agent may appoint local agents. A true general agent is an independent contractor compensated on a commission basis. In practice, in the life and health fields, he or she may receive certain expense subsidies from the company for office operation and training of new agents.

Grace Period

A period of time after the premium due date during which a policy remains in force without penalty even though the premium due has not been paid. Commonly 30 or 31 days in life insurance policies and 7, 10, or 31 days in various health insurance policies.

Guaranteed Insurability Rider

A rider that guarantees the insured can purchase more insurance at specified ages without proof of insurability.

Guaranteed Issue

A requirement that a health insurer must provide health insurance to all applicants without considering pre-existing conditions or other risk factors such as age or medical background.

Guaranteed Renewable

A contract that the insured has the right to continue in force by the timely payment of premiums for a substantial period of time, as set forth in the contract. During the guaranteed renewal period, the insurer may not change any provisions other than a change in the premium rate for classes of insured. A definition of the National Association of Insurance Commissioners (NAIC) specifies that the policy must be renewable to at least age 50 or, if issued after age 54, for at least 5 years.

H

Hazard

A specific situation that introduces or increases the probability of occurrence of a loss arising from an accident or illness, or that may influence the extent of the loss.

Health Maintenance Organization (HMO)

An organization that provides health services to individuals known as subscribers or members. The HMO generally contracts with a group of doctors and other medical practitioners to provide services at agreed-upon costs, prepaid on behalf of the members. Members must rely exclusively on the HMO for all their medical needs in order to qualify for payment.

Home Health Care

Care received at home as part-time skilled nursing care, speech therapy, physical or occupational therapy, part-time services of home health aids, or help from housekeepers and those handling other chores.

Hospice

A facility that provides support services and relief from pain for terminally ill individuals. Hospice care is covered under Part A of medicare.

Hospital Income or Indemnity Policy

A policy that pays a stated amount per week or month directly to the insured while the insured is hospitalized without reference to expenses actually incurred. It is intended to replace income lost when the insured is hospitalized.

I

Immediate Annuity

An annuity on which the income payments to the annuitant are to begin almost immediately after a period of time equal to the period between payments has elapsed.

Implied Authority

Authority of an agent that the public may reasonably believe the agent to have. If the authority to collect and remit premiums is not expressly granted in the agency contract, but the agent does so on a regular basis and the insurer accepts, the agent has implied authority to do so.

Incidents of Ownership

Various rights that may be exercised under the policy contract by the policyowner. Some of the incidents of ownership would be the right to cash in the policy, the right to receive a loan on the cash value of the policy, and the right to change the beneficiary.

Incontestable Clause

A clause in a health insurance policy providing that after the policy has been in force for a specified length of time (usually 2 years), the insurer may not contest the policy as to statements contained in the application except for fraudulent statements. Also states that after that time, no claim may be denied or reduced on the grounds that a condition, not excluded by name at the time of policy issue, existed prior to the effective date. Usually found in policies guaranteeing renewability. Other policies may use a variation titled *Time limit on Certain Defenses*. Both are contained in the Uniform Policy Provisions.

Increasing Term Insurance

A term life insurance policy wherein the death benefit increases but the premium remains level for the policy term.

Indemnify

To restore the victim of a loss, in whole or in part, by payment, repair, or replacement.

Insurable Interest

In life and health insurance, the interest of one party in the possible death or disability of an insured that would result in a significant emotional or financial loss. Such an interest must exist in order for the party to purchase insurance on the life or health of another. In property-casualty insurance, a financial interest in property.

Insurance Commissioner

Common title for the head of a state department of insurance. In some states, the person is known as the *Director* or *Superintendent of Insurance*.

Interest Option

A settlement option under which the insurer keeps the insurance proceeds and invests them on behalf of the beneficiary. The beneficiary receives the interest from the investment. The proceeds remain the property of the beneficiary.

Investigative Consumer Report

A report ordered on an insured or applicant under which information about the person's character, reputation, or lifestyle is obtained through personal interviews with the person's neighbors, friends, associates, or acquaintances.

Irrevocable Beneficiary

A beneficiary that may not be changed without the beneficiary's permission.

J

Joint Life and Survivorship Annuity

An annuity under which payments are made to two annuitants, with the survivor continuing to receive payments after the first annuitant dies.

Joint Life Annuity

An annuity under which payments are made to two annuitants for only as long as both live. When one dies, payments cease even if one remains living.

Jumping Juvenile

Juvenile insurance on which the face amount increases by a multiple, usually five, of the original face amount when the insured reaches age 21.

K

Key Person Insurance

Life or health insurance covering valuable employees whose absence would cause the employer financial loss. The insurance is usually owned by or payable to the employer.

L

Lapse

Termination of a policy because of failure to pay the premium.

Law of Large Numbers

The theory of probability that is the basis of insurance; The larger the number of risks or exposures, the more closely will the actual results obtained approach the probable results expected from an infinite number of exposures.

Level Term Insurance

A term policy in which the amount of insurance protection remains constant during the policy period.

Life Annuity

An annuity that provides a periodic income to the annuitant during his or her lifetime.

Life Annuity Certain

An annuity under which the annuitant receives payments for a specified number of years or for his or her lifetime, whichever is longer. If the annuitant dies before all the guaranteed payments have been made, the beneficiary receives the payments for the rest of the certain period.

Limited-Pay Life

A permanent life insurance policy on which premiums are paid for a specified number of years or to a specified age of the insured. Protection continues for the entire life of the insured.

Living Benefits Rider

A rider attached to a life insurance policy that provides long-term care (LTC) benefits or benefits for the terminally ill. The benefits provided are derived from the available life insurance benefits.

M

Major Medical Insurance

A type of health insurance that provides benefits for most types of medical expenses incurred up to a high maximum limit or provides unlimited lifetime benefits. Such contracts may contain internal limits, a coinsurance or percentage participation provision, and a deductible. Pays expenses incurred both in and out of the hospital.

Managed Health Care

A generic term referring to the oversight by some administrative body of the health care of individuals for the purpose of providing appropriate medical care while containing costs. Health Maintenance Organizations (HMOs) and Preferred Provider Organizations (PPOs) are both sometimes called managed health care systems. May also refer collectively to one or more of various elements of such a system, such as second surgical opinions, precertification, concurrent and retrospective reviews, and outpatient care.

Market Conduct

Used to measure how insurance companies and insurance producers comply with state laws regulating the sales and marketing, underwriting, and issuance of insurance products. Proper market conduct means conducting insurance business fairly and responsibly.

Market-Value Adjusted Annuity

An annuity whose accumulated value is subject to a market value adjustment on surrender. The market value adjustment may be positive or negative depending on the movement of interest rates since the inception of the contract.

Material Fact

In insurance, a fact that is so important that the disclosure of it would change the decision of an insurance company, either with respect to writing coverage, settling a loss, or determining a premium. Usually, the misrepresentation of a material fact will void a policy.

Medical Information Bureau (MIB)

An organization formed and supported by insurers and serving as a clearing house of medical information reported to it by members and reported to them as a source of underwriting information.

Medicare

A government-sponsored health care plan intended primarily for persons age 65 and older who qualify for social security benefits. Is available to specified others, some of whom must pay a monthly premium for both Part A, which is the basic hospital plan and for which no payment may be required of other persons, and Part B, which covers certain non-hospital medical expenses and for which all pay a monthly premium.

Medicare Select Policy

A medicare supplement policy or certificate that contains restricted network provisions conditioning the payment of benefits on the use of network providers.

Medicare Supplement

One of a variety of health insurance plans designed to cover expenses not covered by medicare. Also called *Medigap*.

Medicare+Choice

Options to fill medicare gaps that must usually be paid by a medicare beneficiary. Also known as *Medicare Part C*.

Misrepresentation

On the part of an insurer or its agent, falsely representing the terms, benefits, or privileges of a policy. On the part of an applicant, falsely representing the health or other condition of the proposed insured.

Misstatement of Age

Clause in a life policy that provides that if misstatement of age is discovered after policy issue, the insurer may, if the insured is living, adjust the amount of future premiums and request payment of the additional premium the policyowner should have paid; if the insured has died, the insurer may adjust the face amount of the policy to coincide with the amount of insurance the premium would have purchased had the correct age been known and pay the death benefit claim on that basis.

Modified Endowment Contract

An endowment contract wherein the amount payable upon survival of the endowment period is greater than the face amount and the amount payable at death is the greater of the face amount of cash value. Modified endowment contracts are subject to taxation and subsequent penalties.

Moral Hazard

A condition of morals or habits that increases the probability of loss from a peril.

Morale Hazard

Hazard arising out of an insured's indifference to loss because of the existence of insurance. The attitude, "It's insured, so why worry," is an example of a morale hazard.

Morbidity

The relative incidence of disease.

Mortality Charge

The charge for the element of pure insurance protection in a life insurance policy.

Mutual Insurer

An incorporated insurer without incorporated capital owned by its policyholders.

N

National Association of Insurance Commissioners (NAIC)

Association of state insurance commissioners formed for the purpose of exchanging information and of developing uniformity in the regulatory practices of the several states through drafting model legislation and regulations. The NAIC has no official power to enforce compliance with its recommendations. Originally, National Convention of Insurance Commissioners.

Net Premium

The amount of premium minus the commission.

Network Model HMO

A model wherein an HMO contracts with several physician groups. Physicians may share in savings, but they may provide care for other than HMO members.

Nonadmitted Insurer or Company

Insurance company not licensed to do business in a given state. Also called *unauthorized company*.

Noncancelable Policies

A contract of health insurance that the insured has a right to continue in force by payment of premiums, as set forth in the contract, for a substantial period of time, also as set forth in the contract. During that period of time, the insurer has no right to make any change in any provision of the contract. The NAIC recommends that the term *cancelable* not be permitted to be used to designate any form that is not renewable to at least age 50 or for at least 5 years if issued after age 44. Note that this is in contrast to *guaranteed renewable*, on which the premium may be increased by classes. The premium for noncancelable policies must remain as stated in the policy at the time of issue.

Noncontributory

A general term used to designate any plan of insurance (usually group) for which the employer pays the entire premium and the employee contributes no part of the premium.

Nonforfeiture Option

A legal provision whereby the life insurance policyowner may take the accumulated values in a policy as paid-up insurance for a lesser amount; extended term insurance; or lump-sum payment of cash value, less any unpaid premiums or outstanding loans.

Nonparticipating Policy

Insurance contracts on which no policy dividends are paid because there is no contractual provision for the policyowner to participate in the surplus.

Nonqualified Plan

A benefit type of plan, such as a retirement plan, which may be discriminatory, which need not be filed with the IRS, and does not provide a current tax deduction for contributions.

Nonrenewal

Termination of insurance coverage at an expiration date or anniversary date. This action may be taken by an insurer who refuses to renew or by an insured who rejects a renewal offer.

O

Offer

The terms of a contract proposed by one party to another. In property and casualty insurance, submitting an application to the company is usually considered an offer. In life insurance, the application plus the initial premium constitutes an offer.

One-Year Term Dividend Option

A dividend option under which the insured requests that the insurer purchase 1-year term insurance with the dividend.

Open Access

Allows a participant to see another participating provider of services without a referral. Also called *open panel.*

Open Enrollment Period

A period during which members can elect to come under an alternate plan, usually without providing evidence of insurability.

Other Insurance Clause

A provision found in many life and health insurance policies, stating the disposition of claims when any other insurance contract covers the same events as the policy in which the provision is contained.

Overhead Expense Insurance

Insurance that covers such things as rent, utilities, and employee salaries when a business owner becomes disabled. The insurance benefit is generally not a fixed amount, but pays the amount of expenses actually incurred.

Overinsurance

A condition in which more insurance is in force on the insured or the risk than the potential loss, or so much insurance is in force as to constitute a moral or morale hazard (such as so much disability insurance being in force that it becomes profitable to remain unable to return to work).

P

Paid-Up Additions Option
A dividend option under which the policyowner uses policy dividends as a single premium to buy additional life insurance.

Paid-Up Insurance
A nonforfeiture option in life insurance policies under which insurance exists and no further premium payments are required.

Parol Evidence Rule
A rule stating that a written instrument or contract cannot be modified by an oral agreement. It is based on the concept that written contracts should contain all of the facts and agreements between the parties and, therefore, prevents contemporaneous oral declarations from being included in the contract.

Participating (Par)
(1) Insurance that pays policy dividends. In other words, it entitles a policyowner to participate in allocations of the insurer's surplus. In life insurance there are several options available for the use of such dividends. (2) Insurance that contributes proportionately with other insurance on the same risk.

Payor Rider
A rider to a juvenile life policy providing that if the payor dies or becomes disabled before the insured juvenile reaches a certain age, the company waives the premiums and keeps the policy in full force.

Per Capita
Applied to beneficiaries, it refers to division of policy proceeds among the surviving beneficiaries (Latin: *by heads*).

Per Stirpes
Applied to beneficiaries, it refers to division of policy proceeds among surviving beneficiaries with a full share to the heirs of any deceased beneficiary (Latin: *by roots*).

Peril
The cause of a possible loss.

Permanent Life Insurance
A term loosely applied to life insurance policy forms other than group and term, usually cash value life insurance, such as endowments and whole or ordinary life policies.

Persistency
The staying quality of insurance policies, that is, the renewal quality. *High* persistency means that a high number of policies stay in force; *low* persistency means that many lapse for nonpayment of premium.

Physical Hazard
Any hazard arising from the material, structural, or operational features of the risk itself apart from the persons owning or managing it.

Point-of-Service Plan
A plan allowing a choice of whether to receive services from a participating or nonparticipating provider.

Power of Agency

In an agency relationship, the concept that the actions of an agent may be taken to be the actions of the principal.

Preadmission Authorization

A cost containment feature of many group medical policies whereby the insured must contact the insurer prior to a hospitalization and receive authorization for the admission.

Preexisting Condition

A condition of health or physical condition (and sometimes moral condition) that existed before the policy was issued.

Preferred Provider Organization (PPO)

An organization of hospitals and physicians who provide, for a set fee, services to insurance company clients. These providers are listed as preferred and the insured may select from any number of hospitals and physicians without being limited, as with an HMO. Covers 100%, with a minimal copayment for each office visit or hospital stay. Contrast with *Health Maintenance Organization (HMO)*.

Preferred Risk

Any risk considered to be better than the standard risk on which the premium rate was calculated.

Prelicensing Education Requirement

Statutory requirement of many states that an applicant for an insurance license must complete a specified education program before being eligible for the license.

Premature Distribution

A distribution from an IRA or qualified retirement plan that is taken before the recipient is age 59 1/2.

Pretext Interview

An interview in which the party gathering information refuses to reveal his or her identity, pretends to be someone else, misrepresents the true purpose of the interview, or pretends to represent someone who is not in fact represented. In most cases, federal and state laws prohibit pretext interviews in connection with insurance-related consumer reporting. They are permitted only in connection with investigations into suspected material misrepresentation, fraud, or criminal activity.

Primary Beneficiary

The beneficiary named first to receive proceeds or benefits of a policy that provides death benefits.

Primary Care Physician (PCP)

In a Health Maintenance Organization (HMO) gatekeeper system, the physician selected to provide or authorize all care for a particular member of the HMO.

Primary Insurance Amount (PIA)

A social security calculation that serves as the principal element determining the amount of various social security benefits.

Principal Sum

The amount payable in one sum in event of accidental death and, in some cases, accidental dismemberment. When a contract provides benefits for both accidental death and accidental dismemberment, each dismemberment benefit is equal to the principal sum or some fraction thereof. Examples would be half the principal sum for loss of one arm, half the principal sum for the loss of one leg, and so forth.

Prior Authorization

A cost containment measure that provides full payment of health benefits only when the hospitalization or medical treatment has been approved in advance.

Pro Rata Cancellation

The termination of an insurance contract or bond, the premium charge being adjusted in proportion to the exact time the protection had been in force.

Probationary Period

A period of time between the effective date of a health insurance policy and the date coverage begins for certain conditions. It occurs only once in the life of the policy.

Producer

In many states, anyone who solicits, sells, procures, or gains continuance of insurance on behalf of another. In this regard, embraces agents, brokers, and solicitors.

Q

Qualified Plan

A retirement plan that has been filed and approved by the IRS, which does not discriminate as to participation, and where the contributor (usually the employer) receives a tax deduction for plan contributions, and investment income is tax-deferred until paid out.

R

Rated

Usually used in combination, as in a *rated-up* or *rated policy*. A policy issued with an extra premium charge because of physical or moral impairment.

Rating Bureau

A private organization that classifies and promulgates manual rates and in some cases compiles data and measures the hazards of individual risks in terms of rates in geographic areas, the latter being true especially in connection with property insurance.

Rebate

A portion of the commission returned or anything else of value given an insured as an inducement to buy. The payment of policy dividends, retroactive rate adjustments, and reduced premiums that reflect the savings of direct payment to an agent or home office are not usually considered to be rebates. In most cases rebates are illegal, both for the producer or insurer to give a rebate and for an insured to receive one.

Reciprocal Agreement

An agreement between two states whereby producers of each state can sell insurance in the other state.

Reciprocity

A system of placing reinsurance on a reciprocal basis so that a ceding company will give a share of its reinsurance to a reinsurer who is able to offer reinsurance in return.

Red-lining

Discriminating unfairly against a risk solely because of its location. An example would be refusing to insure a risk because the applicant lives in a depressed area or location. Sometimes these areas are referred to as *blackout areas*.

Reduced Paid-Up Insurance

Option A nonforfeiture option under which the insured uses the cash value of the present policy to purchase a single-premium insurance policy at attained age rates for a reduced face amount.

Reduced Premium Dividend Option

A dividend option under which the policyowner has the dividend deducted from the next premium due.

Reducing Term Disability Insurance

A business disability policy under which, in the event of disability of the owner who has outstanding debt, the policy makes the loan payments.

Reinsurance

Agreement between insurance companies under which one accepts all or part of the risk of loss of the other.

Renewable Term

Term insurance that can be renewed for another term without proof of the insured's insurability.

Representations

On an application, facts that the applicant represents as true and accurate to the best of his or her knowledge and belief. Contrast with *Warranty*.

Rescission

(1) Repudiation of a contract. A party whose consent to a contract was induced by fraud, misrepresentation, or duress may repudiate it. A contract may also be repudiated for failure to perform a duty. (2) The termination of an insurance contract by the insurer when material misrepresentation has occurred.

Residual Disability

In health insurance, a concept that has sometimes replaced partial disability in terms of determining what benefit will be paid. Uses a formula that requires the insured's earnings to have dropped a certain percentage from prior to disability levels.

Respite Care

Normally associated with hospice care, a benefit to family members of a patient whereby the family is provided with a break or respite from caring for the patient. The patient is confined to a nursing home for needed care for a short period of time.

Restoration of Benefits

A provision in many major medical plans that restores a person's lifetime maximum benefit amount in small increments after a claim has been paid. Usually, only a small amount ($1,000–3,000) may be restored annually.

Revocable Beneficiary

The beneficiary in a life insurance policy in which the owner reserves the right to revoke or change the beneficiary.

Rider

An amendment attached to a policy that modifies the conditions of the policy by expanding or decreasing its benefits or excluding certain conditions from coverage. See *Waiver* and *Endorsement*.

S

Second Injury Fund

Special funds set up by each state to pay all or part of the compensation required when a partially disabled employee suffers a subsequent inquiry. Because the compound effect of two injuries can be greater than the effect of the same two injuries in isolation, employers might be reluctant to hire the handicapped if they had to bear the full burden for a second injury. Second injury funds relieve employers of some of this burden.

Secondary Beneficiary

The second person named to receive benefits upon the death of the insured if the first named (primary) beneficiary is not alive or does not collect all benefits before his or her own death. See also *Contingent Beneficiary*.

Separate Account

An investment company (usually a unit investment trust), registered with the SEC, that owns and holds assets for the benefit of participants in variable contracts. Because of the investment risk, insurers are required to keep their variable contract portfolios separate from their fixed investment portfolios.

Service Area

The area, allowed by state agencies or by the certification of authority, in which a health plan can provide services.

Settlement Options

The various methods for the payment of the proceeds or values of a life insurance policy that may be selected in lieu of a lump sum.

Simplified Employee Pension (SEP) Plan

A plan where the employer contributes a specific amount into an eligible employee's IRA on behalf of the employee.

Skilled Nursing Care

Daily nursing and rehabilitative care that is performed only by or under the supervision of skilled professionals or technical personnel. Skilled care includes administering medication, medical diagnosis, and minor surgery.

Speculative Risk

Uncertainty as to whether a gain or loss will occur. An example would be a business enterprise where there is a chance that the business will make money or lose it. Speculative risks are not normally insurable.

Spendthrift Clause

A clause that may be written into a life policy providing that a beneficiary or creditor cannot subject the proceeds or payments received under the settlement option to transfer, commutation, or encumbrance, or to any legal action taken by the creditors against the beneficiary.

Staff Model HMO

An HMO where physicians are employed and all premiums are paid to the HMO, which then compensates the physicians on a salary and bonus arrangement.

Standard Risk

A risk that is on par with those on which the rate has been based in the areas of health, physical condition, and morals. An average risk, not subject to rate loadings or restrictions because of poor health.

Stock Company

An incorporated insurer with capital contributed by stockholders, to whom the earnings are distributed as dividends on their shares. Contrast with *Mutual Insurer*.

Substandard Risk

A risk that for reasons of health, physical conditions, or morals does not meet the requirements to qualify as a standard risk without rating.

Suicide Clause

In a life insurance policy, a clause that states that if the insured commits suicide within a specified period of time, the policy will be voided. Paid premiums are usually refunded. The time limit is generally 1 or 2 years.

T

1035 Exchange

A nontaxable exchange of life insurance policies, as provided under section 1035(a) of the Internal Revenue Code.

Term Insurance

Life insurance that normally does not have cash accumulation and is issued to remain in force for a specified period of time, following which it is subject to renewal or termination.

Tertiary Beneficiary

A beneficiary designated as third in line to receive benefits if the primary and secondary beneficiaries die before the insured dies.

Third-Party Administrator (TPA)

A firm that provides administrative services for employers and other associations having group insurance policies. The TPA, in addition to being the liaison between the employer and the insurer, is also involved with certifying eligibility, preparing reports required by the state, and processing claims. TPA's are being used more with the increase in employer self-funded plans.

Time Limits on Certain Defenses

One of the uniform individual accident and sickness provisions required by state law to be included in an individual health policy. It sets a limit on the number of years after a policy has been in force that an insurer can use as a defense against a claim that a physical condition of the insured existed before the policy was issued, but was not declared at that time.

Time of Payment of Claims Provision

A health insurance provision that requires that claims be paid immediately on receipt of proofs of loss. Some states specify a number of days in place of the word *immediately*.

Total Disability

A degree of disability from injury or sickness that prevents the insured from performing the duties of his or her occupation. Actual wording of definitions vary by policy.

Twisting

Inducing or seeking to induce a policyowner by misrepresentation to terminate an existing policy and buy a new policy, to the detriment of the insured.

U

Unauthorized Insurer

An insurer not licensed to sell insurance within a state. See also *Nonadmitted Insurer or Company*.

Underwriter

(1) A person trained in evaluating risks and determining the rates and coverages that will be used for them. (2) Sometimes, an agent, especially a life insurance agent, who might qualify as a field underwriter. In theory, the agent underwrites "in the field" before submitting an application to a home office underwriter.

Unearned Premium

The portion of an advance premium payment that has not yet been used to provide coverage. For example, in the case of an annual premium, at the end of the first month of the premium period, 11 months of the premium would still be unearned.

Unfair Claim Settlement Practices Law

State laws designed to protect the consumer against unfair practices in the reporting, investigation, payment, and final resolution of insurance claims.

Unfair Trade Practices Law

State laws designed to protect the consumer against misleading, deceptive, monopolistic, or otherwise unfair practices in the business of insurance.

Uniform Policy Provisions

A set of standardized provisions used in health insurance policies, of which 12 are required and 11 are optional. All states use these provisions, although they are permitted to revise the wording as long as it is at least as beneficial to the insured as the original wording.

Uniform Simultaneous Death Act

A uniform law adopted by most states providing that if the primary beneficiary and insured die in the same accident and there is no proof that the beneficiary outlived the insured, the proceeds are paid as if the primary beneficiary died first.

Unilateral Contract

A contract such as an insurance policy in which only one party to the contract, the insurer, makes any enforceable promise. The insured does not make a promise but pays a premium, which constitutes the insured's part of the consideration.

Universal Life

A combination flexible premium/adjustable life insurance policy. The premium payer may select the amount of premium he or she can pay, and the policy benefits are those that the premium will purchase. Or, the premium payer may change the amount of insurance and pay premium accordingly. Many believe this is the only true solution to the "buy term, invest the difference" problem.

Usual, Customary, and Reasonable (UCR)

In health plans, the charges made by medical practitioners that are normally charged in a particular geographical area. Many policies include the UCR wording to keep apace of inflation and avoid revising scheduled amounts as costs of medical care change.

Utilization Review

A cost control mechanism by which the appropriateness, necessity, and quality of health care is monitored by both insurers and employers.

Utmost Good Faith

Acting in fairness and equity with a sincere belief that the act is not unlawful or harmful to others. The insurance contract requires that each party is entitled to rely on the representations of the other without attempts to conceal or deceive.

V

Variable Annuity

An annuity contract in which the amount of the periodic benefit varies, usually in relation to security market values, a cost-of-living index, or some other variable factor in contrast to a fixed or guaranteed return annuity. As a hedge against inflation, the variable annuity presents investment risks to the annuitant.

Variable Contracts

Contracts such as variable annuities or variable life insurance that contain an element of risk for the investor, depending on the performance of the separate account backing the contract. Generally, these contracts are products of insurers but regulated by both state insurance departments and the federal government.

Variable Life Insurance

A form whose face value varies depending on the value of the dollar, securities, or other equity products at the time payment is due.

Variable Universal Life

A combination of the features of variable life insurance and universal life insurance under the same contract. Benefits are variable based on the value of equity investments, and premiums and benefits are adjustable at the option of the policyholder.

Viatical Settlement

The sale and transfer of the legal right to the death benefits of a life insurance policy through an irrevocable beneficiary designation. The policy is usually sold by a chronically or terminally ill person to an insurance company that receives death benefits from the policy at the insured's death.

W

Waiver

(1) A rider waiving (excluding) liability for a stated cause of accident or especially sickness. (2) A provision or rider agreeing to forego premium payment during a period of disability. (3) The giving up or surrender of a known right or privilege.

Waiver of Premium Provision

When included, provides that premiums are waived and the policy remains in force if the insured becomes totally and permanently disabled.

Warranty

A statement made on an application for insurance that is warranted to be true in all respects. If untrue in any respect, even though the untruth may not have been known to the person giving the warranty, the contract may be voided whether or not the untruth or inexactness is material to the risk. Statements on life and health insurance applications are, in the absence of any evidence of fraud, representations rather than warranties. Contrast with *Representations*.

Whole Life Insurance

Insurance that may be kept in force for a person's whole life and that pays a benefit on the person's death, whenever that may be. All whole life policies build up nonforfeiture values, but they are paid for in three different ways. Under a straight or ordinary life policy, premiums are paid for as long as the insured lives. A single premium policy is paid for at one time in one premium. Between these two types there are many limited-payment plans, under which the insured pays premiums for a certain period or until reaching a certain age. Contrast with *Term Insurance*.

Workers Compensation (WC)

(1) A schedule of benefits payable to an employee for injury, disability, dismemberment, or death as a result of occupational hazard. The payments are a liability of the employer. (2) Insurance agreeing to pay the workers compensation benefits required by law on behalf of the employer.

Index

B

F

H

Harcourt Legal and Professional Publishing Web site, 499
hazardous occupation/hobby exclusions, 199
hazards, defining, 3
HCFA (Health Care Financing Administration), 412
health care plans
  ASO contracts, 298-299
  Blue Cross and Blue Shield, 286-287
  commercial insurers, 285
  employer-funded
    501(c) (9) trusts, 299
    cafeteria, 300
    MET, 300
    MEWA, 300
    self-funded, 297
  group, 301-302
  HMO
    basic health care services, 291-293
    closed panel, 291
    consumers cooperatives, 289
    development of, 288
    employer/employee contributions, 289
    enrollment, 289
    federal requirements, 288
    gatekeeper systems, 293
    grievance procedures, 294
    group model, 289-290
    HMO Act of 1973, 289
    IPA model, 290
    member access, 293
    network model, 290
    nondiscrimination, 294
    open enrollment, 293
    open panel, 291
    open-access plans, 295
    open-ended plans, 295
    producers cooperatives, 289
    prohibited practices, 294
    quality assurance, 294
    selecting PCP, 293
    service areas, 289
    staff model, 290
    supplemental health care services, 292-293
  POS, 296-297
  PPO, 295
  prepaid, 286
  reimbursement plans, 285
health care providers, 285-287

health insurance. *See also* group health insurance
  accident only insurance, 284
  AD&D insurance, 282
  blanket, 284
  Blue Cross and Blue Shield, 286-287
  commercial insurers, 285
  credit, 284
  death benefits, 303
  dental expense insurance, 283
  disability benefits, 303
  disability income insurance, 282
  dread disease insurance, 283
  dual choice laws, 289
  elimination periods, 303
  employer-administered plans
    501(c) (9) trusts, 299
    cafeteria, 300
    MET, 300
    MEWA, 300
    self-funded, 297-298
    small business, 299
  government
    Medicaid, 303
    TRICARE, 304
    workers compensation, 302
  group, 301-302
  health care providers
    home health care, 285
    managed health care, 285-287
    skilled nursing facilities, 285
    surgicenters, 285
    urgent care centers, 285
  HMO
    basic health care services, 291-293
    closed panel, 291
    consumers cooperatives, 289
    development of, 288
    employer/employee contributions, 289
    enrollment, 289
    federal requirements, 288
    gatekeeper systems, 293
    grievance procedures, 294
    group model, 289-290
    HMO Act of 1973, 289
    IPA model, 290
    member access, 293
    network model, 290
    nondiscrimination, 294
    open enrollment, 293
    open panel, 291
    open-access plans, 295
    open-ended plans, 295
    producers cooperatives, 289
    prohibited practices, 294

I

inter vivos trusts, 194
interest, determining premiums, 84
interest only settlement option (life insurance), 207
interest-adjusted net cost method (life insurance cost comparisons). *See* net payment cost index method
interest-sensitive whole life insurance policies, 146
interim term insurance policies, 141
intermediaries, 412
intermediate care, LTC (long-term care), 438
internal limits (benefits), 374
Internal Revenue Code
    retirement plans, vesting rules, 266-267
    Section 1035 policy exchanges, 261
Internet insurance distribution, 17
intimidation, Unfair Trade Practices Act, 47
intracompany replacements (policies), 315
investigative consumer reports
    applications, 79
    Fair Credit Reporting Act of 1970, 27
Investment Company Act of 1940, 153
investments (insurance company regulations), 34
IPA (Individual Practice Association) model HMO, 290
IRA (Individual Retirement Accounts and Annuities)
    contribution limits, 269
    distributions, 273-274
    funding, 270
    income deductibility limits, 270
    rollovers, 275
    Roth IRA, 271
    SEP, 272
    SIMPLE, 271-272
    taxes, 269
IRA Plus. *See* Roth IRA
irrevocable beneficiaries, 187, 190

J - K - L

joint life and survivorship settlement options, 232
joint life annuity settlement options, 232
joint life insurance policies, 160
jumping juvenile life insurance policies, 161
juvenile life insurance policies, 161, 168

Keogh plans, 273
key employees, 405
key person disability insurance, 357
key person life insurance, 115
Kluwer Academic Publishers Web site, 498

labor union groups, 92
lapsing policies, 324
last survivor settlement options. *See* joint life and survivorship settlement options
Law of Agency, principles of
    agent's responsibilities to company, 58-59
    agent's responsibilities to insured/applicant, 57
    authority, 56-57
    collection of premium, 57
    company's responsibilities to agent, 59
    E&O insurance, 59
    presumption of agency, 56
    waiver and estoppel, 58
law of large numbers
    defining, 4
    example of, 83
laws
    compensation, workers compensation, 428
    Uniform Individual Accident and Sickness Policy Provisions
        mandatory provisions, 322
        mandatory provisions, Change of Beneficiary, 329-330
        mandatory provisions, Claim Forms, 326
        mandatory provisions, Entire Contract; Changes, 322
        mandatory provisions, Grace Period, 323-324
        mandatory provisions, Legal Actions, 329
        mandatory provisions, Notice of Claim, 325-326
        mandatory provisions, Payment of Claims, 327-328
        mandatory provisions, Physical Examination and Autopsy, 329
        mandatory provisions, Proof of Loss, 326-327
        mandatory provisions, Reinstatement, 324-325
        mandatory provisions, Time Limit on Certain Defenses; Incontestability, 323
        mandatory provisions, Time of Payment of Claims, 327
        optional provisions, 330
        optional provisions, Cancellation, 334-335
        optional provisions, Change of Occupation, 330-331
        optional provisions, Conformity with State Statutes, 335

M

N

S

How can we make this index more useful? Email us at indexes@quepublishing.com

U

V

W - X - Y - Z